To my mother Mrs Khorshed W. Ezekiel
and
my father late Prof. Joe Ezekiel

SACHIN

THE STORY OF THE WORLD'S GREATEST BATSMAN

Gulu Ezekiel

PENGUIN BOOKS

Penguin Books India (P) Ltd., 11 Community Centre, Panchsheel Park, New Delhi 110 017, India
Penguin Books Ltd., 80 Strand, London WC2R 0RL, UK
Penguin Putnam Inc., 375 Hudson Street, New York, NY 10014, USA
Penguin Books Australia Ltd., 250 Camberwell Road, Camberwell, Victoria 3124, Australia
Penguin Books Canada Ltd., 10 Alcorn Avenue, Suite 300, Toronto, Ontario M4V 3B2, Canada
Penguin Books (NZ) Ltd., Cnr Rosedale and Airborne Roads, Albany, Auckland, New Zealand

First published by Penguin Books India 2002

10 9 8 7 6 5 4 3 2 1

Typeset in Aldine 401 by Mantra Virtual Services, New Delhi
Printed at International Print-o-Pac. New Delhi.

Contents

Acknowledgements *ix*
Copyright Acknowledgements *x*

Prologue: The God of Indian Cricket 1
Bombay Boy 4
Schoolboy Prodigy 13
World Record 24
A Boy Among Men 29
Into the Cauldron of Test Cricket 42
12 Runs Short of Glory 53
Hail the Boy King 56
Home, Sweet Home 67
On Top Down Under 77
World Cup Debut 87
Two Little Bits of Cricket History 94
Success at Home and Abroad 102
The Great Friendship 109
The One-day Phenom 116
The Brian and Sachin Show 126
World Cup 1996—and England Again 138
Captaincy-I 149

Defeat and Despair 155
Confrontation 168
Musical Chairs 181
Desert Storm 200
The Don and I 207
On Top of the World 213
Trauma 221
Tragedy and Tears 229
Reluctant Messiah 238
Double—Then Trouble 245
Debacle Down Under 250
Stepping Down 259
Match-fixing and the CBI 268
'The Greatest Series Ever' 278
Foot Fault 286
Year of Controversies 292
Global Brand 311
Man and Myth 318
Epilogue: Qua Vadis, Sachin? 323

Sachin Tendulkar in Figures by S.Pervez Qaiser 330
Select Bibliography 376
Index 378

Acknowledgements

This book would not have been possible without the help and support of a team of friends and family. Chief among them were V.K. Karthika at Penguin India with an attention to detail and dedication that was simply awe-inspiring; my friend Binoo K. John whose constant advice and encouragement were invaluable; fellow journalist and friend Vijay Lokapally who has interviewed Sachin Tendulkar more times than anyone and who gave me wonderful insights; my mother Mrs Khorshed W. Ezekiel for her love and support and my sister Raina Imig who gave me strength through many, many long nights of work with both her Reiki and her love.

Among cricketers I would like to thank Ajit Wadekar, Maninder Singh, Ramakant Achrekar, Abbas Ali Baig, John Wright, Bishan Singh Bedi, Imran Khan, David Boon, Abdul Qadir, Ian Healy and Dave Richardson for providing me with quotes in some cases and extensive interviews in others.

Fellow journalists were of great help, particularly Clayton Murzello, Rizwan Ehsan Ali, Prem Panicker, Joe Hoover, Syed Parvez Qaiser, Paul E. Dyson, David Frith, Rob Steen, Mark Ray, Rick Smith, Pradeep Mandhani, K.Jagannadha Rao, Subhash Malhotra, Sunil Warrier, Patrick Eagar and Don Neely.

I would also like to thank Atmaram Bhende, Shirish Nadkarni, Theo Braganza, Nazim Merchant, Alyque Padamsee and Prof. Nigel Pyne.

Finally, my thanks to 'the man' himself, Sachin Tendulkar, the subject of this book, for being the cricketer and the person that he is.

Copyright Acknowledgements

My publishers and I would like to acknowledge the following periodicals, newspapers and websites for permission to reprint copyright material: *Sportstar, Sportsworld, Sportsweek, Cricket Talk, Outlook, Time, The Week, The Hindu, The Hindustan Times, Mid Day, The Telegraph, The Daily Telegraph, The Age, The Weekend Australian, PTI, The Times of India, Wisden Cricket Monthly, Wisden.com, Wisden Cricketer's Almanack* (extracts are reproduced by kind permission of John Wisden & Co. Ltd.), *The Cricketer International, indya.com, Cricketnext.com* and *Rediff.com*.

Grateful acknowledgement is also made to the following for permission to extract copyright material: Extracts from *Geoffrey Boycott on Cricket: Yorkshire's Greatest Son Hits Out* by Geoffrey Boycott, published by Ebury. Used by permission of The Random House Group Limited; from *Bradman's Best* by Roland Perry, published by Bantam Press. Used by permission of Transworld Publishers, a division of The Random House Group Limited; from *Gavaskar and Tendulkar: Shaping Indian Cricket's Destiny* by Sandeep Bamzai. Used by permission of Jaico Publishing House; from *An Anthropologist Among Marxists and Other Essays* by Ramachandra Guha, published by Permanent Black and *An Indian Cricket Omnibus,* edited by Ramachandra Guha and T.G.Vaidyanathan, published by Oxford University Press. Used by permission of Ramachandra Guha; from *Lord Harris Shield Cricket Tournament: Commemoration Volume, 1897-1997* and *Indian Cricket: The Captains—From Nayudu to Tendulkar* by Partab Ramchand. Used by permission of Marine Sports International Publishing Division; from *Not Quite Cricket* by Pradeep Magazine. Used by permission of Penguin Books India and Pradeep Magazine; and from *Azhar: The Authorized Biography of Mohammad Azharuddin* by Harsha Bhogle. Used by permission of Penguin Books India and Harsha Bhogle.

PROLOGUE

The God of Indian Cricket

The greatest Indian alive—Bishan Singh Bedi

'Sachin Tendulkar is a god in India and people believe luck shines in his hand,' Australia's opening batsman Matthew Hayden told the Sydney *Sun-Herald* in April 2001, shortly after returning from a tour of India. 'It is beyond chaos—it is a frantic appeal by a nation to one man.'

The question was then put to Tendulkar by an Indian journalist: Are you God?

'I don't think anyone can become God or even come close to it,' was the response.

Quite right.

But in a country of a billion plus (with many millions more in the Indian diaspora) where the 'unity in diversity' mantra of the state machinery has begun to ring hollow, Tendulkar has emerged as perhaps the nation's sole unifying force. Columnist C.P. Surendran had this to say about what the batting maestro means to Indians everywhere: Every time he walks to the wicket, 'a whole nation, tatters and all, marches with him to the battle arena. A pauper people pleading for relief, remission from the lifelong anxiety of being Indian...seeking a moment's liberation from their India-bondage through the exhilarating grace of one accidental bat' (*An Anthropologist Among the Marxists and Other Essays* by Ramachandra Guha).

Time magazine chose Tendulkar as one of their 'Asian heroes' and put him on the cover of their Asian edition (29 April 2002) for the second time in three years. Inside, 'The Bat out of Heaven' shared space with human rights activists, freedom fighters and other luminaries.

At 26 Tendulkar was the youngest to be featured by *India Today* in their '100 People Who Shaped India' special issue in 1999 (Millennium Series Vol. I).

In a poll conducted by the *Week* magazine at the height of the match-fixing scandal in 2000, both Tendulkar and Sourav Ganguly were in the list of ten most admired Indians.

The honours have come thick and fast in an international career that began in 1989. Remarkably for a batsman, in these 13 years Tendulkar has never struck a prolonged bad patch. It is this consistency that made Steve Waugh say in awe: 'You take Sir Don Bradman away and he is next up I reckon.'

Just as Sunil Gavaskar reserved his best for the mighty West Indies in the 70s and 80s when they were the best team in the world, so Tendulkar has had some of his greatest moments against world champions Australia. So, Waugh certainly knows what he is talking about.

'The greatest Indian alive' is the tag Bishan Singh Bedi attached to Tendulkar. He clarified his remark when I spoke to him for this book in October 2001. 'I said that in 1998 after his two centuries in Sharjah against Australia that won us the title. I had said then that he should share the title with Lata Mangeshkar. I was struck by the amount of entertainment he provided for the average Indian, thrashing the Australian bowlers to all parts. It was the only thing the common Indian had to cheer about—plus Lata-ji's incredible voice. Sachin for me is God's gift to Indian cricket.'

One of Tendulkar's many admirers was the greatest of them all, Sir Donald Bradman. In April 2002 in the West Indies, the Holy Grail of batting, Bradman's mark of 29 centuries was equalled by his heir apparent. Now only his mentor, Sunil Gavaskar's record of 34 Test tons lies before Tendulkar.

In February 1996, during a television interview Gavaskar 'threatened' to 'personally throttle' Tendulkar if his prediction of 40 Test centuries and 15,000 runs for his fellow-Mumbaikar did not come true. Those awesome figures are now well within the realms of possibility.

Since its international debut in 1932, Indian cricket has been blessed with at least one towering figure for each decade. The 30s belonged to C.K.Nayudu, India's first Test captain; the 40s were the Vijay Merchant decade; the 50s saw the domination of all-rounder Vinoo Mankad; in the 60s it was 'Tiger' Pataudi who gave a new dimension to Indian cricket with his astute captaincy; the 70s belonged to Sunil Gavaskar and the 80s to Kapil Dev.

Sachin Tendulkar made his Test debut in 1989 at the age of 16. He crossed 1000 runs and scored five Test centuries before the end of his teens. Since then he has dominated not only Indian cricket, but the world game as well. And that domination has gone beyond just one decade.

If this book were a work of fiction, the rise of Sachin Tendulkar from middle-class anonymity to global fame in the span of less than a decade would find few takers. But it is true. And that is what makes it awe-inspiring.

'What are the advantages of being Sachin Tendulkar?' he was asked in an interview *(Sportsworld*, May 1995).

'I would like to be humble, be polite to everybody and would like to give respect to my elders. I'm not really expecting anything from the people for the little (fame)...I have earned....I believe rules are there to be observed irrespective of whoever you are.'

That in essence is the man. This is his story.

1

Bombay Boy

I thought there was talent in Sachin.—Ajit Tendulkar

He scored his maiden first-class century on debut at 15; his first Test ton came when he was just 17. But the first person to 'bowl' to Sachin was his nanny. Laxmibai Ghije used to throw a plastic ball at the toddler, all of two and a half years, who would hit it back with a *dhoka* (washing stick). 'We used to go to the terrace and play. I was the first bowler he faced in his life,' the 68-year-old recalled in an interview to the *Week* (29 November 1998).

For 11 years Sachin was under the care of Laxmibai at the writers' cooperative housing society of *Sahitya Sahawas* (roughly translated, the 'community of litterateurs') in the middle-class suburb of Bandra (East). His father, Professor Ramesh Tendulkar, taught Marathi at Mumbai's Kirti College, and mother Rajini worked with the Life Insurance Corporation of India (LIC). Sachin was born on 24 April 1973, 11 years after brother Ajit; sister Savita and brother Nitin were the older siblings. His grandfather named him after the famous Hindi music composer, Sachin Dev Burman. Coincidentally, music would be one of the adult Sachin's three passions, the other two being cricket and his family.

Nitin, Savita and Ajit were children from their father's first marriage. When their mother passed away, Ramesh was left with three young children to bring up, and as is the custom in several parts of India, he married the sister of his late wife.

The family was not particularly sports oriented, with poetry and literature being the abiding passions of father Ramesh, a gold medallist of Bombay University in both the BA and MA examinations. Nitin took after his father and his initial interest in cricket was soon diverted to poetry. Ajit was the first in the family to seriously take to cricket; he captained his school team and also played in college and for various club sides. Both today work for Air India, Nitin as a flight purser and Ajit in reservations.

In the 1970s and 80s, the live telecast of cricket and other sports, notably the finals of Wimbledon, brought the superstars of the sporting world into the homes of Indians who were starved of top quality international sports. The very year Sachin was born, the cricket-mad city of Mumbai for the first time had the privilege of watching a Test match live on TV. It was the fifth and final Test against the MCC (England) side led by Tony Lewis and would be the final Test match to be played at the Brabourne Stadium. Ten years later India won the Prudential World Cup in England—shown live in the country—beating twice-champions West Indies in the final against all odds. Sachin had reached 'double figures' just two months before that epochal victory and was part of the new generation of youngsters fired by one of India's greatest sporting achievements.

Sachin, judging from the memories of his childhood friends, was a hyperactive child. An unusual mix of school-yard bully and sensitive soul, he stood out among his friends even at a young age. Laxmibai recalls his compassion as a little boy and his loyalty to his friends, which has stayed with him all his life. 'After coming home from school, he used to have his milk very reluctantly on the staircase. At times he would give the milk to Ramesh, his childhood friend. I used to feed him while he played,' Laxmibai said in the 1998 interview. And he always insisted on two plates while eating—one for himself and another for Ramesh, the son of the local watchman and his fast friend. Today Ramesh is personal assistant to Ajit and Sachin.

The 11 buildings in the *Sahitya Sahawas* housing complex (the Tendulkars' wing, where Ajit still lives with his mother, is called '*Ushakkal*') had by the standards of the crowded metropolis, a large playground, all of 30 yards by 30 yards. This for Sachin and his close companions constituted the great outdoors.

His brother Ajit recalls Sachin as a restless child who could never stay in one spot for long and was always running around. He had also an early interest in outdoor games.

Childhood photos of Sachin show him with a mass of curly long hair, exuberant and playful. The early neighbourhood gang consisted of Avinash Gowariker (now a photographer) and Sunil Harshe (a contractor) while Atul Ranade (Mumbai Ranji Trophy player) was a friend from kindergarten. The most abiding memory of those childhood days appears to be Sachin's strength and his fondness for 'fights'. Whenever there was a new boy in the housing society or school, Sachin would challenge him physically. He rarely came out on the losing side.

Ranade's first glimpse of Sachin was in junior kindergarten. His long hair had him initially mistaken for a girl. 'But it turned out to be a boy and that too a very strong boy,' said Ranade in *Outlook* (4 January 1999).

By the time he reached the second grade, Sachin had achieved the not inconsiderable feat for a six-year-old of beating up another boy all of two years older than him. 'Bashing them up for no reason' was his own unique way of getting his message across to his peer group, according to Ranade. But he showed compassion too, though this trait was reserved for animals. Gowariker summed up the paradox: 'He was a very tender person. But he was always fascinated with power, speed and things like that.'

Sachin's first sporting hero, though, was not a cricketer; it was tennis superstar John McEnroe. The 1981 Wimbledon final between the brash American and the cool Swede, Bjorn Borg, was the first to be shown live in India. It was the match that saw Borg's five-year reign brought to an end in an epic final. Borg was the sentimental favourite all over the world, India included. But Sachin was rooting for the younger man. McEnroe's victory in 1981 spawned a mini 'Mac' in faraway Bandra. Briefly, the child's fascination was for tennis. With racket in hand and the trademarks of the new Wimbledon champion—headband and two wristbands, not to mention the curly hair—the makeover was complete. It was not long before his friends dubbed him 'Mac'. Fortunately for Indian cricket, the fling with tennis did not last, and before long Sachin had made it to the *Sahitya Sahawas* 'big boys' cricket team.

By the time he was 11, Sachin's obsession with cricket had begun. Every morning at 6 a.m., he would be at the nets in Shivaji Park. Sachin's uncle and aunt, Suresh and Mangala Tendulkar, lived just across the road from the park. Sachin would finish school (Sharadashram English, very close to Shivaji Park) in the morning and then go to his uncle's for lunch and a rest before crossing to Shivaji Park for afternoon practice from 3 p.m. to 7 p.m. The kit would be left at his uncle's house, and with his school bag he would get home by 8 p.m. Studies and dinner followed and then a tired Sachin would be in bed. But the commute from Bandra (East) to Dadar (West) became too strenuous after a while and it was decided that it would be better if he stayed on at his uncle's place. The arrangement continued till he made his first-class debut in 1988.

It was his brother Ajit who first spotted Sachin's natural talent. While Sachin imitated his heroes in other sports (notably, McEnroe), where cricket was concerned, he had a style of his own. Ajit noticed his feel for the game and his ability to read the length of the ball. The talent was most definitely there. And it struck Ajit before anyone else. Indian cricket—indeed, the world of sports—owes a huge debt to Ajit Tendulkar, for it was he who set the first small steps in motion.

To understand the rapid rise of Tendulkar from schoolboy cricketer to international star, you first have to understand the ethos and history of Mumbai cricket. Mumbai has produced more Test cricketers and won the Ranji Trophy on more occasions than any other city or state in India. When the mighty Sunil Gavaskar, first to reach 10,000 runs in Test cricket and scorer of most centuries (34) says, 'Whatever I am in the game today is due to the fact that I have been nursed in the cradle of cricket, that is Bombay,' it is no exaggeration. According to him, the most intense clashes he ever took part in were India v Pakistan, Mumbai v Delhi and Dadar Union v Shivaji Park Gymkhana.

Mumbai's proud record in the Ranji Trophy has faded from the glory days that lasted till the mid-70s. Nor do its players these days dominate the ranks of the national team, as had traditionally been the case since India made its international debut in 1932. Indeed, there have been occasions when Sachin Tendulkar was the sole representative in the Test side from the city that boasts the proudest cricket tradition in the land. The North (particularly Delhi) and the South (particularly Karnataka) caught up with their western rival in the mid-70s. Before that Mumbai remained unbeaten from 1958-59 to 1972-73, a golden streak of 15 years unprecedented in the history of first-class cricket.

To understand the passion that is cricket, take a train to Mumbai. Look out of the window as you approach the city and you will see the evidence all around. On tiny strips of land next to the tracks, on streets and in fields, wherever a little space can be squeezed out, boys of all ages, often with the most rudimentary equipment, can be seen playing their hearts out from dawn to dusk. Veteran cricket journalist Pradeep Vijayakar told me that this passion for cricket in his beloved city was 'unquenchable': 'If I could afford to, I would be at the nets early in the morning, play a match during the day and then coach in the evening.'

The 'Bombay school of batsmanship' is a tradition that has served Indian cricket well. It is founded on technical certitude and a ruthless streak where the bowler is the enemy and occupation of the crease a kind of tunnel vision—a take-no-prisoners style of cricket. And the names of Mumbai's great batsmen read like an honour scroll of Indian cricket—Vijay Merchant, Rusi Modi, Polly Umrigar, Nari Contractor, Vijay Manjrekar, Dilip Sardesai, Ajit Wadekar, Sunil Gavaskar, Sandeep Patil, Sanjay Manjrekar, down to the present generation of Pravin Amre, Vinod Kambli and quite possibly the finest of them all, Sachin Tendulkar.

It was on a beach not far from Mumbai, in the Gulf of Cambay, that the very first game of cricket in India was played. Here, in 1721, British sailors and traders whiling away their time during a fortnight's docking played the occasional game which attracted a smattering of local interest. In 1792, the Calcutta Cricket Club (now the Calcutta Cricket and Football Club) was established, the second oldest cricket club in the world after the MCC. Calcutta (now known as Kolkata) was then the headquarters of the British East India Company. But the action soon switched to Mumbai which witnessed its first match in 1797, thanks to the pioneering efforts of the city's tiny Parsi community, also known as India's Hambledon (the birthplace of cricket) men. The first club, the Oriental Cricket Club, was formed in 1848 by which time the Parsis, who had fled Persia in the sixth century, had made a reputation for themselves in virtually every field from business to sporting. They also followed several British customs and traditions, including the game of cricket.

The first team from India to tour England were the Parsis in 1886. Though they could register just one win from 28 matches, the pioneering steps had been taken and two years later, there was a marked improvement in their record when they toured again. Early enthusiasm among Mumbai's population for cricket was obvious in 1890 when the Parsis beat G.F. Vernon's team from England by four wickets, watched by 12,000 spectators. After they had beaten two more sides from England, a biannual match between the Parsis and the Europeans was instituted in 1895. The Governor of Bombay Presidency, Lord Harris, a former MCC president and England Test captain, was one of the early patrons of Indian cricket, and his name lives on in the Harris Shield inter-school tournament in Mumbai in which Sachin first made a name for himself.

By 1907, the Hindus had joined the fray and the tournament grew to a triangular. By 1912, it was termed as the Quadrangular with the inclusion of the Muslims, and then came the Pentangular with players from other communities (including Christians, Jains, Buddhists and Jews) playing for The Rest. All these matches were played in Mumbai, but eventually the league gave way to the Ranji Trophy after it received the stamp of disapproval from none other than Mahatma Gandhi, who considered anything practised along communal lines anathema.

The bedrock of Mumbai cricket in the twentieth century was the Kanga League which was established in 1948 and which journalist Rajdeep Sardesai (son of Dilip Sardesai) described as the 'heart and soul of Bombay cricket' (*An Indian Cricket Omnibus*, ed. Guha and Vaidyanathan). Rajdeep himself once carried his bat for 19 in a total of 40 for Jolly Cricketers (for whom Ajit Tendulkar also turned out) in a Kanga League match in 1990. Every Mumbai cricketer from Merchant to Tendulkar has cut his teeth in the league which started with eight teams and today has 98 from division 'A' to 'G', attracting over 3000 players, umpires and scorers. The uniqueness of this tournament is that it is played in Mumbai's monsoon season when the rain comes down in unending torrents. 'Play forward on a wet pitch and you will end up with mud splattered on your face,' said Vijayakar who proudly boasts of having claimed Tendulkar's wicket first ball in a club match when Sachin was 12 years old.

Many veterans ascribe the decline of Mumbai's cricketing fortunes to the reluctance of today's players to participate on pitches which are so unpredictable in bounce. 'The top players fear playing on wet tracks...that is why Mumbai's batting standards have dropped. The standards were high because the Kanga League helped them tighten their techniques,' former India opener and Mumbai captain Sudhir Naik told Clayton Murzello in an interview in *Sunday Mid Day* (29 July 2001).

The league attracts intense team loyalty. Former Test batsman Madhav Apte (Jolly Cricketers) is still active at 69, having played every year since the team's inception. Another player, wicketkeeper Mehli Dinshaw Irani who played in the Ranji Trophy, also turned out for his side (Parsi Cyclists) for more than 50 years. In his essay 'Come Rain or Shine' (*An Indian Cricket Omnibus*), Rajdeep Sardesai reports his 1989 conversation with Irani: 'If you can play one hour on a rain-affected wicket, then you can play anywhere. Yet, I find that today's youngsters prefer going to England during the summer. Compared to the Kanga League, English cricket is like a friendly village green.' A major incentive for young cricketers in the league is the hope of seeing their names in the next morning's papers. This is their reward for scores of 30 and above, and bowling figures of three or more wickets.

Former Test umpire Piloo Reporter has been standing in local matches for 40 years. In the same article in *Sunday Mid Day*, he recollects,

'Several years ago, I was standing at square leg, umpiring a game at Azad Maidan. The batsman struck the ball to midwicket and the batsmen ran a couple. I was watching the batsman make his ground. As the wicketkeeper collected the ball, the batsman complained, *"Umpire, yeh apna ball nahin hai"* (Umpire, this is not our ball). He was right, a fielder from an adjoining match had thrown the ball which the wicketkeeper gobbled up!'

Nothing can prepare a first-time visitor for the shock of seeing a dozen games being played simultaneously on the chock-a-bloc Azad and Cross Maidans. Nowhere in the world will you see organized cricket in which a fielder seemingly at mid-wicket is actually positioned at fine leg for his own team.

In Sandeep Bamzai's book *Gavaskar and Tendulkar: Shaping Indian Cricket's Destiny*, the flamboyant former Test batsman Sandeep Patil propounded the theory of two schools of batsmanship within the 'Bombay school of batsmanship': Dadar Union and Shivaji Park. Patil, whose father Madhu also played in the Ranji Trophy for Mumbai (and who agreed with his son's theory), reckoned that Dadar Union batsmen exhibited technical exactitude, while the more devastating version incorporating elan, panache and flamboyance was on show at Shivaji Park Gymkhana. Gavaskar, Dilip Vengsarkar and Sanjay Manjrekar played for Dadar Union, while Vijay Manjrekar, Ajit Wadekar and Sandeep Patil represented Shivaji Park Gymkhana.

While the Kanga League is played every Sunday during the monsoon season, the Times Shield (founded by the *Times of India*) is the inter-office league played during the winter, which attracts an equal number of international and first-class players. The city's cricketing structure is completed by the Harris Shield for boys under 15 and the Giles Shield (under 17) inter-school tournaments, ensuring that cricket is played almost all the year round. And competition is fierce at every level.

Mumbai has often been described as Indian cricket's Yorkshire. But just as West Indian cricket fans preferred to refer to Sir Don Bradman as the 'White Headley' (as against George Headley's popular sobriquet, 'The Black Bradman'), diehard Mumbaikars would no doubt consider Yorkshire English cricket's Mumbai.

2
Schoolboy Prodigy

He was a natural cricketer.—Ramakant Achrekar

If the Kanga League is the heart and soul of Mumbai cricket, the Harris and Giles Shield inter-school tournaments are its roots. When Sachin was growing up, the school scene was dominated by the likes of Sharadashram Vidyamandir, Balamohan, St. Mary's, Don Bosco, St. Xavier's and Anjuman-E-Islam.

Sharadashram has produced four Test cricketers—Chandrakant Pandit, Pravin Amre, Sachin Tendulkar and Vinod Kambli. By the 1980s it had overtaken Anjuman-E-Islam as the winner of the most inter-school tournament titles.

Pandit (a wicketkeeper-batsman) and Lalchand Rajput (opening batsman) were in Ruia College with Ajit Tendulkar and were coached by Ramakant Achrekar, the official Sharadashram coach. Achrekar also ran a few cricket clubs, including the Sassanian Cricket Club and the Kamat Memorial Cricket Club for whom he kept wickets in Kanga League matches well into his 40s.

Achrekar never played first-class cricket. But for many years he was the wicketkeeper-batsman for the strong State Bank of India team in the Times Shield which had in its ranks a future India captain and coach, Ajit Wadekar.

'We used to call him the Bradman of tennis-ball cricket, such was his technique,' Wadekar told me in Mumbai in September 2001.

For those who may scoff at the thought of playing cricket with a tennis ball, try it sometime. Keeping the ball on the ground is devilishly difficult and reaching 20 runs is considered quite a feat.

Ajit Tendulkar felt this was the ideal man to guide the early career of his little brother, who he was convinced had the spark in him to make the big time. According to Ajit, Achrekar's biggest asset was the equal emphasis he laid on both net practice and match practice. The coach ensured most of his boys were busy playing in one tournament or the other right through the year.

Ajit duly approached Achrekar 'Sir' (as he is respectfully referred to) and asked if he could bring his brother along for the net practice which Achrekar held for Kamat Club and the boys of Sharadashram at Shivaji Park. The coach, already well known in Mumbai cricket circles, and soon to become a legend in the cricket world, agreed after first confirming that 11-year-old Sachin had never played with a hard cricket ball. Till then, it had been rubber-ball cricket for the little boy.

On the first day, Achrekar told Sachin to watch in order to get a feel of what playing with the 'big boys' would be like. 'For the first and so far perhaps the only time in his cricket career, Sachin just stood and watched the others play,' remembers Ajit.

Once the batting was over Sachin did, however, get a chance to be part of the fielding drill. For the first time, he got the feel of a hard cricket ball. And Ajit, at least, was impressed. 'I realized once more he had natural talent which should be nurtured.'

I met Achrekar at his modest Dadar flat in September 2001 to get his first impressions of the boy who would be king. Achrekar, now in his 60s, has slowed down after a stroke a couple of years ago. But he was still rushing off to Shivaji Park for the daily coaching sessions. His eyes lit up when I asked him about his most famous product. 'Everything was just right. He was a natural cricketer. I did not have to change much. By the time he was 12-13, I knew he would make the big time. If I told him something, he would be diligent and persevering. I would have to tell him something only once and he would stick to it.' Achrekar also emphasized that it was the Tendulkar family structure that provided the bedrock for Sachin's career. 'His father was always behind him and his brother Ajit would accompany him to the nets. This was essential for the youngster.'

On the way home from that first session, Sachin told his brother with the same confidence with which he would handle the world's best bowlers, 'I can bat better than any of them.'

The next day was the first batting session at the nets and though Achrekar did not express any opinion, he did invite him to continue his practice sessions. Playing with a rubber ball meant Sachin resorted to cross-bat shots to cope with the exaggerated bounce. This led to an overemphasis on leg side play in the initial nets. But Ajit noticed his 'uncanny ability' to judge the length of the ball and middle it.

Like all good coaches, Achrekar was loath to change the natural style of the youngster. He did, however, have a problem with Sachin's batting grip, something he had acquired as a five-year-old when he played around with Ajit's bat. In order to grip a bat that was obviously too big for him, Sachin clutched it at the bottom of the handle, and the habit stuck. The bottom-handed grip enabled him to hit strokes with great power. But Achrekar felt it affected his stance and would cause problems as he grew taller. He tried to persuade Sachin to use the orthodox grip, holding the bat in the middle of the handle with both hands together. But Sachin felt uncomfortable with this new grip and finally, Achrekar relented.

Speaking to me late in 2001, Bishan Singh Bedi narrated an incident that occurred in New Zealand in 1990, during Sachin's second tour. Bedi was the team's coach and was told by former New Zealand batting great, Glenn Turner, that Tendulkar's grip was wrong. 'Turner told me that as coach I should do something about it. But I refused, as this was what had brought so many runs for Sachin at such a young age.'

Two weeks at the nets and Achrekar invited the youngster to play his first organized match, a 50-overs match between two teams made up of his wards. He had fixed Sachin's place as number four in the batting line-up. The first two matches produced ducks. (So would his first two One-day Internationals [ODIs] in 1989.) But those early failures did not faze Sachin one bit. And soon, the runs began to flow. Ajit remembers scores of 51, 38 and 45 (a batsman had to retire after reaching 50), though the diary in which Sachin noted his scores has since been lost. The coach was impressed enough to include him in the Kamat Memorial, one of the teams he managed. The year was 1984.

It is said in Mumbai that if a boy wants to play cricket seriously, he should study in Sharadashram English with its champion cricket team. 'Boys joined the school for cricket. If they wanted to study they could have gone somewhere else,' says Ranji Trophy player Amol Muzumdar who studied with Sachin in Sharadashram. (*Outlook*, 4 January 1999).

Sachin started school in the Indian Education Society's New English School, close to the family home in Bandra (East) where most of his friends also studied. But the school lacked a good cricket ground and coach. Achrekar then approached Professor Ramesh Tendulkar with the suggestion that Sachin be moved to Sharadashram; he was by now convinced the boy had potential. The father turned to Ajit for his opinion. Till now Sachin had played cricket only during the school vacations. Now he would have to combine studies and cricket.

The final decision was left to Sachin himself—a tough one for a boy so young. He would miss his school friends. Commuting every day from his home in Bandra (East) to the new school would take an hour each way, and he would have to change buses. However, it did not take him very long to reach a decision. Cricket was more important than fun and games in the backyard. Sharadashram it would be.

First, though, came the task of buying him a complete kit, under the guidance of his coach. Ajit remembers that Sachin in his child-like excitement picked out the first bat he saw, one that appeared too big and heavy for him. Both Ajit and Achrekar tried to dissuade him. But he was firm in his choice and it has always been heavy bats from then on. Today he wields one of the heaviest in the world, between 3 and 3.2 pounds.

By now Sachin's life revolved around cricket and cricket alone. Studies had begun to take a backseat. Except for a four-month hiatus during the monsoon months, when the only cricket played in Mumbai was the Kanga League. Achrekar did not want to risk his star ward on the treacherous pitches where the ball would get up to all kinds of tricks, mostly of the dangerous variety. But those four months helped Sachin forge what would become one of his closest friendships: with Vinod Kambli. Before long, the two boys would find themselves in the record books.

Sachin made his debut in 1984 in the Giles under-15 tournament for Sharadashram English (he was a reserve in the Harris under-17) against Khoja Khan High School at the Navroze Cricket Club ground on Azad Maidan; he was 11 and a half years old.

His first big match knock produced 24 runs. This included three stylish boundaries—a square cut, a cover drive and a straight drive. Ajit was struck by the power in his kid brother's hands since most cricketers of that age do not have the strength to hit boundaries, getting their runs mainly in singles and two's. But Sachin's timing was so good that he was able to find the gaps in the field, allowing the ball to race to the boundary.

The first person to predict success for Sachin was an umpire by the name of Gondhalekar. He was umpiring the quarter-finals against Don Bosco at Cross Maidan in which Sachin smashed ten fours in a knock of 50. The umpire predicted to Achrekar that the lad would one day play for the country—a prediction Achrekar brushed aside since this was Sachin's first year in competitive cricket. But Gondhalekar insisted. Sadly, he would not be around to see his prediction come true just five years after it had been made.

Achrekar was keen that Sachin get a place in the Bombay Cricket Association (BCA) nets for under-19 boys which were spread across the city and were usually conducted by an ex-Test cricketer. These were very popular during the summer vacations and there was a huge rush for the limited slots.

Ajit took Sachin to the MIG (Middle Income Group) Cricket Club ground, a short walk from their home in Bandra, to meet the coach in charge, a man named Dandekar. But Dandekar was shocked when he heard Sachin was only 12, and bluntly told Ajit his kid brother was too young to get into the under-19 nets.

So the summer was spent in practice sessions with Achrekar, both in the mornings and afternoons. Sessions intense enough for Sachin to say goodbye to a normal childhood with summer vacations filled with childhood pranks and fun and games. At about this time, it was decided that Sachin should move to his uncle and aunt's place near Shivaji Park. The move was triggered by the events of one summer afternoon when Sachin and his friends were playing outside the house while the family watched the Hindi film *Guide* on television. They clambered up a mango tree to steal mangoes but came tumbling down when a branch broke under them. The next day his brother and father sent him for coaching and his career in cricket started.

Years later, Sachin would list the names of his uncle and aunt, with those of Ajit and his father, as his greatest influences.

All through this year of 1985, it was cricket, cricket and more cricket. He ate cricket, drank cricket, slept cricket. Even after he broke into international cricket, Sachin was known to talk—cricket, of course!—and walk in his sleep. And the phrase he uttered most often in his sleep? '*Don-ge*' (Take two)!

The grind would begin at seven in the morning. After a quick breakfast he would be at the ground at 7.30. A batting session would be followed by tips from Achrekar, who was always on hand to guide his favourite student. Bowling was a fascination with Sachin from the early days and even then he bowled an assortment of medium pace and leg spin. Fielding was also taken seriously. The morning session would last till ten and the afternoon one would begin at three and continue till seven. But there was no shortage of practice games either. If he got out early, Achrekar would take him across town on his scooter to the Azad Maidan where his Sassanian Cricket Club was playing, and Sachin would get to bat twice during the day. Thus were his summer months spent, engrossed in the game.

At the age of 12, Sachin played his first match in the Kanga League, scoring five for the Young Parsee Cricket Club in the 'F' division. This was during the monsoon. The season began in right earnest in October and this time Sachin played for another of Achrekar's clubs: Hind Sevak Cricket Club in the Gordhandas Shield, open only to clubs in the suburbs of Mumbai. The team won the tournament with

Sachin scoring 30 in his first game and 43 in the semi-finals, against experienced bowlers with 'A' division experience. A special batting prize was presented to the precocious youngster, still one year short of his teens. By now he had made quite a name for himself and his school fielded him in both the Giles and Harris Shield tournaments. In fact, his maiden century came in the Harris, the senior of the two, in the 1985-86 season.

The landmark came against Don Bosco School, Matunga, at the Bharat Cricket Club ground at Shivaji Park. Sachin was unbeaten on 96 at the end of the first day of the three-day match, coming in after the loss of two wickets. To get over the tension, he decided to spend the night at his parents' home instead of his uncle's. But it was a sleepless night.

Early on the second day, one of the rival team's pace bowlers was square-cut to the boundary and Sachin Ramesh Tendulkar's first century entered the record books.

Sachin was then chosen for the Mumbai under-15 team for the Vijay Merchant inter-zonal tournament to be played in Pune. Joining him in the side was school chum Vinod Kambli. But he was run out for one in a tournament marred by rain and did not make it to the West Zone under-15 team.

By this time, the big names of Mumbai cricket were beginning to take notice of the wonder boy. Former Ranji Trophy captain Milind Rege, who was also a junior selector, assured Ajit that Sachin had the potential to go all the way. The 1985-86 season had turned out to be a notable one for Sachin. A maiden century and a recommendation from one of Mumbai cricket's old guards!

He played a full season of Kanga League cricket in 1986-87 for the 'F' division team of the John Bright Cricket Club. He scored 121 runs for an average of nearly 20 when teams were struggling to reach 100 on the treacherous pitches. Scores of 36 and 83 for the Shivaji Park Gymkhana team against P.J.Hindu Gymkhana and the Dadar Union Cricket Club in the G.R.Visvanath Trophy for under-15 boys saw him secure a berth in the Mumbai under-15 team for the Vijay Merchant Trophy.

It has happened countless times since in newspapers and magazines around the world. But the very first time Sachin's photograph appeared in the papers was when he scored 123 against Maharashtra in just 140 minutes, in the opening game at Baroda. That got him into the West Zone under-15 team as he continued to scale the ladder of success at bewildering speed. West Zone lost to holders South Zone with Sachin's 74 run-out being the highest score.

Now it was back to do duty for Sharadashram in the Harris Shield. In the very first match he registered an amazing score for a boy barely into his teens: 276 against BPM High School, that too in a single day against boys three or four years older than him. Just one rung lower, in the Giles Shield, Sachin had been appointed captain. The first match was against the powerful Balamohan, Ajit's former team. Sachin confidently predicted he would win not only the match, but the title as well.

Sharadashram were struggling at 40 for 3 in reply to Balamohan's 250 when the captain came in and smashed 159 not out in two hours. The team was on its way. And so was Sachin. Centuries came thick and fast as he switched back and forth between the under-17 and the under-15 grade. Against St. Xavier's Fort in the Harris, he hit 123 for his third consecutive inter-school ton. Then came 33 not out against the same school in the Giles, and 156 against Barfiwala High School. In the final of the Harris Shield, Sharadashram English faced their sister institution, Sharadashram Marathi. Sachin scored 42 and 150 not out in his side's victory and finished his Harris season with 596 runs in five innings. Captaining his school in the Giles, Sachin smashed 197 in the semi-finals, and then it was time for the final against Don Bosco, Matunga. His knocks of 67 and 53 were the top scores in a low-scoring game. And true to his word, he had led his school to victory, scoring 665 runs with three centuries in the Giles Shield. Sharadashram English achieved the Harris/Giles double that year, largely due to Sachin's huge scores.

Mumbai's local newspapers have always devoted plenty of space on their sports pages to local cricket, from the Kanga League to school tournaments.

The distinction of being the first journalist to interview the prodigy right after the 'double' fell to Sunil Warrier of *Mid Day*. Warrier, now with the *Times of India*, sent me a copy of that first interview (published in December 1986). He has vivid memories of the meeting, claiming with a laugh: 'I made Sachin famous and then he made me famous.'

'Sachin was making runs by the tons. I went to Shivaji Park in Dadar and met him just around lunch. I told him that since he was fielding I would come later in the evening to chat with him,' Warrier told me. 'I was quite surprised to see his brother too with him in the evening. I was wondering how he had found the time to call his brother to the ground. I suggested we go to a restaurant and have a cup of tea. They agreed and we walked a short distance from the ground to a small Irani restaurant. It is one of the oldest in that area. As we started chatting I realized that Sachin was keeping mum and Ajit was doing all the talking. Every time I asked a question, Sachin would prompt his brother in Marathi, "*Tu sang na*" (You tell him). So I told him, since you go to an English medium school you should speak to me in English and not in Marathi. He smiled politely. We had tea and bun *maska* and the session must have lasted about 25 minutes or so. I did meet Sachin subsequently when he scored debut hundreds in the Ranji Trophy and Irani Trophy. But I was weaned away from cricket to hockey and football and I never met Sachin again.'

Warrier's interview mentioned that Sunil Gavaskar and Vivian Richards were Sachin's favourite batsmen, something he maintains to this day. 'The square cut and the off drive are his favourite strokes,' Warrier wrote. 'He loves to play one-day cricket more than a four-day match. His natural instincts are to attack from the word go.' The interview revealed that 'he thrives on Michael Jackson songs' and concluded with 'Sachin is also a good singer.'

There were so many tournaments to play and Sachin did not want to miss any of them—the Cosmopolitan Shield, the Bombay Junior Cricket tournament, the Mahim-Dadar Shield and the Gordhandas Shield, as well as a few matches for the BCA Colts. He scored his second double-century of the season, 216 in a day, against IES High

School in the Matunga Shield. (Incidentally, it would take him a decade to score his maiden first-class double century and the same number of years to score his first Test double ton.)

But the fantastic season was destined to have a disappointing end. Sachin had scored twice as many runs as any other school cricketer and was the only batsman to have scored a hundred for Mumbai in the Vijay Merchant Trophy. He was the top scorer for the West Zone in the zonal competition for the same tournament. He had been prolific in club cricket against senior bowlers. Yet, he was bypassed for the BCA's Best Junior Cricketer of the Year award. It was a strange decision.

There was consolation, however, in the form of a letter from Sunil Gavaskar dated 3 August 1987, which contained encouraging words and a postscript: 'Don't be disappointed at not getting the Best Junior Cricketer award from BCA. If you look at the best award winners you will find one name missing and that person has not done badly in Test cricket!!'

Even while scoring a mountain of runs, Sachin did not neglect his bowling and picked up quite a few wickets with his medium-pacers. In October of that year, he was part of the selection trials at the MRF Pace Academy in Chennai (then known as Madras), overseen by Australian fast bowling legend Dennis Lillee. But Lillee was not impressed with his bowling and told him to concentrate on batting. Sachin was not selected for the Academy.

The 1987-88 season was a turning point in Sachin's fledgling career.

Even while he was making his mark in every junior tournament in the city, both he and Ajit felt at the start of the season that there was a chance to make it to first-class cricket. Sure enough, at the age of 14, Sachin became the youngest player ever selected for Mumbai in the West Zone Ranji Trophy league.

After useful scores in the Kanga League—where he had now leapfrogged to the 'B' division—he was selected for the Sportstar Trophy for boys under 17. The tournament, organized for schoolboys, featured teams named after famous Indian cricketers. Sachin's scores of 158, 97 and 75 won him the Man of the Series award and took his team (Dattu Phadkar XI) to victory.

On 14 November 1987, the Mumbai Ranji Trophy selection panel of Ajit Wadekar, Sudhir Naik, Bapu Nadkarni and Sandeep Patil announced the names of 36 probables. Sachin's name was on the list. It was just seven months after his fourteenth birthday.

The name of Sunil Gavaskar also figured on the list. But Gavaskar had announced his retirement during the MCC Bicentenary match at Lord's in August and thus the two narrowly missed playing in the same team.

Sachin was in the reserves for the opening West Zone league tie against Baroda on 19 December. Though he got the chance to field as a substitute in some of the games, he was not selected for the playing eleven that season.

Runs continued to flow in junior tournaments. But he failed to gain selection to the Indian team for the under-19 World Cup in Australia. In the Giles and Harris Shield he had a fantastic run: 21 not out, 125, 207 not out, 326 not out, 172 not out, 346 not out, 0 and 14. The 'failures' of 0 and 14, as well as 172 not out, were scored in the Giles Shield. His Harris Shield total of 1,025 runs came to the staggering average of 1,025! The two triple centuries had come in the Harris Shield, in the semi-finals against St. Xavier's, Fort (326 not out) and in the final against Anjuman-E-Islam (346 not out).

3

World Record

He is a sure bet for India in a few years' time.—Raj Singh Dungarpur

The Harris Shield semi-final against St. Xavier's, Fort (Sunil Gavaskar's old school) was played at the Sassanian Cricket Club ground on Azad Maidan on 23-25 February 1988, and it was this match that propelled Sachin into the world record books for the first time.

St. Xavier's had in their ranks leg-spinner Sairaj Bahutule, a future Test cricketer, while defending champions Sharadashram had Vinod Kambli and Amol Muzumdar besides Tendulkar in their team. Muzumdar would go on to captain Mumbai in the Ranji Trophy; he holds the world record for the highest score by a debutant in first-class cricket (260).

Sachin won the toss and took first strike. Opening bowler Sanghani picked up the wickets of openers Atul Ranade (42) and R.Mulye (18) and the score was 84 for 2 when Sachin joined Vinod, who had by then reached 29. At the end of the first day's play, Vinod was batting on 182 and Sachin on 192.

Achrekar was at the ground on the first day to watch his two pupils. But he couldn't make it on the second and his deputy Laxman Chavan was told to keep in touch with him over the phone. It was not long before both batsmen crossed 200 on the second morning and the total mounted to 500. Chavan spoke to Achrekar who told him to pass on instructions to Sachin to declare and give enough time for his bowlers to dismiss St. Xavier's on the second day itself.

'Achrekar Sir's assistant ran all round trying to attract our attention so that he could tell us to declare. Sachin kept telling me not to look at him. We even started singing,' recalled Kambli years later in the television documentary *Tendulkar at 25*.

Finally, a stern warning over the phone during the lunch break forced Sachin to declare at 748 for 2. He was on 326 (one six, 49 fours) and Kambli on 349 (three sixes, 49 fours). The runs had come from just 120 overs: more than a run a ball. The sole maiden was bowled by Sanghani who had the 'best' figures of 2 for 98. Bahutule conceded 182 runs from his 27 overs. By close, a thoroughly demoralized St. Xavier's were 77 for 3.

'Yes, I was angry with Sachin and Vinod as they batted on and on,' Achrekar recalls with a chuckle. 'After all, you cannot bat forever.' Perhaps for the first time, Sachin got a ticking off from his coach. He did not play in the match the next day as he shifted grounds to play in a Giles Shield game. St. Xavier's crumbled to 145 with Kambli picking up 6 for 37 with his off breaks.

A month later, it was revealed in the media that the unbeaten stand for the third wicket worth 664 runs was a world record for any wicket in any class of cricket. The previous record stood in the names of T. Palton and N. Rippon for Buffalo River v Whoroughly at Gapstead in Victoria, Australia in 1913-14.

Thanks to that band of dedicated number crunchers, the Association of Cricket Statisticians and Scorers of India, this feat was recognized as a world record, and the boys got plenty of coverage. They were thrilled to see their names in both the *Guinness Book of World Records* and *Wisden Cricketers' Almanack*.

While Sachin was not a new name for Mumbai cricket followers, he was for most of us in the rest of the country. I was then with the *Indian Express* in Chennai. My brother sent me a cutting from Delhi, of an article on the world record by the late Sunder Rajan that had appeared in the *Times of India*, Mumbai. He wrote across the cutting: 'Watch out for this boy.'

'The world record helped us a lot,' recalled Kambli in an interview to the *Sportstar* (30 September 1995). 'That enabled us to jump the ladder. Previously you had to come through the rungs; we were lucky.'

The Harris Shield final is the most important fixture in Mumbai school cricket. Befitting the occasion, the match is played at Brabourne Stadium, still a favourite with the city's cricket cognoscenti despite the presence of the Wankhede Stadium just across the street. Sharadashram English were up against the formidable Anjuman-E-Islam who had an equally glorious record in the competition. Sachin won the toss and decided to bat. But there wasn't going to be a repeat of the world-beating semi-final. Kambli was out for 18 with the score on 35 for 2. By close, Sachin was batting on 122. He had begun slowly, but gradually played his favourite lofted shots to spread the field. He added a further 144 runs the next day and was on 286 in a total of 511 for 7. The local press had by now latched on to the fact that there was a real talent in their midst and most papers carried Sachin's photograph the next morning. Sharadashram added 79 runs before being all out on the third morning, Sachin's share being 60 to stay unbeaten on 346—his second consecutive unbeaten triple century in the tournament. There was just one life—he was dropped in the covers when on 229.

Anjuman finished the third and penultimate day on 131 for 4. Straight after the rigours of his triple ton, Sachin came on to bowl 22 overs of medium pace on the trot. The match ended with Anjuman on 269 for 8 with Sachin having claimed four wickets in 52 overs (28 maidens). Since even the first innings could not be completed, it was decided that the teams would be declared joint winners.

Tendulkar paid tribute to the Harris Shield and its role in his early development, on the hundredth anniversary of the tournament. In the *Lord Harris Shield Cricket Tournament: Commemoration Volume, 1897-1997* he wrote:

> One cannot but be amazed at the vision and dedication of those who had thought of organizing the tournament for schools....The Harris Shield has a special significance for me. As everyone knows, the unbeaten partnership of 664 between Vinod Kambli and myself brought both of us into the limelight.

Thus, often I wonder what I would have been had there been no Harris Shield tournament. As it has been in my case, the Harris Shield has shaped the destiny of countless cricketers in Mumbai.

The tournament has made Mumbai cricket a great force to reckon with. Its contribution to the game is invaluable. And it has withstood the test of time. There are not many tournaments in the world that can claim to have completed one hundred years.

I particularly cherish the fact that I had the good fortune of leading my school, Sharadashram Vidyamandir (English), to victory in the Harris Shield.

The tournament enabled me to show my cricketing skills at an early age. With the game becoming increasingly popular and with youngsters taking to it in large numbers the Harris Shield assumes added significance as the launching pad for fresh talent.

Sachin was still in school when Raj Singh Dungarpur, one of the doyens of Mumbai cricket and the president of the Cricket Club of India (CCI), took the initiative to make Sachin a member of the prestigious club, whose home is the Brabourne Stadium. The club changed its rules to allow Sachin to play for them in the Kanga League. Club rules stipulated that no one below 18 years was allowed in the pavilion or the dressing rooms. Sachin was just 14!

In an article on Tendulkar by Scyld Berry (*Wisden Cricket Monthly*, June 1996), Raj Singh—then chairman of the national selection committee—looked back eight years on Sachin's innings in the Harris Shield final of April 1988.

'What I recall was his tremendous maturity. He was playing on a full-sized ground for the first time. The field was spread out and he kept driving singles to long off and long on. Then he checked his shot and started taking twos. That was maturity and a high level of confidence.' Raj Singh was also quoted in a more contemporary profile of Sachin by Shirish Nadkarni soon after his school and early Ranji trophy feats, in the *Cricketer International* (April 1989).

> This boy is simply amazing; I have never seen so much concentration and stamina in one so young. He is very strong on the leg side, but otherwise plays strictly in the 'V' to either side of the bowler and all along the ground. His concentration is really astounding—in the two days-plus that he batted while scoring 346 against Anjuman, there was just one blemish and perhaps one uppish square-cut that nearly went to hand. Further, you must remember that he came to the wicket when his team was in a tight corner, having lost early wickets. He played with great responsibility and never lofted the ball. And then he came on to bowl all those tidy overs of medium pace and spin! There is so much of Greg Chappell that I see in him—the batting, the strokes, the bowling style. If carefully nurtured, he is a sure bet for India in a few years' time.

The prediction would come true seven months—not seven years—after the article was published. For Sachin would make his international debut in November 1989.

4

A Boy Among Men

Tendulkar never fails.—Naren Tamhane

Raj Singh Dungarpur, with his eye for talent, played a major role in the formative stages of Sachin's cricketing career. The former Rajasthan medium-pacer (and erstwhile royalty) arranged for a sponsor (the Birla Trust) to enable Sachin to go on his first tour abroad, to England with the Star Cricket Club. The manager of Star was another former Rajasthan medium-pacer, Kailash Gattani, who also had playing experience in England with the Kent second eleven. The tour began in June 1988, when the hot summer months in Mumbai ensured that there was no competitive cricket to speak of.

It was a tight schedule, with 23 matches (all of 50 overs) played in a span of just 30 days. Two days of sightseeing were allotted for the boys, all under 19, during which they visited Edinburgh Castle and the museum at Lord's. Future Test cricketers Vinod Kambli and Sameer Dighe were also in the squad. In the first match against Indian Gymkhana, Sachin scored 49. He followed it up with scores of 41, 81 not out, 44, 63 not out and 73, all scored at a rapid rate.

What is more, he played throughout with an injury: a wart on the left hand between the thumb and the index finger which caused considerable pain and prevented him from gripping the bat properly.

Sachin was back in the UK the following year with Star, and this time he scored his first century on foreign soil. It was in the opening match against Haywards Heath Cricket Club and came from just 77 balls, with 16 fours and two sixes. The team had a few first-class cricketers from Sussex in the side, as well as future South African Test pace bowler Meyrick Pringle. There was nearly another century for Sachin, against Horsham Cricket Club, and this time his 94 came off 75 deliveries.

The two trips gave Sachin valuable exposure to the variable pitches and the changing weather patterns in England. The experience would hold him in good stead, for just 12 months after the second tour he would be back again—this time as a member of the Indian national team.

After returning to Mumbai with the Star team in 1988, it was time for Sachin to play for the CCI in the first division of the Kanga League. He was among the top scorers with 190 runs in six innings. The secretary of the CCI cricket committee and former Mumbai Ranji Trophy captain Milind Rege was suitably impressed by the way Sachin played—like a 'grown-up man'—getting on top of the ball even on a drying track. The seniors in the team paled by comparison.

There was just one more taste of junior cricket before Sachin made his first-class debut. This was as captain of the Mumbai under-17 side in the Vijay Hazare tournament, in which he scored 83 in the final of the West Zone league, against Maharashtra.

A week later, his world would change forever.

There was little doubt now that Sachin would make his Ranji Trophy debut in the season's opening West Zone league game at the Wankhede Stadium against Gujarat. But before that, he had to play in the trial matches. The selection committee of Naren Tamhane, Milind Rege, Sudhir Naik and Ajit Wadekar were suitably impressed, for Sachin scored 55 in the first game and 54 in the second, with nine boundaries. The innings came against an attack that included Test opening bowler Raju Kulkarni, reckoned at the time to be one of the fastest in the country, and that too on a green top.

Years later, Sachin would recall how he irritated Kulkarni by batting without a helmet. It was not meant as a provocation—he simply did not possess one!

Rege wrote in *Sportsweek,* 'We decided to induct Sachin in the Bombay Ranji XI at his usual number four position. Every member in the team was delighted with the way Sachin batted. In fact, he was the only one to drive off the front foot while facing Kasliwal, Kher and Sabnis who worked up a decent pace on the Wankhede practice wickets which are fairly nippy. The reason why I say this is because everybody these days tends to go on the back foot for a medium-pacer.'

Dilip Vengsarkar was captain of both the Mumbai Ranji Trophy team and the national team at the time. He had never seen Sachin bat and needed to be convinced that this boy, who was just 15 and barely five feet two inches tall, could stand up to adults. The Indian team was in Mumbai for a Test match against New Zealand, and Vengsarkar invited the schoolboy to the nets where he got a chance to face the mighty Kapil Dev. Kapil initially bowled off a shorter run-up. But seeing Sachin play him confidently, he stepped up the pace and even slipped in a few bouncers. Sachin was unfazed and stood up to him without flinching.

Asked for his verdict, Kapil was cautious. 'Don't write too much about him now,' he told the newsmen. 'There is some way to go.' Vengsarkar, though, was impressed enough to give the go-ahead for the teenager's inclusion in Mumbai's Ranji fixture against Gujarat.

The experience of facing Kapil left a lasting impression on Sachin. 'I couldn't sleep that night because I had played 15 balls from Kapil Dev. I remember each of those balls like it was yesterday,' he was to say ten years later (*Outlook*, 24 August 1998).

Sachin's debut match was played on 10-12 December 1988 and was the opening match in the Talim Shield, symbol of supremacy in the Ranji Trophy West Zone division. With Vengsarkar on national duty, Mumbai were led by Lalchand Rajput who had earlier opened in Tests for the country. Gujarat's captain was Dhansukh Patel.

Normally, a match involving Gujarat, one of the traditional whipping boys in the West Zone, would evince little interest. But this time Mumbai's cricketing elite turned up in force to watch the prodigy make his debut. The entire selection committee was present as were Gavaskar, Achrekar and Raj Singh—who was at the time the chairman of the national selection committee. The small crowd of about 300 included many boys from *Sahitya Sahawas* as well as from

Sharadashram, all come to cheer their friend.

The match began dramatically after Gujarat won the toss, with S.D. Pathak bowled by Kasliwal from the first ball of the match. Gujarat did not recover from that early shock and were skittled out for 140 before the tea break. By close, Mumbai were 95 for the loss of Shishir Hattangadi's (35) wicket. The fans would have to wait one more day to watch their favourite in action.

Gujarat's total was passed quickly enough on the second day. Alan Sippy and his captain added 159 runs for the second wicket and the pair batted serenely almost till the lunch break. But the spectators had come for one thing only—to watch Sachin bat. With the interval barely 15 minutes away, Rajput going for a third run was run out for 99 at 206 for 2, and Sachin made his way to the crease, heralded by rapturous applause. His moment had arrived.

Seven deliveries later, Sachin faced his first ball in first-class cricket, bowled by off-spinner Nisarg Patel. The batsman defended. The same with the second. The third, tossed up outside the off stump, was promptly driven inside out through the covers for four. Sachin's first scoring stroke in first-class cricket was a boundary. A sign of things to come for bowlers around the world! The next two balls were defended and the last of the over produced another boundary, driven past the bowler and mid-on. At lunch Sachin was on ten. Between lunch and tea his score progressed to the 80s with a full range of attacking strokes as Mumbai strove for quick runs and bonus batting points. Together, Sachin and Sippy added 145 runs to the score, then the left-hander departed for 127, bowled by left-arm spinner Joy Zinto, and Mumbai were 361 for 3.

A mini collapse ensued. Iqbal Khan was bowled for a duck and Suru Nayak was run out for two. Sachin was joined by another debutant, Sameer Talpade, by which time he had progressed to 95. Left-arm spinner Bharat Mistry came on to bowl to a slip, point, cover, deep extra cover, mid-off, long off, mid-on, midwicket and square leg. Mistry tossed the ball up, inviting the drive. Sachin obliged, the shot leaving the fielders rooted as he raced to 99. The tension in the stands was now at breaking point. The next ball was faster and flatter. Sachin went on the front foot and with a neat turn of the wrists to backward square leg, he got the vital run. The century on debut was complete and the stadium erupted in applause. The 100 had come off just 129 balls, with 12 fours. In the next over, Talpade was out for five and Mumbai declared at 394 for 6. The crowd rose as Sachin returned to the pavilion, unbeaten on 100.

At 15 years, 7 months and 17 days, Sachin Tendulkar entered the record books as the youngest Indian to score a century on first-class debut. The match was drawn as Gujarat scored 306 in their second innings and Mumbai finished on 43 for 2, with Sachin not batting a second time. But for once, the result was irrelevant.

There were five days between this opening match and the next against Saurashtra at Rajkot—enough time for more Harris Shield cricket. Against Bandra Urdu High School, Sachin's 191 runs were scored in a mere two hours. That same night he left with the team for Rajkot, where a shock awaited Mumbai. Rajput and Sippy were both out for a duck in the very first over bowled by left-arm medium-pacer Rajesh Jadeja. Unlike in his debut match, this time there was the pressure of a scoreboard reading 0 for 2 when Sachin came to the crease to join opener Hattangadi. He put his head down as the situation demanded, and batted for 156 minutes and 125 balls before getting out for 58. The stand was worth 133 and Hattangadi went on to score 103 in a small Mumbai total of 252. None of the other batsmen could cross 20. Saurashtra gained the rare honour of taking the first innings lead as they scored 297.

In the second innings Sachin came in at number three with the score reading 77 and this time played 120 deliveries for his innings top score of 89 with seven boundaries, the same as in the first innings. He narrowly missed his second century in three innings when he played an overambitious shot, slashing at spinner Virbhadran Gohil to be well caught by Bimal Jadeja at point. A newspaper report the next day commented that 'Tendulkar showed uncanny judgement in meting out the right treatment to every ball.... He danced to hit the ball to the straight field and imparted quite a bit of power to his cover drives and square cuts. He has one flaw. He gets carried away and cannot be curbed even by the non-striker or by advice shouted from the gallery.'

This match too was drawn, with Mumbai declaring their second innings at 250 for 5 and Saurashtra scoring 78 for 4.

Following his first two matches, a remarkable article on Sachin by Mumbai journalist Shirish Nadkarni appeared in the *Cricketer International* (April 1989). The headline was startling: 'As Good As Gavaskar?' After recounting Sachin's scores in the first three innings of his fledgling first-class career, Nadkarni wrote: 'If this is the rate at which Sachin Tendulkar is going to be setting cricketing records, he may even end up putting the great Sunil Gavaskar in the shade....[Sachin] is already being talked about as being better than Gavaskar was at the same age. After all, Gavaskar was not called up for Ranji duty until he was out of his teens, whereas Sachin will only celebrate his sixteenth birthday on 24 April 1989. Until this point the comparison runs very much in his favour, but otherwise it is invidious, since Sachin is basically an attacking batsman whereas Sunny was a master of classical defensive technique.'

Even after making a mark at the first-class level, Sachin continued to play for his school and age-specific tournaments, treating all matches with equal importance. By now, Sanjay Manjrekar, Dilip Vengsarkar and Chandrakant Pandit were back from the Test series against New Zealand and turned out for Mumbai in their third league match against Baroda in Thane. But there was no dislodging Sachin from the team. Baroda were led by Anshuman Gaekwad with wicketkeeper Kiran More and left-arm medium-pacer Rashid Patel (all with Test experience) also in the side. This would be Sachin's most formidable opposition to date.

Baroda batted first and scored 313. Mumbai lost openers Rajput and Hattangadi with only 20 on the board, and Sachin came in ahead of Vengsarkar who was nursing an injured right knee. Patel and Abhay Palkar were both working up a good pace. Sachin quickly hit them both for boundaries. But a lifter from Patel had him caught behind by More for 17, his first failure in first-class cricket. Mumbai gained a lead of 19 runs and the match was drawn, with Sachin not batting in a second innings total of 5 for 1.

The Indian under-19 team was to tour Pakistan for the first time and Sachin was a certainty. He scored 63 in the trial match and also had a double century and a century in the under-19 Cooch Behar Trophy. But the tour was for six weeks' duration and his Secondary School Certificate (SSC) finals were not far off. His family decided that his final year of school had to take precedence. However, he continued touring with the Mumbai Ranji Trophy side since he would be away from home for only a few days. His school books were packed with his cricket gear. 'The school teachers were willing to help me whenever I went to them for guidance,' said Tendulkar in an interview to the *Sportstar* (6 May 1995), looking back on those early years. 'I used to attend those special classes. It was just that I had to miss classes in my last year in school. It was hard to cope with studies. My father had a greater role to play in my success. He told me, "Whatever you want to be, see that you achieve something. Do something where the future is fully secured. I don't want you to try out in every field. If you want to play tennis, establish yourself as a good tennis player. Or prove to be a good cricketer. I don't want to compel you to pursue something."'

Obviously, the late Professor Tendulkar was a man of vision. Sachin did pass his exams but from then on, all further tests would be on the cricket field.

The last West Zone league match was at Aurangabad in January 1989 against Maharashtra. With Ravi Shastri back in the team after Test duty, Mumbai now had eight former, current or future Test players in its ranks. The home side fielded two promising pace bowlers, Salil Ankola and Gregory D'Monte. Ankola had taken a hat-trick in his debut match against Gujarat earlier in the season, while D'Monte had toured Zimbabwe with the India under-25 team.

Maharashtra ran up a huge 575 in their first innings with opener Surendra Bhave scoring nearly half the total off his own bat. Rajput and Pandit gave Mumbai a flying start with an opening stand worth 170 and with Manjrekar also chipping in, they were well placed at 303 for 3. They finished on 435. Tendulkar scored 81 and four not out in the drawn match and Maharashtra finished on top of the West Zone league with 55 points. Mumbai were second, on 46, to join them in the knockout stage. Remarkably, for a 15-year-old in a team full of international stars, Sachin topped the Mumbai batting in the league phase with 349 runs at an average of 87.25. One fascinated viewer of Sachin's 81 was Sandeep Bamzai who wrote about it in his book *Gavaskar and Tendulkar: Shaping Indian Cricket's Destiny*:

> Ankola tried to intimidate the little fella (Sachin), but he took a heavy toll of the wayward bowling. Benign surface or not, it was a stylish knock which still reverberates in the corridors of my mind for the sheer élan and timing displayed. As Ankola bowled on his legs, Tendulkar smashed him to the mid-wicket fence twice, in a trice. The following over, he gave him the same treatment, but this time round, on the off side. He raced to 81 and there was a shot where he bisected the cover fielders, rocking on his backfoot which took our collective breath away in the *shamiana* which served as the press box.

The match was played shortly before the team for the tour to the West Indies was selected and Ankola was on the short-list, though he did not make it. He would eventually play for the country. Mumbai took on Hyderabad next, led by future India skipper Mohammad Azharuddin, in the pre-quarter-finals at Secunderabad in February, and by coincidence I was in Hyderabad to report on the national table tennis championships for the *Indian Express*. With Sachin's reputation having preceded him, every sports journalist in town made a beeline for the dust bowl that was the Gymkhana Ground at Secunderabad, the twin city of Hyderabad.

The large open ground was dotted with shamianas and had no seating to speak of. But Sachin had already become a major crowd-puller and there must have been close to 10,000 spectators—an unusually large crowd for a Ranji Trophy match, even one with so many Test players in both sides. The pitch was a typical turner and the spinners played a leading role from the very first session of the first day. Hyderabad had three spinners of note: Venkatapathy Raju (left-arm), Arshad Ayub (off spin) and M.V. Narasimha Rao (leg spin) while Mumbai could call on the services of Ravi Shastri (left-arm), Suru Nayak (leg spin) and Kiran Mokashi (off spin).

Sure enough, wickets tumbled to spin as Hyderabad were dismissed for 270 (Shastri 4-90, Mokashi 4-65). Mumbai too were struggling at 90 for 4 by the close of the second day. Mokashi was sent in as nightwatchman after Ayub and Raju had accounted for Rajput, Pandit and Manjrekar. But he too fell to Ayub, and Sachin came in at 79 for 4 at the fag end of the day in the company of captain Vengsarkar.

Sachin defended the first ball he faced and drove the next to the boundary. That evening he cornered the team's manager, P.K. 'Joe' Kamath with whom he was sharing a hotel room. Kamath reported the conversation in the *Wisden Cricket Monthly* (July 1990): 'Sir, why did you send a bowler ahead of me? Did you not have confidence in me?' asked Sachin. Kamath confessed that he did not have an answer.

The tiny baby-faced Sachin and Vengsarkar, the towering captain of the national team, were a study in contrast, at least physically. But Sachin matched his skipper stroke for stroke as they added 118 runs to take Mumbai out of the woods and eventually to a narrow first innings lead. Sachin's 59 came in 145 minutes and contained 7 fours. In the second innings, he took 15 runs. Mumbai won the match by six wickets. I recall everyone in the press box, both experienced hands and rookie reporters, being struck by the maturity of the callow youth and the confidence of his stroke play. Many in the fraternity were predicting great things from the schoolboy.

Ravi Shastri was the third Mumbai captain in the season for the quarter-final against Uttar Pradesh which was played at home, as Vengsarkar was unavailable. After an opening stand worth 145 between Rajput and Hattangadi (140), the Mumbai batting collapsed, the next nine batsmen failing to reach even double figures. Sachin was dismissed for just seven by Test off-spinner Gopal Sharma who had the best figures of 4 for 81. But Uttar Pradesh suffered an even more dramatic collapse, crumbling from 104 for 3 to 137 all out. Mumbai piled up 422 in their second innings (Sharma 7-113). There was another half-century by Sachin, his 75 taking four minutes short of four hours, his longest stint at the crease so far. Mumbai won by 224 runs and ran into the formidable Delhi in the semi-finals at the Wankhede Stadium.

Mumbai were weakened by the absence of Vengsarkar, Shastri and Manjrekar, back on national duty in the West Indies. The Delhi side, on the other hand, had a formidable look to it with Madan Lal, Maninder Singh, Manoj Prabhakar and Raman Lamba. Delhi piled up 409 in their first innings. Manu Nayyar (105) and Prabhakar (123) put on 232 for the opening wicket. Tendulkar got his first chance to bowl in first-class cricket (4-0-12-0; 9-2-20-0) and also took his first catch (Manoj Prabhakar for 11 off Nayak's bowling in the second innings). Left-arm spinner Maninder Singh, who had not been considered for the West Indies tour, had the splendid figures of 37-5-105-7 when Mumbai batted. Hattangadi (68) was once again among the runs and was third out at 138. But it was Sachin who took the honours and top-scored with 78. It was his seventh score of 50 plus in the season, in 11 innings, and contained a six and five fours. He began aggressively, hitting boundaries off Maninder and Madan Lal, scattering the field. But the rest of the Mumbai batting could not counter Maninder's spin and at the end of the third day, they were struggling at 258 for 7 with Sachin on 58. His first six came early on the third day, a huge shot that travelled nearly 85 yards from a drive off Sanjay Sharma, an off-spinner. Sachin was last man out and Mumbai were dismissed for 321. The match was drawn, but Delhi were in the final thanks to their first-innings lead of 88 runs.

Maninder, one of the most talented spinners to play for the country, has fond memories of that match. His seven wickets proved to be a match-winning performance. But it was Sachin's 78 that caught his eye.

'The first ball I bowled to him he smashed over extra cover, one bounce four. I was so impressed that for the first time in my entire life I said, "God, I hope he scores runs. I would love to watch him,"' Maninder told me when I interviewed him in August 2001.

'He was so good, so compact at the age of 15 and a half, it was tremendous. When I came back to Delhi after that match, I told my coach that I had just seen a future star in action.'

Despite his outstanding maiden first-class season (583 runs from 11 innings at 64.77, with one century and six 50s) it had been decided that Sachin was too raw to be chosen for the Indian team on their tour of the mighty West Indies. The chairman of the selection board, Raj Singh, admitted the selectors 'seriously thought' about choosing him. 'But we decided to wait till until the tour of Pakistan [later in 1989].'

It was perhaps a wise decision not to expose him to the West Indian quicks at such a tender age. Not that Sachin himself thought so.

Just before the team to the West Indies was announced, actor-journalist Tom Alter interviewed Sachin for a sports video (*Sports Channel*).

> Alter: Are you willing to go to the West Indies?
> Sachin: If I get selected I will go.
> Alter: How will you face Ambrose, Walsh and the others?
> Sachin: I will try my best to face them.

Alter looked back at that interview in *Outlook* magazine (January 1999):

> Four points stood out. Firstly he stated that Gavaskar and Richards were his heroes. Secondly, without hesitation he said that he could read Hirwani's googly, and was ready to face the West Indian fast bowlers (in fact, he said he prefers fast bowling). Thirdly, when asked whether he grew tired of batting while with Kambli in that mammoth partnership, Sachin's reply was an almost unbelievable shake of the head. And fourthly, Sachin made it very clear that being compared to Gavaskar was a bit embarrassing to him, and that he simply wanted to play his own, 'natural' game.

The 1989-90 season kicked off in Mumbai with the Irani Trophy match between Ranji Trophy champions Delhi and the Rest of India for whom Sachin was an automatic choice. It was played on 3-7 November 1989 and was a virtual selection trial for the tour to Pakistan starting later that month. The selection committee consisting of Raj Singh Dungarpur (chairman), G.R.Visvanath, Naren Tamhane, Ramesh Saxena and Akash Lal were to select the team on the third evening of the match, so competition was bound to be intense.

Delhi piled up 461 and by close on the second day, Rest were 79 for 3 with Rajput, Surendra Bhave and Manjrekar the batsmen back in the pavilion. It would be uphill all the way after that. When Gursharan Singh was out for 31 on the third morning, Sachin joined nightwatchman Syed Saba Karim with the total on 119 for 4. Sachin punished the medium pace of Sanjeev Sharma and Atul Wassan, but was troubled by Maninder's accurate left-arm spin. Wassan had picked up two of the four wickets that had fallen at that stage and was bowling with his tail up. After playing himself in, Sachin on-drove and then straight drove Wassan to the boundary. Captain Madan Lal replaced Wassan with Sharma who was promptly smashed for four, followed by a square cut off Maninder that went racing to the boundary for Sachin's fourth four. But Maninder was persisted with and made the breakthrough under rather fortuitous circumstances. As Sachin defended on the front foot, the ball went off the middle of the bat, dropped to the ground and spun on to the stumps to bowl him for a crisply struck 39. Rest were dismissed for 290 to give Delhi a big lead.

That evening, all talk centred on the selection of the team to Pakistan. It was an agonizing wait for the Tendulkar family, but finally they got confirmation of Sachin's selection following a phone call late in the evening from a reporter asking for reactions. The match itself must have seemed anticlimactic after that. There was no stopping Delhi, however, who declared on the fifth morning at their overnight total of 383 for 8. The target of 555 for Rest on the last day was an impossibility. But it did give Sachin another crack at the record books.

Incidentally, during the meeting to select the team for Pakistan, the view was expressed that Sachin might be a failure. 'Tendulkar never fails,' was the reply by the late Naren Tamhane, the West Zone representative.

Sachin went in with the score at 76 for 2 and as if to celebrate the news of his selection, went for the Delhi bowlers. Wassan and Sharma were pretty liberal with the short-pitched stuff, but it didn't seem to bother Sachin. By now, it was virtually Sachin v Delhi as wickets tumbled at the other end. Maninder, who had taken four wickets in the first innings including that of Sachin, was hit over mid-wicket for a huge six. 'It was a brilliant innings. He was hungry for runs and more runs even at that age,' Maninder told me. 'That is what makes him get out of tricky situations. From 15 years onwards, it was his hunger for perfection that was his greatest quality.'

Sachin raced to 50 from just 66 balls, with seven fours, and was rapidly running out of partners. Maninder once again bowled well to claim three wickets. At 132 for 6, the tail was exposed. Sachin tried to retain the strike as much as possible. Razdan and he added 35 runs, Vivek Razdan's contribution being just two. But at 180 for 8, Venkatapathy Raju came out in the form of the last man as Gursharan Singh had fractured a finger on his right hand while batting. Raju was out at 209 with Sachin still 11 runs short of the magic three-figure mark. By this time Raj Singh had told Gursharan to pad up and stay with Sachin till he got his century. He batted with only his left-hand glove on as he could not slip the other glove on. Batting courageously with one hand, Gursharan faced 16 deliveries, finally retiring hurt on five when Sachin cover drove Maninder for his fourteenth boundary to go from 99 to 103. The Rest innings was terminated at 245 and Sachin had registered his second century in eight first-class matches.

It was during this match that Gavaskar presented his ultralight moulded *Morant* fibreglass batting pads to the young batsman who would take over his mantle as the bedrock of the Indian batting in the years to come. At 16 years and 197 days, Sachin had added another 'youngest' record to his collection—the youngest to score a century in the Irani Trophy, that too on debut.

Now for the cauldron of Pakistan.

5
Into the Cauldron of Test Cricket

The lad is a genius.—Abdul Qadir

The selection of the team to Pakistan for what turned out to be the last Test tour by an Indian team (till mid-2002), generated more than the usual share of controversy. The team would be captained in Tests for the first time by Tamil Nadu opening batsman Krishnamachari Srikkanth. His elevation had come under remarkable circumstances, even for Indian cricket, where unusual happenings are commonplace.

India had been beaten 3-0 in five Tests in the Caribbean and swept away 5-0 in the one-day series. After the West Indies debacle, the Indian captain Dilip Vengsarkar had given a taped interview to Mudar Patherya of *Sportsworld* (May 1989) in which he blamed everyone but himself, despite his woeful batting form. To make things worse, he had gone on to the United States, with several other cricketers, to play exhibition matches which had been specifically forbidden by the BCCI. The players were banned on their return to India, and though the Supreme Court subsequently lifted the ban, Vengsarkar's brief reign as captain was over.

Srikkanth can consider himself lucky that midway through the West Indies tour he had his arm fractured by a short ball from Ian Bishop, or he would certainly have joined the team to the US. As it happened, he was the compromise candidate of the Board. The shock omission was that of Mohinder Amarnath. Vengsarkar had ruled himself out of the tour, perhaps anticipating he would be dropped in any case.

The team was widely described as the weakest bowling

combination ever sent to Pakistan. In the event, the fact that the four-Test series was drawn 0-0 is a tribute to the captain and the players under his command. But perhaps the biggest factor in India escaping unbeaten was the appointment of two neutral umpires, John Holder and John Hampshire from England.

This was the idea of Pakistan captain Imran Khan who wanted to put to rest, once and for all, the complaints against Pakistani umpires by visiting teams. The neutral umpires experiment had been tried out in an earlier series in Pakistan when the West Indies were the visitors, with two Indian umpires standing in for the first time. This time round, though neither Holder nor Hampshire was faultless, their supervision reduced the level of tension caused by the umpiring whenever and wherever the two countries had met in the past.

Srikkanth's leadership impressed one and all, but he failed with the bat. And this would prove to be his first and last assignment as captain. Mohammad Azharuddin replaced him for the tour to New Zealand in 1990.

One thing which may have told against Srikkanth was his backing of his players in their protest against the BCCI on the eve of their departure to Pakistan. The Board and the team could not agree on financial terms, and as a protest the entire team decided to forfeit their earnings from the series. Only the three newcomers, Sachin, Vivek Razdan and Salil Ankola were exempted from this action by the players and allowed to pocket their fees. Srikkanth, perhaps, was made to pay the price for supporting his teammates. Certainly, the pay dispute was an unfortunate prologue to Sachin's bow in international cricket. His selection, however, was widely welcomed.

The tour began on 10 November at Lahore with a one-day charity game in aid of Imran Khan's cancer hospital. The next day was the only first-class fixture before the start of the first Test: a three-day game against the Cricket Board Patron's XI at Rawalpindi where Sachin made his first appearance in national colours. The match was drawn, with the tourists scoring 272 in their only innings. Sachin's contribution was a useful 47 before he was stumped off left-arm spinner Iqbal Qasim. His performance removed any lingering doubt over his inclusion in the first Test at the National Stadium, Karachi starting on 15 November 1989.

There were three significant landmarks for India in this Test. At 16 years and 205 days, Sachin became the youngest Indian Test player and the fourth youngest of all time. Laxman Sivaramakrishnan (17 years 118 days) held the previous Indian record. Salil Ankola made his Test debut in the same match. This was also Kapil Dev's hundredth Test match in which he claimed his three hundred and fiftieth Test wicket. Before him, only Sunil Gavaskar and Dilip Vengsarkar had played as many matches for India.

The match also marked the turning point in the career of Azharuddin. He was not originally scheduled to play. But Raman Lamba ruled himself unfit on the morning of the match and Azhar was in. He scored 35 in both innings and also equalled the world fielding record of five catches in an innings.

As far as the age record is concerned, three Pakistanis—Mushtaq Mohammad, Aaqib Javed and Aftab Baloch—were all listed at the time as being younger than Sachin on debut. However, Imran Khan has maintained that all Pakistani cricketers (except him) have routinely taken two years off their age. Unofficially at least, this made Sachin the youngest in history to play Test cricket. There was another significant debutant in the match on the Pakistani side—fast bowler Waqar Younis. The opening day at Karachi was reported to be his eighteenth birthday.

It must have been a strange feeling indeed for a 16-year-old to suddenly find himself among the big names of Indian cricket. Sachin admitted as much in an interview to Sebastian Coe of *Daily Telegraph* (May 2001): 'I remember walking into the changing room and wondering how I would cope with all the famous names around me and they were all about twice my age. My captain, Krish Srikkanth was a great supporter. He sat me down before the game and told me that I belonged in the team, and they were all proud of my achievement. Nobody made me feel like a teenager.'

Srikkanth won the toss in his first Test as captain and put Pakistan in. India had immediate success when Kapil Dev dismissed Aamir

Malik for a duck with four runs on the board. By close on the first day, Pakistan had reached 259 for 4 with Javed Miandad (76) and Imran (17) at the crease. Shoaib Mohammad had shored up the batting with 67. Unfortunately, Sachin's first day in Test cricket was marred by a spectator running on to the field and attacking the Indian captain after first menacing Kapil. The rest of the team grabbed him before security officers took him away, but not before he had torn Srikkanth's shirt.

Miandad could add only two more the next morning before he became Kapil's three hundred and fiftieth Test victim. But there was no stopping Imran, who recorded his fifth Test century—his third against India. The Pakistani total of 409 was a challenging one. It assumed huge proportions when India slumped to 41 for 4. Wasim Akram and Waqar bowled with hostility as Srikkanth, Navjot Singh Sidhu, Manjrekar and Prabhakar all failed to reach double figures.

This was surely a baptism by fire for Tendulkar. As he was to remember in *Outlook* (4 January 1999): 'There I was in the middle, all of 16 years old, absolutely blank and very nervous, butterflies flying around in formations in my stomach! I really didn't know what was happening. Akram was bowling very fast. I think he bowled four bouncers in a row. It was very tough and I thought I was not going to ever play Test cricket again. At times I was beaten by pace, the ball went past my bat before I had completed my shot. I made 15, then a half-century in the next match. After that I don't remember being troubled by pace as such.'

It was a torrid time for the teenager, but he hit 15 from 24 balls in 29 minutes, including two fours, and was bowled by Younis with the score at 73 for 5. In the dressing room, the batsman, perhaps still shell-shocked, walked up to Ravi Shastri and said in Marathi, '*Me khup gahi keli*' (I was too hasty). Shastri reassured him: 'Young man, you don't have to worry about anything. The fact that you are playing for your country at 16 is good enough. Only one thing you must remember. When you are playing at the highest level, no matter how talented you are, you must respect the situation on hand.' (*Mid Day*, 24 May 2001)

Azhar was lbw to Imran, and India were staring the follow-on square in the face at 85 for 6.

This is where the Indian team showed resilience and fighting spirit that had been sadly lacking on recent tours of Pakistan. By close on the second day, the score had progressed to 157 without the loss of another wicket as Shastri (25) and Kapil (49) began repairing the damage. India still needed 53 runs to make Pakistan bat again. Although Kapil could add only six more runs to his overnight 49, the tail wagged effectively and India finished on 262. Shastri and wicketkeeper Kiran More both scored half-centuries and their stand ensured respectability for the tourists. Still, the lead of 147 was substantial and Pakistan enjoyed the upper hand. With two days still to play, they added 103 runs for the loss of three wickets. Shoaib's 95 and Salim Malik's unbeaten 102 helped Imran declare at 305 for 5 and set India the highly improbable task of scoring 453 in a minimum of 102 overs.

Waqar, who had grabbed four wickets in the first innings in a hostile spell, could not bowl in the second because of a strain in the back. That eased the pressure on India. Sidhu's 85 and Manjrekar's 113 not out meant India finished at 303 for 3 and their honour intact in this opening encounter. Tendulkar did not get a chance to bat the second time round. But he did have a chance to bowl on his debut, though without success (1-0-10-0 and 4-0-15-0).

Waqar was not fit for the second Test which was played at the Iqbal Stadium in Faisalabad from 23 November. India brought in medium-pacer Vivek Razdan for his debut in place of Ankola, while Maninder replaced Arshad Ayub. This time, it was the turn of Imran to put the opposition in after winning the toss. But his attack was further weakened with an injured Saleem Jaffar only able to bowl 17 overs in the first innings. Bad light saw only 66.3 overs being bowled on the opening day and once again the Indian batting was in trouble after a useful opening stand of 68 between Srikkanth and Sidhu. Azhar failed to score, Shastri fell cheaply, and there was another crisis at 101 for 4.

The Mumbai pair of Manjrekar (58) and Tendulkar (35) saw to it that there was no further damage; their stand was worth 99 at the close of the first day. Sachin curbed his natural attacking instincts and batted for 150 minutes, perhaps remembering the sound advice given by Shastri after his dismissal in the first Test. The partnership was extended to 143 the next day and Sachin got his maiden Test half-century in only his second innings. This gave him two world records—he became the youngest to be involved in a century stand and the youngest to score 50 in a Test match. Sachin had batted for 244 minutes and 165 balls and hit four fours when Imran, bowling at his best in the series so far, had him beaten comprehensively and got him plumb in front for 59.

India's total of 288 appeared inadequate and Pakistan piled up 423 for 9 declared, with opener Aamir Malik recording his first century. Sachin took his first catch—Akram caught for 28 off Prabhakar. The declaration came 30 minutes after lunch on the fourth day.

The Indian batting came into its own in the second innings as it had at Karachi a week before. Azhar marked his return to form with a streaky 109 (his first century outside India) while Sidhu, Manjrekar and Prabhakar all scored half-centuries as India finished on 398 for 7. Azhar, not for the first time in his career, was like a cat on a hot tin roof in his 90s and caused jitters in the Indian camp as he almost got four batsmen run out, including himself. Sachin (8) was one such victim, rooted a couple of yards outside his crease, uncertain whether to respond to Azhar's call for a single when he was on 99.

Just 15 wickets fell in five days in the third Test which began three days later, a match which was instantly dubbed 'the bore at Lahore'. After the excitement of the first two Tests, it proved to be one of those typical Indo-Pak matches played on a feather bed of a wicket, with plenty of records but little else. India's total of 509 saw Manjrekar reach his first Test double century, his 218 the highest against Pakistan by an Indian batsman. The total was also India's highest in Pakistan. Sachin scored 41 before being bowled by Qadir. Unusually, the off and leg stump were disturbed, but the middle was left standing! But his innings was buried under Pakistan's mammoth 699 for 5.

Miandad became the first Pakistani to play 100 Tests and made the event memorable by scoring a century. This was the same ground where he had made his debut against New Zealand in 1975 when, too, he had registered a century. This made his feat unique. Shoaib's 203 not out made him and father Hanif the first father-son combination to score Test double centuries, something Sanjay's father Vijay had not been able to achieve.

The Indian team was more than satisfied going into the third Test at Lahore without a defeat to their name. Despite better performances in the first half, Pakistan had been frustrated by India's batting strength, with Manjrekar being the outstanding performer.

It would be no different at Sialkot, though for the first time in the series it was India that emerged with the honours. Manjrekar, following his Lahore double-ton, was once again top scorer in the first innings, with 72. All the batsmen except numbers 10 and 11 reached double figures, with Sachin contributing 35. India took the lead for the first time in the series (and only for the second time in 20 Tests in Pakistan) as Pakistan crumbled to 250 with medium-pacer Vivek Razdan—one of Sachin's confidants on the tour—picking up 5 for 79 in only his second Test.

India faced another early-order crisis in their second innings when they lost four wickets for 38 runs, with Akram picking up three. Srikkanth, Manjrekar, Azharuddin and Shastri all fell in single figures. This brought out the best in Sidhu and Tendulkar and they took the score to 104 without further loss at the close of the fourth day, with the opener on 54 and Sachin on 33. The Pakistani pace attack of Imran, Wasim and Waqar used the short ball effectively, especially targeting the teenager. But Sachin stood up to everything they could fling at him and even inspired his senior partner. Then, the unexpected happened. A ball from Waqar did not rise as anticipated; it was top-edged and struck Sachin on the bridge of his nose. He was wearing a helmet without a grill, which he felt obscured his vision. Blood poured from the wound as he slumped to the ground and even the normally hardened Imran showed his concern. The crowd, perhaps the most hostile on tour, was baying for more blood.

Sachin merely threw back his head, pulled out a handkerchief to staunch the blood and carried on bravely. Medical assistance was brushed away. The next delivery, swinging and full pitched, was gloriously square driven for four. The one after that was short outside the off stump. The batsman rose on his toes and the ball was smashed on the up, past the rooted cover fielder for another boundary. It was a stirring performance and the crowd fell silent, stunned and awed in equal measure.

No one after that would ever doubt Sachin's value to the Indian cause. The stand was worth 101 runs before he was caught behind for 57 (195 minutes, 136 balls, five fours) off Imran. Sidhu went on to 97 and India were 234 for 7 when the match was called off. The result: four draws out of four in the series.

Sachin in an interview to *Sportsworld* (January 1996) was to look back at that incident as one that added aggression to his armoury. Replying to the question, 'How did you develop such an aggressive outlook?' he responded: 'It was a good thing that on my first tour I got hurt on the nose off a Younis delivery. I realized that there could be nothing worse than that. There have been worse injuries than mine. But that gave me more confidence and allowed me to be aggressive in my mind. Even if I break my nose, I decided on staying there and not be bothered about fast bowling.'

So Waqar Younis actually did a favour to Sachin Tendulkar and Indian cricket after all! Imran, for his part, claimed he was always conscious of bowling to a schoolboy. That 'schoolboy' finished the series with a highly creditable average of 35.83 for his 215 runs, with two 50s and a couple of other useful scores besides.

In a tribute to him after the Test series, R.Mohan wrote in the *Sportstar* (30 December 1989) under the headline 'The Wonder Boy Is Here to Stay': 'The gut feeling is that Sachin Tendulkar will go places. Much has been predicted for him by many. The projection is that he will go even further than predicted. There is a quality to his game which goes beyond the ordinary talk of talent.'

Mohan, then chief cricket correspondent for the *Hindu* and the *Sportstar*, was prescient when he predicted in the same article: 'This is no young man who will model his batting on Sunil Gavaskar's. He may go beyond that and think of becoming a Viv Richards. He is a born stroke-player.'

The Indian team had emerged with honour intact in the Test series. But there was still the business of the One-day Internationals to be negotiated. Sadly, weather conditions and crowd problems reduced the four-match ODI series to a farce. The opening match at Peshawar on 16 December was reduced to an exhibition game of 20 overs per side to placate the crowd after a combination of bad light and fog held up play. In the second at Gujranwala, only 16 overs could be played by each side because of bad light and a wet outfield and Pakistan won by seven runs. Karachi lived up to its reputation as having the unruliest crowd in Pakistan. The third ODI had to be abandoned as the Indian fielders were constantly being pelted by stones. The end came after just 14.3 overs with Pakistan struggling on 28 for 3, Prabhakar having picked up all three wickets. Weather once again curtailed play in the fourth and final game at Lahore, reduced to 37 overs per side, which Pakistan won by 38 runs.

Even though the Peshawar opener was not considered an official One-day International, it gave Tendulkar the opportunity to play in his first limited-overs game in national colours. And how he made the most of that opportunity is now part of the Sachin legend.

Salim Malik with 75 led the charge as Pakistan raced to 157 for 4, a rate of nearly eight runs per over. After losing their first three wickets for 88, the Indians decided not to exert themselves. Srikkanth had dropped himself down the order and appeared to have given up the ghost when he was joined at the crease by Sachin. The required run rate at this stage was over 15 an over.

The fireworks from the young man's bat had even the fiercely partisan crowd rooting for him. It all started in leg-spinner Mushtaq Ahmed's second (and final) over in which he was smashed for 16 runs by Sachin: two sixes and a four.

'Let me see if you can hit my bowling the same way,' Qadir said to Sachin after Mushtaq's over.

Sachin replied, 'You are such a great bowler, you will not allow me to do that.' (*Sports Channel* video, December 1990)

Qadir got the pasting of a lifetime that evening in Peshawar from a boy young enough to be his son. Three balls in a row were dispatched with power and timing over the ropes. Even Qadir applauded as he turned and saw the second one soaring over his head. Another was hit for four and the next for three. The over produced an astonishing 27 runs as Sachin reached his 50 from 18 balls. Srikkanth, one of the most attacking batsmen in the game, was awestruck by his partner's power. By now it had come down to 17 for victory in the final over bowled by Akram. The Indians fell short by four runs. Srikkanth was left on 13 while Tendulkar's contribution was an amazing 53 not out.

Qadir was generous in his praise. Soon after the thrashing, he told the media: 'The lad is a genius. He is going to take bowlers apart in international cricket for a very long time.' Qadir had a very clear recollection of the match when asked to look back on it for this book. 'I did say in 1989 that Tendulkar will be a great batsman. He was a school kid and looked like an innocent boy. But the way he played against us was enough to convince me that he was going to be a great batsman. I still remember when Waqar Younis bowled him his first delivery when he made his Test debut in Karachi. It was a very fast delivery. Tendulkar came forward and tried to drive the speedster through the covers. He didn't connect the ball and was beaten, but I told myself, "Here is a kid who will make his name in cricket."

'It's a very interesting story (the Peshawar encounter). Firstly I want to clarify that it was not supposed to be an exhibition match. It was actually a One-day International. But it rained heavily in Peshawar. The organizers didn't want to disappoint a large crowd of over 30,000 so that's why they decided to convert the One-day International into an exhibition match. I tied down skipper Srikkanth and didn't allow him to score freely. At that time, Tendulkar was standing at the non-striker's end. At the end of the over, I asked Tendulkar to go after my bowling, so that the world knows that he has the potential of scoring runs against a quality bowler. It was not that I wanted to bowl him loose deliveries, I knew that he could hit me for big sixes. I told him, "Don't feel that a world class leg-spinner is bowling to you. Don't be afraid what will happen if you get out, just think that I am an ordinary bowler and try to score big sixes." When I bowled that memorable over, I didn't bowl badly, but Tendulkar hit me for three sixes and in all collected 27 runs. I still remember that he was dropped in that over, but it didn't stop him from playing his classical shots to all parts of the Arbab Niaz Stadium. It was after that match that I said that Tendulkar will be a great batsman and I wasn't wrong because I knew that he would make his name in cricket.

'A couple of years later I went to Sharjah to play in a double-wicket tournament in which leading players like Salim Malik, Arjuna Ranatunga, Kapil Dev, Ravi Shastri and others were playing. Tendulkar was also there. By that time he had made his name in the cricketing world. That day I again asked him to score runs off my bowling. But he didn't succeed in scoring as many as he scored in Peshawar.

'I love innocent people and those who want to work hard. Tendulkar is certainly one of those players.'

In the first official One-day International at Gujranwala on 18 December, Sachin was out for his first duck in international cricket, caught Akram bowled Younis first ball. Quite shockingly, he was dropped for the next two matches.

At the start of the Test series in Karachi a poster was seen in the stands referring to the new kid on the block. It read contemptuously, *Baccha, tu idhar kya karta hai?* (Child, what are you doing here?).

A month later, at the end of the one-day game at Peshawar, another one popped up. It read: *Ek sher aya hai* (A tiger has arrived).

6

12 Runs Short of Glory

I cried so much when I was out I could not see.—Sachin Tendulkar

A month later, the Indian team were in New Zealand under a new captain, Mohammad Azharuddin, and a new coach, Bishan Singh Bedi. The team had a fresh, youthful look to it—it was, as Raj Singh would describe it, the 'team for the 90s'. Tendulkar scored 13, 47, 4 (not out) and 30 in the two warm-up games prior to the first Test at Lancaster Park, Christchurch. And in the first innings against New Zealand President's XI at Pukekura Park, New Plymouth on 22 January 1990, he became the youngest to reach the landmark of 1000 first-class runs.

It was a miserable batting performance by the visitors in the first Test at Christchurch as they were beaten by ten wickets with Tendulkar out for his first duck in Test cricket, in the first innings. Of the Indian players, only Kapil Dev had previous playing experience in New Zealand. India crumbled to 164 all out in reply to New Zealand's 459 and, following on, could muster only 296 (Tendulkar: 24). Sir Richard Hadlee became the first bowler in Test cricket to reach the landmark of 400 wickets when he bowled Manjrekar in the second innings. Hadlee was arguably the best bowler in the world at the time and facing him at such an early stage of his career was an education for Sachin. He felt that Hadlee was the kind of bowler who made batsmen think all the time and after only his second tour, rated the Kiwi master as the best bowler he had faced till then.

After that early setback, the Indian batting clicked in the second Test at Napier where over two days were lost to rain and a draw was the only verdict possible. W. V. Raman was out to Hadlee off the first ball of the match and it was Prabhakar (95) and Manjrekar (42) who did the early repair work, adding 92 for the second wicket. Azharuddin chipped in with 33 and his departure brought Tendulkar in at 152 for 4. Both Vengsarkar and Kapil came and went cheaply, and when wicketkeeper Kiran More joined Sachin at the crease, the score read 218 for 6. More (73) played the dominant role as he and Tendulkar put together a record seventh-wicket stand worth 128 runs. Several airy-fairy shots outside off stump marked the early part of Tendulkar's innings and he could have been out on numerous occasions. But his boyishness faded away gradually, and the longer he stayed at the wicket, the more decisive he grew. By the close of the third day India were 348 for 7 and Tendulkar had batted five hours for his unbeaten 80. All the speculation overnight centred on whether the long-standing record set by Pakistan's Mushtaq Mohammed against India in 1960-61, for the youngest Test century-maker, would be broken on the fourth day. Mushtaq was 17 years and 82 days when he reached his maiden century in Delhi. Sachin was still two months shy of his seventeenth birthday.

A teammate, unnamed by Sachin, perhaps added to the pressure when he told the not-out batsman that he was 20 runs short of history as he returned to the dressing room that evening.

The next morning, the first ball of the day from Danny Morrison was dispatched to the cover boundary and then Sachin ran four runs to a shot to deep mid-off as he moved quickly to 88. Perhaps over-confidence and youthful exuberance got the better of him, for the very next ball was driven firmly but uppishly to captain John Wright at mid-off who took a comfortable catch on one knee. Sachin had batted for 324 minutes, faced 266 balls and hit four boundaries. 'I cried so much when I was out, I could not see. The entire team consoled me,' said Sachin. 'I could have worked my way to the century. I suppose I got carried away, wanting to take on the bowler.' (*Sports Channel* video, December 1990)

'I had two feelings when I caught him,' recalls Wright, now coach of the Indian team. 'Firstly one of relief, as at the time I was captain of New Zealand and he was batting so beautifully we looked like we would never get him out. It was the second Test and we had won the first. My second feeling was one of almost feeling sorry for him as he was only a lad really and he had batted so well and deserved a century.... I was surprised, as he had hit the ball in the air, it was an easy catch and it came straight to me at mid-off.'

'[Sachin's innings] left experienced members of the New Zealand team agog,' wrote Don Neely, the convenor of the New Zealand selection panel, in the *New Zealand Cricket Almanack* (1991).

The third Test at Auckland, a high-scoring match in which Tendulkar could score only five, was also drawn and New Zealand won the series 1-0. There was no second chance at the record for the youngest Test centurion as the next Test series (against England), was five months away.

The Auckland Test was followed by a one-day tri-series also involving Australia. Tendulkar played in the opening match against New Zealand at Carisbrook but once again failed to score. Which meant he had got out for a duck in his first two One-day Internationals.

He was dropped for the next match against Australia but in the one after that, against New Zealand at the Basin Reserve on 6 March, he scored an attractive 36 from 39 balls, with five fours, as India won by one run. These were his first runs in One-day Internationals. India had to beat Australia in the next match two days later at Hamilton if they were to make the final. Tendulkar was once again dropped for the match and Australia won by eight wickets to complete an unsuccessful tour for the Indians.

Hadlee was impressed enough by the end of the series to proclaim the presence of amazing natural ability in Sachin. He thought it was extraordinary how one so young could hold his own in the world of men and in such difficult circumstances.

The summer drew to a close with the six-nation Austral-Asia Cup in April-May at Sharjah. It was a disappointing tournament for both Sachin and the team as India lost both its league matches, to Sri Lanka and Pakistan, in Group B and failed to reach the semi-finals. Sachin scored 10 (run out) and 20 in the two games. At the end of the season, he had just 66 runs from his first five ODIs.

7

Hail the Boy King

He played like an old pro.—Graham Gooch

Despite three half-centuries in his first six Test matches, there was some speculation that Tendulkar would be dropped for the tour of England in the summer of 1990. Fortunately, better sense prevailed. After the two tours with Star Cricket Club, this was his third visit to England in as many years. India were to play three Tests and two One-day Internationals apart from two months of first-class and one-day games against the counties. After scoring 19 in the opening one-day match against League Cricket Conference at Sunderland, Tendulkar was rested for the first county game versus Yorkshire at Headingley. Against Hampshire he had scores of 32 and 58 not out as the Indians lost by seven wickets.

With the first Texaco series ODI on 18 July, Sachin ran into form and followed the unbeaten half-century against Hampshire with scores of 92 and 70 (v Kent); 65 (v Minor Counties); and 10 not out (v Scotland). His first century on tour was an unbeaten 105 in the two-wicket win over Derbyshire in the one-day match at Chesterfield, the day before the first ODI. The victory came in the final over when Tendulkar pulled West Indian fast bowler Ian Bishop for his second six. There were also seven fours from the 149 balls he faced.

Derbyshire captain Kim Barnett (who scored 115) would be the first of many Englishmen to be impressed by this awesome talent. 'It was quite simply an astonishing innings. Even the great players of the game would have been proud of that,' he said in appreciation (*Indian Cricket Annual*, 1990).

Sachin's knocks of 92 and 70 against Kent at Canterbury were significant as they were the first for him in the role of opener. Regulars Navjot Sidhu and W.V. Raman were indisposed and Sachin opened with wicketkeeper Kiran More in a makeshift arrangement. According to manager and former Test stumper Madhav Mantri, Sachin had volunteered for the slot, keeping the team's interests in mind. The Indians won the game by seven wickets. By now the media was all abuzz with talk of India's latest boy wonder and a full house turned up to watch the first ODI at Headingley.

Mike Atherton fell early after England were asked to bat first. Then captain Graham Gooch, in an ominous portent of the flood of runs to come in the Test series, and with the help of 50s from David Gower and Allan Lamb, took the score to 134 for 2. Debutant leg-spinner Anil Kumble struck two telling blows at this stage and India were back in the game. Just 19 years of age, Kumble then bowled Gower and had Robin Smith caught behind for six. In the end, England's total of 229 all out (in the last of the 55 overs) was a credit to the Indian bowlers' persistence.

After lunch Phil DeFreitas opened the bowling for England with a no-ball. Immediately afterwards, India lost Raman to the first legitimate delivery of the innings, but they managed to reach the target with two overs to spare, for the loss of four wickets. Though Tendulkar scored only 19, his straight six off spinner Eddie Hemmings was a massive one, clearing almost 100 yards. He departed at 115 for 3 and after that it was left to Manjrekar (82) and Azharuddin (55 not out) to steer the side home quite comfortably. Former England captain Geoffrey Boycott sprang a pleasant surprise by picking Kumble as the Man of the Match for his figures of 11-2-29-2.

Another full house for the second game at Trent Bridge, another toss won by the Indian captain and another victory with exactly two overs to spare, this time by five wickets. Gooch was bowled cheaply. But Robin Smith's 103 and 50s from Atherton and wicketkeeper Jack Russell helped England to a formidable 281 all out in exactly 55 overs. Manjrekar followed up his 82 in the first game with 59 and Vengsarkar hit a rapid 54 with two sixes as all the batsmen scored usefully. India needed 145 runs from the last 20 overs to win and got them in some style, thanks in part to a delightful little innings of 31 from 26 balls (two fours) by Tendulkar. He added 63 runs in seven overs with his captain, with driving described by one newspaper as 'wondrously potent'. Azhar smashed 63 not out from 44 balls and took the Man of the Series award for India.

In the first Test at Lord's, Azharuddin won the toss and asked Gooch to bat first. The English captain probably couldn't believe his ears, for the wicket was a beauty and there appeared to be runs galore for the asking. Indian manager Bedi promptly disassociated himself from his captain's decision. It was an indication of the rift in the Indian camp that did not auger well for the rest of the tour. Later in the match, Gooch had another opportunity to be grateful to Indian generosity when, on 36, he edged medium-pacer Sanjeev Sharma behind and More floored a straightforward chance.

From the very first day India was fighting to save a Test which could have turned out very differently if not for a startling bit of misjudgement by their captain.

The tourists started promisingly enough, with Kapil Dev bowling Atherton for eight to leave England at 14 for 1. Gower and Gooch then added 127 runs and the left-hander was most displeased at being given out for 40, caught at silly point by Manjrekar off Hirwani. It was uphill for India all the way after that. By close on the opening day, England were 359 for 2 with Gooch on 194 and Lamb on 104. Lamb raced to 139 at more than a run a ball, his partnership of 308 with Gooch an all-wicket record for England against India. After that early lapse, nothing got past Gooch's bat which assumed ever-larger proportions for the toiling Indian attack. He reached the first triple century in a Test at Lord's and now Garry Sobers' world record of 365 not out was in his sights. But the 37-year-old was beginning to feel the fatigue of an innings of more than ten hours. After adding 192 with Robin Smith, he was out to a tired stroke, bowled by Prabhakar for 333. England declared at 653 for 4 as soon as Smith reached three figures and the Indian openers, Shastri and Sidhu, held on to score 48 by the end of the second day. India used five bowlers during England's onslaught and all save Shastri—who gave away 99—conceded more than 100 runs. The target was now clear: 454 to avoid the follow-on. And India did indeed reach that score in a glorious manner.

Shastri held the top order together with a determined 100. Vengsarkar, who had scored hundreds in each of his previous three Tests at Lord's, this time contributed 52. But at 288 for 5, the follow-on was still looming large. Tendulkar came in to bat, his first visit to Lord's, and had to return disappointed, bowled middle stump for ten between bat and pad by Chris Lewis. Now it was up to the captain to atone for his blunder with the toss. He did so in the only way he knew, unleashing a torrent of dazzling strokes that had the English bowlers wringing their hands in despair and the media singing his praises. Once Azhar was bowled by Eddie Hemmings for 121, it was left to Kapil to make England bat again. With nine wickets down and only Hirwani for company, it was a do-or-die situation. Hemmings was the bowler, and in four deliveries the follow-on had been saved in astonishing fashion—all four balls were sent over the boundary for six!

England raced to 272 for 4 declared to set an impossible target for India. Gooch entered the record books once again as the only batsman in the history of first-class cricket to score a triple and single century in the same match. The Indians, the second time round, could not repeat their first-innings heroics and crumbled to 224 all out to lose by 247 runs. Tendulkar displayed rare application in an innings of 27 in which he struck four boundaries. He occupied the crease for 93 minutes, showed copybook technique and was willing to wait for the loose ball. But he got one from Fraser that took off from a good length spot and was caught at slip by Gooch.

The match produced a record for the most runs in a Lord's Test—an amazing 1603 at more than four runs an over. It was glorious entertainment for the spectators. And amidst all the landmarks and achievements recorded by both sides, there was one moment that is remembered clearly even today by those who witnessed it. Lamb, batting in the second innings, had clouted Hirwani, but slightly miscued the drive. Tendulkar raced across from the wide long off boundary, past the sight screen where the ball was heading. It was a 40-yard dash worthy of a Carl Lewis. As the ball dipped seemingly out of his grasp, he thrust out his right hand and the ball stuck in his palm. A TV commentator gushed, 'Oh my goodness gracious me. He didn't look like he had any chance of reaching it.' Harsha Bhogle, writing in *Mid Day*, called it 'the greatest catch I have ever seen'. John Thicknesse, in *Wisden Cricketers' Almanack* (1991) called it 'as wonderful an outfield catch as Lord's has seen'. David Frith in *Wisden Cricket Monthly* (September 1990) called it 'An amazing one-hander which deserved isolated billing in a meaningless drawn match rather than inclusion among such competing headlines.' Only someone of Tendulkar's youthful exuberance would have attempted such a catch, let alone successfully executed it.

The three-day game against Gloucestershire at Bristol, just before the second Test, finished in a draw. Tendulkar's scores were 13 and 47. He was also given his first long spell of bowling on the tour, indeed in his entire first-class career to date. In 32 overs in Gloucestershire's first innings, he picked up the wickets of Hodgson, Romaines and Alleyne, three top order batsmen, for 79 runs. This was after left-arm spinner Raju had ended his tour with a broken hand while batting in the first innings.

The second Test at Old Trafford, Manchester, which started on 9 August would finally see the promise of youth translate into a display of greatness—a match-saving century from the youngest Test cricketer in the world. Centuries from Gooch—his third in succession—and fellow opener Atherton saw England finish the opening day on 322 for 3, inducing a sense of déjà vu among the Indian bowlers who had suffered a similar pasting at Lord's less than two weeks ago. Smith weighed in with a ton and England's massive score of 519 once again meant that India could only hope to save the Test match. They found themselves on shaky ground at the end of the second day, with the first three wickets falling for 57. But Azhar took over from where he had left off at Lord's, and his domination of the bowling was such that the English attack was made to look pedestrian. His 179 was his third century in successive Tests as captain, something no Indian captain had achieved. His 189-run stand with Manjrekar (93) took the score to 246 for 4 and was followed by another worth 112 for the fifth wicket with Tendulkar. The captain was around to guide the young man through a tricky initial period at the crease. It took Sachin 54 minutes and 38 balls to get his first run. His contribution to the century partnership was just 24 as Azhar ran amok. But with the last five wickets going down for 74, his innings of 68 (eight fours) in 216 minutes was enough to see England's lead cut to a manageable 87 runs. It was also Tendulkar's highest score so far in Tests. A mark that would be obliterated just two days later.

Gooch failed for the first time in the series in the second innings, but England's 320 for 4 left India with a huge task ahead of them. To win, they needed 408 runs from a minimum of 88 overs. Sidhu's dismissal for a duck saw the top order crumble for the second time in the match, and now the only thought was of survival. Defeat here would reduce the third and final Test at the Oval to a formality. When Prabhakar joined Tendulkar at 183 for 6, there were still two and a half hours remaining for England's bowlers to mop things up. But their fielders muffed two chances that would have sewn up the match and the series. Hemmings dropped a sitter off his own bowling from Tendulkar at ten and Gooch floored Prabhakar at slip. That was all the pair needed. Tendulkar was watchful, considering the perilous position the team was in. But he did not fail to punish the loose ball and reached his second half-century of the Test from 100 balls. The landmark was reached with three shots to the boundary off Chris Lewis in one over.

At the start of the last 20 overs, the score was 255 for 6 and the field was still an attacking one. Tendulkar off-drove Fraser for four, then cut him high and hard over the waiting slip cordon for another, to move into his 90s. An elegant back-foot boundary off Fraser took him to 96 and then at 97 there was just that tiny sign of nerves as he ducked Fraser and left his bat sticking up, getting a single to long leg in the process. Another off drive for three runs, and the magic moment had arrived. Sachin's maiden century had taken 171 balls, 14 of which had been crisply dispatched to the boundary.

With a shy half-smile he lifted his helmet to acknowledge the applause from the small crowd and a frenzied Indian dressing room where his mentor Sunil Gavaskar had raced from the commentary box to witness the moment. Sachin was too young to vote, too young to drink alcohol, too young to sign his contract with the Board which his father had done for him less than 12 months ago. But not too young to save his side in battle, overshadowing his teammates, some almost twice his age, who had recklessly thrown away their wickets on the final day. The line between prodigy and genius—the word Dennis Compton used to describe him—had been crossed in only his ninth Test.

The stand with Prabhakar was worth an unbroken 160, the all-rounder not out on 67. And despite the five other centuries in a Test dominated by the batsmen, the critics had eyes only for the sixth and last one. In all, Tendulkar had batted for 225 minutes, faced 189 balls and struck 17 boundaries. It made him at 17 years and 112 days the youngest to score a Test century in England and the second youngest ever. Fraser, the pick of the bowlers at Old Trafford and the most successful in a series awash with centuries, told Scyld Berry of *Wisden Cricket Monthly* (June 1996), 'He never looked raw or out of place, even at Lord's in the first Test. Some batsmen come in and freeze or seem unsure, but not him—not that he was cocky. It just didn't feel as if you were bowling to a 17-year-old. His temperament allowed the talent to flow.'

'Fraser Denied by Tendulkar's Breathtaking Brilliance' was the headline in the *Cricketer International* (October 1990). Wrote Christopher Martin-Jenkins, 'Coming in at 109 for 4, with Hemmings turning the ball and Lewis fresh and firing, Tendulkar batted with quite astounding skill and composure.' The headline to David Frith's report in *Wisden Cricket Monthly* (October 1990) proclaimed a new batting master on the world stage: 'Hail the Boy King'.

Founder and former editor of WCM (and editor of the *Cricketer International* before that), author of over 30 books on cricket and one of the game's greatest historians, Frith readily agreed to contribute his memories of one of cricket's finest batting displays.

'It was a considerable privilege to have witnessed Sachin

Tendulkar's maiden Test hundred. Although the England attack was scarcely the greatest ever fielded by that country, there was a crisis to be overcome on the final afternoon when India, needing 408 to win after Gooch's declaration, had slipped to 127 for 5. Tendulkar had failed at Lord's in the first Test but had scored 68 in the first innings here at Manchester. Now he showed astonishing maturity in batting for almost four hours to make 119 not out, his match-saving stand with Prabhakar realizing 160. He was only 17 years and 112 days—the second-youngest Test centurion, after Mushtaq Mohammad—and we wondered what he might be capable of doing in the next ten years or so.

'Reverting to my notes from that Test match, I find the sense of wonder was real. How could anyone so young be so good at the highest level? He was wearing Sunil Gavaskar's off-white fibreglass pads, which made him appear to waddle rather like one of television's cuddly toys. His first innings in this match was worth 68, and he had had to struggle for almost an hour for his first run. That, for a start, told us something important about him. He stayed with his captain, Azharuddin, through a century stand, and finally gave his wicket away after three and a half hours at the crease. Most notable innings owe almost everything to a fielding error. In his second-innings century Tendulkar escaped a chest-high caught-and-bowled to off-spinner Eddie Hemmings when he was only 10. He inside-edged the next ball, as England piled on the pressure, but emerged to play calmly and reassuringly.

'India really had seemed doomed. Kapil Dev got out to a wild shot, causing one of my neighbouring writers, a senior from India, to slap his forehead and exclaim, "Oh, my God!" That's how bad it was. But young Tendulkar stood solid, and so did Prabhakar. The youngster even showed himself to be street-smart, for almost every time the bowler turned, preparing to bowl, he was still studying the field, or adjusting his gear, or marking his crease. With the fielders clustered around him like members of the fan club that was soon to make his life difficult, Tendulkar dealt with everything England dished out, driving powerfully and cutting like a flash. The hundred came with an off-drive for three off Angus Fraser. I was quite affected by this wonderful performance from one so young. He saw India to safety, and half-an-hour later, he was stepping forward in the pavilion to receive his Man of the Match award. Under the glare of the spotlights he gave the first discernible sign of nervousness. His lower lip seemed to tremble as he stepped forward to receive his magnum of champagne, and he was soon explaining that he was too young to drink.

'At the press conference which followed, he replied to the kindly, almost patronising questions in a quiet voice, one which had not as yet fully broken. Always prepared to gaze into years distant—past or future—I simply had to write: "A smile came readily to his unrazored face, and already those with rich imaginations were envisaging the sophisticated grown-up face and the deeper voice which would respond to questions at some far-distant press conference to mark his breaking of Gavaskar's Test records." The young prodigy had helped India turn the tide in the match, transforming the seemingly inevitable disappointment of millions into jubilation at his wondrous act. The finest compliment of all probably came from England's dour skipper Gooch: "He played like an old pro."'

Said Richie Benaud on TV after Tendulkar had received his award from David Lloyd: 'We'll see a lot more centuries from his bat. I hope I'll be around to see them.' Bedi commented, 'He applied himself magnificently and showed maturity beyond comprehension.' Bedi told me he had observed during the tour that even Bradman at that age was no match for Sachin. 'Of course, the white cricket world was not too pleased with that statement. And as it turned out, by the time Sachin reached his 20s, he was way behind what Bradman had achieved at that age with his numerous double and triple centuries.'

The Indian manager by then had made quite a name for himself with his numerous controversial comments. One such must have been acutely embarrassing to Sachin himself. 'The English media reported that I said that every Englishwoman would like to seduce Sachin. Actually I said they would like to mother him. At that age he was so adorable,' Bedi clarified to me.

After all that excitement, the third and final Test at the Oval was almost anticlimactic. This would be the high noon for the Indian batting machine, at a ground with happy memories for the country. (India's first Test victory in England was at the Oval in 1971.) Never before had India scored over 600 against England and for the first time at home England were forced to follow-on against India. The massive total of 606 for 9 declared was built around opener Shastri's 187 and Kapil Dev's 110. All but number ten Hirwani reached double figures and there were 50s for Azhar and More as well. Tendulkar was out to debutant medium-pacer Neil Williams for 21 (including three boundaries), slashing to Lamb at first slip. England followed on after trailing by 266 runs. But any hopes India may have harboured of forcing victory were thwarted by Gooch (80 in both innings) and a majestic unbeaten 157 by David Gower. Gooch garnered over 1000 Test runs over the summer, including three Tests earlier in the season against New Zealand. Tendulkar was third in the averages with 245 runs at 61.25, after Azhar and Shastri. It was a summer full of tons and runs and yet it was Tendulkar's match-saving knock at Old Trafford that continued to be the talking point of the year.

There was the formality of one more first-class match to be gone through before the Indians could fly home after a tour lasting two months. It was a privately arranged match by TV personality and journalist Michael Parkinson, played in the festive atmosphere of Scarborough, but it was a first-class game nonetheless. The match was billed as Michael Parkinson's World XI v Indians and ended in a draw. The World team was a motley bunch, including Kiwi Mark Greatbatch (who slammed unbeaten centuries in both innings), Mudassar Nazar, Gordon Greenidge (the captain) and Chetan Sharma. The Indians were set to score 388 in four and a half hours and in a virtual replay of the last day at Old Trafford, once again it was Tendulkar who saw them to the safety of a draw with 108 not out. The bowling attack in the hands of Ezra Moseley, Mike Whitney, Meyrick Pringle, Chetan Sharma, Roger Harper and Peter Sleep was nothing to sneeze at. The century was reached from 131 balls, including 17 fours, and was the perfect end to a perfect summer of batting.

Tendulkar finished with the highest aggregate for the touring side, with 945 runs from 11 matches (19 innings) at the impressive average of 63. This included two centuries and six 50s. There was also a century in the one-day game against Derbyshire. As in the Test series, only Azhar and Shastri finished ahead of Sachin in the tour averages.

The tour of England was a huge step forward in the cricket education of Tendulkar. Now he had other worlds to conquer.

8

Home, Sweet Home

It is impossible to fathom what the youngster is capable of.—R. Mohan

It was exactly 12 months after he made his international debut that Sachin Tendulkar finally played a Test match on home soil.

That 12 month-period saw the Indian team play an amazing ten Test matches, as well as One-day Internationals in Pakistan, New Zealand, England and Sharjah. After all that hectic activity, the Indians would play just one Test in the next 12 months. Indian fans longing to get a glimpse of the teenager who had wowed audiences around the world finally got their opportunity with the one-off Test against Sri Lanka at Chandigarh in November 1990.

Sri Lanka were still the pushovers of international cricket, a far cry from their post-1996 status. The prosaic sounding Sector 16 Stadium in Chandigarh was hosting its first Test match, which would also be its last. (From 1994 international cricket in the city moved to the suburb of Mohali on the outskirts of Chandigarh. Expansion at Sector 16 was ruled out due to local building laws and the Punjab Cricket Association now has one of the best stadia in the country.) The match had been shifted from Jalandhar at short notice due to political unrest there. For the first time in India security was so tight that the police outnumbered the spectators on a couple of days. Both teams were guarded day and night at the stadium and their hotel by 3000 policemen. It was a pointer of things to come.

The under-prepared pitch was the talking point of the Test that India won by an innings with a day to spare. Azhar won the toss and batted first. Ravi Shastri's 88 was the lone half-century of the match even as India struggled to reach 288. But that score was more than enough as the visitors crumbled to 82 and 198 all out.

The Man of the Match was left-arm spinner Venkatapathy Raju. In only his third Test he had figures of 6 for 12 and 2 for 25 from 53.5 overs. It was Azhar's first win as captain and the first for the Indian team after playing 14 Tests abroad.

Sachin managed only 11. But it was a heady experience being on the winning side for the first time since his debut a year before. The Indian dressing room was a joyous sight with champagne corks popping, though the captain and the prodigy were among those abstaining from the bubbly.

Sri Lanka's plea for an extra Test match was turned down by the BCCI, citing short notice. With Pakistan subsequently cancelling their visit to India on security grounds, this remained the lone Test of the 1990-91 season.

India took the three-match ODI series against Sri Lanka that followed the one-off Test with a 2-1 margin. For the first time, Tendulkar showed glimpses of his prowess with the ball.

India won the first ODI at Nagpur by 19 runs with Tendulkar contributing 36. The second at Pune on 5 December saw him pick up his first wickets in international cricket, those of openers Roshan Mahanama and Dhammika Ranatunge, returning figures of 9-0-39-2 with his gentle medium-pacers. To add to his wickets, Tendulkar recorded his first ODI 50 (53) which saw India win comfortably by six wickets. He reached his half-century in just 38 balls and hit seven fours and a six in a sparkling innings. His stand with Azhar for the third wicket was worth 80 runs in only 9.4 overs. The all-round performance—which included two catches and the run-out of skipper Arjuna Ranatunga—earned Sachin the first of his numerous Man of the Match awards. It was one of those games in which everything he touched seemed to turn to gold.

The final game at Margao was played on an under-prepared pitch and halfway through the innings, Azhar and Tendulkar had to call for helmets to play the Sri Lankan spinners as the ball turned and jumped alarmingly. Tendulkar's 30 was the top score in a miserable Indian total of 136 all out. The visitors romped home by seven wickets after the pitch had dried out.

There was success at home for the Indians in the Asia Cup which followed. But with Pakistan pulling out, the tournament was robbed of its glamour and India fought it out with Sri Lanka and Bangladesh. Tendulkar had a quiet tournament, though he equalled his highest score of 53 in the final at Kolkata, in which India beat Sri Lanka by seven wickets.

The lack of international cricket for the rest of the season was a blessing in disguise for Indian cricket. Finally, the big names in the country like Kapil Dev, Ravi Shastri, Dilip Vengsarkar, Sachin Tendulkar and others would be available to assist their state and zonal teams in the domestic tournaments. The result was some gripping cricket after a gap of many years. Sachin enjoyed being a member of the Mumbai team that won the Wills Trophy and the West Zone team that lifted the Deodhar Trophy, both limited-overs tournaments. Both these tournaments were a novel experience for him, as was the zonal first-class Duleep Trophy in which West Zone lost in the final to North Zone under highly contentious circumstances.

The quarter-finals against East Zone at Guwahati from 11 to 15 January 1991 saw Sachin complete a unique treble. With an innings of 159 in the first innings he entered the record books as the first and still the only batsman to score a century on debut in the Ranji, Irani and Duleep Trophy. The first two feats had been achieved before the start of his international career. Now, after a year in world cricket, he had made it three out of three in domestic cricket's first-class set-up.

The East Zone bowling attack was certainly no great shakes and had no big names to speak of. Their batting was marked by Sourav Ganguly's maiden century in his seventh first-class match. Uniquely, there were two future India captains in this match, Ganguly and Tendulkar, as well as two from the recent past—Ravi Shastri and Dilip Vengsarkar.

The West Zone batting, on the other hand, was formidable, with the first six batsmen in the line-up as well as number eight Kiran More having international experience. Little surprise then, that on a placid track there should be massive scores. Lalchand Rajput (82), Sanjay Manjrekar (122) and Vengsarkar (72) all cashed in while Tendulkar top-scored with 159. East were no match for the West total of 604 and were all out for 317. The match was drawn with West advancing on their huge first innings lead. Tendulkar's innings, his fifth century in 31 first-class matches, was divided in pace. It took him 226 minutes to reach three figures, but he lashed out after that. The last 59 runs included nine fours and two sixes and came from a mere 30 balls.

The semi-finals between West Zone and South Zone at Rourkela produced a typical run-feast. South piled up 515. But that was dwarfed by West's 747 and once again West advanced on the basis of their first innings lead. This time the bowling attack was certainly more challenging than in the previous match. South had in their ranks Javagal Srinath, Venkatapathy Raju, Arshad Ayub, Robin Singh and Anil Kumble. Not that it bothered Tendulkar. His contribution this time was another century: 131.

The stage was set for the battle of the giants of domestic cricket, North Zone and West Zone, at Jamshedpur. It was a match that was destined to go down in history, but for all the wrong reasons.

North Zone, led by Kapil Dev, were more than a match for West in batting and bowling. Their total of 729 was beyond the reach of even the formidable West batting line-up which could muster 'only' 561 against a bowling attack that was virtually that of the Indian team itself.

Tendulkar failed this time, and that may have made all the difference. Both sides had three century-makers. But Tendulkar's contribution was just 25 and with his dismissal, West's hopes faded. The North second innings was a formality. But it ended in an ugly brawl between bowler Rashid Patel from Gujarat and batsman Raman Lamba from Delhi. There had been plenty of bad blood spilled in the match already, with the North bowlers resorting to beamers and deliberate overstepping, and the air thick with foul language. Patel decided to give the North batsmen a taste of their own medicine in the short time left for them to bat out the match, and bowled some menacing bouncers and beamers. Hot words were exchanged between batsman and bowler and for the first time, cricket witnessed a bowler assaulting a batsman with a stump on the field of play. Both Lamba and Patel received bans of varying degrees from the BCCI for their behaviour even as the match was abandoned by the umpires.

In one of those strange twists of fate, the Delhi opener, one of the most prolific batsmen in domestic cricket, died eight years later, in 1998, after being struck on the head while fielding in a club match in Dhaka.

Indian cricket spent almost as much time in the law courts as out on the field of play in this particular season, with controversies galore. There was a two-month gap between the first two and last two quarter-finals as a dispute between Karnataka and Bengal dragged on and on. Even during the league stage, a legal dispute between Punjab and Delhi in the North Zone had threatened to disrupt the tournament. The end result of all this acrimony was that the tournament for the first time dragged on till May.

Tendulkar had missed the West Zone league stage in the Ranji Trophy. But with Mumbai qualifying as the second team in the league after Maharashtra, he returned to assist them in the knockout stage.

After beating Uttar Pradesh by ten wickets in the pre-quarter-finals, Mumbai faced the might of Delhi in the quarter-final tie at the Feroze Shah Kotla. The match was played in the middle of April.

A number of Delhi players had been contracted to play league cricket in England that summer. Conflicting interests led to a fixed match, as the Delhi players admitted to the Central Bureau of Investigation (CBI) a decade later, during its investigations into match-fixing and corruption in cricket. At the time, of course, no one suspected anything, and the Mumbai-Delhi match was widely thought to be one of the most exciting Ranji Trophy matches of all time. Tendulkar top-scored with 82 in Mumbai's total of 390. Bantoo Singh's century for Delhi guided them to 386 for 9. But when Wassan was bowled by Patil for 32, Mumbai were assured of a place in the semi-finals on the basis of their first innings lead of one run. And the Delhi cricketers could happily book their tickets to England. Failure to arrive on time would have invited hefty fines from their clubs.

Mumbai made a mountain of runs in their second innings: 719 for 8 declared. Tendulkar's 125 was his third century in five first-class matches. Though Delhi's second innings was a formality, there was enough time for Tendulkar to make his mark again, this time with the ball.

He had bowled just one over in the first innings. Now, in the second, he got one to leap from the placid pitch and hit Bantoo Singh, fracturing the nose of the first-innings century-maker. Tendulkar had fancied himself as a fast bowler till Dennis Lillee told him to concentrate on his batting. But it is doubtful whether even the great Australian would have been able to extract such life out of a dead Kotla pitch on the final day.

Even by the batting standards of Indian domestic cricket, Mumbai's 855 for 6 declared in the semi-finals against Hyderabad at the Wankhede Stadium four days later was an awesome figure. Sanjay Manjrekar's 377 was the highest ever by a Mumbai batsman in the Ranji Trophy. There were centuries from Vengsarkar and Kambli as well, while Tendulkar's contribution was 70 and 88 in Mumbai's second innings of 446 for 4 declared. Hyderabad stood no chance at all.

For the first time Sachin would experience the thrill of playing in the final of the National Championship, that too at home at the Wankhede Stadium. Mumbai's opponents were Haryana, who under Kapil Dev had made short work of Bengal in the other semi-final. Kapil, Chetan Sharma and Ajay Jadeja (yet to make a mark in international cricket) were the only known names in the Haryana line-up. Mumbai, on the other hand, was a virtual who's who of Indian cricket and the red-hot favourites. It turned out to be one of the best Ranji finals of all time. Haryana's huge 522 was built around opener Deepak Sharma's 199 while both Jadeja and Chetan Sharma fell in the 90s. Most of the top Mumbai players made useful runs, Tendulkar contributing 47 before he was lbw to Chetan Sharma. It was nightwatchman Sanjay Patil who top-scored with 85. However, Mumbai's 410 was well short of Haryana's total and it looked like curtains for the side. But their bowlers turned in a strong second-innings performance and had Haryana on the ropes at 100 for 5 before Ajay Banerjee (60 not out) rallied them to 242. The target was 355 for Mumbai to win back the Ranji Trophy they had last claimed in 1984-85. The run rate was stiff, more than five an over.

At 3 down for 34, Tendulkar and Vengsarkar got together in a rollicking stand worth 134 runs. Sachin took the bowling attack spearheaded by Kapil Dev and Chetan Sharma apart. He reached his 50 from just 49 balls, taking over the attacking role from his captain and senior partner. The Haryana bowling was dispatched all around as Tendulkar raced towards a century which appeared inevitable till he was caught by Jadeja off the bowling of off-spinner Yogendra Bhandari for 96. Sachin was going for the boundary that would have got him his ton. The last 46 runs had come from just 26 balls and the sparkling innings was studded with five sixes and nine fours. A crowd of 4000 had turned up to watch the final day's play—a large number for a domestic match in India. They had pinned their hopes on the young hero of Mumbai. Such was his dazzling stroke play on the last day that even Kapil Dev was seen shaking his head in bewilderment. Just two and a half years earlier, the schoolboy Sachin had faced the champion bowler in the nets at the Wankhede Stadium. Now he was dictating terms to him.

Sachin's dismissal at 168 for 4, followed by that of Vinod Kambli (45), triggered another collapse even as Vengsarkar marched towards a majestic century. When the ninth wicket fell, debutant pace bowler Abey Kuruvilla joined the captain with 50 runs still needed for victory. As tension mounted, the pair added 47 before the last man was run out. Victory was Haryana's by two runs. Though Vengsarkar's 139 not out was the top score for Mumbai, the run chase would have been given up as futile if it hadn't been for the teenager's batting pyrotechnics.

Tendulkar would have to wait some more time to be part of a Ranji Trophy winning side. He ended the season with 577 runs from four matches at the outstanding average of 82.42. There were also two individual honours for him. He was named as the Association of

Cricket Statisticians and Scorers of India (ACSSI) Cricketer of the Year and one of the five Cricketers of the Year by *Indian Cricket Annual*.

The cancellation of Pakistan's visit to India meant there would be no international cricket till October 1991 when India were scheduled to be back in Sharjah for the three-nation Wills Trophy. There would be non-stop action for the next six months, culminating in the 1992 World Cup in Australia.

The opening match for India in the Sharjah three-nation Wills Trophy against Pakistan on 17 October 1991 saw the side record a rare win over their arch-rivals. Manjrekar was the top scorer with 72. But it was Tendulkar's 52 not out from 40 balls, with five fours, that provided the impetus towards the end of the innings. The match also marked the international debut of Vinod Kambli, three and a half years after he had been involved in the world-record partnership with his school chum for Sharadashram Vidyamandir.

In the final league match, which India lost to Pakistan under dark skies and in controversial circumstances, Tendulkar fell one short of another 50. But he failed in the final, lbw first ball to Aaqib Javed. That completed a hat-trick for the medium-pacer who had figures of 7 for 37, a world record in One-day Internationals that would last for ten years. West Indies were beaten by India in both their league games. In the second of these, Sachin got the Man of the Match award, but not for his batting. He returned his best bowling figures of 4 for 34 as the former world champions crumbled to 145 all out. Tendulkar accounted for opener Clayton Lambert, captain Richie Richardson, Gus Logie and Jeff Dujon. His success with the ball meant he was now an integral part of the team's bowling plan.

Meanwhile, in faraway South Africa, dramatic events were rapidly unfolding that were soon to bury the evil of apartheid. India had been in the forefront of the movement to ban South Africa from international cricket in 1970. Until then, South Africa only played Test cricket against the 'white' nations of the ICC. After the ban, they found themselves in exile for 21 years. With the release of Nelson Mandela, the dismantling of apartheid and the advent of multiracial sports, it was once again India that took the lead at the ICC meeting at Lord's which saw South Africa return to the fold. South African cricket supremo Dr Aaron 'Ali' Bacher showed his gratitude by agreeing to tour India. He hurriedly assembled a team under the captaincy of veteran Clive Rice and flew to India to play three ODIs at the request of BCCI secretary Jagmohan Dalmiya.

The first match at Eden Gardens, Kolkata on 10 November 1991 in front of over 90,000 spectators was truly a historic event, going beyond mere sporting clichés. All but Kepler Wessels, who had previously represented his adopted country of Australia, were making their international debut. On the ground, the emotion was palpable and the enormous crowd, the likes of which the visitors had never seen, egged the home side to victory.

Though the South African total of 177 for 8 in 47 overs was hardly threatening, India made heavy weather of it initially. South Africa's spearhead Allan Donald blasted out the top order to capture the impressive figures of 5 for 29 as India lost their first four wickets with just 60 on the board. At this stage, a dream victory for the debutants was very much on the cards. The damage for India was repaired by the Mumbai pair of Tendulkar and debutant Praveen Amre in a rollicking stand worth 56 runs that snatched the initiative from the visitors. (Amre was the third of coach Ramakant Achrekar's students to make it to the big league, following the examples of Tendulkar and Vinod Kambli. His 55 at Kolkata would be followed a year later by a century on Test debut against the same opponents at Durban. It was a feat that Achrekar's other two prodigies had been incapable of.)

R.Mohan was effusive in his praise of Tendulkar's many talents (he also picked up the wicket of South Africa's top scorer Wessels) in the *Sportstar* (23 November 1991): 'It is impossible to fathom what the youngster is capable of. He is a match winner pure and simple. The manner in which he adapted to the slow wicket and played the shots few others could strike with any great conviction is a clear pointer that he is the jewel in the Indian crown. Soon, very soon, people will be turning up only to watch Tendulkar play. He has so much of the champion phenomenon in him. And he is not capable of playing for records because he has such a positive approach. If he continues to bat like this he will be the leader of the new era in which the raw power of batting is going to dominate cricket as it has baseball. Only Tendulkar would use that dominance in that refreshingly orthodox way of his.'

The Man of the Match award was shared by Donald and Tendulkar, an unusual occurrence in international cricket, but one in keeping with the spirit of the occasion.

9

On Top Down Under

This boy is from heaven. He will do anything.—Tim Laine

The hastily arranged South African tour gave the Indians precious little time to acclimatize and prepare for their Test tour to Australia. The Indian team flew out straight after losing the third and final ODI in New Delhi on 14 November 1991. The South Africans won the game, but the series ended 2-1 in the home team's favour.

India were slated to play five Tests Down Under for the first time since 1977-78. In between the Test series, West Indies would join India and Australia for the WSC one-day tournament. And after that was the big one—the World Cup. It would be the most gruelling tour ever undertaken by an Indian cricket team.

Just how unprepared the Indians were to take on the might of Australia was cruelly exposed in the first Test at Brisbane. This, after they had been shot out for 64 in a one-day game against Western Australia and beaten by New South Wales inside of three days in the only first-class match before the Test series. The formidable Aussie fast bowling attack of Craig McDermott, Mike Whitney and Merv Hughes blew away the Indians in the space of three and a half days by the thumping margin of ten wickets. Still, there were two inspiring individual achievements on the Indian side. On the third day, Kapil Dev produced what Australian opening batsman David Boon described as 'the best three balls bowled consecutively that I have seen in Test cricket'. Boon was at the non-striker's end as Kapil bowled an in-swinger to Allan Border of such perfect length that any left-hander would have been bowled off-stump. The second ball, an outswinger to Dean Jones, beat bat and stump by a coat of varnish. The next ball was brought back and bowled Jones for a duck. There were also some batting heroics from Manoj Prabhakar who stayed at the crease for over five hours. The Test marked the debut of Javagal Srinath who picked up three wickets.

The traditional Boxing Day Test at Melbourne followed much the same pattern, the margin of victory for Australia this time being eight wickets. The destroyer-in-chief was Bruce Reid who replaced another left-arm seamer, Whitney, in the attack. Reid had figures of 12 for 126 and once again the Test was over in four days. Tendulkar had been a disappointment so far, as was the Indian batting as a whole. His first three innings had produced scores of 16, 7 and 15. But in the second innings at Melbourne, he hit a cultured 40 with five fours before a rush of blood saw him caught in the deep off spinner Peter Taylor. Border took a brilliant catch, running back over a hundred feet to clutch the swirling ball. It was a chastening experience for the young man, who vowed never again to hit the ball in the air.

The Sydney wicket with its reputation for aiding spinners has always provided welcome respite from the generally bouncy tracks found across Australia, for touring Indian teams. It was surprising then that India went in for the third Test with only one spinner (Ravi Shastri), with Venkatapathy Raju and Narendra Hirwani having to cool their heels. Shastri emerged as the Man of the Match for the first double century by an Indian against Australia and four wickets in the second innings, which almost saw India pull off a shock victory. But it was Tendulkar's sublime century that had the critics once again eating out of the palm of his hand. David Boon's 129 not out was the standout innings in Australia's total of 313.

India lost Navjot Singh Sidhu for a duck. But they had a stroke of luck when their tormentor in the previous Test, Bruce Reid, limped off with a torn muscle in the side after bowling just four overs, and took no further part in the Test. That was just the chance the Indian batting needed to finally come good after the defeats at Brisbane and Melbourne. Opener Shastri batted nearly ten hours for his 206 before becoming the only victim of leg-spinner Shane Warne who finished with 1 for 150 on his Test debut. Even as Shastri dropped anchor and sought to repair the early damage with a little help from Manjrekar and Vengsarkar, it was the silken skills of Tendulkar that had all of Australia suddenly taking notice of the Indian team. The record stand for the fifth wicket between Shastri and Tendulkar was worth 196 in 198 minutes and as Shastri moved towards his first Test double century, Tendulkar took centre stage with an array of dazzling shots that had the spectators riveted. The fourth day's play belonged to Tendulkar as he reached his century in 226 minutes from 171 balls, the youngest to do so on Australian soil. Once again, as at Old Trafford in 1990, the bat was lifted, the helmet taken off, and a shy half-smile crossed his lips.

At 18 years and 256 days, Sachin had surpassed the previous record held by Australian left-handed legend Neil Harvey who had made 153 against India at Melbourne in 1948, at the age of 19 years and 121 days, 25 years before Tendulkar was born. Harvey himself led the chorus which rang out across the country. He thought Sachin's performance had been quite brilliant and expressed his belief that he would be around for a long time and would break a few records before he was finished.

'He is the best player I have seen for ages. I love the way he places the ball past fieldsmen and his back-foot technique is superb. He also seems to have a good temperament. Given his ability and the number of Test matches they play these days, he could play 200 Tests before he's finished.'

There was something else Sachin had in common with Harvey. He forced a fielding captain to accept an offer of bad light, something Harvey had achieved in South Africa. With just a handful of Tests behind him, Sachin's innings displayed a maturity that put the vastly experienced batsmen who came before and after him to shame. Virtually everything came off the middle of the bat and he drove and cut with panache and precision.

The Aussies, meanwhile, had been giving a hard time to both Shastri and Tendulkar with their patented form of abuse known euphemistically in Australia as 'sledging'. 'I had just reached my hundred and I was having a verbal duel with the Australians,' recalled Shastri in *Mid Day* (May 2001). 'At the end of the over he came over to me and said in Marathi, "*Thumb, mazha pan shambhar hounde*" (Wait till I get my hundred). And I said, with your brilliance young man, you don't even have to do that. What happened is history. The Waugh brothers were made to eat humble pie.'

India declined to declare on their overnight 445 for 7 (Tendulkar: 120 not out) on the final day and added a further 38 runs to swell their lead to 170. Tendulkar was now improvising and got 28 of the last 38 runs. His 148 not out from 216 balls with 14 fours took a shade under five hours. Needing 171 to avoid an innings defeat, Australia finished on a precarious 173 for 8 with captain Border hanging on for 53. With the wicket taking plenty of spin on the final day, Azhar in desperation turned to Tendulkar to bowl some off spin. And he claimed his first Test wicket in his only over when he had the obdurate Merv Hughes caught by Prabhakar for 21. The draw was a huge turnaround from the crushing defeats India had suffered in the previous two Tests and prevented the clean sweep which many Aussie supporters had been predicting. Victory could have been India's but for some strange tactics and also time lost to rain. Azhar was criticized for delaying the declaration till early on the fifth day. In hindsight, the 36 minutes he batted on and the ten minutes for the change of innings may have proved the difference between victory for the Indians and a draw.

David Frith summed up the match eloquently in *Wisden Cricket Monthly* (February 1992): 'Tendulkar's creamy elegance, power and precocity had even the local partisans cooing…It was bad luck for Shastri that his double-century and his wickets will take second place in public memory behind Tendulkar's beautiful century. The boy wonder's talent is so great it's almost frightening.'

Between Test matches, India, Australia and the West Indies were involved in the World Series Cup (WSC) in which India had lost in the finals in 1985-86. The tournament marked the start of the decline of the mighty West Indies, World Cup champions in 1975 and 1979 and virtually invincible in one-day games in Australia until now. Led by Richie Richardson, West Indies were without the one and only Vivian

Richards for the first time since the mid-1970s. Veterans like Desmond Haynes and Malcolm Marshall were coming to the end of their careers, and Brian Lara was yet to set the cricket world alight. Indeed, it was India who had first pricked the bubble of Caribbean invincibility, first at Berbice in 1983 and then later the same year at Lord's in the World Cup finals.

The tri-series began in sensational style at Perth on 6 December 1991 with Sachin Tendulkar getting the last West Indies wicket to earn a tie for India. It was the first time in 692 ODIs that both sides were all out for exactly the same score—a perfect tie. In conditions ideal for swing and seam bowlers, both sides made their lowest total against each other. Shastri took a laborious 110 balls to score 33, the highest score in the match. There were just two boundaries in the entire Indian innings of 126 all out in 47.4 overs and Shastri hit both. West Indies were quickly in trouble too, as debutant medium-pacer Subroto Banerjee picked up three wickets, including Lara for 14. The score was 76 for 8 before the unlikely pair of Curtly Ambrose and Anderson Cummins came together in the biggest stand of the match (37). Cummins and last man Patrick Patterson had pieced together 13 runs when Tendulkar had Cummins brilliantly caught in the slips by a diving Azhar, with the scores level. It was his only over of the match and made up to some extent for his failure with the bat.

Two days later, it was Australia's turn to collapse for their lowest score against India, a measly 101, as India scored a thumping win by 107 runs against the reigning world champions. Shastri's 5-15 from 6.5 overs were the best ODI figures for India till 1993-94. Tendulkar gave away just eight runs from his four overs and also scored a useful 36 in India's score of 208 for 7. After the shock at Perth, Australia came back strongly to crush India by eight wickets at Hobart and then edge West Indies out by nine runs at Melbourne. Manjrekar and Tendulkar hit identical scores (57) and their stand of 102 stood out starkly in a paltry Indian total of 175 for 8 at Hobart.

West Indies' poor run continued as they were beaten by ten runs by India at Adelaide. The Indian total of 262 for 4 would be the highest in a tournament in which the ball generally dominated the bat.

Srikkanth—who was making a comeback after being unceremoniously dumped following the Pakistan tour—smashed 84 at almost a run a ball with Manjrekar (55) and Tendulkar (48) helping to boost the score. Australia by now were on a roll, and they flattened both their opponents. It would be a fight between India and West Indies for the other slot in the final. West Indies finally broke their wretched run as Cummins' 5-31 bowled them to victory by six wickets against India at Brisbane. Tendulkar's 77 was his highest score in 27 ODIs and he was now emerging as the most reliable of the Indian batsmen. Each time he looked set to get a bigger score, though, he got out to impetuous shots. With the West Indies beating Australia and then India losing to Australia, it came down to the last game. The winner of the final league game at Melbourne would be in the final.

West Indies crawled to 48 for 3 from 25 overs and three run-outs ensured that they could only reach 175 for 8. Though he did not claim any wickets, Tendulkar gave away just 38 runs in his full quota of ten overs. The Indian batting was pinned down by an outstanding opening spell by Ambrose: 6-4-3-1. But Man of the Match Tendulkar helped break the shackles with 57 not out, which saw India home by five wickets and into the finals.

Australia romped home by eight wickets in the first final at Melbourne. The second at Sydney could have gone either way. India needed 13 off the last over bowled by Whitney. They lost by six runs. Tendulkar once again top-scored with 69 from 100 balls, though he had some lucky escapes. He was dropped by Steve Waugh, who had earlier 'caught' him off a no-ball. Waugh floored a skier off his own bowling even as TV commentator Tony Greig was saying, 'No way in the world will he drop that.' Then Tom Moody's throw from square leg hit the stumps and the TV replay showed Tendulkar was short of his ground. This was before the advent of the third umpire with the benefit of TV replays. Ironically, just ten months later Tendulkar would become the first to be given out (run out) to this technology.

With 401 runs from ten innings (one not out) Sachin was the leading Indian batsman. The WSC one-day games were an ideal warm-up to the World Cup, though they did add to the fatigue of the players.

But for now it was back to the Test series with India down 2-0 after three Tests. Shastri had suffered a knee injury during the WSC and his absence from the last two Tests of the series was a major setback for the team. The Indian bowling had come in for much flak at the start of the tour. But the bowlers had performed creditably, and it was their batting that was the bane of the Indians. The bowlers had their finest hour in Australia's first innings in the fourth Test at Adelaide after Azhar had won the toss and put them in. Memories of a similar decision 18 months ago may have been on his mind. But this time, it paid off handsomely. Kapil Dev and Raju picked up three wickets apiece. And Tendulkar broke the back of the batting with two vital wickets at the start of the innings. He bowled opener Mark Taylor for 11, and then had Border caught by Pandit for his second duck of the series. Australia crashed to 145 all out.

Kapil was having a vintage series with both bat and ball, and his 56 was the first half-century of the match. But with the top six batsmen swept away by Hughes and McDermott with just 70 on the board, it looked like Australia would take the lead after all. However, this time the Indian tail wagged and a lead of 80 runs was their reward.

The Australian umpiring sunk to new depths during the series and was a persistent grouse with the tourists. When Boon was on 1, Kapil rapped him on the pads, but he was given not out. It seemed an unjust decision at the time to the Indians and they would certainly have cause to rue it, for Boon (135) and Taylor (100) added 221 for the second wicket, helping Australia cross the 400 mark for the first time in the series.

Indeed, eight Indian batsmen would be given out leg before in this Test, against two for the Australians. But it was the shocker which Vengsarkar received in the second innings, stretching well forward to Hughes, that took the cake and led commentator Ian Chappell to blurt out on air, 'If that was not outside the line of the off stump when it hit, then I'm a Dutchman.' This from a true-blue Aussie!

The normally diplomatic Indian cricket manager Abbas Ali Baig asked cuttingly if there had been any changes in Law 36 which his team were unaware of, and about which he wished to speak to the umpires for the fifth Test.

Azhar's form in the series had also become the topic of discussion amongst the team and back home. He had eked out just 51 runs so far and there were murmurings that he was not worth his place in the side. It hardly helped matters that the side contained four former captains—Shastri, Kapil, Vengsarkar and Srikkanth—perhaps still nursing a desire to get back the captaincy.

In his authorized biography of Azharuddin, Harsha Bhogle hinted at this while stressing that the younger members of the team were behind their skipper. 'Sachin Tendulkar told me, "If only Azzu could score runs, it would make such a difference. For his sake, we all want him to get runs. You know, the other day, I just couldn't control myself and I went and told him that if he batted like this, it might help. Perhaps I shouldn't have done it but all of us so badly want him to score"' (*Azhar: The Authorized Biography of Mohammad Azharuddin*).

The final day, and the equation was clear. India had all their wickets intact and the target was now 340 from 90 overs. Azhar had dropped himself down to number six to accommodate Tendulkar at four, since the team had decided to go all out for victory in the hope of keeping the series alive. It was make or break for both the team and their leader, and Azhar responded with the most dazzling batting exhibition so far. Just as he had done in England and New Zealand in 1990, he went for the bowling and tore it apart. Prabhakar (64) put on 101 with him for the seventh wicket in less than 90 minutes, and while they were at the crease an improbable Indian victory suddenly loomed large. Azhar smashed 80 between lunch and tea, at which point the score was 252 for 6, with 120 more needed. It took a tremendous burst with the second new ball by McDermott and another diabolical umpiring decision to thwart the victory charge. Azhar was snapped up at slip by Mark Taylor for 106 as McDermott took the final four wickets to fall, including Prabhakar lbw off an inside edge. With five wickets in both innings, the Man of the Match award was his. The series could so easily have been 2-2 going into the final Test at Perth. Instead, Australia had pocketed it 3-0 and the Indians were to rue several missed opportunities, not to mention the umpiring that did them in at crucial moments.

Despite there being little to play for at Perth, the Test produced some glorious personal milestones and achievements. The result—Australia's victory by a whopping 300 runs—seemed almost inconsequential. Three Australian batsmen—David Boon, Dean Jones and Tom Moody—reached three figures (it was Boon's third century of the series) and Mike Whitney took the bowling honours (4-68 and 7-27). But it was Tendulkar and Kapil who had the media and the fans enthralled. When Kapil had Taylor lbw for 16 on the fourth day, he became only the second bowler after New Zealand's Sir Richard Hadlee to reach the milestone of 400 Test wickets. With four wickets in the Test, the medium-pacer who had made his debut in 1978 had his best overseas series with 25 victims in all. Only McDermott with 31 topped that.

The fourth day also saw Tendulkar progress from his overnight 31 not out to his second century of the series, and already predictions were being made by journalists and former cricketers about the glittering career that lay ahead of him. After Australia's 346, it took Tendulkar's daring strokes to get his side to within 74 runs in the first innings. A total of 400-plus in the fourth innings was always beyond India's batsmen. But their capitulation to a mere 141 all out after an opening stand of 82 stunned one and all.

Tendulkar's century came from only 135 balls, with 14 fours, as he cut the formidable Australian pace attack to size in a breathtaking display of aggression. The second 50 of the innings came from 55 balls with six boundaries. He was like the boy who stood on the burning deck, for every other batsman in the side struggled to cope with the steepling bounce. There would be two more boundaries before he was caught knee-high by Moody at second slip off Whitney. He had scored 114 out of the 140 runs made while at the crease. The innings was marked by cutting and driving of ferocious power and timing. Often he would go up on his toes to smash the ball to the distant square boundaries. The series saw some dazzling batsmanship on both sides. But they all paled in comparison to Tendulkar's third century in 16 Tests.

The Tendulkar fan club was now growing rapidly. Former Australian Test batsman Norman O'Neill had this to say: 'The difference between an ordinary and a class player is the time he has even to make last second adjustments to play his strokes. Tendulkar has it. He is all class. I enjoyed every moment of his innings.' Said Border, 'If he could play like this at 19, I shudder to think what he will be at 25.' In fact, he was still a couple of months shy of his nineteenth birthday at the end of the Perth Test. Even ABC radio commentator Tim Laine's gushing praise did not seem out of place: 'This boy is from heaven. He will do anything' (*Sportstar*, 15 February 1992). Nearly a decade later, even after his twenty-fifth Test century, Tendulkar himself rated this knock as among his top three (*Cricket Talk*, 9 December 2000).

David Boon told me, 'It was quite amazing that someone so young could show the maturity he did. His shot selection and execution were of someone who would normally be much older and more experienced.'

Cricket manager Abbas Ali Baig shared his memories of the tour and of Tendulkar in particular with me in his office in New Delhi in October 2000. 'At Sydney he had a senior pro (Shastri) with him to nurse him along—not that he really needed it at that stage of his career. The wicket at Sydney was also rather slow. At Perth it was another matter. It was a very nasty and fast wicket and the Australian fast bowlers were playing havoc with our batsmen. But Sachin was hooking them with impunity; he was cutting and driving them. I rate this innings very, very highly. The Australians secretly adored him but on the field they gave him a bit of stick as is their wont. They always pick out the best player and target him. But he never flinched and gave it back to them.

'At team meetings he would be very involved. He would sit quietly but then his little voice would suddenly pipe up. He would be to the point and didn't waste your time. Even at that age you had to take note of his suggestions. He was remarkably mature for his age.'

10

World Cup Debut

Inzamam is a much better batsman against fast bowling.—Imran Khan

There was some speculation at the end of the Test series that the Indian team would return for a short break before their opening World Cup game at Perth against England on 22 February, just 17 days after the fifth Test at the same venue had ended. Many of the players were homesick after so many weeks away from their families, and the prospect of another month of travelling the length and breadth of this vast land for the World Cup was a daunting one. However, it was decided that they should stay on and play a couple of warm-up games, though the team was hardly short of match practice. Ajay Jadeja and Vinod Kambli joined the team for the World Cup and Ravi Shastri was back from Mumbai, having been declared fit after the knee injury that had kept him out of the last two Test matches.

The fifth edition of the World Cup to be staged in Australia and New Zealand, or the Benson and Hedges World Cup to give it its full name, was unique in many respects. For the first time on the world stage, matches would be played under lights with the players donning coloured outfits and using two white balls from either ends. This would set the trend for future World Cups. There was also considerable excitement over the debut of post-apartheid South Africa. Also, there was a new round-robin league format, with all the nine teams facing each other.

The tournament could not have got off to a more sensational start. New Zealand, which had failed to make the semi-finals in 1987, stunned World Cup holders Australia by 37 runs in Auckland, with

Kiwi skipper Martin Crowe stroking a masterly 100 not out—and surprising one and all by opening the bowling with off-spinner Dipak Patel. On the same day at the Western Association Cricket Association (WACA), India came within a whisker of upsetting the 1987 runners-up England, ultimately losing by just nine runs. This was a match that swung back and forth as India became the first team to bat under lights in a World Cup game. With Graham Gooch (51) and Robin Smith (91) to the fore, England made a brisk start and were looking good for a big score. Smith was out at 197 for 4 and the last six wickets then crashed for just 27 runs. The English tally for the last seven overs was 39 runs for the loss of six wickets and a total of 236 for 9 appeared eminently achievable. That certainly seemed the case as openers Shastri and Srikkanth put on 63 in contrasting styles. There were seven boundaries in the latter's 39, while Shastri top-scored with a rather laborious 51. Azhar's nightmare run with the bat continued, as he got out on the first ball. At 63 for 2, it was left to the Mumbai pair of Shastri and Tendulkar to put the innings back on the rails. This they did in a stand that doubled the score by the thirtieth over.

Now Ian Botham swung the advantage back England's way with an inspired spell of bowling that would win him the Man of the Match award. Just as Tendulkar was looking like he would win the game single-handed, Botham tied him down and then foxed him with a slower one. The perfectly pitched away cutter had him playing forward and well caught by wicketkeeper Alec Stewart for a smart 35 from 44 balls, with five fours. The experienced Botham was delighted; the young Tendulkar anguished. It was a dismissal he would forever look upon with considerable chagrin, for he did not have a clue to the delivery. Botham also accounted for Vinod Kambli and the equation came down to 51 from seven overs, then to 36 from three with the last wicket pair of Banerjee and Srinath at the crease. Some amazing shots saw them needing 11 from the last over from Chris Lewis. But England had the last laugh.

India's next match against Sri Lanka at Mackay was abandoned due to rain after just two balls had been bowled and both teams were awarded one point. Australia had suffered another shock defeat, following their loss to New Zealand in the opening game. This time they were handed out a nine-wicket trouncing by South Africa who could not have marked their World Cup debut in greater style.

The India-Australia bout at Brisbane on 1 March was thus a needle match with both teams looking for their first win. It turned out to be one of the greatest games of cricket ever, at the venue of the first ever tied Test (in 1960).

Australia batted first. Dean Jones hit 90 from 109 balls, while Border's miserable form with the bat continued, and they finished on 237 for 9. Kapil Dev and Prabhakar turned in identical figures of 3-41 from ten overs. India, in its innings, had reached 45 for 1 (Srikkanth the batsman out, bowled for a duck by McDermott) after 16.2 overs, when there was a 21-minute delay on account of rain. The rain rule came into play then, and the revised target (under the 'highest scoring overs' formula) was now 236 from 47 overs. While only two runs had been knocked off the target, India would have three overs less to play. The damp ball after the rain made things slippery for the Aussie bowlers. Azharuddin played one of his gems, a rare occurrence in a tour of horrors for the Indian captain. Kapil Dev was promoted to push the scoring along and slammed 21 in a run-a-ball cameo. This after Shastri had got bogged down, plodding to 25 from 70 balls.

It was Manjrekar, coming in at number six, who gave his captain the necessary support to go for the win. Azhar played typically glorious, wristy shots all round the ground and raced to 93 from 103 balls (ten fours) before becoming the first of four run-out victims in the innings: Border's rocket-like throw caught him short of the crease. His stand with Manjrekar was worth 66, and when he fell the score was 194 for 5. With eight overs and six wickets in hand, the target had come down to 77. Manjrekar lifted the tempo and it was now down to 42 from five. He hit Hughes for a six and a four and raced to 47 from 42 balls, then he too was run out at 216 for 7, with 20 runs still needed for what seemed an improbable win. Tendulkar's failure (he was out for 11) put further pressure on the lower order.

It was now left to the tail-enders and they took the team to the very doorstep of victory. A miscalculation by Border saw his main strike bowler McDermott bowl the penultimate over from which he conceded just six runs and now 13 were needed from the last over by off-spinner Tom Moody. Kiran More smashed the first two to the boundary. But he was bowled next ball, trying to finish the game with another four. Prabhakar scored a single from the first ball he faced and was run out from the next. Four runs were now needed from the last ball. Srinath swung hard and connected cleanly, sending the ball soaring down to the fine leg boundary for what appeared to be a certain six and victory. Indeed, last man Raju was already doing a victory jig. Then came the final breathtaking twist. At full tilt, Steve Waugh ran round and reached for the catch, only to drop it even as the crowd gasped in disbelief. Waugh grabbed the ball as it slid towards the gutter while Srinath and Raju ran for their lives, and threw as the batsmen were crossing for the third run that would have tied the game. The throw was wayward and Boon, keeping in place of the injured Healy, had to drag it in, but he managed to remove the bails a split second before Raju could complete the run. Australia had won by one run, just as they had at Chennai in the opening match of the 1987 Reliance Cup, which they went on to lift. Finally, it looked like their defence of the title was back on the rails. India could only curse the wretched rain rule.

The round-robin format of the World Cup ensured that all the teams played each other before the knockout stage. Thus, for the first time in five World Cup tournaments, India and Pakistan would come face to face. Until now, organizers had made sure to place the traditional rivals in different groups. Even as India were looking for their first win in the tournament, Pakistan were decidedly lucky to be saved by rain against England, at Adelaide, after crashing to 74 all out.

The two teams met at the Sydney Cricket Ground on 4 March 1992. The pressure on both sides was intense. The crowd of 10,000 was almost entirely made up of expatriate Indians and Pakistanis.

Azhar took first strike on winning the toss. The Indian total of 216 for 7 was built around Ajay Jadeja's 46 (he opened in place of Shastri) and Tendulkar's 54 not out from 62 balls. Kapil Dev provided the impetus towards the end with a quick-fire 35. Pakistan began their run chase with Azhar setting an attacking field from the start. Inzamam-ul-Haq and Zahid Fazal both fell for two and at 17 for 2, the Indian bowlers had gained the upper hand. Opener Aamir Sohail and Javed Miandad began the rescue act in a partnership of 88, punctuated with a confrontation between wicketkeeper More and Miandad. It was Tendulkar who made the breakthrough, getting Sohail caught low down at midwicket by Srikkanth for 62. Once Miandad had been bowled by Srinath for a painstaking 40, the rest of the batting fell apart and subsided to 173 all out, leaving India winners by 43 runs and Tendulkar with his first Man of the Match award in the World Cup.

After all the frustration with the rain rule in the match against Australia, things evened out for India in the next match against Zimbabwe in Hamilton, New Zealand. The match was initially curtailed to 32 overs. Zimbabwe's innings was terminated by another downpour, at 104 for 1 in 19.1 overs. Though India's score at the same stage was 106 for 3, their 'best' 19 overs had produced 159, hence the strange calculations and victory to India by 55 runs.

India opened with Kapil Dev, but it was Tendulkar who stole the show. He smashed his highest ODI score of 81 from 77 balls, with eight fours and a six, that saw them to 203 for 7. He mastered all the bowlers except veteran off-spinner John Traicos, who was 26 years older than him. Traicos claimed 3-35 from his six overs. Though this contrived result kept their hopes alive, India were struggling and it was no surprise when they lost their next three matches against the West Indies, New Zealand and South Africa, and made their exit from the tournament.

Tendulkar failed against the West Indies at Wellington, caught behind off a perfect leg-cutter from Curtly Ambrose as India went down by five wickets. He came roaring back against New Zealand, overtaking his previous highest score of 81 by three runs. He was dropped early at short cover, after which he unleashed a range of sparkling strokes with six boundaries in his knock of 84 from 107 balls. His stand of 127 in 30 overs with Azhar produced some dazzling batting in front of a crowd of exactly 9000. But it wasn't enough, as the hosts won by four wickets to make it six wins in a row. The Indians weren't helped by the freezing conditions: Carisbrook in Dunedin is cricket's closest venue to the South Pole. The defeat finally dashed whatever slim hopes India may have harboured of reaching the semi-finals. Their last match at Adelaide against South Africa was once again reduced by rain. South Africa won in the thirtieth and final over to make it to the last four in their maiden World Cup.

It was an unhappy end to a disappointing campaign by the 1983 World Cup champions.

Tendulkar's personal total of 283 runs came from seven innings at an average of 47.17, with three 50s. He was now emerging as the team's potential match winner. 'His contributions were consistent, but not enough,' summed up manager Abbas Ali Baig.

Pakistan were the surprise winners of the World Cup final at the Melbourne Cricket Ground (MCG) on 25 March. Led by Imran Khan, they would have been eliminated in the league stage itself, but for rain during the match against England at Adelaide. The virtually unknown Inzamam-ul-Haq's dazzling 60 from 37 balls in the semi-finals against New Zealand at Auckland helped them pull off an improbable victory. The 22-year-old hit 42 in the final against England, following which his captain predicted he would be the world's number one batsman in the near future.

Ten years later, this is Imran Khan's analysis of the two batsmen from the subcontinent who promised to rule the world:

> I feel both Tendulkar and Inzamam are great players. When Tendulkar first came to Pakistan in 1989, his timing was very good. Tendulkar's innings management is much better than Inzamam's. He times the ball very well and he manages his innings to perfection. But I still say that Inzamam is a much better batsman against fast bowlers. He has played a number of match-winning innings for Pakistan against quality fast bowlers, whereas I don't think Tendulkar has played that many match-winning knocks for India. There are lots of other batsmen I would like to mention. Allan Border and Javed Miandad were not that talented, but the big plus of these

batsmen was that they were very good at building their innings—a quality which certainly Tendulkar has.

11

Two Little Bits of Cricket History

No one could have done a better job of breaking the ice.
— Geoffrey Boycott

Few Indian cricketers have enjoyed long stints in English county cricket. Kapil Dev, Ravi Shastri and Azharuddin played briefly for Northamptonshire, Glamorgan and Derbyshire respectively, while in more recent years Javagal Srinath, Anil Kumble, Rahul Dravid and Sourav Ganguly have turned out for various teams with mixed results. Sunil Gavaskar played just one season, and that was in 1980 for Somerset. The only Indian who made a career out of county cricket was wicketkeeper-batsman Farokh Engineer who was part of the Lancashire squad that enjoyed much one-day success in the 1970s. Sachin Tendulkar had made a huge impression on the English public and the media on his first tour in 1990. His century at Old Trafford at the age of 17 had captured public imagination. It wasn't surprising, therefore, that he should receive an offer to play county cricket. The real surprise was that the offer came from Yorkshire.

While county cricket had been thrown open to foreign professionals from the 1960s—and many played in England long before that too—the only county that did not allow 'outsiders' to be part of their team was Yorkshire, also the most successful team in county cricket history. Cricket is part of the Yorkshire ethos, much as it is in Mumbai, or in Victoria and New South Wales in Australia. Great pride is taken in being able to wear the Yorkshire colours and there is a saying that 'When Yorkshire is strong, England is strong.' Yorkshire, in fact, extended their ban on outsiders to anyone born outside the boundaries of the county. Along with their pride came a sense of parochialism and in more recent years, charges of racism. It is ironical given the large population of Pakistani immigrants, particularly in Bradford, that Yorkshire has never awarded a county cap to even those Asians born within its boundaries. To add to their reputation, the crowd at Headingley, Leeds was often virulent in its taunts and slurs.

While other teams were marching ahead with their overseas stars, Yorkshire cricket went from bad to worse. They had last won the county title in 1968 and in 1983 they took the wooden spoon for the first time. The team was also riven asunder by internal squabbles that caused immense bitterness in the 1980s and beyond. In frustration, many of its best players migrated to other counties. Finally, Australian fast bowler Craig McDermott was signed up on a three-year contract starting from 1992. But injury forced him to pull out. Former Yorkshire captain Geoffrey Boycott, the focus of a great deal of controversy at the club during his playing days, then decided to sign up Tendulkar in place of McDermott. He came up against opposition from another former captain, Brian Close, the chairman of the Cricket Committee. Close was adamant that a fast bowler should replace McDermott. But with time running out, a lack of international fast bowlers to choose from, and sponsors Yorkshire Television keen on a big-name signing, the final choice remained Tendulkar. And it proved to be an inspired one, more off the field than on it.

The deal was worth £30,000 to Sachin. Yorkshire Chief Executive Chris Hassell flew to Mumbai in April 1992 for the signing, which Tendulkar agreed to after receiving the stamp of approval from coach Ramakant Achrekar and mentor Sunil Gavaskar. Yorkshire were keen to shake off the racist tag and also to attract more Asians to their matches. But, while they may have succeeded to a limited extent in the PR department, there was hardly a surge of interest among the immigrants. As Michael Calvin pointed out in the *Daily Telegraph*, the immigrants mainly consisted of Pakistanis who were not particularly enthused by the presence of Tendulkar. For his part, Tendulkar fitted in remarkably well, considering he was just 19 and aware that there was a fair amount of opposition to the century-old 'no outsiders' tradition being dismantled in his favour. A *Press Association* photograph that was published in virtually every Indian newspaper showed him gamely attired in a Yorkshire flat hat, in his hand a glass of Tetley Bitter beer, one of the team's sponsors.

On the field, he was consistent without being spectacular. There was just one century (exactly 100 v Durham) and seven 50s in a total of 1070 championship runs from 25 innings at 46.52, placing him fortieth in the year's averages. In the Sunday League (40 overs), his best was 107 from 73 balls against Lancashire. The century against Durham powered Yorkshire to victory after they had been set a target of 262. Teammate Phil Carrick was quoted on that innings by Scyld Berry in *Wisden Cricket Monthly* (June 1996):

> I walked over to have a chat with him as he came in and I remember him staring at me quite intently—perhaps he couldn't understand me! I passed on some information, then I thought: 'what am I doing telling him?' You could tell he had a fantastic talent, class oozing through every vein.
>
> I told him it was the sort of wicket where you couldn't hit it on the up, and shortly after he came in he smashed one straight past Ian Botham. It was a full-length ball, so I thought, 'well, he might have heard me,' and he went on to win the match. The only criticism that you could make was that sometimes he'd be a bit impetuous, he'd get to 60 or 70 and set the game up, then get out in ways he wouldn't do now. He'd never play for himself—in fact we wished he would bat for himself a bit more. Otherwise he made an ideal first overseas player, for us and him. He contributed a few ideas and in the dressing-room he used to fiddle with his bats—tremendously heavy bats—or listen to his music, and just get on with it.

Against Essex he struck a classy 93 as Yorkshire won by a huge margin of an innings and 55 runs. The Roses match saw him strike 56 not out and 48 as Yorkshire beat traditional rivals Lancashire by four wickets. In addition, he struck 86 against Hampshire and a brilliant

92 against Gloucestershire. Yorkshire's downward slide, however, continued as they fell two places to finish sixteenth in the county championship and eight places to fifteenth in the Sunday League.

Sachin's real success was in breaking down barriers and creating goodwill wherever he went, with colleagues, fans and the media. Boycott summed it up in his book, *Geoffrey Boycott on Cricket*: 'He had a lot to prove. If he had failed with the bat or behaved carelessly, the outcome would almost certainly have been disastrous. Happily, we picked a winner. Unfailingly well-mannered and charming, with a shy smile on his lips, he settled quickly into the dressing room, and the Yorkshire public, shrugging off their reservations, took him to their collective heart. No one could have done a better job of breaking the ice on behalf of the imports.'

The positive reaction in the Yorkshire county circles paved the way the next year for West Indian captain Richie Richardson to join the team. In 2001, Yorkshire won the county title for the first time since 1968. Their match winner throughout the season was Darren Lehmann, an Australian left-hander not good enough for the Australian touring side, but good enough to finish second in the national averages that season.

Tendulkar has always looked back on his county stint with affection. 'It was a tremendous experience and exposure and, in many respects, a highlight for me, particularly as I was the first overseas player to play for Yorkshire,' he told Sebastian Coe of the *Daily Telegraph* (6 May 2001). 'I'm sorry I couldn't stay longer, but there was just no way I could combine five months' commitment to the Indian team with a county season. I don't think it will be possible for me to play for a county again.' According to Boycott, writing in *Outlook* (4 January 1999): 'Yorkshire supporters loved him. Sachin played well for a medium team but at the age of 18 he was not the finished article. We didn't expect him to be but he created an enormous amount of interest and left behind tremendous goodwill. I wouldn't have swapped him for any other player.'

Tendulkar's season was curtailed when on 21 August he was summoned by the BCCI to play in the Duleep Trophy. As if he were still on trial! He was interviewed by Andrew Collomose for the *Cricketer International* (November 1992), at Scarborough, during his last game against Nottinghamshire. Wrote Collomose of 'Yorkshire's Fresh Spice': 'Tendulkar's warmth, courtesy and obvious enthusiasm for the cause quickly made a nonsense of unspoken pre-season fears that the racist element among Yorkshire followers would sour his season before it really got underway. "It is a time I will treasure," said Tendulkar...."Everywhere I have played, both in Yorkshire and elsewhere, people have gone out of their way to be friendly. Yes, I was a little nervous when I first arrived in England. Yorkshire is such a famous county and I was going to be their first overseas player. It was a big responsibility. But my only regret is that it took me so long to score a hundred. At one stage it seemed I would never do so."'

He shared a flat in Dewsbury with old school chum Vinod Kambli who was playing with Spen Victoria in the Bradford League. Despite the numerous Indian restaurants in the county, they ate mostly Chinese, or a pizza, or maybe a Kentucky Fried or something at McDonald's. 'The Indian food over here is not quite the same as I am used to at home. Not enough fresh spices.'

In late 1992, India were invited to be the first team to play in South Africa since the apartheid ban imposed in 1970. With Nelson Mandela all set to assume leadership of the 'new' South Africa, it was a historic visit in many ways. Indeed, from the moment they landed till the end of the tour, the Indians were feted and felicitated wherever they went, particularly by the local Indian community which tended to go overboard in its enthusiasm. One of the Indian team's sponsors who travelled with the team confided to me that such was the hectic round of parties and functions, there were occasions when Sachin would hide in his room to avoid attending them!

Dr Ali Bacher dubbed the visit 'The Friendship Tour'. It may have been so off the field. But the cricket itself was very hard fought, at times even bitter, with the home side determined to give their fans a taste of victory after more than two decades. The Indian team had earlier made a brief stopover in Harare en route to South Africa, where Zimbabwe gave a pretty good account of themselves in their maiden

Test. The Test marked the second occasion on which Tendulkar was out for a duck, caught and bowled by master off-spinner John Traicos.

The one-day festival match at Raadjasfontein that kicked off the South African tour saw Tendulkar score a century against Nicky Oppenheimer's XI. The series began in right earnest at Durban with South African opener Jimmy Cook out to the first ball of the series, caught by Tendulkar at third slip off Kapil Dev. This was South Africa's second Test after readmission, having been stunned earlier in the year by the West Indies in Barbados. The weather had the final say at Durban, with more than a day lost to rain, and the match ended in a tame draw. But there were quite a few interesting events that captured the attention of cricket historians. Left-arm spinner Omar Henry, at 40 South Africa's oldest debutant, also became the first non-white to play for his country. South African captain Kepler Wessels, who had earlier represented his adopted country, Australia, in Test cricket, became the first to score a century for two different countries. Ramakant Achrekar's 'boy' Praveen Amre became the ninth Indian to score a century on Test debut.

The most dramatic moment of the match came on 14 November 1992, the second day of the Test. Tendulkar was on 11 and the total on 38 for 2. He played a ball from Brian McMillan backward of point, set off for a run and then changed his mind as Jonty Rhodes swooped and threw the ball to Andrew Hudson. The batsman tried to make his ground even as short leg Hudson, up at the stumps, took the flat throw on the bounce and broke the wicket. It appeared desperately close and South African Cyril Mitchley at square leg passed the decision to the umpires' room, outlining the shape of a TV screen with his hands. Third umpire Karl Liebenberg was sitting in front of the TV, and 29 seconds later came his response: a green light flashed (for 'go' rather than red for 'stay'—the reverse works now) and Tendulkar made his way back, the first cricketer to go through a trial by TV. So close was the verdict that he may well have gained the benefit of the doubt if the on-field umpire hadn't had the benefit of calling for the replay. Cricket had entered the technological age, at last.

The fact that this new technology did not find universal acceptance even among the umpires may well have cost India the second Test at Johannesburg. West Indian Steve Bucknor was the neutral umpire standing in the series. Ironically, it was Jhonty Rhodes who gained the reprieve. South Africa were 61 for 4 in their first innings, with Rhodes on 28, when Srinath threw down the stumps with a direct throw. But Bucknor ruled it not out without consulting the third umpire, despite pleas from the fielding side. The TV replays showed Rhodes clearly short of the crease. He went on to score 91 and took his side to the respectable score of 292. It was a mistake no international umpire would make again.

India too lost early wickets. It was 27 for 2 when Tendulkar walked in. Two more wickets fell for the addition of 50, and at 77 for 4, there was the looming threat of a follow-on. Tendulkar started hesitantly. He took 20 balls to get off the mark and was dropped at ten by Craig Matthews off Donald. His 50 came from 84 balls, his century from 243, and there were 19 fours in his 111 before he was ninth out at 212, caught Hudson by Cronje. He had been at the crease for 372 minutes. His fourth Test century made him the youngest in Test history to reach 1000 runs, at the age of 19 years 217 days. Teammate Kapil Dev at 21 years 27 days was the previous record holder. It was Tendulkar's nineteenth Test and twenty-eighth innings.

These are the bald statistical details. They do not convey his power that day at the Wanderers where the mighty Donald was blasted out of sight. Once again, Sachin played a lone hand, battling to pull his team out of a hole, making full use of his favourite square cut and square drive. Time and again, Donald and McMillan bounced at him and Tendulkar went up on his toes and used his powerful wrists to play attacking strokes to deliveries that were at least shoulder high. In an Indian total of 227, Tendulkar scored virtually half the runs off his own bat. Thanks to his effort and 6 for 53 from Anil Kumble in South Africa's second innings, India gained a face-saving draw. Once again, the luminaries of cricket were ecstatic in their reaction to Tendulkar's batting. One of South Africa's best all-rounders, Eddie Barlow, had this to say: 'He has the technique which is the hallmark of a great player. Everything indicates that he will be a great player and I am sure he will prove me right. Under incredible pressure, he batted superbly. Like Barry Richards he is very straight, very compact. He moves his feet very quickly into position and can adjust to the pace and bounce superbly' (*Sportstar*, 12 December 1992).

Between the second and third Tests, India and South Africa played a series of seven One-day Internationals. Tendulkar was a major disappointment, with only 144 runs from seven innings, and a highest score of 32. India were beaten 5-2.

Donald came into his own in the third Test at Port Elizabeth and India were crushed by nine wickets. There was an extraordinary century by Kapil Dev in the second innings. But it was not enough to stop Donald bowling South Africa to their first victory in 22 years with the devastating figures of 5 for 55 and 7 for 84. There were, unfortunately, plenty of umpiring disputes during the match, with the visitors feeling they had got a raw deal. Perhaps the most shocking was umpire Rudi Koertzen's decision to give Tendulkar caught behind first ball off Donald in the second innings, when the ball had brushed his pad. The departing batsman was horrified and non-striker Shastri dropped his bat in disgust and had words with the umpire.

Much of the cricket played in the three Tests had been dreary. But the fourth and final match at Cape Town made a dubious entry into cricket's record books as the slowest of all time. The Indian batsmen were wary of the South African pace attack. The hosts were keen to hang on to their lead in order to wrap up the series. This they achieved even as the Test produced an average of 159 runs per day at 1.83 per over. Tendulkar was his side's top scorer in the match with 73. But even his normally attacking batsmanship was curtailed, the 50 taking him 167 minutes. For Kepler Wessels and his countrymen, the series marked a triumphant return to Test cricket. The story was starkly different in the rival camp, with Azharuddin seemingly on his way out as captain after another series defeat and a lacklustre batting performance.

12

Success at Home and Abroad

If they want me to be captain, I'm ready.—Sachin Tendulkar

England's tour to India under the captaincy of Graham Gooch saw Mohammed Azharuddin placed on probation, in a manner of speaking. His appointment was confirmed only till the first Test in Kolkata in January 1993. Two ODIs were played before the opening Test, with honours even.

The season unfolding would be an extraordinary one for Vinod Kambli. Briefly, he would gallop ahead of his old school friend. The trend was set in the first ODI at Jaipur, which England won by four wickets after a scrambled single from the last ball of the match. It was Kambli's twentieth birthday and he celebrated it in style with his first century in international cricket. His score of 100 not out came from 149 balls and there was some adverse comment at the end of the game over the manner in which he crawled through the 90s. The feeling was that India lost precious momentum which cost it dearly in the end.

The old Sharadashram pair got together at Jaipur after Prabhakar, Sidhu and Azharuddin had been sent back with just 59 on the board. They batted till the end of the innings with Kambli reaching his century in the last over. Sachin stayed unbeaten on a rapid 82 and was on hand to congratulate his friend. Once again, an ODI century had proved elusive for him. The unbroken stand was worth 164 (in 28 overs)—exactly 500 less than their world record for Sharadashram just five years earlier!

Kambli was quick to give credit to Tendulkar while receiving the Man of the Match award. He told the media emotionally that it was his friend's calming influence at the wicket that had helped him to the landmark. 'I will never forget Sachin's birthday gift to me,' were his words.

Both batsmen failed in the second ODI at Chandigarh, though India won by five wickets to draw level. The sword which has traditionally been placed over the head of the Indian captain was perilously close to cutting short Azharuddin's reign when the teams moved to Kolkata for the first Test. It was here, against England at the Eden Gardens, that Azhar had first dazzled the cricket world with his century on debut in the 1984-85 series, followed by two more on the trot. Now, once again, the lucky charm that had always followed him to Kolkata seemed to work its magic. The captain's dazzling 182 crushed England's spirits and victory was India's by nine wickets. Tendulkar's 50 in the first innings promised much more before he had a lapse of concentration and fished at a wide delivery from Devon Malcolm. By then, the stand with his captain was worth 123 runs. Kambli on his Test debut had scores of 16 and 18 not out. With just a handful of runs needed for the win after England had followed on, Sachin and Vinod were at the crease when India wrapped things up before lunch on the fifth day.

Just as Eden Gardens in Kolkata was Azhar's favourite venue, the MA Chidambaram Stadium in Chennai is where Tendulkar has scored the maximum runs. In February 1993, Chepauk was witness to Tendulkar's first century at home and his fifth overall. This was in his twenty-third Test match, of which only two—one at Kolkata and before that the Chandigarh one-off against Sri Lanka—had been played at home. In 1998, an outstanding innings against Australia saw Sachin master Shane Warne at Chepauk. But there was heartbreak in 1999: another masterly ton took India to the doorstep of victory against Pakistan before Sachin's back gave way and India fell just short. Three years later, in March 2001, Tendulkar recorded his twenty-fifth Test century at Chennai as India stunned world champions Australia to take the series 2-1.

There was drama even before the start of the second Test in Chennai in 1993. England's captain Graham Gooch was forced out by sickness, thanks to a plate of prawns he had eaten the night before. The demoralized Englishmen were forced to follow-on for the second time in successive Tests and lost by an innings. This, after their bowlers had conceded the highest total against India at home. The massive 560 for 6 declared was built around centuries by Navjot Singh Sidhu and Tendulkar, who made the highest of his five Test centuries in an innings spanning nearly six hours. Kambli (in his second Test), Amre and Kapil Dev also chipped in with half-centuries.

Already there was talk of how Tendulkar in the years to come would challenge Allan Border's record Test aggregate. And for the first time the comparison with the great West Indian Viv Richards, one of Tendulkar's heroes, was made, this time by the former England all-rounder Vic Marks. I noticed too, for the first time, that Tendulkar was taking over some of the field-placing chores from his captain who looked on benignly. There was no talk at this stage of Tendulkar assuming the captaincy. But there were moves to groom him in the role of vice captain. There were a couple of incidents on the field during this match which showed Sachin's versatility. Though he bowled just two overs in each innings, he surprised the cognoscenti by bowling genuine leg breaks. He even pulled off the perfect googly for good measure. And there was a dazzling catch to top it all. Paul Jarvis flicked Kumble hard and low in the second innings, only to be gobbled up at short leg by Sachin, an outstanding catch at ankle height from a legitimate shot. There was no doubt after that, about the choice for the Man of the Match.

India had won the series. And the third and final Test in Mumbai proved to be the final nail in the coffin for the English team. A new record total by India at home, and another innings victory. For the first time, India had accomplished a series whitewash. The Test was a triumph for the Mumbai trio of Kambli, Tendulkar and Amre, particularly the left-hander. In only his third Test match, Kambli had compiled the highest score by an Indian batsman against England: 224. He joined a band of 25 others whose first three-figure knocks were over 200, among them two legendary left-handers, Garry Sobers and Brian Lara. Kambli stayed at the crease for nearly ten hours and faced 411 deliveries. The English bowling attack of Phil DeFreitas, Chris Lewis, John Emburey and Phil Tufnell could hardly be called threatening. The third wicket stand with Tendulkar was worth 194 runs in 44 overs, with the senior partner somewhat subdued. His 78 took nearly four and a half hours and was not nearly as flawless as his batting in the previous Test. Kambli had two reprieves, at 39 and 119. Nerves got the better of him as he approached the highest score (at the time) by an Indian in Tests: 236 not out by Sunil Gavaskar. Till then, his daring stroke play was a wonderful treat for the fans at the Wankhede Stadium.

The action now switched back to the one-day game and at least here there was some consolation for the tourists. The series finished level at 3-3, with neither Kambli nor Tendulkar being able to make much of an impact.

Before the series began, the selectors had named Tendulkar captain of the under-25 side which played against England at Cuttack prior to the first Test. But a minor foot injury had forced him to miss that game and Ajay Jadeja had taken over. He got his chance to lead in the three-day game at Visakhapatnam between the first and second Test, captaining the Rest of India. Also in the team were W. V. Raman, Sanjay Manrejkar and Salil Ankola, all with Test experience. Still two months shy of his twentieth birthday, Sachin appeared comfortable in a role he was handling for the first time, and termed the experience 'interesting'.

'I had to lead a relatively new side. There were players like Ananthapadmanabhan and Utpal Chatterjee whom I had never seen before, so it took me some time to settle down. I just wish it had been a five-day game instead of a three-day one,' he recalled in *Sportsworld* (February 1993). No doubt the experience at Visakhapatnam gave him the necessary confidence going into the Chennai Test. And perhaps Azharuddin was instructed by the selectors to allow the youngster a little leeway in setting fields. In the same issue of *Sportsworld*, chairman of the Selection Committee G.R.Visvanath denied that Sachin was being groomed for captaincy. 'Basically Sachin is a very, very mature cricketer. We have noticed this maturity. It is not that he is going to captain overnight, we're just trying to put a little confidence into him. The fact is that he's going to be around for quite a while and if he comes good as captain earlier than expected then it's good for Indian cricket.'

The article proclaimed him the future captain of India. 'I don't mind taking up the challenge (of captaincy) anytime,' was the confident reply from the teenager when asked what would be the right time for such a move. 'It's not a question of whether I want to be captain or not. It's like whatever the country needs I'm ready to do. If they want me to be captain, I'm ready. If they want me to play in the side, I'm ready. If they think I'm not good enough to be in the side, I'm ready to step down.' Confident words from the 19-year-old.

The first step was taken with Sachin's appointment as vice captain for the tour of Sri Lanka following the England series. But before that, there was a one-off Test against Zimbabwe in New Delhi and once again this was a triumph for Kambli—and how. He suddenly saw his name up alongside those of Wally Hammond and Don Bradman as the only other batsman to score two consecutive Test double centuries. He followed up his 224 at Mumbai with 227 in New Delhi, once again coming agonizingly close to Gavaskar's all-time highest score. It was heady stuff. He was the first Indian left-hander to score more than one Test century and that too, in only his fourth Test. There was yet another century stand with Sachin (62), and Amre also contributed a half-century as did Sidhu. India completed another innings victory against the hapless Zimbabweans for their fifth win in a row at home.

Tendulkar's start to his Test career had been steady without being extraordinary, though of course his youth had given it a romantic sheen. It had taken Kambli nearly four years to follow in Sachin's footsteps. But the impact he made was immediate and spectacular. That spectacular run would continue in Sri Lanka where India won a Test and a series abroad for the first time since England in 1986 (an achievement they have not been able to equal, till the end of 2001).

The first Test against Sri Lanka, at Kandy, was a washout with only

12 overs bowled. India won the second Test at Colombo's SSC by 235 runs as Tendulkar and Kambli both recorded centuries, though not in the same innings. But incessant appealing and a great deal of resentment and rancour on the part of the Indians marred the match. The objects of their ire were the umpires who the Indians accused of adopting different standards for the two teams. The conflict led to match referee Peter Burge bringing the two teams together at the end of the match and issuing them a stern warning about their conduct in the next Test. Kambli was issued a reprimand by Burge for showing dissent after being given caught behind in the second innings. Tendulkar too had got a dicey decision in the first innings when he was adjudged caught at short leg for 28, when it was doubtful whether he had played the ball.

Kambli's third hundred saw India score 366 in their first innings. Anil Kumble picked up five wickets as the home side trailed by 112. Tendulkar was determined to make amends in the second innings as the Indians went for quick runs and a declaration. There were three centuries (and four near-centuries) in the Test. Tendulkar's was the most attractive by far. At 37 he was dropped by Warnaweera at deep fine leg off Wickramesinghe. Nothing could stop him from reaching his sixth hundred after that. While Sidhu played the anchor role, Tendulkar punched and drove the bowlers with ease and power. One shot in particular stood out amidst the 11 fours and a six—he lofted a half volley from Warnaweera over long on, with a fielder stationed on the boundary. It was audacious stuff and allowed Azhar to declare at 359 for 4. Tendulkar remained not out on 104. Sidhu recorded an identical score, while Prabhakar struck 95.

The unlikely target for Sri Lanka was 472 and the best they could do was hang on for a draw. By close on the fourth day, they had lost both openers with 86 on the board. Aravinda de Silva's 93 held up the Indians on the final day and they finally finished it off after tea. It had been close, though the final margin of victory was substantial. It was Azhar's first win abroad after taking over three years ago, and would end up being India's only victory on foreign soil in the entire decade.

The third Test ended in a high-scoring draw. But not before Kambli had recorded his fourth century in five Tests (including Kandy where he did not bat). He was involved once again in the now almost obligatory century stand with his friend who managed 71. That helped Tendulkar finish the series with an awesome average of 101.50, though it was Kambli who had the best aggregate.

With Azhar off the field with flu, the vice captain got his chance to lead the side on the final day of the third Test. Writing in the *Cricketer International* (September 1993), Sri Lankan journalist Mahinda Wijesinghe observed that 'It was refreshing to see young blood calming frayed tempers and soothing unrequited appeals.' Sachin became the youngest to lead a side in Test cricket—albeit in an acting capacity. He was a year younger than the Nawab of Pataudi Jr. was when he led India to the West Indies in 1961-62. Tendulkar enjoyed the experience as he told Vijay Lokapally of the *Sportstar,* in September that year: 'I was a little bit satisfied. But they played negative cricket and I hardly got a chance to play a commanding role you expect a captain to play. Yet I was more involved than I am normally.'

India would have to wait seven years before they could emulate the feat of another win abroad. Tendulkar would be part of that match at Dhaka, but not Azhar. A lot would change in Indian (and world) cricket in the intervening years.

13

The Great Friendship

He took the elevator to the top and I took the stairs.—Vinod Kambli

Sachin Tendulkar first met Vinod Ganpat Kambli when he made the switch from the New English School to Sharadashram Vidyamandir (English) at the age of 11. Kambli was a year older than Sachin and played in the same school team, for Mumbai and West Zone junior (under-15) teams and then for the Mumbai Ranji Trophy side and finally for India. Except perhaps for the odd match here and there, they have not found themselves on opposing sides in nearly 18 years of knowing each other and playing cricket together.

The names Tendulkar and Kambli became inextricably linked after the semi-final of the Harris Shield against St. Xavier's Fort at Azad Maidan. That game, played on 23-25 February 1988, saw them involved in the world-record partnership of 664 (unbroken) for the third wicket—a mark that is unlikely to be erased for a long, long time. Suddenly the pair were the talk of Mumbai cricket circles. At school level Vinod often outscored his friend. But Sachin made a rapid transition from school to first class and then Test cricket, while Vinod lagged behind. Achrekar, who coached them both, told me: 'Vinod scored more runs at school level. But he did not have the dedication or perseverance of Sachin, and also developed bad habits. Sachin, on the other hand, always had a very sensible attitude and a strong family background, especially with his father and brother Ajit always behind him.'

Sachin made his Test debut in November 1989 in Pakistan and less than a year later, in his ninth Test, scored his maiden century.

Kambli would follow him into Test cricket in the home series against England in 1993. But while Tendulkar would have to wait till late 1999 to score his first Test double century, Kambli's very first three-figure knock was 224—in only his third Test.

As we have seen in the previous chapter, Kambli followed up that 224 with 227 in the next Test and then two centuries in three Tests in Sri Lanka. It was scintillating cricket. And suddenly comparisons were being made with Tendulkar, not all of them flattering for the younger man. 'He took the elevator to the top and I took the stairs,' is the way Kambli described their varying journeys to the world of international cricket. Kambli made his international debut in October 1991 in Sharjah with scores of 23 not out, 40 and 30. A year later, he was chosen for the World Cup in Australia and New Zealand after being passed up for the Test series in South Africa and Australia. The story goes that when Kambli landed in Sydney for the World Cup, he was disappointed that his chum had not come to the airport to receive him. But Sachin had stayed up the whole night in his hotel room, reading and watching television to keep himself awake for the late night arrival. They spent the night chatting.

If Tendulkar's debut in first-class cricket was a remarkable one for a schoolboy, Kambli's early career was notable for the mountain of runs he scored in his first three seasons, starting with his debut in 1989-90. He piled up 2400 runs from only 20 games at the amazing average of 85.71. The tally included nine 100s (with a highest score of 262) and 12 half-centuries. So why did it take him four years to break into Test cricket? To put it bluntly, Kambli had rapidly acquired an 'image' problem. His West Indian-like appearance and hero worship of Desmond Haynes had earned him the nickname of 'Dessy'. Haynes used to sport a bracelet on his wrist with the words 'Live, Love, Laugh' inscribed on it. Kambli perhaps took these words literally, particularly when he first broke into big-time cricket. Achrekar has always felt that Kambli's flamboyant ways held him back in a cricket set-up that continues to be conservative. Flamboyance is acceptable on the field. But once stories of off-field shenanigans began circulating, progress was stymied.

There was an incident in the 1992 World Cup that was held against Kambli for quite sometime. It occured during a rain break in the match against Sri Lanka at Mackay when the cheerleaders were out on the field keeping the crowd entertained. Kambli joined in the dancing and the photographers had a field day. But many thought that for someone so fresh to the team, it was inappropriate behaviour, even brash. Much has also been made of Kambli's social background and childhood. It would be best to quote the man himself on this sensitive aspect of his life. In an interview in 1998 he revealed, 'I come from a very, very poor family. My father was a machinist, worked in Bhandup [in Mumbai]. We lived in a *chawl* in Kanjur Marg. Dad was a good fast bowler and played against many former Mumbai players, even Test cricketers. He had to look after seven of us, but he never made us feel that we lacked anything.' (*Rediff.com*, 15 December 1998)

Cricket elevated Kambli to a lifestyle he could only have dreamed of. Subsequent reports of 'temptations' and 'distractions' during the 1992 World Cup didn't do his career any good. And the contrast with Tendulkar could not have been starker. In an interview to the *Sportstar* (30 September 1995), Kambli himself explained the difference in their outlook to life: 'He [Sachin] is reserved. I am the outgoing type. I like to enjoy life. I always enjoyed life. People say I am fascinated with jewellery. But I like wearing it and I earned the money to buy it. I may go to a disco to unwind. There is life after cricket hours. People love clothes. Some wear sober clothes. I suppose I am the type who likes colourful clothes. It all depends on your liking. I will not like to change my lifestyle.' Kambli certainly could not be accused of hypocrisy. He did nothing to hide his flamboyant ways. But this very frankness had a negative effect on the authorities.

In the early years, Vinod and Sachin often found themselves batting together when one or the other reached a personal landmark, almost as if fate were playing a hand. The bonds of friendship were thus strengthened and made public. Tendulkar was at the other end when Kambli got his maiden century in One-day Internationals against England at Jaipur in 1993. They were together when Vinod got his first Test 50 in the second Test at Chennai shortly after that. And the very next Test at Mumbai saw them involved in a stand worth 194 as Kambli struck his double ton. The second Test at Colombo later that year which India won, saw them score centuries in the same match for the first and only time so far.

By 1994 there were rumours that Tendulkar was feeling pressurized by Kambli's success. This question was put to him by *Sportstar* (26 March 1994), at which stage he was yet to score a century in One-day Internationals. 'Rubbish, there is nothing like that,' Tendulkar shrugged off the suggestion. 'These things take place because people just assume things.' Kambli, for his part, has always expressed his gratitude to Sachin for his help and support. 'Sachin is my friend, philosopher and guide,' he would repeatedly emphasize in interviews.

The no-ODI-century monkey was taken off Tendulkar's back in the Singer Cup match against Australia in Colombo on 9 September 1994. It was five years since his international debut. And sure enough, Kambli was at the non-striker's end to embrace him on reaching the landmark.

But the contrast in their batting form was the starkest in the Hero Cup five-nation tournament which India won at home in November 1993. Kambli and Azhar were the outstanding batsmen in the tournament. Kambli had scores of 78, 10, 55, 86, 4 and 68. Tendulkar, on the other hand, could only score 26 (not out), 2, 24, 3, 15 and 28 (not out). But if one is to believe them, the competitive streak extends only to their respective music collections. This is another shared passion and it became a race to see who had the bigger and better collection. As Kambli put it in his interview on *Rediff.com* (December 1999), 'Actually, whenever Sachin is there at the other end, the understanding between us is so good that if he hits a four, I don't take it as a challenge. If I get a loose delivery, I am going to whack it, anyway, but if I don't get one, no big deal. There has been no competition between us as such. I know people expect a lot of runs from me, just like they do from Sachin. I try my best to fulfil their expectations. It's not that I don't try. I try, I try and I try. If I don't succeed, even I feel bad about it. Everybody does.'

In the same interview Kambli explained how Sachin's presence in the team acted as an inspiration to him. 'He is such a thinking cricketer and a perfect team man. When I play alongside him, he helps me so much. Of course, he helps others as well. He provides a lot of motivation to other players. His presence is very, very important in the side for the others. Whenever we are together, we talk a lot about cricket. And I hope when I finally make a comeback, we will again do the same. It will not only motivate me, it will help keep me upbeat.' Kambli's first seven Tests fetched him 793 runs at an average of 113.29. He was the quickest Indian to reach 1000 Test runs, in 14 innings from 12 Tests. The earlier Indian record had stood in the name of Sunil Gavaskar (21 innings/11 Tests) while the only batsmen quicker than Kambli were Everton Weekes, Herbert Sutcliffe (both 12/9) and Don Bradman (13/7). In contrast, it took Tendulkar 28 innings from 19 Tests to reach 1000. Of course, he was the youngest to do so. In fact, it was not till his forty-third first-class match (first Test v West Indies at Mumbai, November 1994) that Kambli was dismissed for a duck. 'I'm no longer just Sachin's batting partner, I'm Vinod Kambli,' he proudly asserted after his second double century on the trot. But it did not last very long.

The visit to Sri Lanka in 1993 was one of the stormiest and most contentious tours an Indian team has undertaken. As one of the leading Indian batsmen, Tendulkar was targeted by the appalling umpiring. While he refused to be provoked by some atrocious decisions, Kambli could not keep his cool and received a reprimand from the match referee for showing dissent. This provided yet another reminder of their contrasting temperaments. Also, despite all those runs early in his career, there was always a lurking suspicion that Kambli would find himself in trouble against top class fast bowling. The bulk of his runs had come in the subcontinent against the weaker bowling attacks of England, Zimbabwe and Sri Lanka. The West Indians soon sorted him out when they toured India late in 1994. Walsh and company peppered him with the short stuff. And suddenly, suspicions about his ability to face quality fast bowling appeared to have been proved true. He scraped together a miserable 64 runs from six innings in the Test series.

Later, in 1996, one of the most enduring and poignant images of the World Cup was that of Kambli coming off the field after the semi-final at Kolkata had been awarded to Sri Lanka followed crowd disturbances. The tears flowed freely that night. For Kambli wears his heart on his sleeve. There was more anguish off the field too, during the World Cup. Unruly behaviour at the team hotel, including public shouting matches with his newly married wife, left a very poor impression on the team management. He was left out of the team that toured England after the World Cup, apparently on disciplinary grounds, and not for the last time.

It has been a virtual see-saw since then. He was picked for the playing XI ahead of Sourav Ganguly for the Sahara Cup in Toronto in 1996—which inevitably led to whispered allegations of nepotism against Tendulkar who was captain then. In April 1998, a serious ankle injury while fielding as a substitute in the one-day game against Australia at Cuttack saw him out of action for the rest of the year. He was back for the visits to Sri Lanka and Singapore in September 1999 for one-day tournaments. This was soon after Tendulkar had been asked to lead for the second time.

The new captain reacted angrily when asked the question by G. Viswanath for the *Sportstar* (21 August 1999): 'The selection of Vinod Kambli. People have linked it to your friendship?'

Sachin replied, 'If I were to pick friends, then my brother [Ajit] should be there in the Indian team. He can also play cricket. It just says about the mentality and petty-mindedness of the people who think that he [Kambli] is there in the team because I am the captain. I am the captain of the Indian team and my only interest is to win matches for India. There is no question of friendship. Kambli might be my friend, but off the field. On the field, there are no friends. Everyone is playing for the country. Even a captain of a Club team will pick the best side. There have been occasions when I have not played him in the eleven.'

Kambli has been in and out of the team a dozen times since his debut. His last appearance was in Nairobi and Sharjah late in 2000. In the public eye, Sachin and Vinod are still closely associated. Their joint appearance in a Fiat Palio TV commercial only reinforces that image. And while Tendulkar was going great guns in South Africa in 2001, Kambli was busy acting in his first movie—as a 'villain'. (Tendulkar too has received movie offers, all of which he has politely and consistently turned down.)

It was manager Ajit Wadekar who took Kambli under his wing when he hit the purple patch in 1993. The famous code of conduct was drawn up to keep a rein on the players, and Kambli was made to toe the line. Wadekar and Kambli enjoyed a special relationship. Both being left-handed and both being from Mumbai may have helped. Wadekar was like an indulgent uncle keeping an eye on his wayward nephew. But today, ask Wadekar why Sachin zoomed ahead and Kambli has only played 17 Tests till date, and the former manager will sum it up with one word: 'attitude'.

Journalist Vijay Lokapally of the *Hindu*, who knows both Sachin and Vinod well, told me that the 'real' Sachin could be seen only in the presence of his great pal. 'He is totally relaxed in Vinod's company. There are plenty of jokes and leg-pulling. What struck me was that even at noisy and crowded functions when it is hard to hear anything, the two would be conversing comfortably.'

4

The One-day Phenom

It was quite satisfying.—Sachin Tendulkar

The Hero Cup five-nation tournament in November 1993 saw India reach the semi-final against South Africa despite being trounced by West Indies in their league game and held to a tie by Zimbabwe. The Indians seemed to be peaking at the right time, as they beat South Africa easily by 43 runs in the final league game at Mohali. Two days later, they met again in the last four. The sole team to be eliminated was Zimbabwe, with the other semi-final pitting West Indies against Sri Lanka. Both the semis and the final were played in Kolkata under lights for the first time.

Tendulkar had scores of 26 not out, 2, 24 and 3. He failed with the bat in the semis too, caught behind by Dave Richardson off medium-pacer Richard Snell for 15. But he would play a crucial hand in the very last over of the game. On a slow track, India had mustered a total of 195 in their 50 overs, with skipper Azharuddin top-scoring with 90. More than the bowlers, it was the Indian batsmen themselves who made a hash of things with four run-outs. This was the first ODI with a third umpire in charge of replays, and there was no escape. Vinod Kambli was the first such victim in limited-overs cricket.

The South African batsmen appeared overcautious in chasing the small total, and the crowd of nearly 100,000 gave them little respite. Srinath got captain Kepler Wessels out early, but fellow opener Andrew Hudson survived two chances to make 62 as they inched their way towards the target. The Indians hit back through Ajay Jadeja and Anil

Kumble who picked up two wickets each to break the back of the top order and reduce the score to 130 for 5. The asking rate had climbed to eight an over as the batting subsided to 145 for 7, with three run-outs, including that of Hansie Cronje at 13. Then came the first of many dramatic twists.

In three overs, the burly Brian McMillan and Richardson plundered 32 runs to take their side to within just seven runs of victory. When Richardson got out for 15, it was down to the last over, with six runs standing between South Africa and the final. Srinath had conceded 23 runs in his last two overs and Prabhakar had gone for 16. Kapil still had two in hand. Who would bowl the last over to McMillan, a man capable of finishing things off with one mighty blow? It looked like a toss-up between Srinath and Kapil. Then wicketkeeper Vijay Yadav suggested the name of Tendulkar. The problem was that he had not bowled a single over so far.

This is manager Wadekar's version of what happened next: 'I had sent a message to Azhar that Kapil, being most senior and experienced, should bowl the last over. When Sachin saw Kapil slightly hesitating, he snatched the ball from his hand and told Azhar that he would bowl the last one. Azhar had no choice.' Millions of TV viewers saw it that way too. The young man had grabbed the challenge as he always has done in his career.

There were two wickets standing and six balls to go, with six runs to get. Bowling tantalizingly slow medium-pacers, Tendulkar induced panic from the first ball. Fanie de Villiers was run out going for a second run. Five from five, and last man Allan Donald to face. All he had to do was take a single and give McMillan the strike. He did so, but only off the penultimate ball—for three balls he swung and missed. The last ball, and a boundary was what South Africa required. Tendulkar managed to squeeze the ball between the bat and leg stump. And McMillan could get just one from the edge down the leg side as he swung and failed to connect. The Indian players mobbed Tendulkar, hugging and kissing him as the crowd erupted with joy.

'We had to win the match for the spectators. They cheered us throughout and we owed it to them,' said Tendulkar, his voice choked with emotion. Watching on TV in his hotel room, West Indies captain Richie Richardson thought Azhar had got it wrong. 'I would have given it to my best bowler. But the young fellow bowled intelligently,' he said. Sachin spoke about that last over in an interview to *Sportsworld* (December 1993). 'Some team members had suggested I try and bowl leg-spin. But I decided to bowl leg cutters at military medium pace. The idea was to frustrate the batsman going for a big hit, as the ball wouldn't come onto the bat. I only had one apprehension, that in trying to restrict the batsmen I don't end up bowling a wide or a no ball. Especially before I came in to bowl the last ball, I was ultra cautious. The last ball that I bowled was slightly faster. The line was outside the off stump. I varied my pace, to unsettle the batsman who was expecting a slower delivery.'

West Indies brushed aside Sri Lanka in the other semi-final and ten years after their historic World Cup encounter, it would be India v West Indies again.

This time it was leg-spinner Anil Kumble who emerged the hero. His figures of 6 for 12 are still the best by an Indian in ODIs and saw West Indies crumble to 123 in reply to India's 225 for 7. Kambli capped a brilliant run with the top score of 68. Tendulkar chipped in with his highest in the tournament, 28 not out, and then bowled Brian Lara for 33 just as the West Indian batsman looked to be taking command. Tendulkar had done enough—just about—to silence the critics who were beginning to ask where his next big innings would come from. He had proved his utility to the team. Still, that elusive century was nowhere in sight.

The subject of his relative lack of success in ODIs was posed to him by a reporter with the *Sportstar* (26 March 1994), just before the ODI series in New Zealand where he opened for the first time.

> Q: How do you explain your failures in one-day internationals as opposed to your success in Test cricket? Are you aware this is causing the misimpression that you have been failing in international cricket for a while now?
>
> A: It is very difficult to analyse why you fail in the one-day

games. It is also difficult to know what you have to do when you go out to the middle. You go out to bat in the 40th over, or even in the 30th over, and you don't know whether you have to go after the bowlers or hang on there, give the strike to the set batsman and play your shots later. That is what has been happening to me in the one-day internationals. I have tried playing shots and got out early. I have not been able to get too many runs. But then I am as serious about the one-dayers as I am about Test cricket and so the failures are not coming from lack of seriousness. So, maybe, things will change with a big innings or two. As far as I see it, there is nothing wrong with my technique so far as one-day cricket is concerned. It is just that a few failures have made it even more difficult for me. It is not as if I am getting out only in one way. Then you have to think and sort out the problem. Otherwise, I feel it is quite okay. I know I can succeed in one-day cricket also.

The specific issue of his low position in the batting order was discussed in an interview (*Sportsworld*, December 1993) shortly after the Hero Cup.

Q: Why don't you request the captain to promote you up the batting order? You could also try and do a 'Brian Lara' by opening the innings in one-dayers and then go in at number four in Test matches?
A: Well, I've no problems about that. Tomorrow if they tell me that my opening the innings in one-dayers will help the team, I'll surely open. If they say 'no', I won't press for it either. I'm quite flexible as a cricketer.
Q: What do you mean 'they'? You're the vice-captain of the side. If you think by opening the innings you would be able to help the team, why aren't you suggesting that? After all, the vice-captain comprises the management.
A: No, I'm not going to do that. I'm not going to go out of my way. But as I told you, if they ask me to open the innings, I will.

'They' would 'ask' him soon—and in somewhat freakish circumstances. The moment came in the Bank of New Zealand series of four one-day matches early in 1994, which followed the one-off Test. New Zealand won the first match at Napier by 28 runs with openers Jadeja and Sidhu putting on 66 runs for India. Tendulkar was out for 15. Two days later, on 27 March 1994, the Indian think tank faced a crisis when Sidhu woke up with a stiff neck in Auckland and found himself unfit. Azharuddin explained the circumstances in his column in the *Sportstar (*11 February 1995).

> Sidhu and I had gone shopping down the main street of Auckland the previous evening and there had been no thought that a fitness problem would develop and that the extraordinary event of opening with Sachin would take place. Poor Sidhu woke up with a stiff neck and had to sit down and Tendulkar came up and asked me whether he could try his hand at opening. This was discussed at the team meeting just before the match and all agreed this was well worth trying since we had to win the second match to keep our chances of winning the series.

This is what Wadekar told me about the turn of events: 'Sachin and I used to talk about his opening the innings in one-dayers so that he would get more overs to thrash the opposition. However, the team management thought of not risking his wicket with the new ball as he would be more useful in the middle order. When Sidhu pulled out, the three of us—Azhar as captain, Kapil Dev as a senior member and myself—had an emergency meeting on the ground before the toss and when I told them that Sachin would not mind opening, they agreed willingly. Sachin jumped in the air with joy and celebrated his promotion to the opening slot with a swashbuckling innings. Thus a star opening batsman was born for India in ODIS.'

And how! It was Tendulkar's seventieth ODI and one that would change the face of modern cricket. This is how New Zealand selector and journalist Don Neely recalls the match and Tendulkar's innings:

New Zealand made a dismal 142 and in the course of 49.4 overs only managed to hit 9 fours and one six. There was a surprise for the spectators who had almost been comatose by the local batting.

Jadeja's partner was Tendulkar. The young man played shots of technical excellence and plundered the attack. The Indian 50 was posted in 7.4 overs, the 100 in 12.5. An experienced group of bowlers was exposed as being good at containing most batsmen but powerless to curb the brilliance of the young Indian. His innings of 82 consisted of just 22 scoring shots and he was back in the pavilion in 69 minutes and the game was over with 26.4 overs to spare.

No one who witnessed the batting of Tendulkar that day will ever forget it. He was calm while all around him was in chaos. He was composed, fast on his feet, a master batsman displaying his wares. There were no crude, innovative creations. Just textbook perfection. Power came from sublime timing.

The effect on followers in New Zealand was that the grounds were almost full before the toss was made. No spectator wanted to run the risk of arriving at the ground late and missing Tendulkar.

As he has done repeatedly since then Tendulkar has shown that in both forms of the game he is an exceptional batsman. One innings of such class is burned into the memory banks, to be replayed at will for the rest of one's life.

In the batsman's own words in the *Sportstar* (23 December 1995), 'I thought I could play a few lofted shots and scatter the field. Mentally, I was prepared to go for the bowling. I waited for the first three or four overs. I realized the onus was on me and Ajay Jadeja to give a good start. I gauged the bowling, gained in confidence. I started striking the ball very well. The rest happened automatically.'

What happened 'automatically' was the decimation of the Kiwi attack consisting of Danny Morrison, Chris Pringle, Gavin Larsen, Matthew Hart and Chris Harris. The most experienced of the lot,

Morrison, was singled out for special treatment and smashed for five imperious boundaries. At Napier, in the first ODI two days earlier, he had taken New Zealand's first ODI hat-trick. Now he was carted for 46 runs from six overs. 'It was pleasing to get runs off Morrison. But actually the Kiwis bowled the way I expected them to. I was picking the line easily. It was sheer instinct.' In panic and not knowing where to pitch the ball, Morrison bowled a bouncer so high that it went way over Tendulkar's head. It was done deliberately to deny him the chance of making contact, such was the bowler's desperation.

Larsen was considered the tightest of the Kiwi bowlers. He was taken off after two overs which cost him 24 runs, including two sixes. The opening stand with Jadeja was worth 61 runs—Jadeja's contribution was 18. The 100 came up in an amazing 12.5 overs. 'The captain and the manager had said the score should be 100 by the 25th over. I said, "Fair enough. We will try and do it." I still remember when the score reached 100, it was 12.5 overs. It was quite satisfying.'

The target of 143 was now a mere formality. The only question was whether Azharuddin's world record of the quickest ODI century—off 61 balls against New Zealand at Baroda in 1989—would be beaten. Tendulkar raced to 82 from 49 balls (22 scoring shots) before being caught by skipper Ken Rutherford off Pringle. Rutherford was the first to applaud—perhaps as much in relief as in awe—as the crowd rose in tribute to one of the great ODI innings. 'I was thinking about a hundred, but it didn't matter. The team won, that's more important. To me the team always comes first.' Once again, Vinod Kambli was witness to the fireworks from the other end. The two had added 56 for the second wicket. This was the sequence of scoring shots: 2, 4, 4, 4, 4, 3, 4, 4, 4, 4, 6, 4, 4, 6, 4, 4, 4, 4, 2, 4, 2, 1. Even umpires Brian Aldridge and Chris King joined in the applause from the crowd and the New Zealand players.

Seven years later, in April 2001, after becoming the first player to cross 10,000 ODI runs, Sachin was asked by Vijay Lokapally of the *Sportstar* about the thrust his career had got after opening the innings. 'It was a big change,' Tendulkar said. 'Batting at number six I thought I wasn't getting enough opportunities. I was capable of delivering more than I was doing at that time, batting so low in the order. Something inside me would always tell me that I was cut out to bat higher in the order to be able to give more and more to the team.'

The series was drawn 2-2. In the next game at Wellington, India won by 12 runs and once again, the openers did their job admirably. Jadeja (56) and Tendulkar (63) put on 103. There was an opening stand of 61 in the final game at Christchurch, which the home side won by six wickets. The series was levelled, but the gain for the Indian team was immeasurable.

The hectic schedule of the team took them to Sharjah less than a fortnight after the one-day series had ended in New Zealand. The six-nation Austral-Asia Cup was an opportunity for Tendulkar to test his new found skills as opener against the formidable bowling attacks of Pakistan and Australia. New Zealand, Sri Lanka and the UAE were the other teams in the fray.

The opening match between India and the UAE was their maiden One-day International. In the course of his 63, Tendulkar broke another record: he became the youngest player to make 2000 ODI runs.

India had stayed away from Sharjah for nearly three years for a variety of reasons. The India-Pakistan match was, therefore, more eagerly anticipated than ever.

Tendulkar gave India a blazing start. He raced to his 50 from just 42 deliveries, and after the match Pakistani captain Salim Malik conceded that he had been worried India would reach 280-plus, the way the top order went for the bowling. In the end, they could only get to 219, which was hardly a challenge for the strong Pakistani batting line-up. As he had done just a couple of weeks earlier, Jadeja was content to watch from the other end as Tendulkar went at the bowlers hammer and tongs. His contribution in a stand of 62 was just 19. Even the pro-Pakistani sections of the crowd cheered Sachin's audacious stroke play. He hit ten fours and three sixes, one of which, off Wasim Akram, was a real beauty. The ball was picked clean from the middle stump and sent soaring over midwicket. Even Akram had to confess: 'It was stunning.' Rarely had an Indian batsman treated the Pakistani bowling with such contemptuous ease. But just when he was beginning to look unstoppable, a careless shot brought the entertainment to an end. In off-spinner Akram Raza's first over, Sachin tried to hoist him over midwicket only to present a catch to Basit Ali in the deep. He was out for 73 from 64 deliveries. It was Raza's only wicket in the match, but what a vital one!

With Sidhu and Azhar following Sachin's cue, India were well placed at 164 for 3 when wickets began to fall in a heap. Pakistan eventually cantered home by six wickets.

In the semi-final against Australia, Tendulkar was dismissed cheaply by Glenn McGrath, though India won by seven wickets. With Pakistan beating New Zealand by 62 runs in the other semifinal, it was once again an India-Pakistan final, just what the organizers and fans had hoped for. The Pakistanis took 250 in their innings, a total which could have been overhauled easily if the Indians had received another good start from Jadeja and Tendulkar. It was not to be. Akram removed Jadeja for a duck and then Ata-ur-Rehman struck the vital blow when he had Tendulkar caught by Aamir Sohail from a full toss for 24. Kambli's 56 was the top score as Pakistan completed their twelfth win over India in 15 matches in Sharjah, to win the title for the third time running. Tendulkar's position at the top of the batting order was, however, cemented by now.

But when would that elusive century finally arrive?

The answer came on 10 September 1994 at the R.Premadasa Stadium at Khettarama in Colombo. The Singer Cup was the first major one-day tournament to be staged in Sri Lanka, the hosts competing with India, Australia and Pakistan for the top prize. The tournament was badly hit by rain with a number of matches being cancelled, postponed or curtailed. The players spent long periods cooped up in their Colombo hotel. Perhaps this gave them ample time to indulge in non-cricketing activity. For, as the murky match-fixing saga unfolded over the years, events off the field in the Singer Cup would acquire notoriety.

After losing the opening match to Sri Lanka by seven wickets,

India were desperately looking for a win to keep their hopes alive when they met Australia. This was Tendulkar's seventy-eighth ODI. His record before the match stood at 2053 runs from 74 innings (nine not out) at 31.58—useful rather than world-class. The day-night game at Colombo would change all that.

India's opening match had been reduced to 25 overs because of rain. Wadekar was confident his boys would prove their worth if given the full quota. He was proved right as India won against Australia by 31 runs. Tendulkar had a new opening partner in the tournament in all-rounder Manoj Prabhakar. Their stand was worth 87 and India's total of 246 for 8 was built on Tendulkar's 110. Craig McDermott, Glenn McGrath and Shane Warne were at their wits' end on where to pitch the ball. Good deliveries as well as bad were treated with equal contempt as Tendulkar launched an attack on Warne that saw him go for 53 runs from his ten overs. Repeatedly, he hit over the top and through the line and when he reached three figures, the Australians joined in the applause. He raced to 50 from 43 balls, but slowed down a little after that, once the century was in his sights.

The sight of non-striker Vinod Kambli (43 not out) embracing his friend on reaching the long-awaited ton was a sight to warm every Indian heart. 'It came a little late but I am glad to have got over that mental pressure of not having achieved the distinction,' said the relieved Man of the Match. India went on to win the rain-reduced final against Sri Lanka, though Tendulkar was out for a duck.

From October 1994 following the Singer Cup to December 1995, Tendulkar played in all of India's 19 one-day games. Only in one of these did he not open. The 19 innings brought him 931 runs at an average of 49, with three more centuries and five 50s as well.

The one-day phenomenon had arrived.

15

The Brian and Sachin Show

I hate comparisons.—Sachin Tendulkar

Sachin Tendulkar hates comparisons. He has made this clear in interview after interview. Indeed, these comparisons—often ridiculous—have been made ever since his school days. In 1996, when Sir Donald Bradman created a sensation in the Indian media by going on record that the Indian master's batting reminded him of his own, Tendulkar was honoured. But even then he protested, saying Sir Don was being 'unfair' in making the comparison. Among his contemporaries, comparisons have most frequently been made between Tendulkar and the West Indian batting genius, Brian Lara.

Lara is a left-hander. But since the 1990s, the Indian and the West Indian have emerged as the greatest batsmen of their generation, good enough to be part of many all-time World XIs. Even as this chapter was being written, Lara scored his sixteenth century in his eighty-first Test, at Galle, Sri Lanka. It was his first Test century in 11 months. In the third and final Test of the series at Colombo, he scored 221 and 130, and finished the series with an astonishing 688 runs (average 114.66)—a record-breaking 44.68 per cent of his team's total aggregate and the second highest for a three-Test series. Yet, the West Indies were beaten 3-0. After the series, champion Sri Lankan off-spinner Muthiah Muralitharan was quoted as saying he found it more difficult to bowl to Lara than Tendulkar. 'Lara and Tendulkar are the hardest batsmen to bowl against, but the West Indian has troubled me more. Tendulkar is positive and difficult to bowl against, but I have an advantage over him because he is a right-hander. I have been working hard against left-handers. Part of the problem is I am turning the ball too much and find it difficult to get leg-before decisions.

'Lara is a wonderful player. He can play all shots. Most batsmen are restricted in some way and, as a bowler, you can focus on their weak points. But he can do anything—cut, late-cut, drive, sweep and the lofted drive. When you are playing a good bowler, you have to be patient and pick the right ball to hit and Lara does that well. We had a really good battle. I won it twice, but he was the winner most of the time.'

Sadly for Lara, the tour ended prematurely, following a dislocated elbow during a one-day game (followed by more girlfriend troubles back home). He became only the sixth batsman to score a double century and a century in the same Test (Graham Gooch had made a triple century and a century). Still, he has a long way to go to catch up with Tendulkar's current record and has rapidly fallen behind after his golden year of 1994. A Test average in the 60s at his peak had slipped below 47 by mid 2001, and only the wonderful run of scores in Sri Lanka pushed it marginally past 50. In 1997, Lara scored 394 runs at 39.40 while Tendulkar's figures were 1000 runs at 62.50; in 1998 it was 429 at 39 (647 at 80.87 for Tendulkar); in 1999 Lara's 737 runs were scored at an average of 27.29 compared to Tendulkar's 1088 at 68. In 2000 the comparative figures were: Tendulkar: 575 runs at 63.88; Lara: 497 at 29.23; and in 2001 Lara had 1151 runs at 63.94 while Tendulkar's record was 1003 at 62.60.

Lara tends to skip tours with alarming frequency on the flimsiest of grounds. The most recent instance was the tour to Zimbabwe and Kenya in 2001 from which he made a late withdrawal, ostensibly due to an injury.

In the fifth Test against England at St. John's, Antigua in April 1994, amidst scenes of unprecedented jubilation, Lara broke the world Test record of fellow West Indian Sir Garfield Sobers. The record individual score of 365 not out had been set in 1958. Now Lara eclipsed it with a powerful innings of 375. Then, inside of 50 days, he broke the 500-run barrier for the first time in the history of first-class cricket with an astounding innings of 501 not out for Warwickshire against

Durham at Edgbaston in the English county championship. It made Lara the first batsman after Bradman to simultaneously hold the record for the highest Test and first-class score. Suddenly the Prince of Trinidad was being proclaimed the king of cricket. And the cricket world had eyes for only one man.

Lara had first announced himself with a sublime innings of 277 (run out) against Australia at Sydney in December 1992, his maiden Test century. Tendulkar, it may be recalled, had taken more than ten years to score his first double century. The Trinidadian's appetite for massive scores appeared insatiable while Tendulkar's seeming impatience at the crease saw him fail to build on his centuries.

Lara is four years older than Tendulkar. He made his debut a year later (1990), also in Pakistan. But it took him two years to establish himself in the West Indian team. No cricketer before or since has enjoyed as spectacular a year as Lara did in 1994. It not only brought him tons of runs and records galore, but also fame and wealth the likes of which cricket had rarely seen. Sponsors lined up to sign up the master batsman and, back home in Port-of-Spain, Trinidad, the government gifted him a vast plot of land to build a house for himself and his family. It was the stuff of fairy tales, the classic rags to riches story. But how long would it last?

A friend warned Lara in 1994 that his troubles were just beginning. The prediction turned out to be spot on. Just a year later, the pressure proved too much. Lara announced his retirement, walked out of the tour of England and told manager Wes Hall: 'Cricket is ruining my life.' It was a startling confession. He was persuaded to return, but was fined ten per cent of his fees at the end of the tour, and he pulled out of the tour to Australia later in the year in protest. It was during that series in England in 1995 when things were spiralling downwards that Curtly Ambrose bluntly told the star batsman at a team meeting: 'It seems like you don't want to bat long again. Where is the hunger, will and determination? They cannot get you out unless you get yourself out. You are not the same man, so get hungry.' He showed his hunger after that with Test scores of 87, 145, 152, 20 and 179. After being dismissed for a pair by a part-time bowler against Kent in one of the touring team's warm-up matches, he railed, 'Everyone expects me to go out and at least get close to breaking those records every time I bat.' Such is the price of fame. At various times Lara has consulted psychiatrists in a bid to overcome his demons, and in conversation with former England captain Mike Brearley in 1995, he complained of 'frustration, and mental and physical tiredness'.

There were more troubles ahead after the West Indies were edged out of the 1996 World Cup semi-finals by Australia. The West Indies Cricket Board reprimanded Lara after several verbal outbursts by him. By now, he had made it clear to one and all that he was determined to be captain of the West Indies and that he would allow nothing and nobody to get in his way. Lara did get his chance in the Barbados Test against India in March 1997. With Walsh injured, he led the team astutely to a thrilling victory. Leading India was Tendulkar. But the West Indian authorities appeared in no hurry to make Lara's appointment a formal one. That decision was finally made for the home series against England in 1998. Things seemed to be looking up as the West Indies won the Tests 3-1 and the ODI series 4-1.

But the fall from grace was to come a year later, in South Africa. Lara led a pay dispute by the team that saw him stripped of his captaincy, only to get it back once the matter was resolved. The West Indies were humiliated on their first tour of South Africa, crushed 5-0 in the Test series and 6-1 in the ODIs. Now he was living on borrowed time. He was retained for the home series against Australia in 1999 after being castigated by the Board for his 'weakness in leadership', and placed on probation as captain for the first two Tests.

What happened next was one of the greatest turnarounds in sporting history. Bowled out by Australia for an all-time low of 51 and crushed by 314 runs in the first Test, the end appeared near for the West Indies and not for the last time either. Lara had not scored a century in 13 Tests. In the next three he would reel off three. Two of them—213 and 153 not out—inspired amazing victories. The third, 100 in Antigua in the final Test, could not prevent Australia from levelling the series. But single-handedly, Lara had restored the pride of West Indian cricket, and his own reputation in the bargain, with his breathtaking batting.

The downslide, however, came back to haunt the team as they crashed out in the league stage of the 1999 World Cup. Both Tests and all five ODIs were surrendered in New Zealand. And on 24 February 2000, Lara submitted his resignation from the captaincy as he took another break from cricket. It had become too much. Back home in India around the same time, Tendulkar too resigned from the captaincy that had been thrust on him for the second time, late in 1999. The pressure on the two superstars was having its effect.

The similarity, however, ends there. Lara lacked the comfort of a stable family life, which has benefited Tendulkar so much, and given him much needed peace of mind. Lara's father, who was an early influence, died before he made his Test debut. Lara did have a daughter from his girlfriend in 1994, but they have since parted ways. In Australia, during the 2000-01 season, he was accused of spending more time with an 18-year-old English model (who has since moved in with him) than on his cricket. Golf, too, had become an obsession, distracting him from cricket.

Almost every current and ex-cricketer ranks Tendulkar above Lara in contemporary cricket, though as we have seen, it was not always that way. Allan Donald, for one, thought that Tendulkar was in a different class to Lara as a professional cricketer. He was a model cricketer, and despite the intolerable pressures he faced back home in India, remained a really nice guy. He also considered Tendulkar the best batsman in the world, pulling away from Brian Lara every year. Writing in *Sportsworld* (May 1995), 'Tiger' Pataudi commented: 'Tendulkar, I reckon is even more talented than Lara, but he is yet to develop the latter's temperament and so often pleases to tease.' And in *Geoffrey Boycott on Cricket*: 'The way in which he [Tendulkar] reacted [to losing the captaincy in 1998] at a time of great stress illustrates the difference between Tendulkar, who did not cause a moment's fuss or trouble, and the petulant Lara. The product of a careful upbringing in India, Tendulkar, despite his superstar status, simply refused to waste his time in altercations with the Indian board and selectors.' And finally, Sir Donald Bradman in Roland Perry's *Bradman's Best*: 'Lara and Tendulkar have proved to be the two best batsmen in the 1990s.

Tendulkar has a very strong defence. He's very tight. But he can be aggressive, as he showed in that one-day series against Australia early in 1998 and in the Tests in India. On balance, however, Lara has probably proved more aggressive, though more mercurial. Tendulkar is proving more consistent.'

As though to clinch the issue, Tendulkar was the only contemporary cricketer to find a place in Sir Don's controversial 'Dream Team' released by Perry shortly after the legend's death in February 2001.

Lara and Tendulkar came face to face in a Test series for the first time when West Indies toured India late in 1994 under Walsh's captaincy. The three-Test series was drawn 1-1. But Tendulkar certainly had the better of the exchanges, averaging double that of Lara (67 to 33), with a century and two half-centuries. Lara had two 50s with a top score of 91 in the third Test at Mohali, which West Indies won to square the series. The tour was the first for Lara following his twin world records. But it turned out to be something of a nightmare both on and off the field. He failed to register a century in either the Tests, the first-class tour matches or the numerous ODIs. And he was suspended for one ODI by match referee Raman Subba Row. This followed his request to the umpire to consult the replays after being given out stumped against New Zealand in the Wills World Series match at Margao.

Before the series against the West Indies, it was Sri Lanka's turn to be flattened by the Indian steamroller early in 1994, losing all three Tests by an innings. It was another whitewash by Azhar and his merry men—on home soil, that is. The series was notable for Kapil Dev first equalling and then overtaking Sir Richard Hadlee's world Test record of 431 wickets. The onslaught began at Lucknow. Opener Sidhu battered the Sri Lankan bowlers as he smashed eight sixes in his 124. But it was Tendulkar's 142 that was a class apart.

'Sidhu helped me a lot,' said Tendulkar after his seventh Test century. 'He smashed the bowlers and that gave me enough insight into the bowling. I was under a bit of pressure because the Sri Lankans concentrated on getting me out.' Poised at 88 at the end of the first day, Sachin reached his ton the next morning from just four balls from medium-pacer Pramodya Wickramasinghe. The century came with two cover drives. He admitted the 100 had been on his mind when he resumed his innings with Azhar for company.

The West Indies under Walsh were expected to give India a run for their money in the winter of 1994. India had not lost a series at home since 1987; West Indies had not lost a series anywhere for 15 years. Ultimately, both sides kept their records intact. Indian cricket fans were also keen to see world record holder Lara in action. But as mentioned earlier, he was a major disappointment. The first Test at Mumbai was played on a pitch of such variable bounce that the West Indies batsmen used chest pads even while facing the spinners. It was tenacious batting in both innings by the Indians and an outstanding spell of fast bowling in the second by Srinath that swung the match India's way. Victory early on the fifth morning was the tenth for Azharuddin, a record for an Indian captain. But the margin of 96 runs was deceptive; the finish was actually quite tight.

Walsh and Benjamin got an alarming lift on the first day and the score of 99 for 5 would have been even more disastrous but for plucky batting by Kambli (40) and Tendulkar (34). Both Prabhakar and Azharuddin failed to score. Wicketkeeper Nayan Mongia (80) was the unlikely top scorer and his sixth-wicket stand of 136 with Manjrekar (51) took India to the respectable total of 272. Left-arm spinner Raju then picked up five wickets to give India a lead of 29 runs. This was nullified, however, by the end of the second day when India were reduced to 11 for 3, Benjamin bowling with real fire.

There was a delay of 45 minutes to the start of the third day due to damp patches near the bowling crease. This allowed the sting to be drawn from the wicket, and that was all the Indian batsmen needed. Sidhu and Azhar failed for the second time, making it 88 for 5. But as the day wore on, the pitch eased out and the Mumbai pair of Manjrekar and Tendulkar took the game away from the West Indies. Tendulkar's 85 (he was the joint top scorer in the Test with Junior Murray) was a perfect blend of attack and defence, while Manjrekar came up with his second 50 of the match. Tendulkar straight drove Walsh and worked him off his pads for fours and then forced the removal of leg-spinner Dhanraj, hitting him for a six over long on and a four over mid-off. Both the batsmen looked in total control as they added 74 for the sixth wicket before they fell to attacking shots. Tendulkar's 85 came from 139 balls before he sliced an off break from Hooper to be caught behind. The tail wagged furiously with Kumble (42) and Srinath (60) flogging the bowling. The target for the West Indies (363) was beyond their reach, and Srinath finished with 4 for 48 and the Man of the Match award.

India's safety-first approach possibly cost them the second Test at Nagpur and a series victory. The West Indies, let off the hook then, staged a fightback at Mohali in the third and final Test to salvage their pride and unbeaten record. Nagpur saw Tendulkar score his first century against the West Indies as India built up a formidable 546 for 9 declared and claimed a first innings lead of 118 runs. He added 177 for the third wicket with Sidhu and a further 202 with Azhar (97) for the fifth. But India consumed nearly two full days in compiling their huge score.

'I gained in confidence watching Sachin bat,' said Sidhu. 'I consider him as the living legend. I am his fan. It helps batting with Sachin.' This was Sidhu's sixth century, and in the last four he had been joined on three figures by Tendulkar. The two were proving to be India's batting mainstays. Tendulkar had come off two ducks in a row at Faridabad and Mumbai in the one-day series and had been feeling the pressure. He was delighted with his century and for once showed emotion by leaping and pumping his fist in the air when he got to three figures—going from 99 to 105 with a hooked six off Walsh. But he was disappointed at missing his first Test double century, out for 179. Now that his first ODI century was behind him, this was a fresh landmark preying on his mind. 'People forget easily, but not me. It's in the back of my mind. But I have an extremely positive mind.'

Sidhu and Tendulkar wrested control of the West Indies' attack after off-spinner Carl Hooper had got rid of Prabhakar and Kambli cheaply. Tendulkar's back-foot shots went like bullets, as did his straight drives. So good was his timing and so powerful his shots that a rare defensive stroke off Walsh bounced over fielder Benjamin and raced to the fence. The double century partnership with his captain was the first over 200 in which Tendulkar was associated. The 179 was his highest Test score till then and it took a brilliant, diving catch by Lara at mid wicket off Walsh to terminate it; he faced 319 balls and hit 24 fours and a six. But the overcautious Indian batting in the second innings and a late declaration allowed the visitors to escape. There was another century stand between Sidhu (76) and Tendulkar (54) in the second innings, for the third wicket. But this time the runs came at a much slower pace even as the Windies' bowlers slowed down the over rate. The declaration when it came on the final day allowed the Indian bowlers just four hours—in which they grabbed five wickets.

The West Indies stormed back to take the third Test at Mohali and draw the series. Walsh and Benjamin unleashed a barrage of hostile bowling to which the Indian batting had no answer, particularly on the final day when they collapsed for 114. Adams was the batting hero and the Man of the Series. But it was their furious fast bowling that had once again won the day for the visitors. The West Indies had a first innings lead of 57. The Indian innings was marked by a maiden century by Manoj Prabhakar. Manjrekar and Tendulkar both chipped in with 40 while Srinath (52) was once again a revelation with the bat. Lara (91) in the role of opener finally sparkled in the second innings when his team was looking for quick runs. He took four fours off a Srinath over. But just when he seemed set to reach his first century in the subcontinent, he walked after nicking the ball to the keeper. His gesture came in for plenty of praise after what had been a taxing tour for the entire team.

The target of 359 was quite beyond India's reach and they lost both openers on the fourth evening. Prabhakar was taken off bleeding after being hit on the mouth by Walsh before he had opened his account, while Sidhu was out for 11. The fifth day collapse was spectacular. Seven wickets tumbled in the first ten overs and the match was over five minutes before lunch. India looked to Tendulkar, as usual. But he played a loose cover drive after a deliberate field change by Walsh for

Benjamin. The air of invincibility surrounding Azhar's boys at home had been blown away. The disappointment of the Test series was offset to some extent by winning both the ODI tri-series (New Zealand were the third team) and the one-day series against the West Indies, that too by a convincing 4-1 margin. The two series were played simultaneously.

Tendulkar started off the ODI series against the West Indies with two successive ducks. But he followed up those failures with scores of 54, 88 and 105 (at Jaipur). There was also a century at Baroda against New Zealand in the Wills World Series. In the final against West Indies at Calcutta, Man of the Match Tendulkar was top scorer with 66 and returned figures of 1 for 35 from eight overs as India won by 72 runs.

Lara and Tendulkar came head-to-head again in the Carribean in 2002. The media was rife with comparisons once again, just before the series. West Indies captain Carl Hooper admitted the pressure got the better of Lara in the second Test which India won.

There was rare success for India in Sharjah in April 1995. Despite losing once again to Pakistan, they made it to the final thanks to an upset win by Sri Lanka over the Pakistanis. Tendulkar scored his fourth ODI century of the 1994-95 season in the league game against Sri Lanka which India won by eight wickets. In the process, he became the youngest to cross 3000 ODI runs. The margin of victory was repeated in the final, though this time Tendulkar's score was 41.

Meanwhile, back home Tendulkar had been appointed captain of Mumbai for the 1994-95 Ranji Trophy season, and it turned out to be a season of triumph for both the team and the captain, culminating in a century in both innings in the final against Punjab. The first-innings century was reached in 83 balls, the second from a mere 66—the fourth fastest in Ranji history. (The next season he would score the fastest century in domestic one-day cricket—from 69 balls for Wills XI in the Wills Trophy quarter-final against Hyderabad in Rajkot.) In the five Ranji matches that season (seven innings) he had 856 runs with five centuries at 122.28. It was not just the bulk of runs but the ferocious rate at which they were scored that was amazing. Those 856 runs were scored from 859 balls with 23 sixes and 106 fours. Mumbai had won all their West Zone league matches for the first time in 37 years. At 21, Sachin became the youngest captain to win the Ranji title in the history of the championship.

Tendulkar had been away in New Zealand when Mumbai regained the Ranji Trophy after a gap of ten years in 1994. So, being part of a winning Mumbai team was special for him. Before the Ranji Trophy triumph, Mumbai had also won the Wills Trophy limited-overs tournament. Tendulkar scored 116 in the final against Haryana, which Mumbai won by nine wickets. Chasing a total of 263 in 50 overs, Mumbai reached the target in 36.4 overs. Apart from 856 runs in the Ranji Trophy that year, he had struck his first ODI century as well as tons against New Zealand at Baroda, West Indies at Jaipur and against Sri Lanka in the Asia Cup in Sharjah. The Wills Trophy saw him score 57 and 116 for Mumbai. He had 285 runs in the Wills World Series, 247 in the Pepsi one-day series against the West Indies and 402 runs in three Tests against the same team. No wonder he told Vijay Lokapally (*Sportstar*, 6 May 1995) that it was his 'best season'.

The key to his new found success in ODIs was, of course, the decision to open the innings. No longer would he be left with less than ten overs in the middle order. As he said in that interview to the *Sportstar* (6 May 1995): 'I was happy the way I performed in Tests and one-day matches. There was much to learn and I was really satisfied that there were occasions when I lived up to the expectations of my teammates. My overall performance was better and I think I improved technically as a batsman.'

All those runs and tons gave a huge boost to the Indian side. They started the season by winning the Singer Cup in Sri Lanka in September 1994 and ended it with the triumph in the Asia Cup in Sharjah in April 1995. At home, the West Indies were beaten 4-1 in the ODI series, and India also won the Wills World Series triangular tournament. For Sachin, it was a memorable year: his first ODI century, first Ranji Trophy triumph, first century against the West Indies, the Asia Cup...and there would be one more, even more cherished moment.

On 25 May 1995, at the Jewel of India hall in Mumbai, Sachin married Dr Anjali Mehta, a paediatrician whom he had been dating since 1990. She was five years older than him. The wedding and numerous receptions that followed had all of Mumbai agog. Star TV offered him a huge amount to telecast the marriage live. But Sachin flatly turned them down. Other TV crews were turned away at the venue of the wedding. As always, he drew a very firm line between his personal and professional life. It took a great deal of persuasion from one of Mumbai's senior sports journalists before he allowed photographers a brief session on the lawns of the hotel, with the bride, following the wedding ceremony. Naturally, the city's cricket fraternity as well as politicians and film stars were present at the celebrations.

Ex-Yorkshire captain Phil Carrick represented Sachin's old county team at the wedding. This is what he told Scyld Berry of *Wisden Cricket Monthly* (June 1996): 'It was the nearest I'll ever get to going to a royal wedding. There were banners and neon signs saying congratulations to Sachin and Anjali. The wedding itself was for only a few close friends and relatives, but there were about seven receptions and there must have been a thousand at the one I went to on a hotel rooftop.'

There was to be another landmark in Tendulkar's life that year. In November he signed a five-year deal with Mark Mascarenhas's WorldTel for an astronomical sum.

16

World Cup 1996—and England Again

He plays much the same as I played.—Sir Donald Bradman

The World Cup returned to Asia in 1996, a decade after the Reliance World Cup, and as in 1987, under stormy circumstances. India, Pakistan and Sri Lanka won the right to co-host the sixth edition in the face of fierce opposition from England. Then, on the eve of cricket's mega event, terrorist bombs struck in the heart of Colombo, and Australia and West Indies refused to play their Group A matches in Sri Lanka due to security concerns. But it turned out to be another magnificent tournament, nonetheless, won in grand style by the Sri Lankans who defeated Australia in the final at Lahore. For the first time there was a quarter-final stage, though with only 12 teams in the fray there was not much doubt as to which eight teams would qualify for the two groups.

India were once again led by Azharuddin. Their batting challenge was now firmly in the hands of Sachin Tendulkar who had matured from 'promising' prior to the 1992 World Cup, to one of the best batsmen in the world four years later. This, despite struggling in the run-up to the World Cup. The home series against New Zealand, late in 1995, had been bedevilled by rain. India had won the three-Test series 1-0 with precious little play possible in the second and third Tests. Tendulkar's scores of 4, 0 (not out), 52 (not out) and 2 were disappointing. The inexperienced Kiwis ran the hosts close in the one-day series that followed, losing 2-3. Here again, Tendulkar failed to fire, and ended with just one half-century. A total of 142 runs from five innings as opener forced him to rethink some aspects of his technique. There were a few months between the series and the World Cup which enabled him to iron out the technical flaws which had crept into his batting. 'Mine is a floating technique,' he commented after the lean patch. 'Sometimes the balance of the body weight is on the front foot and sometimes on the back foot. But I knew all I needed was one big innings to sort things out.'

That innings came in India's opening World Cup tie against Kenya at Cuttack; he was 127 not out, at nearly a run a ball. India, needing 200 to win, coasted to victory with seven wickets to spare after Tendulkar's opening stand of 163 with Ajay Jadeja. It was his maiden World Cup 100 and won him the Man of the Match award.

India's first big test would come three days later, at Gwalior, where they met the West Indies, champions in 1975 and 1979 but by now in rapid decline. For the first time, the Indian team was being seen as a 'one-man army'—uncharitable though this was to Tendulkar's talented teammates. But it was true that for Indian fans, Sachin was the main event. Inevitably, the match was seen as a Tendulkar v Lara clash.

In the event, it was a no-contest. Not only did India maintain their recent supremacy over the twice-world champions by winning by five wickets, but Tendulkar also outshone his famed rival. The scores: Lara-2; Tendulkar-70.

It was a far from blemishless knock, though. Chasing Windies' 173, India lost two early wickets and it could so easily have been three: Tendulkar was dropped at square leg when on 12, and then on 22 in the tenth over. His skied leg side shot hovered in the air for ages before wicketkeeper Browne floored the sitter. The roar of relief from the crowd must have rocked the nearby fort. Had the catch been held, India would have sunk to 35 for 3. It was the slice of luck the side desperately needed and after that, the West Indies were shut out of the game. Tendulkar slammed 79 for the third wicket with Azhar in 16 overs and then added 31 with Vinod Kambli before being run out for 70 after a mix-up with his chum. By then, India were comfortably placed at 125 for 4 and the Man of the Match award was Sachin's again.

It was two weeks before the World Cup came up with its first classic match. The India-Australia World Cup encounters had gone down to the wire both in 1987 at Chennai and in 1992 at Brisbane. The match in Mumbai on 27 February did not quite produce such thrills. But the cricket played by both sides was out of the top draw. If India v West Indies was billed as Tendulkar v Lara, this one was the Tendulkar-Warne show. This time Sachin won the individual honours against the leg-spinner. But he was outshone by Mark Waugh and the Australians who won the contest by 16 runs.

It was Mumbai's first floodlit match and it was a privilege to watch the classic from the Wankhede Stadium press box. Australia won the toss and were into their stride right away with an opening stand worth 103 between captain Mark Taylor and Mark Waugh. The total of 258 was challenging, though it might have been much more but for a collapse which saw the last seven wickets fall for 26 runs. Waugh's 126 followed on from his 130 against Kenya four days earlier, making him the first batsman to make back-to-back centuries in the World Cup. Even though it came at virtually a run a ball, there was never the slightest hint of a slog in his imperious innings. It was all wristy stroke play and even the 40,000 partisans in the stadium could not fail to appreciate its quality.

The contrast between Waugh and Tendulkar could not have been greater. With Jadeja and Kambli sent back for next to nothing, a sense of desperation crept into the Indian master's batting. The result was batting which was not exactly crude, but certainly brutal. Faced with a big target, Tendulkar decided to chance his arm and play some audacious shots. It was not pretty in the way Waugh's innings was, but under the trying circumstances, it was perhaps the only method available. Especially since the top Indian order, with the exception of Sanjay Manjrekar (62), was fast crumbling in the face of Damien Fleming's accuracy and aggression. McGrath missed a tough caught-and-bowled chance and was promptly carted for 27 runs from two overs. There were a couple of other half-chances too, and some wild shots which stayed in the air but landed safely. The Mumbai boy was living dangerously, willing to take risks in a desperate bid for victory.

It was a magnificent spectacle under the lights and the crowd was in a frenzy. It seemed only Sachin could save India as he raced to his 50 from 41 balls. He jumped from 12 to 56 off just 25 breathtaking balls—it all appeared to be happening in the blink of an eye, so surreal was the atmosphere. Warne's very first delivery was hit straight and hard for six and suddenly Tendulkar was on 90 from 88 balls. This is where Mark Waugh had the last laugh. Bowling innocuous off breaks, he saw Tendulkar charge out and bowled wide down the leg side. Ian Healy whipped off the bails and the life had gone out of the Indian batting.

Watching this innings by Tendulkar on TV at home in Adelaide, Sir Donald Bradman was struck by a sense of déjà vu. He told his wife that he felt Tendulkar's batting technique was similar to his own.

There were more fireworks to follow in India's next match against Sri Lanka in New Delhi, but the Indians were outplayed on this occasion as well. Tendulkar and Azhar were in devastating form, plundering 99 runs from the last ten overs. Tendulkar was run out in the last over for a blazing 137, his highest ODI score which took his aggregate in the World Cup to 424 runs for three times out. There were five sixes and eight fours and the runs came from 137 balls. India's total of 271 for 3 was seemingly insurmountable. Certainly, nothing could have prepared the Indian bowlers and the 25,000-strong crowd for the onslaught that followed.

Sanath Jayasuriya and Romesh Kaluwitharana had proved to be hugely effective in the short time they had opened the innings together. Under overcast skies, they reduced the crowd to silence with their first 50 coming in an incredible 4.4 overs. Only 23 overs had been bowled when Sri Lanka lost their fourth wicket at 141. That would be the last success for the Indians as Arjuna Ranatunga and Hashan Tillekeratne strolled to victory. Only Kumble (2-39) and Tendulkar, who conceded 41 from his ten overs, were spared the carnage in a show of might by the Sri Lankans that was a sign of things to come.

Tendulkar's only failure in the entire tournament came against Zimbabwe in the last league game, when he was bowled by Heath Streak for three. But Kambli's 106 gave the home side victory by 40 runs and this set up an electric encounter with Pakistan in the quarter-finals.

If any sporting event epitomized George Orwell's description of sport as 'war minus the shooting', the India-Pakistan match was it. Normal life came to a standstill in both nations and the tension was evident on the field too. It soon became obvious that the team that would hold its nerves best would win the match. Minutes before the start came the dramatic announcement that Pakistan captain Wasim Akram had pulled out with an injury and Aamir Sohail would lead the side. It was a lucky break for India. Openers Sidhu and Tendulkar made a cautious start and 90 was on the board before the latter dragged one from Ata-ur-Rehman on to his stumps for 31. By then his partner had reached 50. It was a sedate innings by Tendulkar's standards, taking 59 balls, as the openers weathered a hostile opening spell of four overs from Waqar Younis. All the top order batsmen got a good start with Sidhu holding the innings together with 93. Ajay Jadeja provided the first fireworks of the day when he punished Waqar for 22 runs from one over. His 45 from 26 balls helped India to a huge 287 for 8.

As in the match against Sri Lanka, the rival openers made merry and the total suddenly appeared inadequate. What Jayasuriya and Kaluwitharana had done to the Indian bowlers at the Kotla, Sohail and Saeed Anwar now replicated. The crowd was suddenly silent as 84 runs were smashed from the first ten overs. Anwar was the first to go for 48 from 32 balls while Sohail continued to attack. The acting Pakistan captain was known for his abrasive behaviour on the field. He smashed Venkatesh Prasad for four, then promptly offered the bowler some gratuitous advice. Prasad kept his cool, his next ball was full and straight and bowled Sohail for 55. The Bangalore boys were doing the trick and the crowd was beside itself with joy. Prasad picked up two more wickets, Anil Kumble grabbed three, and the Pakistani challenge subsided and died out. Judging by the celebrations on the streets of Bangalore and indeed throughout the country, one would have thought India had won the World Cup. But there was still the hurdle of Sri Lanka to overcome before they could reach the final.

If the Bangalore match had brought pride and joy to the country, the Kolkata semi-final brought only shame. Unruly behaviour and bottle throwing by the massive crowd at Eden Gardens forced match referee Clive Lloyd to award the game to the Sri Lankans by default, the first and only time this has happened in the history of cricket. Coincidentally, the Sri Lankans had started the tournament with two wins by forfeit.

The crowd's frustration got the better of it as India slid to certain defeat. At 120 for 8 in 34.1 overs, in reply to Sri Lanka's 251 for 8, there could have been only one winner. It was a sad end to a promising campaign by the co-hosts who looked to be peaking after their memorable match against Pakistan. Vinod Kambli on ten walked off with tears streaming down his face and he was not the only one to show his feelings. The Indian dressing room was the picture of dejection.

Yet, it could have been so different. Azharuddin went against all advice in opting to field on winning the toss. Then, for a brief while, the Indian bowlers looked to be on top when they got rid of the top three batsmen with just 35 on the board. But Sri Lanka recovered to post a healthy total, with Tendulkar looking the most impressive of the bowlers with 2 for 34 from his ten overs. India lost Sidhu early in front of a crowd of 110,000—the biggest ever for a cricket match. Once again, the onus was on Tendulkar and he found an able partner in Manjrekar. He reached his 50 in the seventeenth over with the score on 71 for 1. By the twenty-third over it had gone up to 98 and the time for acceleration had arrived. Left-arm spinner Jayasuriya replaced Muralitharan and slid one down the leg side. The ball brushed Tendulkar's pad and he moved out of his crease, looking for a leg bye. Kaluwitharana behind the stumps quickly gathered the ball and removed the bails; the third umpire confirmed the batsman's backward lunge had come too late. His 65 had been another masterly display under immense pressure. The Sri Lankan openers who had blazed a trail throughout the tournament had scored a solitary run between them this time. But they had now combined to pull off the turning point of the match.

The Indian batting after that defied all reason. Seven wickets went down for 22 runs as one after the other, the batsmen committed hara-kiri. Lloyd's decision was almost an act of mercy, although Indian cricket would take a long time to live down the ignominy. The brilliant Sri Lankans went on to lift the World Cup four days later at Lahore.

Tendulkar finished with the most runs in the tournament: 523 runs at 87.17 from his seven matches—still the only instance in the World Cup of a batsman exceeding 500 runs. Only Ranatunga (120.50) and De Silva (89.60) had a better average. Anil Kumble captured the most wickets (and took the most catches, too). But no doubt, both men would gladly have exchanged these individual honours for the prize that really counted.

Just a fortnight after the World Cup finals, India, Pakistan and Sri Lanka were at it again. The hectic schedule of international cricket had brought the three teams together in Singapore, where big-time international cricket was being played for the first time. The tiny Pedang ground was tailor-made for big scores and the newly crowned world champions set the ball rolling in the opening match. Jayasuriya broke one world record after another while racing to his century in 48 balls against Pakistan, the fastest in ODIs till then. But Pakistan stormed back to beat them in the final. India beat Sri Lanka by 12 runs to atone in some measure for the two World Cup defeats at their hands. But they were beaten by eight wickets by Pakistan and edged out of the final on net run rate. Tendulkar's round 100 was his first century against Pakistan in either form of the game.

There was bad news off the field for him, though. For the first time he was fined 20 per cent of his match fees by the match referee H. Gardiner of Zimbabwe. His 'fault' was the MRF logo on his bat, which infringed the International Cricket Council's (ICC) ruling prohibiting logos of a particular size other than that of the bat manufacturer.

From Singapore it was over to Sharjah once again for India and Pakistan, joined for the first time by South Africa. This time it was India's turn to pip Pakistan on net run rate and reach the final against South Africa, who made it a debut to remember by winning the match by 38 runs. There was, however, the considerable consolation for India of beating Pakistan in the return match by 28 runs, having lost the opening game by 38 runs. It was the first time in five years that India had turned the tables on Pakistan in their traditional desert stronghold and only the third time in the last 12 years.

Not surprisingly, it was Tendulkar who led the charge with his second century in the last three matches against Pakistan. He also picked up two wickets, including the last one of Saqlain Mushtaq's, lbw. This led to an uncharacteristically aggressive reaction from the bowler, no doubt fuelled by the thrill of beating Pakistan in Sharjah. As a result, Tendulkar received a warning from match referee Ranjan Madugalle for the abuse and pointed finger directed at the departing batsman. Madugalle also issued him a friendly warning when the issue of the logo on his bat cropped up again and Tendulkar quietly removed it to avoid another fine.

The match saw India record its highest total to date (305 for 5) while the stand for the second wicket (231) between Tendulkar and Sidhu was India's best for all wickets. Azhar, by now, appeared preoccupied with matters of a more personal nature. Under these circumstances, Tendulkar, the trusted lieutenant, was already being perceived as the de facto captain with Azhar often letting him set the field and handle the bowling change. Azhar's batting form was in tatters too, and the story goes that Tendulkar virtually led him by the hand to the dressing room door in Sharjah when India recorded their rare triumph over their arch-rivals. Azhar's confidence had sunk so low he was trying to push himself lower and lower down the order. But his deputy's faith was repaid when the captain smashed 29 (remember, India won by 28 runs) from ten balls, including 24 from the last over bowled by Ata-ur-Rehman. The anti-Azhar campaign, which received its biggest boost after the captain's blunder in the World Cup semi-final, had by now reached fever pitch. It appeared to be only a matter of time—and not much at that—before he would be replaced in Indian cricket's hot seat by the man who could seemingly do no wrong.

Tendulkar had made his first Test century at Old Trafford on the 1990 tour of England. Now India returned for three Tests and three ODIs. And Azhar was still in charge, though barely. The run-up to the first Test at Edgbaston could hardly have been worse for the tourists. They were beaten 2-0 in the ODIs (the first was a no-result after being disrupted by rain). And to make things worse, the experienced Sidhu stormed out of the tour and flew back home after a row with the captain.

England drew first blood in a Test that had seven debutants, four of them from India. Though Nasser Hussain took the Man of the Match award for his maiden Test century, it was Tendulkar who stood out with his 122 out of an Indian second-innings total of 219. 'The real Man of the Match,' as *Wisden Cricket Monthly* aptly put it.

The rest of the Indian batting in both innings ended up in shambles, with number nine Srinath being the only other to pass 50. Trailing by 99 after the first innings, it would have been a total rout but for the Indian vice captain's ninth Test 100. With wickets falling in a heap around him, Tendulkar went for the bowling on a track that offered plenty of help to the seamers. It took him 50 balls to get to his 50, with 40 of the runs coming from boundaries. Manjrekar and Kumble gave him a modicum of support and enabled him to reach three figures, which came with a straight six off Mumbai-born spinner Min Patel. It was a flawless innings with strokes all around the wicket. The bowlers were treated with disdain as he hit 19 fours plus one six. With batsmen on both sides struggling to cope with the uneven bounce and movement off the pitch, this was a batting display that finally cemented his place as the best in the world.

Tendulkar was ninth out when he skied a bouncer from outside off stump from Chris Lewis to Graham Thorpe, who caught it running backwards at midwicket. Geoffrey Boycott summed up the way he rose head and shoulders above the rest of the Indian batting: 'The best way for India to beat England would be to have Sachin Tendulkar bat at number one, two, three, four and five.'

The *Sportstar* spoke to Tendulkar (29 June 1996) and asked him to rank his nine Test tons. He put the Edgbaston innings at number two, after his 114 at Perth in 1992. At number three was the 111 against

South Africa at Johannesburg in the same year. At fourth spot was his maiden century, 119 not out, against England at Old Trafford in 1990. His century at Sydney in 1992 was placed number five, followed by 179 v West Indies (Mumbai, 1994); 165 v England (Chennai, 1993); 142 v Sri Lanka (Lucknow, 1994) and finally, 104 not out, also against Sri Lanka (Colombo SSC, 1993).

The second Test at Lord's was drawn and was notable for the Test debuts of Sourav Ganguly (131) and Rahul Dravid (95). Tendulkar was bowled by a beauty from Lewis for 31. The third and final Test was another high-scoring draw at Trent Bridge as England repeated the 1990 series scoreline of 1-0. Both teams scored 500-plus in the first innings and there were four century makers. Ganguly followed up his debut ton with 136 while Tendulkar came the closest he has ever been in his career to making two centuries in the same Test. The first-innings 177 was his fourth against England and tenth overall, a remarkable feat for a 23-year-old. In the second, he skied an intended pull off Lewis and was out for 74. The combined match aggregate of 251 remains his highest and made him the top scorer by far on either side in the series. Dropped at slip on zero and then surviving a confident lbw appeal off Dominic Cork, Tendulkar appeared to have been coasting to his maiden double century. But as in the second innings, it was a careless lofted shot which saw his dismissal.

He also led India on the field for nearly the entire duration of the England innings. Azhar was hit on the ankle by Stewart while fielding on the third day and only returned to bat on the fifth and final day. England amassed 564, a lead of 43, and there was already some criticism of Tendulkar's captaincy. This is how he defended himself in an article in the *Times of India* nearly a year later (June 1997):

> By the end of the Indian cricket team's England tour of 1996, my name was being mentioned for captaincy for the forthcoming season. Hence on the third day of the third Test match against England when captain Azharuddin reported unfit and I took charge of the team, my captaincy received special

attention.

After India had scored 500 runs in the first innings it was expected of me to put pressure on England by placing an attacking field and making proper bowling changes. Contrary to this, it appeared I was adopting tactics which had slowed down the pace of the game. Obviously, my moves were not appreciated by cricket lovers. The fact was that things were not so easy. Centuries scored by Atherton and Hussain reduced chances of our possible lead in the first innings considerably. At this stage I thought it would be unwise if we got England out quickly. This would have made India bat in their second innings rather too early, which could have created problems for us. Rathore was unfit to bat; Manjrekar and Mongia were to open the innings and were not in good form; Ganguly and Dravid were playing only their second Test; Azharuddin was injured and was not in good form. He was to bat only if needed. I thought one or two quick wickets could have changed the complexion of the game and the situation could have been reversed. These two days of experience made me realise the ordeal of captaincy that I would have to face if I was selected captain of the team.

There was no doubt, however, that Tendulkar was streets ahead of all the other batsmen in the series, so it didn't come as a surprise when he was chosen as one of the five Cricketers of the Year by *Wisden Cricketers' Almanack* (1997).

17

Captaincy-I

It's only for my team's sake that I cannot sleep.—Sachin Tendulkar

It was a virtual *fait accompli* following the England tour that Sachin Tendulkar would be asked to take over the captaincy from Mohammad Azharuddin. Azhar's unbroken spell of seven years was one of the longest for an Indian captain. The youngest in the history of Test cricket to take on the responsibility was 'Tiger' Pataudi. He was just 21 when the captain's job was thrust on him after a near fatal injury suffered by captain Nari Contractor on the 1962 tour of the West Indies. Appointed vice captain for the series, Pataudi was groomed for the top post, as was Tendulkar. But while Tendulkar had three years as the number two, Pataudi did not enjoy the luxury of even one full series.

'Time for Change' was the headline in the *Sportstar* (27 July 1996), and in it R. Mohan summed up the mood of Indian cricket followers: 'The way forward for Indian cricket is to appoint Sachin Tendulkar captain now. His cricketing powers and his cricket faculties are in acute focus and there is no better time to hand over charge to a young man. A young man in charge of a young team is the only route forward.' Sure enough, on 8 August 1996, when the squad for the Singer Cup one-day tri-series in Sri Lanka and the Sahara Cup 'Friendship' one-day series against Pakistan in Toronto was announced, Sachin was named captain.

In his debut series in Pakistan in 1989, Sachin's captain K.Srikkanth had told him, perhaps only half-jokingly, 'When you are captain, remember who was your first.' Now, the appointment received a unanimous welcome. The question on everybody's mind was, could Tendulkar, the batsman with the golden touch, transfer those skills effortlessly to the captaincy as well? This is what Sunil Gavaskar wrote in his column in the *Sportstar* (September 1996): 'My gut feeling is that the responsibility [of the captaincy] will see greater consistency from him and less throwing of the wicket to casual, experimental shots. It might make him a marginally less attractive player, but if he tightens up he will play longer. And which one of us would complain to seeing more of his batting?' There was also concern over how Azhar would fit into the scheme of things now that he was no longer in charge.

These doubts were dispelled—at least for the time being—upon Tendulkar's debut as captain against Sri Lanka at the R.Premadasa Stadium in Colombo, on 28 August. Though India were routed by nine wickets, Tendulkar marked the day with his ninth ODI ton and added 129 runs for the third wicket with Azhar. It was the world champions' first home game, five months after winning the title, and once again it was the explosive opening pair of Jayasuriya and Kaluwitharana that knocked the stuffing out of the Indian bowling. The Indians made short work of Zimbabwe in their next match before being edged out by Australia in the last league game to decide who would meet Sri Lanka in the final (the result was a repeat of the World Cup final).

In his book *Indian Cricket: The Captains—From Nayudu to Tendulkar,* Partab Ramchand wrote about Tendulkar's first stint in charge:

> Really there can be nothing but praise for the manner in which Tendulkar conducted himself in his various capacities as captain. He made every attempt to get to know and understand his players, their needs, their requirements, their comforts. He made every attempt to goad his players on the field and, by now, leading by personal example was second nature to him. He made every attempt to be accessible to the media and in the public relations aspect he was a big improvement over his predecessor. India's failure to gain, very narrowly, a berth in the

final, did not in any way make a dent in his popularity.

From Sri Lanka it was straight to Toronto, where big-time cricket would be played in Canada for the first time in the inaugural India v Pakistan five-match one-day series. India could have wrapped things up after leading 2-1. But Pakistan, under the experienced Wasim Akram, stormed back to win the fourth and fifth games and the series. Though his captaincy was praised as positive, Tendulkar's batting fell away after he won the Man of the Match award for an unbeaten 89 in the first match, which India won by eight wickets. Thereafter, he had scores of 20, 2, 3 and 23 on sub-standard batting pitches which were severely affected by incessant rain.

There was some controversy during the series, about the preference of Vinod Kambli over Sourav Ganguly for the third and fourth matches. Kambli had scores of 3, 29 and 6. Neither Sourav nor he got a chance to bat in the first match. Ganguly was 11 not out in the second and when he replaced Kambli in the fifth and final game, he could manage just 12. The criticism (not surprisingly, mainly from West Bengal) obviously stung. Tendulkar reacted angrily. He had no intention of grabbing the captaincy, he said. If the selectors had confidence in him, they should let him do things his way, without interfering. He defended his choice of Kambli by saying that he was the best batsman for that wicket, and if Ganguly wasn't upset, why should other people?

Asked in Toronto to give his views on his counterpart's captaincy, Wasim Akram was measured in his response: 'Yeah, he has the makings of a very aggressive captain. Give him at least six more months before you start judging him. He is attacking and energetic but the Test matches in the season ahead will be his greatest challenge.' (*Sportsworld*, October 1996)

There would be a one-off Test for the inaugural Border-Gavaskar Trophy in New Delhi in October, followed by a three-Test home series against South Africa. In between, India lifted the Titan Cup one-day title in the tri-series involving Australia and South Africa. The Australians were weakened by the absence of the injured Shane

Warne who no doubt would have licked his lips in anticipation had he taken one look at the Feroze Shah Kotla pitch.

It was a new Indian team management that was in charge. Madan Lal had replaced Sandeep Patil as coach while the visitors too had a new coach, with Geoff Marsh taking over from Bobby Simpson. The Australians were ill-equipped to exploit a wicket that turned from the first session and they were outclassed in three and a half days. Tendulkar failed with the bat (10 and 0) in his first Test as captain. But everything else went his way as India won by seven wickets, their first victory over Australia since 1981 in Melbourne. The state of the pitch—which was to find its way into the CBI report into match-fixing four years later—was defended by the new Indian captain. 'There is no harm in playing to your strength. We need not worry about what kind of pitches we might get in South Africa and West Indies.' Understandably perhaps, Mark Taylor's views were not quite so positive.

Australia's poor form continued in the Titan Cup as they lost all their league matches. South Africa, on the other hand, appeared unstoppable as they flattened India and Australia in the run-up to the final. Tendulkar was in sparkling form and had three half-centuries in the league phase. The final was expected to be one-sided—and it was. Surprisingly, it was the Indians who came out on top. The captain may have had an inkling the day before when he told the media: 'The South African batting can collapse.'

This it did, folding up for 185 in reply to India's 220 for 7, with the only 50 of the low-scoring game inevitably coming from Tendulkar. Tendulkar's proactive approach while defending the small total must have come as a pleasant surprise to most of the team, as they were used to Azhar's low-key approach to captaincy. It started with Sachin giving a short pep talk to his team as they went out to field under the lights. And it continued till last man Allan Donald was bowled. Tendulkar was more than just active, he was a touch hyperactive, whether in advising bowlers, handling the field placements with elaborate care, or even taking advice at on-field meetings. This gave the impression of his being hands-on and in charge, and impressed the critics no end.

But a year later, when the defeats outstripped the wins, the same style of captaincy was condemned as naïve and over the top.

Sachin's first full series in charge against the strong South Africans was a topsy-turvy affair. India won the first Test at Ahmedabad, were crushed by 329 runs in the second at Kolkata, and then stormed back to win the decider at Kanpur by 280 runs. It turned out to be the worst series of Tendulkar's career with the bat to date (the one against New Zealand the year before, at home, had been severely curtailed by rain), and fortunately for India, it still remains his worst. He had scores of 42, 7, 18, 2, 61 and 36 to go with his twin failures in the one-off Test against Australia. His two knocks at Kanpur showed a new Sachin to the Indian public. It was a Sachin who eschewed stroke play for occupation of the crease, in an echo of his mentor Gavaskar's prediction in his column. In the first innings, he batted for three and a half hours to hold the shaky innings together and top-scored in a total of 237. In the second he played the uncharacteristic supporting role, occupying the crease for 123 minutes as Azharuddin reeled off his second successive century following his dazzling 109 at Kolkata.

Wrote R.Mohan in the *Cricketer International* (February 1997), at the end of the series, 'The change at the helm effected during the year proved far reaching while also bringing in a twin benefit. Sachin Tendulkar's captaincy, dynamic in most parts, and Mohammad Azharuddin's batting touch, a splendid recreation of all that is good about Indian batsmanship, came about because the switch at the top was made well in time.' Added Mohan, 'The most positive aspect to emerge from the series is that a young captain is prepared to play positive cricket. He has learned his lessons quickly. He may have hit a low in the negative cricket he made his team play in the second Test in Calcutta but he came out of that mindset, in time to go for the series win in Kanpur.'

It was the first time South Africa had been beaten in a full series since their return to Test cricket in 1992. For India, the unbeaten run at home now stretched to almost a decade. But the real test would come when the Indians moved to South Africa for the second leg of the contest.

There was just enough time at the end of the tour to squeeze in one more match. The Mohinder Amarnath benefit game at Mumbai was given official status at the eleventh hour, much to the fury of Cronje and his men who were keen to get back home after a strenuous tour. Tendulkar led the assault with his tenth ODI century and South Africa were routed.

Four years later, the real story behind this match would emerge.

18

Defeat and Despair

It was a privilege to be there.—Dave Richardson

That old tag, 'Tigers at home, kittens abroad,' which has attached itself to the Indian team over the 1990s must have been at the back of Sachin Tendulkar's mind as he prepared himself for his first tour as captain. The one-off Test against Australia and the three Tests v South Africa at home had given him the time and breathing space to get used to the rigours of his new role. Nothing, though, could have prepared him for the shocking capitulation in the opening Test at Kingsmead, Durban.

The South Africans had been aggrieved by the pitch they encountered at Ahmedabad. Now, within a fortnight, it was time for revenge. And a brutal reality check for Sachin.

The match was over shortly after tea on the third day. India crumbled to 100 and 66—the lowest ever score against South Africa in Test cricket. Both innings together lasted a total of 72.3 overs—less than a full day's play—with Allan Donald taking 9 for 54 in the match. South Africa too struggled on a brute of a pitch, scoring 235 and 259. But even their first innings would have been sufficient. In the end, they won by 328 runs and the Indian team was in disarray at the start of the series. Even Man of the Match Andrew Hudson (80 and 52) was forced to admit: 'You were never really in on that wicket.'

As has often happened in Tendulkar's career, the rival bowlers and fielders reserved their best for when he was at the crease. In the first innings he was bowled by a beauty from Donald for 15. In the second, it was an astonishing catch by Gary Kirsten at gully off Shaun Pollock that sent him back for four. Donald felt the ball that got Sachin got was one of the most lethal he had ever bowled in a Test match. Following two half-volleys which were driven regally to the boundary, Tendulkar got one that pitched on a perfect length just outside off stump. It jagged back at such speed that the batsman was still in the process of bringing down his bat when the stump was sent cartwheeling in the direction of the stunned wicketkeeper. 'I always get fired up a bit extra when I bowl at Sachin and the Waughs,' said the delighted bowler in a rich tribute to his victim.

In the second innings, a sliced drive at Pollock was flying at great speed and some distance from gully. An airborne Kirsten clutched it on the dive.

India were crushed again in the second Test at Cape Town, this time by 282 runs as the home side sealed the series 2-0. But this time, two Indian batsmen produced a partnership fit for the gods, of which players on both sides still speak in awe.

The batsmen were Tendulkar and Azhar, the stand was worth 222, the runs came in 40 overs and produced 175 minutes of some of the most exhilarating batting seen in the history of Test cricket. Yet, India were soundly beaten once again as they capitulated for 144 in the second innings. South Africa had piled up a massive 529 for 7 declared with Kirsten, Brian McMillan and Lance Klusener all striking centuries. But even these paled in the face of the onslaught launched by the current captain and his immediate predecessor. They came together with India reeling at a hopeless 58 for 5. Once they were parted the innings folded up for 359 with only two others reaching double figures.

Instead of grinding it out, two of the most gifted stroke players in the modern game decided to fight fire with fire. Azhar played with a care and abandon not seen since his magnificent series in England in 1990. His batting was exotic and unorthodox, and more than a little risky. Tendulkar's was more along classic lines, though no less attractive. Both had their chances. With the stand worth 197 Azhar was dropped by Cronje at extra cover; a run later, it was Tendulkar on

80 who was reprieved by Hudson at gully. Hudson had also missed Azhar on 55. But the crowd did not seem to mind one bit. They cheered every stroke as if they were being executed by their own batsmen. Such was the spell cast by the two Indians. Klusener was hammered out of the attack, smashed for four boundaries in his first over after lunch and for 60 runs from six overs. The follow-on mark was still 50 runs away when Azhar was run out by a Hudson throw from backward point. He had batted for just under three hours and raced to 115 off 109 balls with 19 fours and a six. Tendulkar looked determined to reach his first double century. Instead, he was out to a catch of such dazzling quality by Adam Bacher deep on the square leg fence—leaping backwards and plucking the ball with one hand as it sped to the boundary—that Tendulkar could only stand shaking his head, hand on hip. He was the last man out for 169 (26 boundaries) off McMillan after a stay of 331 minutes. It was perhaps fitting that it took such a magical catch to end such a magical innings.

It was not only the South African spectators who were dazzled. The man with the best view was South African wicketkeeper Dave Richardson and this is what he told me about Tendulkar's innings: 'I can say it was the only occasion when I have honestly enjoyed an opposing player scoring a century. It was a privilege to be there. It obviously helped that despite the century SA was still in a strong position in the game.'

Richardson was not the only South African player to feel that way. Allan Donald described the innings as 'fabulous', and admitted that for once he had detatched himself from his role of fast bowler to appreciate the stroke play of his opponent.

Englishman John Woodcock has reported on more Test cricket than any other journalist alive. Even he could not think of any partnership to match this one. Another English journalist, Matthew Engel (then the editor of *Wisden Cricketers' Almanack*) wrote in *Wisden Cricket Monthly* (February 1997):

> For a few hours in Cape Town on the first Saturday of 1997 the game of cricket got as near as it perhaps can ever get to being

> sublime....Tendulkar's innings was what one expects from him: mature, controlled, commanding—the weight of his country's expectations resting lightly on his shoulders. The extra dimension came from the other end. Azharuddin played what you might call an ex-captain's innings....He was determined to go out there and indulge in the carefree pleasure of showing everyone how to hit a cricket ball.

The visitors had their best chance to pull one back in the third and final Test at Johannesburg but were thwarted by weather and a defiant unbeaten 122 by Daryll Cullinan. South Africa, who set a target of 357 in 95 overs were at 228 for 8 when play was called off under dark skies with four overs remaining. Earlier, 152 minutes were lost to rain and this robbed the Indians of a well-deserved victory. Tendulkar was clearly disappointed at being denied, but felt the draw had boosted the confidence of his young side on the eve of the one-day tri-series.

The ODIs produced some splendid contests with South Africa storming into the final with an all-win record and India edging past Zimbabwe. The outsiders held India to a tie in their first match and then beat them in the penultimate game to push the league phase down to the wire. India not only had to beat Zimbabwe in Benoni, but also had to do it fast enough to push their net run rate above that of their opponents. It was touch-and-go and once again, it was the captain who showed the way.

Zimbabwe reached 240 for 8 in their 50 overs and the Indian target was 241—from 40.5 overs. That they got home by six wickets in 39.2 was largely due to Tendulkar's rip-roaring 104, ably supported by Ajay Jadeja (56 not out). Dravid had opened with Ganguly in the previous matches, but now Tendulkar was back at the top of the order to give the run chase the launching pad it needed. The final had to be replayed after the first one was washed out with South Africa well on top. It was different altogether in the replay, and India came pretty close to pulling off a sensational victory thanks to the batting of Tendulkar and Dravid.

South Africa piled up 278 for 8 in 50 overs. Rain intervened again and India's target was altered to a stiffer 251 from 40 overs. Tendulkar set the tone with a lightning 45 from 33 balls and his stand of 66 with Dravid came at eight an over. Dravid carried the fight almost to the end with a superb 84 which won him the Man of the Match award. But India fell 16 runs short with South African tempers rising and their behaviour on the field getting worse as the match seemed to slip out of their grasp.

The tourists had shown considerable spirit in coming back strongly, both in the Test and ODI tri-series, after the early setbacks. However, the lack of success weighed heavily on the captain's mind.

R.Mohan revealed Tendulkar's fatalistic state of mind midway through the tour in the *Sportstar* (1 March 1997): 'Sachin was speaking to a friend in his room that evening, asking him if he should consider stepping down from the captaincy. The very thought, fleeting though it may have been, was reflective of the emotional state of mind he was in then.'

Mohan admitted that the captain's frame of mind improved after the latter stages of the tri-series. But the experienced journalist got it wrong when he repeatedly stated in the article that Tendulkar's captaincy would be safe for many years to come. There were already rumblings that the captain was unhappy with the team that he had been presented with for the five Tests and four ODIs for India's first visit to the Caribbean since losing 3-0 in 1989.

Despite the fact that the West Indies were a shadow of what they had been eight years earlier, virtual back-to-back tours to South Africa and the West Indies was a challenge for both the team and the captain. In the interview that accompanied Mohan's article in the same issue, Tendulkar expressed concern at the enormous workload imposed on the Indian players. Indeed, 1997 would probably be the most hectic ever, with tours to South Africa, West Indies, Sri Lanka, Pakistan, Toronto and Sharjah for Test and ODI tournaments, as well as home games. There was also an uncanny quote from Tendulkar. 'If any of them [Srinath and Venkatesh Prasad] breaks down in the West Indies—I hope it doesn't happen—it's going to be very tough.'

Sure enough, within two days of the team landing in Kingston,

Jamaica, the main strike bowler Srinath had to quit the tour because of a rotator cuff tear in his shoulder that had been troubling him for some time. It was a crippling blow to the team's hopes. Apart from Venkatesh Prasad, debutant Abey Kuruvilla, the raw D.Ganesh, and all-rounder Robin Singh were the only medium-pace bowlers left in the squad. To make things worse, there followed a quixotic move by the selectors which foxed one and all. Srinath's replacement was Hyderabad's Noel David, an off-spinning all-rounder, even though medium-pacer Salil Ankola was on standby, and was the first choice of the team management. David was not even a front line spinner for Hyderabad.

Ironically, Tendulkar had been keen on an off-spinner at the selection meeting for the West Indies tour, as Prem Panicker of *Rediff.com* testified.

> I was at the CCI that day, when the selectors were picking the side to tour the West Indies. I do remember Sachin storming out of the meeting before it was less than half over—I happened to be standing in the carpark enjoying a quiet smoke when he came stomping out and I asked him what happened...and he uncharacteristically burst out with 'If they don't want to listen to my opinions, why do they bother asking me to attend these meetings?' and he got into his car and slammed out of there.
>
> For me that was the first sign that something was going wrong between Sachin and the selectors.
>
> He never did say 'Noel who?' when Noel David was named to replace Srinath—that is apocryphal, a media creation. But he did get rather bitter and in a team meeting, said something to the effect that the selectors had deliberately named a bowler who has never bowled off spin.
>
> I know one thing for sure—he was very, very upset then, he believed the team had a superb chance to beat the Windies with spin and wanted to, and he thought selectorial politics was what kept him from pulling it off.

Poor David would sit out the whole Test series and get his chance only in the ODIs that followed.

India, with their limited bowling attack, did well to draw the first Test at Kingston. Though West Indies were on the decline, they were no pushovers, with Ambrose and Walsh still firing away and the batting in the safe hands of Lara and Chanderpaul. Half the final day was washed out and India, set 323 to win, finished on 99 for two after an overnight declaration by Walsh. Tendulkar pointed out that this was the first time an Indian touring side had escaped defeat in the opening Test of a series abroad since he made his debut in Pakistan in 1989. It had, in fact, happened once before, in the Kandy Test in 1993. But that was severely curtailed by rain with just 50 minutes' play possible in all.

If this series was to be a match up between Lara and Tendulkar, the West Indian had certainly won the first round. He was at his best in the first innings when he cracked a delightful 83 and followed it up with 78. Tendulkar had scores of 7 and 15 not out.

Traditionally, Port-of-Spain has been the venue where touring Indian sides have had their best results, thanks to a pitch which is spin friendly. Only twice before had India won Test matches in the Caribbean and both were played in the Trinidad capital.

Just as the home side had the better of the draw in the first Test, India, it could be said, won the second on point. But then, this was cricket, not boxing, and it appeared from the very first ball that the tourists would be more than satisfied with another draw.

Playing in his fiftieth Test match, Tendulkar ground out one of his slowest batting displays after the West Indians had been dismissed for 296 in their first innings. The Indian batting received a jolt when Laxman was out to Ambrose from the second ball of the innings. Thereafter, it was safety-first tactics with Navjot Singh Sidhu—back for the series after serving his sentence following the episode in England—recording the second slowest double century in Test cricket. Dravid and Sidhu did the initial rescue act in their second wicket stand of 171. This was consolidated by the captain when he joined the opener to pile up a further 174. But at no time did the batsmen seek to accelerate the scoring. And Ganguly was one of the main culprits.

Tendulkar had occupied the crease for 306 minutes when Walsh ran him out for 88. He struggled to find his touch and had several close lbw appeals go in his favour as he padded up. The closest was from the second ball he faced. Ambrose was the bowler and the only person on the ground who did not think it was out was Australian umpire Steve Randell. The lead was a substantial 140 for the Indians. But too much time had been consumed and a draw was inevitable from then onwards, which seemed to please the Indians.

But their world came crashing around them in the next Test at Bridgetown, Barbados with a shocking fourth innings collapse. This sealed not only the Test, but effectively the series as well for the West Indies. The pitch was sub-standard, the ball seamed all over the place and the uneven bounce caused all sorts of problems for the batsmen. But after the dreary draws in the first and second Tests, it did at least produce a result.

Lara led the West Indies for the first time, since Walsh was declared unfit. Tendulkar won the toss and opted to field and the seam attack of Prasad, Ganesh and Kuruvilla rewarded their captain by getting the West Indies out for 298. The innings was held together by Shivnarine Chanderpaul whose 137 not out was his first century following 13 50s. For the second time in a row, the Indians gained the first innings lead, even if it was only 21 runs. Tendulkar played a classy innings, and was eight short of his first century in the West Indies, when umpire Lloyd Barker failed to call Ian Bishop for over-stepping. The resulting 'catch' was a brilliant one by Sherwin Campbell at deep gully.

After his tentative batting in the early part of the tour, this was classic Tendulkar all over again as he and Dravid established a record for the third wicket for India in the West Indies, of 170 runs. At least half of Tendulkar's 14 fours from 147 balls came from cuts, and his six was a pull off Rose. His batting was superb as he dispatched anything loose with outstanding shot selection. Twice he hit balls that were just short of a length off the back foot through extra cover—one of the most difficult shots in the book.

The Indian seamers were back in action in the second innings to rout West Indies for 140, their lowest score against India at home. Lara counter-attacked to top score with 45 and then a last wicket stand worth 33 between Ambrose and Dillon pushed the target for India to 120. Their runs made all the difference in the end and Tendulkar was criticized for his defensive field placements during the stand.

There was tremendous tension all round at the Kensington Oval on the fourth (and final) day as India sought to earn only their third victory in nearly 50 years in the Caribbean. It was not to be. The tourists were all out for 81, even if their captain said at the end that it was 50 per cent due to the pitch and 50 per cent due to their poor batting. In a mere three hours, the Indian batsmen had thrown away all the good work of the previous three days. 'I still can't believe we couldn't make 120 runs,' said the shattered skipper after a defeat that he still looks back on as one of the most disappointing moments in his career. 'It you can't score 120 to win you deserve to be punished,' was the harsh verdict from Madan Lal, the disgusted coach.

Lara manipulated his bowlers in a masterly manner with only Ambrose, Bishop and Rose (debutant Merv Dillon did not get to bowl) being entrusted with the task of bowling out the Indians. The score of 81 was their lowest in the West Indies. Overnight two without loss, Sidhu was the first to go on the fourth morning. Once again, umpire Barker erred in not calling a no-ball. The opener desperately tried to fend off one from Rose which was climbing towards his throat. Watching from the dressing room, panic set in among the batsmen as they allowed the unpredictable pitch to prey on their minds.

If Sidhu was forced to fend for his life, Azharuddin was shocked by one from Ambrose that crashed into his stumps at shin level. Tendulkar was done in by the bowler, rather than the pitch. A perfectly pitched late out swinger from Bishop saw him caught low down to his left by Lara at the lone slip. Only Laxman (19) reached double figures as the Bajan crowd celebrated late into the night. Vijay Lokapally summed up India's dismal performance in the *Sportstar* (12 April 1997): 'There was no attempt to push oneself beyond the expected levels. There was not a single partnership worth mention in the second innings and the disgraceful display left a sour note on a tour which had been quite encouraging till then.'

Back in the solitude of his hotel room after the defeat, a journalist was shocked to see Sachin break down and weep. It had been a shattering blow. *Wisden Cricket Monthly* (May 1997) compared the performances of the two 'superstar captains'. It gave Lara nine out of ten and his Indian counterpart seven out of ten—a fair assessment.

After all the excitement of Barbados, the series petered out with the last two Tests at St. John's, Antigua and Georgetown, Guyana producing rain-dominated draws. Tendulkar finished second in the averages behind Dravid with 289 runs at 57.80. Three times he came close to a century. A five-Test series without a single century was certainly unusual for the master.

Looking back on the series in an interview with Lokapally in the *Sportstar* (3 May 1997), he would rue the loss at Barbados. 'I think it was a combination of good bowling by the West Indies, bad batting by us and a terrible track,' he said when asked 'What really went wrong at Barbados?'

'It was very tough batting in the fourth innings. It was mainly the batting which let us down. I can only hope that such mistakes are not repeated.'

Inevitably, the question of whether the captaincy had inhibited his 'strokemaking instincts' cropped up.

> There were situations when we would have lost early wickets and naturally I was required to hang in there….I like the ball to come onto the bat. Since I became captain, it is only in South Africa that I have played on wickets where the ball was coming on and once in Barbados…. On slow tracks, where you have two players in catching position and a deep point, I have to curb myself. I just can't go and slam the ball because runs in international cricket are not easy to come by. I would rather wait than try to prove I am not bothered by pressure and play my natural game. I would prefer getting slow 70s or 80s than a quick 20 or 30.

The matter of team selection was also raised and here Tendulkar's words were to haunt him soon, considering the storm just ahead.

> Q: How much say do you have in selection matters, or planning an itinerary?
> A: Nothing at all. Not even in the selection matters. I only make suggestions and the decisions are taken by the selectors. The captain and the manager have no vote at all.
> Q: Would you like to have one?
> A: Most definitely because I have to play with the side and not others. I am the one who is to handle the side and I must have the players I want.

Sadly, the tour which had started on a promising note would end on a bitter one. The four ODIs that followed the Test series had more than their fair share of controversy. Ganguly had crawled to 3 from 55 balls in the second Test at Port-of-Spain when quick runs were needed. This was apparently held against him by the tour management and he found himself dropped for the fifth Test and the first ODI at Port-of-Spain. Predictably, this led to a storm back home in Kolkata which had also reacted in fury when their favourite son had been dropped a few months earlier in Toronto.

West Indies easily won the opening game by eight wickets but were stunned in the second at the same venue.

Tendulkar admitted he had misread the pitch on winning the toss in the first match. But he sought to make amends with the bat and smashed nine fours in his 44 (43 balls), audaciously stepping out to the fast bowlers, knowing full well how difficult the pitch was. It took an atrocious decision by umpire Eddie Nicholls to halt him in full flow, adjudged caught behind when the ball had grazed his right shoulder. After the match he showed the red mark where the ball had hit him.

Ganguly was back for the second match. A brilliant bowling display by Prasad, Kuruvilla and debutant David skittled out the West Indies for 121, their lowest against India in an ODI. With rain interruptions, the target was revised to 113 from 40 overs and the runs were promptly rattled off by openers Tendulkar (65 not out) and Ganguly from just 23.1 overs even as more rain threatened.

All the good work was undone by two awful batting displays as the West Indies ran away 3-1 winners. 'Incredible,' was all a stunned Tendulkar could utter at the end of a shocking collapse in the third game at Arnos Vale, St. Vincent.

Chasing 250 for victory, the Indians were coasting with Ganguly and Dravid at the crease. Their stand was worth 130 from 29 overs and the score was 157 when the second wicket fell. It came down to 65 off 68 balls with eight wickets in hand. Unbelievably, those wickets fell in a heap for India to be all out for 231. After the good start, the batsmen simply lashed out at the bowling when the target was well within reach. Azharuddin was out to a terrible shot when well set on 24, and the rest followed suit.

There had been ugly scenes in the Indian dressing room before the match when Sidhu declared himself unfit due to a knee injury suffered during the warm-up. Even as he prepared to go out to the toss, those on the scene reported that Tendulkar was forced to separate a furious Madan Lal and Sidhu, with the coach accusing the batsman of 'not wanting to play for the country'. Hardly the sort of thing to put the team in the right frame of mind. And things went from bad to worse after that.

'I gave the batsmen instructions,' said the captain who was so furious that no team member dared to approach him at the dinner table in the hotel in the evening. 'Don't hit in the air,' he sent repeated instructions. But they continued to play airy shots. 'I thought it was lack of cricketing sense. As a captain I can only tell them and expect them to follow my instructions. I can't go play for them in the middle.' Madan Lal too was left fuming at the way the potential lead had been thrown away so callously.

West Indies returned the compliment from the second match by crushing India by ten wickets in the final game, at the venue of their sensational Test triumph five weeks earlier. By then the fight had gone out of the Indian camp and the overwhelming emotion at the end of another disappointing tour was one of relief that it was all over.

19

Confrontation

The Indian skipper is powerless.—Sachin Tendulkar

The most high-profile victim of the West Indies debacle was Mohammad Azharuddin. It was not only his miserable form on the tour, but the way he threw away his wicket on more than one occasion that forced the selectors to take the decision prior to the Independence Cup four-nation tournament staged in India in the summer of 1997. 'Let it be said that Sachin Tendulkar had it up to here,' wrote R. Mohan, a staunch Azhar supporter, in the cover story of the *Sportstar* (3 May 1997), headlined: 'He Had It Coming.'

> He could not wait anymore for results from Azhar's bat and greater support to the younger men of the middle order. Any residual sympathy may have been washed away in St. Vincent where Azhar simply did not take charge of the business end of the chase as he should have.
>
> Here was a great opportunity for him to pay back his skipper for all the support and the understanding on two tours that have been the toughest in many years. One good knock from him in the second and third Tests and one in St. Vincent would have given India at least a half share of the one-day series. One knock, just one knock from the country's most experienced cricketer would have enabled the side to make history.
>
> What did it get in return but careless strokes played as if winning matches was not his concern? The flailing shot that

ballooned to cover in St. Vincent was the last straw.

The writer dismissed the talk of bookie influence behind that 'flailing shot' as 'so many straws in the wind'. Subsequent events may have given some extra credence to that theory, though. Mohan later called for Azhar to be rehabilitated in the Indian team after the Independence Cup.

Tendulkar appeared to put all these cares behind him in India's opening match against New Zealand at Bangalore. The Kiwis had stunned Pakistan in the tournament opener at Mohali. Now their bowling was simply torn to pieces as India romped home by eight wickets. New Zealand scored 220 for 9 and India made the target in 42.3 overs. The captain's 117 and his opening stand of 169 with Ganguly destroyed the bowling, especially medium-pacer Heath Davis who was belted for 4, 6, 4, 4 by Sachin in his third over.

But the wheels starting falling off the Indian campaign after that. The next match in Mumbai was a replay of the previous year's World Cup semi-final and once again, it was Sri Lanka who came out on top.

'Get Tendulkar early' had by now become the winning mantra for all opposing teams, and it was no different this time. The Indians never recovered from losing both openers with just four on the board. Ganguly was bowled first ball by Vaas and then in the fourth over came the breakthrough the Sri Lankans had sought so eagerly. The captain was out for two in the fourth over, top edging a cut from Sanjeeva de Silva straight into Kumara Dharmasena's hands at third man. After that it was Sanath Jayasuriya all the way; his unbeaten 151 made it a one-sided contest.

The key game of the tournament was inevitably the India-Pakistan clash at Chennai and it created a feast of runs and a world record. If Pakistan came out on top by 35 runs, it was almost entirely thanks to opener Saeed Anwar's 194, which remains the highest score in an ODI. Pakistan's huge 327 for 5 was always going to be a challenge, and once Tendulkar went early, this time for four, it was left to Rahul Dravid to keep the match alive with his maiden century. Vinod Kambli (65) gave him good support. But Pakistan's record total was beyond the

Indians. Anwar was helped considerably by the generosity shown by the Indian captain in allowing him to use the speedy Shahid Afridi as a runner after he had reached 75. The heat and humidity in the Chepauk Stadium made the game as much a test of stamina as of skill. Anwar had a history of illness going into the match and was overcome by heat exhaustion and fluid loss, as were many other players. Having someone to do most of his running was no doubt a factor in his world record, though it took nothing away from his dazzling strokes and domination of the bowling.

In the finals a few days later, Sri Lanka confirmed their status as world champions by beating Pakistan 2-0.

The simmering discontent between the Indian selectors and the captain exploded into the open when the team was announced for the Asia Cup to be held in Sri Lanka in July, the next stop in the crazy schedule that the Indians were subjected to in 1997. It came down to this—Tendulkar wanted Mongia and Kambli in the team, the selectors did not. Back in were Azharuddin and Sidhu, with newcomer Syed Saba Karim replacing the experienced Mongia. Tendulkar was on his way to London to attend the international captains' annual meeting when he heard the news. In an interview over the phone to Kolkata daily *Aaj Kal*, he declared that it was time to 'speak the truth', and that 'lies do not serve any purpose'. But the statement that rocked Indian cricket was this: 'I've been given a B grade team. It's not the best. It was imposed on me.'

The interview was, of course, splashed on the front page. Among other statements much out of character for the usually laconic and non-controversial captain: 'I will not be a scapegoat anymore. Why shouldn't the captain get the team he wants when he receives the flak?'; 'I won't be used any longer. I'm going to speak the truth'; 'I'm not enamoured of the captaincy. They can take it away. The Indian skipper is powerless'; It's my prerogative what I do on the field. I'm not answerable (to the selectors).'

A fortnight before this interview an extraordinary column under

Tendulkar's byline, syndicated by Sunil Gavaskar's Professional Management Group, had appeared in the *Times of India* (28 June 1997). It was largely a series of justifications for his captaincy record. And it had appeared, surely not by coincidence, the day the selectors were discussing the captaincy. The article is reproduced in its entirety below.

> Mumbai: By the end of the Indian cricket team's England tour of 1996, my name was being mentioned for captaincy for the forthcoming season. Hence on the third day of the third Test match against England when captain Azharuddin reported unfit and I took charge of the team, my captaincy received special attention.
>
> After India had scored 500 runs in the first innings it was expected of me to put pressure on England by placing an attacking field and making proper bowling changes. Contrary to this, it appeared I was adopting tactics which had slowed down the pace of the game. Obviously, my moves were not appreciated by cricket lovers.
>
> The fact was that things were not so easy. Centuries scored by Atherton and Hussain reduced chances of our possible lead in the first innings considerably. At this stage I thought it would be unwise if we got England out quickly.
>
> This would have made India bat in their second innings rather too early, which could have created problems for us. Rathore was unfit to bat; Manjrekar and Mongia were to open the innings and were not in good form; Ganguly and Dravid were playing only their second Test; Azharuddin was injured and was not in good form. He was to bat only if needed. I thought one or two quick wickets could have changed the complexion of the game and the situation could have been reversed.
>
> These two days of experience made me realise the ordeal of captaincy that I would have to face if I was selected captain of the team.
>
> I entered the test arena in 1989 and today when I am at the helm, I find most of the senior players Kapil Dev, Dilip

Vengsarkar, Krishnamachari Srikkanth, Ravi Shastri, Manoj Prabhakar and Kiran More with whom I played at the start of my career, have left the scene. Two experienced batsmen, Sidhu and Manjrekar, have been in and out of the side for some reason or the other.

During the last year, the Indian team, barring Mohd. Azharuddin, Anil Kumble, Nayan Mongia and Javagal Srinath comprised of a large number of newcomers. Laxman, Abey Kuruvilla, David Johnson, Dodda Ganesh and Noel David all made their debut during the year. Rathore, Ganguly, Dravid, Prasad and Joshi had played hardly two to three Test matches.

This scenario clearly indicates that the team has been passing through a transitional period.

Further, Sidhu was not in the team until the tour of the West Indies. In the circumstances, Raman who had not played Test cricket for a long time, opened the innings in South Africa. Srinath's injury and subsequent return to India at the start of the West Indies tour was a big blow to India's bowling attack.

The Test season began with victory in the solitary Test match against Australia; my first Test match as captain. Although I was delighted we won, to be fair to Australia, they were playing on a turning track which does not suit their style at all. But the victory against South Africa in the first Test at Ahmedabad meant much more to me, from the viewpoint of captaincy.

At 65 runs for the loss of four wickets and 170 runs needed to win, victory seemed within their reach. Their strategy, perhaps, was to curb the spin of Kumble and Joshi on the turning track.

Sensing this I decided to bring Srinath back into the attack, and it did the trick. In their second innings South Africa were all out for a meagre 105 runs. In his interview after the match, skipper Hansie Cronje was generous enough to compliment me on my captaincy, and confessed that his team was not prepared mentally for this move.

At the start of the tour of South Africa, we played only one practice match, a three-day match against a local team. The wicket happened to be the slowest of all the wickets that we came across on that tour. After Test matches at home, where we had got used to playing on the front foot because of the low bounce on our wickets, we looked forward to getting some practice on the bouncy wickets in South Africa. But it didn't happen. South Africa simply crushed us in the first two Test matches. Incidentally the wicket at Durban for the first Test was perhaps the fastest that I have ever played on.

Past records indicate that Indian teams have found it difficult to adjust their game on foreign wickets and perform to the best of their ability at the beginning of the tour. At the same time they have not only done better in the latter part of the tour but have also won Test matches. It appears that we do take time to adjust. As if to prove this we came close to winning the third and final Test, but the rains came to South Africa's rescue in their second innings on the last day. Two crucial hours between lunch and tea were washed out. At the end of the day South Africa had lost eight wickets, but had managed to save the game.

On that occasion weather had certainly deprived us of a win in South Africa; but let us not deprive ourselves of better performances abroad by preparing fast and bouncy wickets at home along with traditional turning wickets. Also we must play more practice matches at the start of a tour; this will give the team time to adjust to the conditions and more importantly to the pace bowlers abroad.

When we went to the West Indies, Srinath had to leave the team because of a shoulder injury. For a five Test series we were left with only two specialist bowlers in Prasad and Kumble. Abey Kuruvilla was making his debut; the other two bowlers, Sunil Joshi and Dodda Ganesh, hadn't been in the playing eleven regularly. Obviously most of the cricket lovers in this country ruled out our chances of even giving a good fight. But except for the first Test match when the West Indies took the lead and put us under pressure, in the remaining four matches we had the upper hand. This seemed to be overlooked in the light of our failure to reach the target of 121 runs in the third Test at Barbados.

I get a feeling that the assessment of our performance on the entire tour is being decided by the happenings on the fourth day.

In this match too we had put West Indies under pressure on the first three days. We had taken a lead of 21 runs in the first innings and then skittled them out for a mere 140 odd runs. But at the end of the third day the wicket had deteriorated considerably and the experts like Sunil Gavaskar, Geoff Boycott and Michael Holding were unanimous in their opinion, even before our innings started, that it was going to be very difficult to score those runs. The beginning of our second innings was going to be of the utmost importance. Sidhu got out first, to a perfectly-pitched ball which rose suddenly giving him no chance at all to defend. The ball hit him on the glove and went straight into the hands of the gully fielder. The team's score had not even reached double figures then.

Sidhu's wicket confirmed our doubts about the deteriorating pitch. I will not blame the wicket entirely, but some accurate bowling, excellent field placing, and to some extent bad batting contributed to our loss. I remember a similar situation when in 1982 one of the strongest batting line-ups of an Australian team comprising Greg Chappell, Doug Walters, Allan Border, Kim Hughes, Graeme Wood, John Dyson and Rodney Marsh, could not achieve a target of only 129 runs against India on a bad Melbourne wicket.

As I have mentioned earlier, our present team has many newcomers who have played very few Test matches as yet. The team needs time to improve and develop their skills.

Even the 1996 World Cup winning Sri Lankan team has developed into a winning combination over a period of time and has reached such heights in one-day cricket only recently and in Test cricket too their present performances indicate that they are a side to reckon with.

The first six players, Sanath Jayasuriya, Aravinda de Silva, Gurusinghe, Arjuna Ranatunga, Roshan Mahanama and Tillekratne of the Sri Lankan team had played around 125 matches each before the World Cup. Jayasuriya himself took almost 100 matches to prove his potential, which in my mind was never in doubt. I happened to witness his batting during Sri Lanka's tour of India in 1993-94. He was not known to many as a batsman of the calibre as he is known today. Also he used to bat lower down in the middle order. But even in those days his ability of playing breath-taking strokes against the likes of Kapil Dev was enough to give proof of his talent.

After so many years of struggle, patience, and organized efforts the Sri Lankans have struck a good performing combination. We too are at the beginning of our efforts to build a young team of talented players. Let us continue.

By now the selectors were aware that they were not dealing with a rubber stamp, as Tendulkar's predecessor was often considered to be. He was younger, with a mind of his own and obviously not afraid to speak it. This did not go down well with the selectors, or at least some of them. Reportedly, the meeting took more than an hour to decide to retain him as captain and the vote could not have been closer: 3-2. What saved him evidently was that there was no viable alternative at that stage.

The panel at the time consisted of Ramakant Desai (chairman) Sambaran Banerjee, Shivlal Yadav, Kishen Rungta and M.P. Pandove. They were joined on 7 July for the team selection meeting in Bangalore by Tendulkar, Madan Lal and BCCI secretary J.Y. Lele. It was more than two hours before the 14 were announced. When Desai was asked if he was happy with the way the meeting went, he said: 'I think so.'

Three days later, Desai admitted in Mumbai that there had been a major dispute. He said he too wanted Kambli and Mongia in the team but that they (Desai and Tendulkar) were helpless in the face of stiff opposition from the other selectors. (He would subsequently deny these comments.) 'Everybody agrees that Mongia is the best wicket-keeper in the business. The fact that he was not selected will create a lot of heartburn and soul searching,' Desai added.

However, he questioned the credibility of the interview in *Aaj Kal*. 'Tendulkar has a wise head and knows the futility of crying over spilt milk in public. If at all he had to speak, he would go guardedly about it and not scream from the roof top.' Reportedly, Desai and Tendulkar on two occasions during the stormy meeting lost their cool with the other selectors. Lele too was certain that Tendulkar would distance himself from the interview and fall back on the 'I was misquoted' line so beloved of Indian cricketers and officials.

In fact, on reaching London, Tendulkar gave an interview to *Press Trust of India* in which he virtually corroborated his *Aaj Kal* comments. 'The skipper should get the team of his choice as it's his head which is on the chopping block each time there is a reverse. The selectors dropped Kambli despite his innings of character during the Independence Cup in Chennai.'

There were some half-hearted attempts to disassociate himself from the stinging remarks by the time the Indians reached Colombo. But it was a case of too little, too late. The general consensus was that Tendulkar was going public with his grievances over team selection just when his captaincy was under threat. It was felt that now he had made his feelings clear, the selectors could not take action against him without it being perceived as an act of revenge. By this time, the media was full of match-fixing, bookies and bribery revelations and by the time the Indians landed in Colombo, former Pakistan captain Rashid Latif had named names in an interview from London.

Latif claimed four Indians—Azharuddin, Sidhu, Venkatapathy Raju and Mongia—were involved in betting on matches. Azhar immediately issued a denial and Latif too denied his earlier statement in a fax to the Indian team hotel, in which he claimed he had been misquoted. But with the captain's remarks still ringing in their ears, the team was not in the best of spirits and were routed by Sri Lanka in the final of the Asia Cup. Madan Lal's public lashing of his team after the defeat did not go down well either. While a gag order had been placed on the players speaking to the media, the coach gave an interview in which he castigated virtually every member of the team. Things went from bad to worse on the tour, with the two Tests being drawn and Sri Lanka making it a clean sweep in the three-match ODI series. The Indians returned empty-handed from a dismal tour.

Tendulkar was in form in the two Tests, scoring 143 in the first and 139 in the first innings of the second. But all other feats were overshadowed by Sri Lanka's world record total of 952 for 6 wickets in the first Test at the R.Premadasa Stadium. Roshan Mahanama (225) and Sanath Jayasuriya (340) broke all partnership records for Test cricket with their second wicket stand of 576 runs. The Indian bowling, still without Srinath, had run out of answers. Indian cricket was at a pretty low ebb. The year was turning out to be a disaster for both the team and the captain. The BCCI, under public pressure, constituted a one-man enquiry commission to probe into the allegations of corruption in Indian cricket. But former Chief Justice Y.V. Chandrachud came under a lot of fire for what turned out to be a farce and a whitewash. All the findings of the commission and the pious pronouncements of the Board officials would be thoroughly exposed by the CBI report three years later.

Ironically, the first to be axed was not a cricketer, but a journalist. R.Mohan, the experienced and high-profile cricket correspondent for the *Hindu* and the *Sportstar* for more than 15 years, was summarily sacked by his employees in the wake of rumours that he had links with bookies.

The next stop on the Indians' whistle-stop calendar was Toronto, for the second annual Sahara Cup ODI series against Pakistan. Considering what had transpired in the previous ten months, there was little scope for optimism.

But it turned out to be the one silver lining in the dark clouds that had gathered over Indian cricket. And the hero of India's successful campaign was none other than Sourav Ganguly, the man who had been left fretting on the sidelines a year earlier, in Toronto. The Indian attack was pretty raw, with Srinath and Prasad both unfit and Kumble 'rested' by the selectors. Pakistan too were without their two strike bowlers, Wasim Akram and Waqar Younis. In the end, it was Ganguly's innocuous medium-pacers that did the trick. They got him 15 wickets, including two in the third match which was declared a 'no-result' due to rain. No wonder the captain referred to him as the 'secret weapon'. Added to these wickets was Ganguly's total of 222 runs, more than enough to make him the obvious choice for Man of the Series.

The wickets were seamer friendly, and the batsmen struggled in the first four matches. Pakistan captain Rameez Raja condemned them as unsuited to one-day cricket, and no wonder. His team was swept aside in the first four matches, his own form plummeted, there were non-cricketing problems for his team as well, and at the end of the tournament he was promptly sacked as captain. For once, India came out on top despite Tendulkar not being among the runs. It was not till the last match that he managed to cross 50. 'As long as the team performs well and wins matches, I don't worry about my batting. I would say that these wins against Pakistan have been the most satisfying to me in my career,' said the winning captain.

Just a week later, though, Pakistan would exact revenge, that too at home. The Wills Challenge Cup series of three matches was the first time since his debut in 1989 that Tendulkar was playing in Pakistan. His poor form continued with scores of 2, 21 and 7 and this was a factor in Pakistan winning 2-1. Beaten by five wickets in the first ODI at Hyderabad (Sind), India came storming back to win the second at Karachi in the last over. Once again, Karachi lived up to its poor crowd reputation and Tendulkar was forced to take his team off the field after the third incident of stone throwing. Pakistan had reached 265 for 4 in 47.2 overs at that stage. Ganguly once again did the star turn with 89 before Rajesh Chauhan hit Saqlain Mushtaq for a six in the last over to make it safe for India. The decider at Lahore saw Ijaz Ahmed blast the Indians out of the game and make it 2-1 for the home side.

Sri Lanka had been whitewashed 3-0 when they toured India in 1994. Now, just three years later, they were a changed side after their epochal triumph in the World Cup the year before. This time, all the three Tests they played in India were drawn. So was the ODI series, played on India's return from Sharjah. India won the first at Guwahati by seven wickets and lost the third at Margao by five. In between, the second at Indore had to be abandoned after just three overs because of a dangerous pitch. This meant that India had played 12 Tests (just three at home) in 1997 without a single victory, though at Mumbai in the third Test against Sri Lanka they were thwarted by rain when well on top, as had happened earlier in the year in South Africa.

Tendulkar was feeling the heat as pressure on his captaincy mounted. There was a campaign in certain sections of the media to bring back Azhar and by now the selectors, backed by some Board officials, were gunning for him too. But all the talk of the captaincy affecting his batting was nonsense, at least in Test matches. He had exactly 1000 Test runs in the year at an average of 62.50, with four 100s and three 50s. The ODI figures for the year, though, did show a decline—1011 runs in 39 matches at 30.66, with two 100s and five 50s. And of those 39 matches, India had managed only ten wins. There were 23 defeats as well as one tie and five 'no-results'. India's win percentage of 30.88 per cent for the year was below that of Kenya and above only Bangladesh. It did not make for pretty reading.

At the end of the year, England sprang a surprise by winning the Akai Singer Champions Trophy four-nation tournament on only their third visit to Sharjah. This turned out to be the final nail in Tendulkar's captaincy coffin. How it came about set new low standards for intrigue even in the history of Indian cricket, which is replete with such sordid tales. India hit the depths, beaten by England (seven runs), Pakistan (four wickets) and West Indies (41 runs). To add to his humiliation by the selectors, Tendulkar had also now been ordered to bat lower down the order. It did not do much good. He had scores of 91, 3 and 1. The nadir was reached in the third and final match against the West Indies. Chasing 229 for 6, India crumbled to 188. Azharuddin, for one, appeared in a tearing hurry. His running between the wickets shocked everybody and it was no surprise when he was run out for four, going for a non-existent second run. Sunil Gavaskar, commenting on TV, summed up the feelings of every Indian cricket fan when he said: 'Azhar has just run himself out of the Indian team.'

Three weeks later, Azhar was to be appointed captain again.

20

Musical Chairs

He has played me better than anybody.—Shane Warne

The third ODI against Sri Lanka at Margao on 28 December 1997 was Sachin Tendulkar's last in charge before he was sacked on 2 January. India lost the match by five wickets and there were rumours that the captain had asked to be relieved of his duties. The disastrous Sharjah tournament was played in between the Test and the three-match ODI series against the Sri Lankans at home. The defeat meant Tendulkar had lost 31 of the 54 ODIs in which he had led since taking over in August 1996. Only 17 were won, five were abandoned, and one was tied.

His batting record in the 54 matches was below par—1739 runs at the average of 37, with four 100s and ten 50s. In 17 Test matches as captain, he had 1195 runs at 45.96, with four 100s and four 50s. There were three wins, four defeats and ten draws in these Tests. The figures suggest that while his Test performance remained largely unaffected, his batting in ODIs had suffered to some extent. Harsha Bhogle had this to say in the *Sportstar* (25 October 1997), nearly three months before Tendulkar's sacking: 'It is not the number of runs that he has scored, or hasn't, that causes as much concern as the personality he seems to project now. Tendulkar could always punish good ball and bad alike and offer more than one shot to a ball. He demolished bowlers, he didn't kill them softly. Today he seems to stumble momentarily in the gulf that has ruined the best; in that brief moment where he asks himself, "should I or shouldn't I?"'

Of equal concern to genuine cricket fans was the change in appearance that Bhogle pointed out. 'Tendulkar had a carefree boyish look to him two years ago. Today, he seems a worried man. Look at a photograph of him then and place it alongside one of today's and you will see two different men.' Tendulkar was interviewed by the *Telegraph* (1998) and asked if it was easier not being captain. 'Let's say you have more time, or well, all the time to think about your own game. Perhaps as captain, I didn't get the time to think about my own game. I kept thinking about everybody else. I'm not complaining, still....' As for his first reaction to the sacking: 'Initially, yes, I was upset. But those first few days I fell back on my family.'

The reinstatement of Azhar was not the first instance of its kind in Indian cricket. The circumstances, though, were certainly unusual, for the BCCI officials had, just a few weeks before his reappointment, said they would be giving him a dressing down for his irresponsible batting in Sharjah.

Ramakant Desai dismissed all talk of Tendulkar having tendered his resignation. He said: 'We removed Tendulkar because he could not take the pressure of both batting and captaincy.' This is something Tendulkar and his supporters have always denied.

Prem Panicker of *Rediff.com* was ruthless in his criticism of the selectors in an article published on 2 January 1998, the day of the drama (which came to be called 'musical chairs'). It is worth reproducing in full as it vividly conveys both the drama of the occasion and the double standards and subterfuge of the National Selection Committee.

Sachin Sacked, Azhar Back!
By Prem Panicker

Sachin Tendulkar was today removed as India's cricket captain.

Mohammad Azharuddin was reinstated in the job he lost at the conclusion of the England tour of 1996.

And the selectorial cow jumped over the moon!

New year or no, some things never change—and the

With Vinod Kambli after their world-record partnership for Sharadashram Vidyamandir in the Lord Harris Shield (February 1988). *Courtesy: Marine Sports Publishing Division.*

Pradeep Mandhani

On his first tour (Pakistan, November-December 1989). Standing (l. to r.): Manoj Prabhakar, Navjot Singh Sidhu, W.V.Raman, Kiran More, Vivek Razdan, Arshad Ayub, Sanjay Manjrekar, Vishwas Raut (physio). Middle row (l. to r.): Chandu Borde (manager), Kapil Dev, K.Srikkanth (captain), Ravi Shastri, Mohammad Azharuddin, Maninder Singh. Front row (l. to r.): Salil Ankola, Sachin, Ajay Sharma, Raman Lamba.

Pradeep Mandhani

Test debut v Pakistan at Karachi (November 1989).

Patrick Eagar

Cover-driving on the way to his maiden Test century at Old Trafford (August 1990)

Pradeep Mandhani

In action during his 148 not out in the third Test at Sydney (January 1992).

Pradeep Mandhani

Phil DeFreitas stands by as Tendulkar gets to his first Test century at home in the second Test at Chennai (February 1993).

Pradeep Mandhani

Heading for his first One-day International century v Australia at the R.Premadasa Stadium in Colombo (9 September 1994).

Pradeep Mandhani

Vinod Kambli congratulates his batting partner after the century.

Pradeep Mandhani

First Test as captain (playing for the Border-Gavaskar Trophy) with Australian captain Mark Taylor and match referee John Reid at Feroze Shah Kotla, New Delhi (10 October 1996).

Pradeep Mandhani

Holding the Border-Gavaskar Trophy, with the batting legends on either side of him.

Pradeep Mandhani

With mentor Sunil Gavaskar in Colombo (1993).

Pradeep Mandhani

Ian Healy watches as Tendulkar drives past a diving Shane Warne during his unbeaten 155 in the second Test at Chennai (February 1998).

Pradeep Mandhani

Adam Gilchrist is behind the stumps as Tendulkar goes on the rampage in Sharjah. Warne is the bowler (24 April 1998).

Pradeep Mandhani

Ravi Shastri looks on as Warne congratulates Tendulkar at the end of the Sharjah final.

Pradeep Mandhani

Australian captain Steve Waugh adds his congratulations as Tendulkar's teammates look on.

Pradeep Mandhani

With the late WorldTel chief Mark Mascarenhas after the victory.

With father Prof. Ramesh Tendulkar (to his left) and Vinod Kambli (extreme left) during a function in Mumbai in February 1996. Also in the photo are former Test cricketers Ajit Wadekar and Madhav Mantri (partly visible). *Courtesy: Mid Day*

Gulu Ezekiel

Brother Ajit Tendulkar who played a major role in the formative stages of his career (September 2001).

Pradeep Mandhani

Sachin and Anjali at their wedding reception in Mumbai (May 1995).

Pradeep Mandhani

Receiving the *Khel Ratna* from President K.R.Narayanan at Rashtrapati Bhavan (29 August 1998).

Pradeep Mandhani

With his hero Sir Vivian Richards during the Commonwealth Games at Kuala Lumpur (September 1998).

Pradeep Mandhani

Batting with captain Mohammad Azharuddin in Mumbai (November 1995).

Pradeep Mandhani

The vital wicket: Pakistan off-spinner Saqlain Mushtaq is ecstatic after capturing Tendulkar's wicket for 136 in the second innings of the first Test at Chepauk (31 January 1999).

Pradeep Mandhani

Batting against Kenya at Bristol in the 1999 World Cup, soon after returning from his father's funeral in Mumbai (23 May).

Pradeep Mandhani

Captain Tendulkar with coach Kapil Dev in New Delhi (November 1999).

Pradeep Mandhani

Chatting with Brian Lara in Singapore (September 1999).

Pradeep Mandhani

Giving thanks after Test century number 25: third Test v Australia at Chennai (20 March 2001).

Pradeep Mandhani

The first to get 10,000 runs in One-day Internationals: v Australia at Indore (31 March 2001).

Pradeep Mandhani

Celebrating One-day International wicket number 100: Steve Waugh at Margao (6 April 2001).

With Leander Paes during a shoot for Adidas. *Courtesy: Adidas*

Khorshed W. Ezekiel

The author with Ramakant Achrekar 'sir' in Mumbai (September 2001).

Pradeep Mandhani

The 'new Sachin'? With Virender Sehwag during his century knock on debut at Bloemfontein (3 November 2001).

alarmingly contradictory face of Indian cricket is first on that list.

Consider recent history. After a dream run leading India in Tests and one dayers on home soil, the first cracks appear in Azharuddin's captaincy when, flying in the face of perceived wisdom, he wins the toss and opts to bat second against Sri Lanka in the World Cup semifinal at the Eden Gardens, Calcutta. The clearly underprepared track crumbles and Sanath Jayasuriya has India in a spin, leading to a riot and the abandonment of the game, which is awarded to Sri Lanka by match referee Clive Lloyd.

The cracks widen during India's disastrous tour of England. The team stumbles from one bad performance to another, Navjot Singh Sidhu adds controversy to confusion when he abandons the tour, media reports and, indeed, the report of the tour manager speak of a disinterested captain who has totally cut himself off from the rest of the team and spends all his time with his inamorata.

Ironically, at that point in time, Azhar has really done little wrong. The defeat in England owed to factors other than the captaincy—the cold weather told on the bowlers, especially the spinners; batsmen found their fingers cramping, fielders lumbered around in clothing more suited to an arctic expedition....

Look back at that tour, and you realise that as the biting cold of winter eased towards the end of the tour, both batsmen and bowlers began performing a lot better—though the improvement came too late to do any good in terms of overall results.

The team returns. And Azharuddin is sacked. The selectors replace him with Sachin Tendulkar—and the nation goes into collective frenzy, expecting the master batsman to produce miracles. Sachin for his part records fine wins over Australia and South Africa in Tests at home, then leads the team to the Titan Cup ODI triangular against the same opponents, before taking off to South Africa where the team is caught on the backfoot on the fastest wicket in the world, and goes down 1-0 before it can even catch its collective breath. From there on, it is all downhill, till the third Test, when India's bid for victory is thwarted by a combination of rain and what can best be described as 'patriotic' ground staff.

Again, after a bad start, India storms into the final of the SBI ODI series—and an exciting run chase made more difficult by rain and a consequent readjustment of the target later—lose, but emerge the real heroes for a brilliant performance.

From there to the West Indies—and an eminently forgettable performance by the team. And in retrospect, it is here that Tendulkar's troubles with the selectors begin. Ahead of the tour, he asks for an off spinner to combat the Windies array of left-handers. The request is turned down by selectors on the grounds that there are no off spinners of quality in India (never mind that the same bunch, later, rediscovered Rajesh Chauhan). Tendulkar protests. Protests again when the totally unknown Noel David is flown over after Srinath breaks down.

His protests, for the first time, lead the selectors to realise that he is no rubber stamp, to meekly toe the line.

Meanwhile, master batsman Mohammad Azharuddin slides. Badly. Initially it is seen as loss of form. Then, as the run outs mount, as instances of his over-ruling the captain's instructions surface (for instance, in the St Vincent's one dayer), the groundswell of opinion turns against him.

He is dropped from the Indian side to play the Independence Cup quadrangular. And the selectors—the same bunch, mind you, who are doing duty right now—explain that it is his lack of commitment, his apparent disinterest in the game, that has led to his ouster.

Reinstated for the Asia Cup and the Test series in Sri Lanka, Azharuddin comes good with the bat.

At this point, a section of the selectors openly come out in favour of the sacking of Tendulkar and reinstatement of

Azharuddin as India's captain. The timing is important, here—this is *before* Toronto. At this point, Sachin Tendulkar is doing very well with the bat. And yet, sections of the media carry on the inspired campaign—that Tendulkar is feeling the pressure of captaincy, that his batting is falling apart, that India's losses are attributable to this factor and this factor alone.

The five game Sahara Cup in Toronto sees Azhar still in fine touch—while Tendulkar hits a bad patch. Pakistan, and the three ODIs for the Jinnah Cup, and Azhar is still doing okay, if a shade under the form he showed in Sri Lanka and Canada.

However, the selectors, who have been making a case for the sacking of Tendulkar, fail to muster a majority within the committee. Further, the 5-3 win record in eight games on the trot against Pakistan make it rather embarrassing, for them, to talk of the sacking of the skipper. And board president Raj Singh Dungarpur steps in to read the riot act, and indicate firmly that Tendulkar should not be tampered with.

Then comes Sharjah—and a performance from Azharuddin that is so downright shocking that international television commentators of the order of Geoffrey Boycott and Mark Nichols comment adversely. Sunil Gavaskar, also on live television, is scathing. The media reports are uniformly condemnatory.

And as Mohammad Azharuddin gets run out—in a fashion that would discredit a novice—in the key game against Pakistan, a section of fans at the ground hold up a banner that sums up the collective mood. 'Manoj Prabhakar, you are right!', reads the banner, referring to the former all-rounder's allegations of bribery and match-fixing within the Indian squad.

The national selectors, shaken by the storm, summon Azharuddin to a closed door meeting. And at the end of it, Ramakant Desai, chairman of selectors, announces that he has been reprimanded, and pardoned.

Board secretary Jaywant Lele, who was in Sharjah at the time of the selection committee meeting in question, announces on his return that he believes Azharuddin should have been sacked. Saying that he was basing his views on the evidence of having seen Azhar play, at first hand, in Sharjah, Lele says, 'The national selectors should have shown more courage and dropped Azharuddin. Reputations should not count, only performance should be the criterion....'

Follows three more ODIs, against Sri Lanka. Azhar's bad run of form continues.

At the end of it, Azharuddin is made captain of India!

Not just for the three-nation tournament in Bangladesh beginning January 10. But also for the three Test series against Australia to follow. *And* for the triangular ODI tournament after that.

Contrast this with Sachin Tendulkar, who was recently appointed 'captain for 27 days.'

Lele is totally, completely silent.

So, interestingly, is Ramakant Desai, chairman of selectors, who stumbles in the face of acerbic, at times angry, questioning by the media at the press briefing after the selection committee meeting in Bombay on Friday.

Desai opens his account in style, by saying 'There was no pre-determined move to sack Tendulkar. All five selectors felt it would be a great disservice to Indian cricket if he continued his lean trot in one dayers because of the extra burden of captaincy.' No pre-determined move? When, both before and after the Asia Cup, two selectors have systematically, under the guise of anonymity (the heck with the no names policy—the two selectors in question are Sambaran Bannerjee and Shivlal Yadav) spoken to the media about their determination to sack Tendulkar? No 'pre-determination'? When the board president, then in London, is constrained to telephone the national selectors ahead of the Sharjah tournament to insist that they do not sack Tendulkar? No 'pre-determination'? When national news magazine *The Week* carries a cover story, quoting a national selector and an unnamed BCCI official as saying that there was a move, with sanction from a section of the board, to sack Tendulkar? And when the same magazine, and others, openly allege that a cartel of bookmakers, unable to make any headway with Tendulkar, have begun exerting monetary influence on the selectors to axe him?

The 'no pre-determination' number by Desai is flayed by the media. A volley of questions follow. Desai subsides into silence. Finding him lost for answers, his colleague, Kishen Rungta, steps into the breach. And comes up with some of the best specimens of double-talk seen in living memory. We present samples:

'The reason why the selectors fell back on Azharuddin was that he was the only player, other than Tendulkar, to be a certainty in both forms of the game....'

Oh really? Granted that Rahul Dravid has been dropped—never mind, for now, the wisdom or lack thereof of that particular move—how about Sourav Ganguly, to name just another certainty? Again, wasn't this the same bunch of selectors who, just a while ago, spoke of having one captain—Ajay Jadeja—for one-dayers and another for Tests? So why does the captain for Bangladesh have to be a certainty in 'both forms of the game'?

No reply.

Wasn't Azharuddin originally dropped because he was seen to be an unimaginative captain? No, says Kishen Rungta. 'He was sacked due to a turbulent period in his personal life. He had remained tense and preoccupied, which showed in his leadership. He is now settled back as a family man, married to Miss Bijlani, he has got an amicable divorce from his first wife and his parents have also accepted him,' is Rungta's reasoning.

In other words, the most essential qualification for becoming captain of India is a happy married life. Which, of course, rules out the bachelor boys, Dravid, Jadeja et al. But last we heard, Sachin Tendulkar was perfectly happy with wife Anjali and newborn daughter Sara. And Ganguly, to cite another name, was very happy with wife Dona. Or do the selectors know something about the personal lives of these players that the rest of us don't?

Was there any doubt about Azhar's commitment to the side? Of course not, says Rungta. Then why was he summoned to the selectors' meeting, ahead of the Sharjah tour? 'We simply wanted to give him a pep talk, to boost his spirits which seemed low after so many negative things were written and spoken about him in the media and on television.'

There was no question of his ability and his sincerity? 'No, that was never in doubt by any of us!'

The statement is a downright lie.

'Azharuddin was pardoned,' Desai told the press at the end of the meeting on December 18. The members of the national press were present. The words were quoted, verbatim, in all media reports the last day.

However, there is more still. Asked why Tendulkar was sacked, Rungta on behalf of Desai said that the only criterion was bad batting, and not any perceived defects in the captaincy.

If that is the case, then why is Tendulkar not captain of the Test side, considering that he is aggregating over 1,000 runs, and averaging over 63, in Tests this year—the highest of any of the Indian batsmen?

No reply.

But more of the same. 'We wanted to make a last ditch effort to avoid the unpleasant step of axing Tendulkar, so we asked him to bat lower down in one dayers. This, however, failed to produce any extraordinary results, he got only two 50-plus scores in six innings, so we were forced to take this step.'

So the selectors determine these things on the basis of runs scored. Interesting.

Now examine the facts. The selectors ask Tendulkar to bat lower down. He does so, in six matches. His sequence of scores, beginning with Sharjah, are as follows: Versus England, 91 off 87 deliveries. Versus West Indies, 1 off 2. Versus Pakistan, 3 off

4. Versus Sri Lanka in the first ODI, 82 off 86. Second ODI, abandoned. Third ODI, 6 off 13. And one of those innings, the 82 off 86 undefeated, is a match-winner.

Compare Azharuddin's sequence, in the same period, in the same order: 3 off 19, 4 off 8, 39 off 57, 28 not out off 46, 24 off 36. In fact, against Sri Lanka, Azhar is ranked below Tendulkar, who tops with 88, Ganguly (73), Jadeja (60) and Sidhu (53), with 52 runs to his name. In other words, Azharuddin, whose form and commitment are not in doubt by the selectors, ranks last among the 6 specialist batsmen in the side.

Therefore, he—deservedly, in the opinion of the national selectors—gets to lead the side. Because for the selectors, statistics are not a beacon light but a crutch—to be used, selectively, when they do not have a logical leg to stand on.

It is not my intention here to belittle the achievements of Azharuddin—who, by any yardstick, deserves to be ranked among the top five batsmen India has produced in contemporary (even, perhaps, in all time) history. In fact, a look through our own archives will indicate that at the conclusion of the England tour of 1996, when there was a collective demand for his head, *Rediff* consistently argued that his personal life should not be the yardstick used to judge him, that the team failure in England was collective and could not be laid at the door of the captain alone, and that it was bad policy to sack him at that point.

However, applying the same yardstick, we maintain that it is even worse policy to reappoint him now. His form is suspect, his commitment even more so (Rungta notwithstanding, do keep in mind the selectors' move in calling him for a 'reprimand and pardon'). If captaincy can have a negative impact on Sachin Tendulkar, how much more then, by the same logic, could it impact on an already struggling Azharuddin? Wherein lies the logic, here?

Meanwhile Desai, once the storm of questioning about the appointment of Azhar subsides, takes over from Rungta to mouth an extempore elegy to Sachin Tendulkar. Samples:

'All of us have tremendous respect for Tendulkar, and not since Gavaskar has anyone received so much admiration from all as Tendulkar has got. But unfortunately, the selectors could not come to any other conclusion for his batting failures in one-dayers, except that it was due to the 'problem of captaincy.'

Interesting. How then do they account for the fact that Tendulkar's average in Tests this year is *higher* than his lifetime average? The 'problem of captaincy' adversely affects a player when he is playing one-day cricket, and beneficially when he is playing Test cricket?

More from Desai: 'The selectors have gone on record appreciating Tendulkar's sportsmanship of taking all the blame on himself. He is the type to carry on the battle. Very few captains put their head on the block as he did, but we want him more as run-scorer than as captain.'

And—as television anchors are so fond of saying—with this, we come to the end of today's programme. The next installment will be brought to you on Saturday, when the national selectors meet to finalise the team for Dacca.

Tailpiece: Two peripheral issues need passing mention, here. On Friday, the national selectors unveiled their latest theory to explain why Sachin had done badly as captain, and why Azharuddin was doing badly as a batsman. 'The media has been writing irresponsibly, and putting pressure on the team,' says Desai.

Right. The media chopped and changed teams at will. The media held a gun to Tendulkar's head and asked him to bat at number four (interestingly, Desai before the Sri Lanka series vehemently denied that the selectors had asked Tendulkar to bat lower down, and said that was a media-propagated lie; today, Rungta confirms that the selectors had indeed done so in a 'last ditch attempt' to avoid sacking him—so who is lying, here?). The media consistently refused to give Tendulkar the team he asked for. The media dictated that Prasad should not play in certain games. The media dropped Dravid. The media got Azharuddin run out with some bad calling.... and so on.... Right on, Mr Desai!

Meanwhile, was Sachin sacked, or did he quit? The last 48 hours have brought a spate of denials. From Desai, from Lele, from Shivlal Yadav. Every denial is couched in the same way... 'No, we have not *officially* been informed of Tendulkar's resignation....'

Nice. The media reports, since denied with extreme heat, were specific. They said in so many words that after the third ODI against Sri Lanka, Tendulkar has told the selectors that he would like to step down. He did not put it in writing, to 'whomsoever it may concern'. And so the BCCI establishment kept harping on not having been informed 'officially'.

The most illuminating statement on this issue comes from Desai. 'It is true that for some time now we have been debating a change in captaincy. However, it must be made clear that any decision on the matter will be our own decision, and not Tendulkar's.'

In other words—'Sorry, Sachin, you can't quit, because we want to sack you!'

By the way, friend Desai, when he said on Thursday that 'it is true we have been debating a change in captaincy,' could not foresee, poor chap, that 24 hours later, he would inform the press at the briefing that there was 'no pre-determination about the move to change captains'.

There was to be a tragic footnote to Desai's travails at the hands of his fellow selectors and the media. Two months after Tendulkar's sacking, he resigned on health grounds. A month later he was dead, at 58.

For Indian cricket, on its sickbed throughout 1997, the new year would be one of robust health as it went on a title-winning spree. And for the ex-captain, who would celebrate his twenty-fifth birthday in April, it was perhaps his *annus mirabilis*. Whether this was a result of the unburdening of the heavy baggage that the captaincy entailed, is open to debate. But there is no doubt that in 1998 he was back to 'demolishing' bowlers.

There appeared to be twin benefits to Indian cricket with the change at the top. Tendulkar was back to his best in one-day games while Azharuddin's added responsibilities appeared to bring out the best in him again. At Dhaka in January 1998, the Indians recorded the most amazing run chase in nearly 30 years of one-day cricket. The occasion was Bangladesh's somewhat belated Silver Jubilee Independence Cup in January. Both the captain and the ex-captain had an outstanding tournament and combined to beat the hosts in the opening match. With Bangladesh playing against India and Pakistan, there was little doubt about who would contest the best-of-three finals. It was the outcome that would be a surprise.

After their century stand in the first match, Azhar and Tendulkar were once again involved in a big stand as India beat Pakistan by 18 runs in the preliminary game. Azhar was Man of the Match for his 100. But it was Tendulkar who made it a match to remember. His fiftieth score of 50-plus (he made 67) was smashed from 44 balls as the two raced to a stand worth 112 from just 14 overs, taking India to 245 for 7 from 37 overs (the match was shortened by fog).

Pakistan's hopes rested on Inzamam-ul-Haq. Their top scorer with 77, he was caught and bowled by Tendulkar—his fiftieth ODI wicket. Sachin also held three more catches to round off a sparkling all-round display. India took their form into the first final, coasting home by eight wickets with nine overs to spare. Once again, Tendulkar was in the thick of things. He had bowling figures of 7-0-45-3 and then he put the Pakistani bowlers to the sword with 95 runs from 78 balls, with five sixes and six fours. In this innings he became the youngest to make 6000 ODI runs. His opening stand of 159 from 25 overs with Ganguly made the task of chasing 213 for victory an easy one.

Coach Anshuman Gaekwad had given Navjot Singh Sidhu the task of attacking off-spinner Saqlain Mushtaq. But Tendulkar would have none of it. Though Saqlain was the most successful bowler of the tournament, Tendulkar went after him with a vengeance. In the second final, when he was bowled in the second over by Azhar Mahmood for 1, the batting folded up for 189 and Pakistan wrapped it up easily to take the tournament to the decider.

There too, it appeared to be Pakistan all the way as Saeed Anwar and Ijaz Ahmed went after the bowling and helped amass 314 for 5 from 48 overs. The target seemed out of India's reach, though they were given a flying start with Tendulkar smashing 41 from 26 balls. Azhar gambled by promoting Robin Singh as the pinch hitter. Amazingly, the ploy worked. Amazing because it had been tried by Tendulkar a month earlier at Sharjah against Pakistan. Robin had got out first ball on that occasion and the captain faced the flak for his decision. This time, the left-hander stayed long enough to score 82 in a stand of 179 runs from 29.5 overs with centurion Ganguly. That took the score to 250 for 1 in 38 overs and now the chase was on, with ten overs remaining. Six Indian wickets tumbled in the gathering gloom. The winning hit came from the penultimate ball and the world record for the highest winning total and the title was India's. (Australia would go on to equal and then break the record.) Ganguly was Man of the Match for his superb 124 while Tendulkar took the Man of the Series award.

Tendulkar has pointed out in subsequent interviews how the captaincy can hinge on decisions like the promotion of Robin Singh coming off or not. That was not the only irony of the final match. At 258 for 2 in 39.3 overs, the umpires and the Pakistanis left the field with the light fading fast. But skipper Azhar stood his ground. India would have lost if the match had been called off at that stage as they needed 289 in 40 overs. But the match referee persuaded the umpires to continue the match which was then played with the floodlights switched on. This was before the National Stadium was equipped with floodlights for cricket. The lights the Indians played under were meant for football. And the match referee was a gentleman by the name of Mike Denness, the former England captain who would play a major role in Indian cricket three years later. One of the keys to the team's success was the restoration of Tendulkar to the opening slot.

The new captain had been very particular about it and the selectors had had to acquiesce.

The visit of the Australian team to India a month later was keenly anticipated. While India went without a Test win in 1997, Australia were sweeping all before them. Their record since 1994-95 had elevated them to the status of undisputed world champions. It was 12 years since the Aussies had been in India for a full series. In 1996 there was the one-off Test on an under-prepared pitch in Delhi which India easily won. But Shane Warne was injured and not on that trip. This time too, their bowling would be weakened in the absence of Glenn McGrath and Jason Gillespie, with Paul Reiffel fit only for the first Test. The focus was on Warne who had come a long way since his disastrous debut series against the Indians in Australia in 1991-92. He was now considered the greatest bowler in the world, just as the tag of greatest batsman rested on Sachin's shoulders. Their duel would be the battle within the bigger battle and its outcome was expected to tilt the series one way or the other.

Before the series, Tendulkar's preparations consisted of getting some local leg-spinners to bowl to him on a pitch where the area outside the leg stump had deliberately been roughened. The practice held him in good stead. The tourists' opening match was against Ranji Trophy champions Mumbai at the Brabourne Stadium. Led by Tendulkar, they inflicted a crushing ten-wicket defeat on the Aussies and the captain's own contribution set the tone for the series. In a decade of first-class cricket, Tendulkar had not come close to a double century. That would change now as he went after Warne to put the visitors on the back foot at the very start of their campaign.

Australia declared at 305 for 8 in their first innings. The fireworks came after that. Warne had figures of 16-1-116-0, his worst in first-class cricket. Tendulkar was 204 not out, his best in first-class cricket. Mumbai declared on 410 for 6 and a demoralized Australia crumbled to 135 in their second innings to go down by ten wickets. From the Indian team's point of view and from Tendulkar's too, this performance was vital. It put a scare into the Aussie camp and it was downhill all the way for them after that. Warne was hit for 23 runs in his first two overs. Tendulkar reached his first 50 from 46 balls and his century came from 90 with 15 fours and a six. By the time he declared, Tendulkar was on 204, scored in 269 minutes from 192 balls, with 25 fours and two sixes. The first bout against Warne had ended in a knockout.

Less than ten days later, it was time for the real thing—the first Test at Chennai. Once again, Tendulkar employed the rough-outside-the-leg-stump tactics at the Chennai nets. This time, though, he had bowlers of the calibre of Kumble and L.Sivaramakrishnan bowling to him.

India won the toss and took first strike. Openers Mongia and Sidhu gave them an excellent start with a stand of 122. But the innings fell away after that and 257 was a disappointing total. Warne picked up four wickets and the prize one was that of the master himself. In the space of five balls, the full house at Chepauk first roared with delight and then was stunned into silence. All the Warne v Tendulkar hype had obviously got to Sachin. The first ball was smashed past the bowler. The fifth dipped as he rushed the bowler and turned just enough to take the edge of his flailing bat. The ball flew to Taylor's right at slip and the captain clung to it as if his life depended on it. The Aussies were naturally cock-a-hoop. Tendulkar had been too hasty in trying to assert his authority over Warne and had paid the price. Australia had a first innings lead of 71. But they were to bat last on a spinning track and it wasn't enough. India piled up 418 for 4 declared in their second knock and then ran through the unofficial world champions, to come out winners by the convincing margin of 179 runs.

Tendulkar walked to the wicket half an hour into the fourth day, with the score on 115 for 2, after Sidhu had softened up the bowlers with a hard-hitting 64. His ability to find the smallest gaps in the field allied with the power of his shots resulted in an unforgettable innings of 155 not out—the only century of the Test. It was the fifteenth of his career, in his fifty-second Test. By now the pitch was wearing rapidly and Warne would no doubt have been in his element against any team except India at home, and any batsman except Tendulkar.

Sachin's two previous tons against Australia in the 1991-92 series, at Sydney and Perth, had only contributed to a draw and a heavy defeat. This time it played a crucial part in India's victory. 'Taking into account the pitch conditions and the fact that he was facing arguably the best wrist spinner of them all, Tendulkar's 199-ball innings was one of the greatest batting exhibitions of modern times,' wrote D.J. Rutnagur in *Wisden Cricket Monthly* (May 1998).

Warne was reduced to desperation by Tendulkar's uncanny judgement of the direction and degree of spin from the bowler's hand. Leg-spinners pitching on the stumps were left alone, while a googly was read early and ruthlessly disposed of. To make things worse for the bowler, his flipper wasn't working either. All those hours spent playing against the leggies in the 'nets', pitching in the rough, now paid off for Tendulkar. Bowling round the wicket, Warne pushed Dravid into his shell. But Tendulkar was determined not to allow the bowler to gain the upper hand in their absorbing personal duel. Batsmen around the world for many years had floundered against the leg-spinner pitched on the rough on a turning wicket. But the Indian master was made of sterner stuff. He smashed the ball over midwicket, had a narrow escape—then did it again. The calculated risk had come off splendidly and now he was unstoppable. The Aussie bubble had been burst and from then on an Indian victory was almost inevitable. So was Sachin's Man of the Match award.

The first Test had been a contest till Australia's last-day capitulation. The second at Kolkata turned out to be a rout, the visitors suffering one of their biggest defeats of all time. India's 633 for 5 declared was their highest against Australia and the biggest total by any side at Eden Gardens. Australia crumbled to 233 and 181 and were crushed by an innings and 219 runs. This time it was the captain who played the leading hand with the bat. Azhar's 163 not out was his fifth in seven Tests at Kolkata. Laxman, Sidhu and Dravid all came close, but fell short of their tons. Once again, Tendulkar was in a murderous mood and once again Warne was his main target. He reached his 50 from 60 balls and hit 12 fours and two sixes before playing an impetuous shot to be out for 79.

India maintained their mastery on their own soil. The Australians admitted that India at home was their biggest challenge. The series was decided, and Azharuddin held the Border-Gavaskar Trophy that India had first won in 1996.

Australia salvaged some of their wounded pride by claiming the 'dead' third Test at Bangalore by eight wickets. It was a case of too little too late, and once again Tendulkar proved he was peerless, with a sparkling 177. It was the sixth time in 16 centuries that he had crossed 150 and the double ton would have been his but for a rush of blood. A measure of his domination was that he scored 177 out of a total of 281 made while he was at the crease, and struck an extraordinary 29 boundaries plus three sixes.

There could only be one candidate for the Man of the Series.

In his autobiography published three years later, Warne admitted that Tendulkar had had the best of their exchanges during the series. His immaculate footwork and his confidence to go for his strokes were admirable, and bowling to him was actually a pleasure, said Warne.

Tendulkar carried his form against the Aussies into the Pepsi tri-nation one-day series, where Zimbabwe joined the two teams. The surprise came in the opening match at Kochi which India won by 41 runs. This time Tendulkar won his customary Man of the Match award for his success, not with the bat but with the ball—a first for him. The huge Indian total of 309 for 5 was built around Ajay Jadeja's 105 not out.

The challenge was taken up by the Australians who started off with an opening stand of 101. They lost three quick wickets after that before captain Steve Waugh and Michael Bevan put them back on track with a partnership that threatened to take the game away from India. Azhar introduced Tendulkar into the attack more out of compulsion than anything else. He made an immediate impact and slowed the run flow in tandem with Kumble. Mixing up his slow medium-pacers with leg breaks, he foxed Waugh with a slower one and the ball was gently tapped back into the bowler's hands. Next, he had Darren Lehmann plumb lbw for eight. Bevan and Tom Moody struck a flurry of boundaries before Bevan stepped out to Tendulkar in a bid to increase the run rate. He was stumped by Mongia for 65 and was followed by Moody, also stumped, from the first ball of Tendulkar's next over to put him on a hat-trick. He almost got it when Damien Martyn hit the ball just wide of the bowler. From 201 for 3, the batting had crumbled to 254 for 8 in 11 overs. Tendulkar got his first five-wicket haul when Martyn was caught at deep mid-off. Australia were soon all out for 268. Tendulkar's analysis was 10-2-32-5, beating his previous best of 4-34 against the West Indies at Sharjah in 1991. 'I am myself surprised by this show,' he said later, at the awards presentation.

Not so surprising was another Tendulkar ton in the Kanpur game against the hapless Australians, who must have been sick and tired of the sight of his broad bat by now. The Australian total of 222 for 9 was made to look insignificant by an opening stand of 175 between Ganguly and the century-maker. But the Green Park track was not an easy batting surface; the ball turned and kept low. Tendulkar decided the best way would be to get to the pitch of the ball and go for the bowling if India had to qualify for the final. He did just that, with devastating effect. His seven sixes (plus five fours) were an Indian record, beating the six sixes hit by Kapil Dev against Zimbabwe in the 1983 World Cup. The innings took just 89 balls. Waugh admitted that his bowlers could do little with the batsman in such brilliant form. 'He played a great innings,' he conceded.

Australia won two and lost two of their league matches, India won all four, while the Zimbabweans were gallant in defeat, losing all four by narrow margins. The victory in the final for Australia then was certainly against the run of play and came as a huge consolation to the exhausted tourists who had criss-crossed the country for six weeks.

Waugh and his men had a plan for the final in Delhi and it worked. With the star openers sent back with just 58 on the board, they steadily tightened their grip on the match and then sealed it with Bevan and Waugh batting them through to victory.

But if Australia, and Warne in particular, were relieved at the end of the tour, they could hardly have foreseen what was awaiting them in Sharjah just days later.

21

Desert Storm

I'll be having nightmares of Sachin just running down the wicket and belting me back over the head for six.—Shane Warne

A mere three days after India lost to Australia in the final of the Pepsi Cup, the two teams were in Sharjah for the Coca-Cola Cup, with New Zealand joining the fray. For the first time in ten years, Pakistan was not part of the Sharjah tournament. Just four months before, the Indian team had been the object of derision, and the captain had been displaced after they had crashed to three defeats in a row. Now Tendulkar was determined to prove a point to the spectators who had insulted him and his team in December 1997.

The format of the tournament had each team playing the other twice in the league stage. The start was low-key, hardly indicative of the fireworks that were to follow. New Zealand ran India close despite Ganguly's century, before fading out and losing by 15 runs. It was India's first win in Sharjah after five straight defeats. The next day, the Kiwis were brushed aside by six wickets by Australia, and now it was the turn of the Big Two to clash in their first league encounter, which was expected to be a dress rehearsal for the final. Once again, it was Tendulkar who played the lone hand, though a losing one. His 80 was the highest score of the match and won him the Man of the Match award. But it was little consolation as the Aussies ran out easy winners by 58 runs. The nightmare of December 1997 seemed to have returned to haunt the Indians; the very next day, they went down by four wickets to New Zealand. The Kiwis excelled in the field and three of India's top batsmen—Tendulkar, Azhar and Jadeja—were run out. Suddenly, there was the unexpected possibility of India not making it to the final.

Australia rested some of their key players when they faced New Zealand for the second time, and yet emerged easy winners to book their place in the final. As has so often been the case before and since, India now brought it down to the last game. They would have to either beat Australia outright, or raise their net run rate above that of New Zealand to reach the final. The organizers were hoping for an India-Australia clash for the title, as the crowds had been disappointing till then. But the Australians were in no mood to oblige in the return game.

For the first time in the tournament, the stadium was full. Many Indian fans felt this might be their last chance to see their team in action. Their pessimism was only heightened when Australia effortlessly made the highest total of the tournament, a huge 284 for 7. Michael Bevan remained not out on 101 and Mark Waugh took 81.

The target: 285 to win, 254 to qualify on run rate. These were revised to 276 and 237 after a sandstorm lopped off four overs from the chase. In the end, India lost, but still made it to the final. Thanks to Tendulkar, the real winner of the dramatic night. 'Second Only to Bradman' was the headline of the tournament report in the *Cricketer International* (June 1998), and few who were there at Sharjah or watched the match on TV would argue with that assessment.

The morale of the Indian team was already low after the defeat by the underdogs, New Zealand. It was compounded by the sandstorm that disrupted play after they had lost their four top batsmen, Ganguly, Mongia, Azhar and Jadeja. Their cause now looked more hopeless than ever. The score at that stage was 143 for 4 in 31 overs. To reach the final on better run rate, India needed 94 runs from the next 15 overs. Laxman hung around to give Tendulkar some support. But it was clear to Tendulkar himself that only he could turn the tide. He proceeded to attack the bowling as though it were a club side. He played every shot in the book and some that had never been seen on a cricket field. The Australians were sent reeling by the murderous assault and wilted in the desert heat. As millions watched at home in India on their TV sets, they must have missed a heartbeat or two. One shot landed in no man's land, another was dropped on the boundary. But the gods were smiling on the champion that day. By the time he was given out to a highly dubious decision, caught behind off Gillespie, the deed had been done. India were in the final. His masterly 142 had come from 131 balls and had nine fours and five sixes in it. The next highest score was Mongia's 35. Tendulkar was stunned by the decision that sent him on his way and lingered for a moment in disappointment. Still, he knew he had done his job, and there was an unmistakable swagger in his walk up the steps as his teammates rushed to pat him on the back. 'I wish we had won the match,' he said later that evening, after receiving yet another Man of the Match award for his fourteenth century.

Looking back on that night, having watched the match on video, Tendulkar expressed surprise at the manner in which he strode into the pavilion. 'Though India lost the match, we qualified. When I came back inside, I was angry because of my dismissal. But I realized that we had a chance against the Australians in the next match. What I can't forget about the incident is the swagger with which I walked into the dressing room. I was walking like Viv Richards. I don't think I will ever forget that walk,' he said (*Outlook*, 24 August 1998).

Unbelievable as it may seem, 48 hours later, Tendulkar matched that magical innings of his, stroke for stroke. India had lost in the Pepsi Cup finals at home, after winning all their preliminary matches. Now it was the turn of Australia to suffer the same fate in the Coca-Cola Cup.

The occasion was perfect. It was Sachin's twenty-fifth birthday. The stage was just right—India v Australia in front of 25,000 Indian fans. The result was fitting—another match-winning century from the birthday boy. Australia's 272 for 9 had set up another challenging target for the Indians. In the end, they made it relatively easily, winning by six wickets with nine balls to spare. Tendulkar's share this time round was 134 from 131 balls, with 12 fours and three sixes. And once again, it was a dubious umpiring decision that saved the bowlers from further humiliation.

Even the Aussies waxed eloquent after the match. Steve Waugh confessed that Tendulkar had to be the best after Bradman: 'We were beaten by one man. It is difficult to control Sachin when he is on song. What sort of field can one set for a batsman who has so many shots to play?' This was echoed by the long-suffering Warne whose ten overs in the final went for 61 runs: 'He was unstoppable. I don't think anyone, apart from Don Bradman, is in the same class. He is just an amazing player.'

Richie Benaud was another awestruck Aussie, calling Sachin's two centuries the most glorious exhibition of batting he had ever seen in limited-overs cricket, ranking with two other innings he had seen from Viv Richards.

Later that year, Sachin revealed that he had set himself a goal before the tournament: to win it for India. And he succeeded.

Sachin had scored 1130 (average 113) against the best team in the world, in ten matches in both forms of cricket over a two-month period. This included one double century, five centuries and two 50s. And the land that produced the one and only Don realized what it felt like to be on the opposite side of a batting legend.

Back home, mass Sachin hysteria had broken out across the country. The nation's favourite son had marked his twenty-fifth birthday with a dominating display, the likes of which Indian sports lovers had never seen before. And all of it live on television. Harsha Bhogle writing in the *Sportstar* (9 May 1998) sounded a note of caution: 'The issue with Sachin Tendulkar is not whether he can keep his sense of balance amidst the uncontrolled hysteria that surrounds his existence. It is whether we can keep ours. It is not how he reacts to the persistent scrutiny that is important. It is the quality of the scrutiny itself.' Wise words. But then, who was listening?

There was no stopping the comparisons with Sir Donald Bradman now. One news magazine even brought out an entire special issue dedicated to Sachin, complete with a specially commissioned poem and painting and an artist's rendering of a stamp. It was all a bit over the top. Tendulkar's greatness lay in his feats in both forms of the game. In Test cricket, several others had achieved far more by the time they turned twenty-five.

What was phenomenal was the amount of cricket Sachin had played in the last nine years. Though his average at the same age was less than that of Bradman (23 Tests; average 99.71), Viv Richards (23/62.41), Garry Sobers (37/59.86), and Javed Miandad (40/54.36), Tendulkar had played 62 Test matches (average 54.03)—50 per cent more than Miandad. On top of that was the huge number of ODIs (nearly 200) he had played in. This was the twin load borne by the modern player, especially by those playing for India, who over the last few years had been saddled with a massive schedule of international matches.

The Coca-Cola tri-series at home with cricket babes Kenya and Bangladesh generated more interest in the cola wars than in the action itself. Held at the height of summer, this was a tournament where the eventual winner was never in any doubt. Tendulkar was rested for the first two matches, apparently much against his own wishes. Certainly, the organizers were keen to have him back as the Indians also rested some other big names and tried out a number of new faces—28 players in all were fielded in the five matches. Tendulkar's return for the second game against Bangladesh ensured a full house at the Wankhede Stadium. He contributed 33 as India won by five wickets, as they had done in the first match.

There was a shock in the return match against Kenya at Gwalior. Already assured of a place in the final, the Indians were beaten by 69 runs, with Tendulkar falling for 18. Fired by this defeat and his two failures with the bat, Tendulkar led a resurgent India in the final against Kenya at Eden Gardens. The Kenyan total of 196 was overhauled in double-quick time—35 overs, to be precise. The former captain's contribution was 100 not out from 103 balls. He was now only one step removed from the world record of 17 ODI tons held by West Indian opener Desmond Haynes.

The amazing title run of the Indians continued in Sri Lanka where, the year before, they had had a dismal tour. But now, with Azhar back at the helm, they could scarcely do wrong. They won their fourth title in seven months after finishing with just one the year before. The

Singer Akai Nidahas (meaning 'independence' in Sinhalese) Trophy tri-series with New Zealand as the third team, was the latest of the subcontinent's celebratory tournaments—none of which were won by the celebrants themselves. India, Pakistan and Bangladesh had all previously failed to please their home fans and the trend was carried into Sri Lanka.

As with all tournaments held here in June-July, rain played a major role. This time round, all three league matches at Galle had to be called off without a ball being bowled. Colombo also saw two 'no-results', and New Zealand gained points without winning a single match.

The opening game of the tournament saw India record one of its most emphatic victories over Sri Lanka. Openers Ganguly (80) and Tendulkar (65) put on a sparkling 115 in 18 overs, easily overhauling Sri Lanka's 243 for 6, with eight wickets and plenty of deliveries to spare. But the Indians were almost done in by the rain rule, in their next match against New Zealand. They had raced to 131 for 2 in 24.2 overs, Tendulkar (53) galloping to his 50 in 33 balls, in reply to New Zealand's 219 for 8. That's when the rain came down with only four balls needed for it to be considered a contest. If that had happened, India would have needed 147 runs in 25 overs to be deemed winners!

After a week of nearly non-stop rain at Galle, the action moved back to Colombo, and this time it was Sri Lanka who nosed out India by eight runs in a match reduced to 36 overs a side. The two sides expectedly met in the final, which proved to be a real humdinger. The Indian innings was marked by a world record opening stand of 252 runs from 43 overs by Ganguly and Tendulkar. Both got centuries, with Tendulkar in his one hundred and ninty-sixth ODI now level with Haynes after his 128 from 131 balls. It was Tendulkar's third century and third Man of the Match award in three consecutive tri-series finals in the span of three months, India having won all three. The pair were out to successive deliveries, though there was an element of doubt in third umpire Peter Manuel's decision against Tendulkar. Manuel took his time over the stumping appeal off Jayasuriya, even as it appeared that the batsman's right toe was within the crease.

A heroic century by Aravinda de Silva, hobbled by a groin strain, took the home side within a few runs of India's 307 for 6. But Agarkar picked up four wickets and they fell short in the last over of a pulsating final, by six runs. It was heady stuff for Azhar and his men. In five ODI tri-series in the year so far, they had won four and lost only the final of the Pepsi Cup at home to Australia.

And there was still more to follow.

22

The Don and I

He spoke and we listened in awe.—Sachin Tendulkar

At his home in Australia, the legendary Sir Donald Bradman watched Sachin Tendulkar on television and saw in his batting a reflection of his own style. This was during the 1996 World Cup match against Australia at Mumbai, a match in which Sachin scored 90. 'He plays much the same as I played,' were Sir Don's exact words during a rare television interview on Australia's *Channel Nine* (May 1996). The interview was accompanied by split screen shots of Bradman and Tendulkar and their similar stroke play.

Sir Don played his final Test in 1948. In the decades since, he had paid fulsome praise to many batsmen who followed him, notably West Indians Sir Garry Sobers and Sir Vivian Richards, South African Barry Richards, and Indian opener Sunil Gavaskar, the only man to score more Test centuries than Bradman himself.

However, he obviously felt a special affinity for Tendulkar. Both were icons in their respective countries, both short men whose first instinct was always to attack and dominate the bowlers. They were also both precocious talents, though in this regard Tendulkar made an impact at a much younger age than the Australian legend. Averse as Sachin is to comparisons, he gently chided Sir Don for making an 'unfair' comparison, in a television interview. It was said with a wry smile on his face. For Tendulkar knew that while he could shrug off such comparisons made by journalists, it was a different matter when the world's greatest batsman himself went on record with such a telling comment. Tendulkar also made the point that he would be happy if he could retire with an average half that of Bradman's—an astounding 99.94.

Bradman played 52 Tests from 1928 to 1948, interrupted by World War II. In fact, at the same stage (52 Tests), Tendulkar's average was precisely half that of Bradman's. These are their comparative records: Bradman: 52 Tests; 80 innings; 10 not out; 6996 runs; 99.94 average; 334 highest score; 100s: 29; 50s: 13; 0s: 7. Tendulkar: 52 Tests; 79 innings; 8 not out; 3534 runs; 49.77 average; 179 highest score; 11 100s; 17 50s; 4 ducks. Still, after his fabulous exploits in Sharjah, the comparisons flew thick and fast. Naturally, then, there was huge excitement when Sir Don invited Tendulkar to his Adelaide home on the occasion of his ninetieth birthday on 27 August 1998.

The Indian team was at the training camp in Chennai for the Sahara Cup, when the invitation came. Tendulkar received special permission from BCCI president Raj Singh Dungarpur to fly to Australia. One of the few dissenting voices was surprisingly that of Sunil Gavaskar who, in his syndicated column, publicly urged Tendulkar not to leave the camp. He also revealed that during the 1991-92 tour to Australia, Tendulkar had turned down Gavaskar's invitation to join him on a visit to Sir Don.

The day was marked by a charity dinner in Bradman's honour, which was attended by 1,100 guests—but not by the great man himself. His celebrations were private, a quiet dinner with his son, daughter and two grandchildren. In the afternoon, Tendulkar and Shane Warne, attired in matching suits, dropped by to spend time at Sir Don's home. Bradman had also expressed his appreciation of Warne's leg-spinning skills, though he always maintained that another Australian leg-spinner, Bill O'Reilly, was the greatest bowler he had seen. It was the first time either of the two giants of the contemporary game were meeting cricket's all-time legend; both were understandably nervous.

'I was tense. I did not know where to begin, what to ask. But Sir Don made us feel easy. He spoke and we listened in awe,' Tendulkar told Sanjay Rajan of the *Sportstar* (2 September 1998) on his return to Chennai. The meeting lasted for an hour and both Warne and Tendulkar were pleasantly surprised to learn of Sir Don's high regard for the modern game. 'Sir Don, who watches a lot of cricket on television, spoke about the present-day game. He said the standard now is very high and competitive and the fielding very good. He said one-day cricket is attacking and exciting, though he loves Test cricket,' said Tendulkar.

There were two aspects of Bradman's career that Sachin was curious about. 'I asked him what was his initial movement while playing quick bowling and then his approach to the spinners. He said, to fast bowlers his initial movement was back-and-across and for the spinners an initial front-foot movement, though not a front-foot commitment.' Sir Don, in turn, asked Sachin if he moved before the ball left the bowler's hand. 'I don't know,' was his reply. But Sir Don was insistent. 'I think you do. You begin your movement before the bowler bowls, otherwise you wouldn't have the time to play the kind of shots you do,' reported Tendulkar in *Outlook* (12 September 1998). (A year later, Tendulkar himself spoke of his ability to anticipate the bowler's action depending on the previous few deliveries, and even to 'compel' the bowler to bowl in a certain way—just as Bradman was said to have done in his own playing days.)

Bradman also expressed surprise that Sachin had been coached. 'I have had three coaches, one in school, one at the state level and one at Test level,' Tendulkar told him. 'I didn't think you were coached,' confessed Sir Don, 'because anybody who's been through coaches is told to play with the left elbow pointed towards mid-off. You don't do that. I didn't do that. That gives you the flexibility to play in any direction anywhere.'

The second question Tendulkar posed to Sir Don was on his 'mental preparation' before a big match. The answer surprised him. 'He told me he would work in office between 7 and 10 in the morning, play the match and go back to work again.'

Sir Don repeated once again his observation that Sachin was the best batsman in the world at the moment and the closest in style to the way he himself had played. He felt that among contemporary batsmen, Brian Lara took more risks, and Warne agreed: 'Yes, he takes more risks. I think I can get him out anytime I want. He has so many openings. But with Tendulkar the problem is that there are no openings. He can spot the length of a delivery better than any other human being.'

Sir Don did not give Sachin any particular advice on batting. 'Before leaving, I told him that India was scheduled to play a series in Australia in 1999, to which he said, "Hopefully, I should be able to come and watch."'

Tendulkar's lasting impression was of 'the kindness of that remarkable person. Though the greatest batsman of all time and Australia's greatest sportsperson, Sir Don is so down to earth. He has stayed away from publicity and controversy all these years.' On a personal note, the photograph of Tendulkar, Warne and Sir Don together—and signed by all three—is the favourite item in my cricket memorabilia collection.

The charity dinner that evening was marked by another Tendulkar-Warne duel—this time at the bidding for an autographed photograph of Bradman dating back to 1948. The batsman emerged the winner with a bid of $A 4000 (about Rs 100,000).

When Sir Don passed away on the eve of the first India v Australia Test at Mumbai in February 2001, Tendulkar and Warne led the tributes with their memories of that August afternoon two years earlier. And it emerged a few months later that Sir Don had posthumously paid Sachin Tendulkar the ultimate compliment. He was the only contemporary cricketer to figure in his all-time World XI.

Tendulkar flew straight from Australia to New Delhi after meeting Bradman. Here, he was to receive the Rajiv Gandhi Khel Ratna award, the nation's highest sports-specific honour, from President K.R.Narayanan at Rashtrapati Bhavan, on 29 August. The *Khel Ratna* had been instituted by the government in 1991-92 as a sort of 'super' Arjuna Award, the annual award given to meritorious sports persons since 1961. Surprisingly, for such a cricket-mad nation, Tendulkar was the first cricketer to receive the *Khel Ratna*, and the only one so far.

For some weeks before the function, the private television company I was working for was in touch with WorldTel in order to get Tendulkar into the studios for a series of interviews. Everything was agreed upon and we arrived at the Rashtrapati Bhavan with our camera crews, ready to bring Tendulkar back with us. Sourav Ganguly and Ajay Jadeja were among the Arjuna Awardees. With three cricketers at the function, there was pandemonium in the normally staid environs of the President's official residence.

The first shock came when the press discovered that all their reserved seating had been taken by the President's staff and family. Once the awards were presented amidst all the pomp and ceremony, it was time for the informal tea session hosted by the President for the various dignitaries, sports officials, the press, and the awardees and their families. I was just a few feet away from the President and was shocked to see him standing alone in a corner, teacup in hand. He seemed equally shocked, judging by his expression.

The President of India had been abandoned by his security staff, ministers and VIPs—all of whom had made a beeline for the only person who seemed to matter on the day. Sachin was accompanied by his wife Anjali and a family friend. They found themselves hemmed in by hundreds of hysterical autograph hunters. He turned to her, whispered a few words, and the next thing we knew, they had bolted—with fans in desperate chase. It was the quickest of quick singles as they reached the car and sped off, leaving behind hundreds of unsigned autograph books. Even Jadeja and Ganguly had all but been forgotten. Inside, the other sports persons were grumbling and muttering. Once again, their moment of glory had been hijacked by cricketers.

My colleague and I, and our camera crew, piled into our vehicles and followed Tendulkar to the hotel. There, we were told he would not be able to make it to the studio and we would have to be satisfied with a quick 'shoot' by the hotel swimming pool. Apparently, Anjali wanted her husband to accompany her on a shopping excursion into town. We were none too happy, as may be imagined.

A harried looking Sachin joined us after some time, after having changed from formals into jeans and a checked shirt. He snapped at the camera crew with a *'jaldi kar'* (be quick) as they set up the equipment—though he was courteous to me and my fellow reporter. I did notice that Viv Richards swagger return as I greeted him in the lobby and escorted him outdoors. I thought to myself, how is it possible for a young man constantly in the spotlight and adored by millions to keep his head? And what a year it had been already—the thrashing of the Australians and the taming of Shane Warne at home and abroad, Man of the Match at the Diana Memorial match at Lord's, a private audience with the Don—and now the Rajiv Gandhi *Khel Ratna*.

These were the topics we covered in an interview that lasted just over four minutes, as foreign tourists sunbathing in the background looked on curiously. As the cameras were being set up, I mentioned to him something I had read in the papers—that Sir Don's son John had turned to his father as Sachin left their residence and commented: 'What a bonzer!' With a grin Sachin asked me what 'bonzer' meant, and I explained to him it was Australian slang for an all-round great guy.

Tendulkar was polite but obviously impatient—wife and shopping were waiting. He answered all the questions put to him briefly. But after that day, he has made it a point to wave or greet me whenever our paths have crossed.

Perhaps he was pleased with the interview.

23

On Top of the World

It was as though he was having a net.—Allan Donald

The MCC v Rest of the World match at Lord's on 18 July 1998 was held to commemorate Dr W.G.Grace's hundred and fiftieth birth anniversary. Officially, however, it was known as the Diana, Princess of Wales Memorial Match, as all proceeds (£750,000) were contributed to the Memorial Fund. Although it was an exhibition match, 22,861 people turned up to see a glittering array of 22 of the world's best cricketers.

Tendulkar found himself leading the Rest of the World XI. The MCC XI were led by Mike Atherton and had in their ranks the current Indian captain, Mohammad Azharuddin, as well as Anil Kumble, Javagal Srinath and Sourav Ganguly. Though the usual tension associated with an official international match was obviously missing, the cricket was played seriously.

MCC XI scored 261 for 4 in the allotted 50 overs, with West Indian left-hander Shivnarine Chanderpaul top-scoring with 127 not out. Azhar contributed a delightful 61. The MCC attack was formidable, with Allan Donald, Srinath, Glenn McGrath and Kumble. Sanath Jayasuriya opened with Tendulkar, but was soon lbw to Srinath and Donald picked up Saeed Anwar cheaply to leave the Rest of the World at 54 for 2. Aravinda De Silva then joined his captain of the day for the most entertaining part of a delightful game. The two added 177 and ensured their team won the match by six wickets with plenty to spare. Tendulkar was initially scratchy and was troubled by Srinath. But he was soon into his stride and was particularly severe on the part-time left-arm spin of Aamir Sohail, whose two overs were smashed for 37 runs. By the time he was bowled by Kumble for 125, he had batted for 114 balls, with 15 fours and four sixes. Even the bowlers were impressed. At one point, Allan Donald actually said, 'Good shot!', something he had never said to a batsman at any time in his career. He thought Sachin the best looking batsman he had ever seen; everything was right in his technique and judgement, entirely without a fault.

'I do not think even W.G. would have played like Sachin,' exclaimed the normally taciturn Atherton. 'Perhaps a hundred years from now MCC will stage a Tendulkar Memorial match.'

For an Indian cricketer to play for his country for nearly a decade and not be involved in a major controversy, is one more 'record' Tendulkar could have claimed. Except for a publicity-hungry politician-cum-career-sports-official who attempted to tarnish his reputation and implied motives to him that had the cricketing fraternity up in arms.

It was a clash of egos and dates that set the Indian Olympic Association (IOA) and the BCCI on a collision course. For the first time, cricket was to be played at the Commonwealth Games (it would also be the last time) at Kuala Lumpur. Unfortunately, the dates for the Games clashed with those for the India v Pakistan annual Sahara 'Friendship Series' in Toronto, which had been launched with much fanfare in 1996.

The success of cricket and the amount of coverage it gets in the media has always been a sore point with those representing other sports, who react with a mixture of envy, awe and resentment. At the same time, the officials of the IOA have always resented the fact that the BCCI is the only autonomous sporting federation in the land. And all thanks to the huge amount of money that flows into its coffers while other sports associations have to go with begging bowl in hand to get meagre funds from a hard-up government.

The Commonwealth Games was not recognized by the International Cricket Council as an official event, while the Toronto event was. The IOA, backed by the government, insisted on a full-strength team being sent to Kuala Lumpur; the Sahara Cup was to be either postponed or fobbed off with a second-string team. Suddenly, the IOA converted the issue into one of patriotism v commercialism. There were no such qualms on the part of the Pakistanis who sent a B-grade team to Kuala Lumpur while their top players went to Toronto, awaiting India's challenge.

In fact, England, as the founders of the Commonwealth, did not even bother sending a team to Kuala Lumpur. Yet, once the IOA and BCCI locked horns, charges and counter charges began flying back and forth. The BCCI resented being dictated to by the IOA and was loathe to shed its autonomy, which it had zealously guarded for so many decades. Truth to tell, there was just one player the IOA would have been happy with—the rest could have been a bunch of juniors as far as they were concerned. That one player, naturally, was Sachin Tendulkar. Sadly, he was made a pawn in the BCCI–IOA power struggle.

Ultimately, the BCCI caved in and Tendulkar was packed off to Kuala Lumpur. Ajay Jadeja (the captain), Robin Singh and Anil Kumble were the other star players in the squad. It was agreed that if the Indian team made an early exit, the players would rush to Toronto in a bid to play in at least a couple of games in the five-match series. It was a compromise that was doomed to failure. India were knocked out in the preliminary stage at Kuala Lumpur and lost 4-1 to Pakistan at Toronto.

The conditions for cricket at Kuala Lumpur were sub-standard, especially the pitches. The weather was appalling too. It was a novel experience for the cricketers, having to stay in the Games Village rather than in the luxury of five-star hotels. But they didn't complain. In fact, Tendulkar and the others quite enjoyed the atmosphere.

India were struggling at 30 for 2 in 9.4 overs when rain washed out their opening match against Antigua and Barbuda, spearheaded by Curtly Ambrose, with Sir Viv Richards as their coach. The West Indies were competing as separate nations as they do at the Olympics. The Antigua pace attack was augmented by Eldine Baptiste and Kenneth Benjamin and it was Baptiste who got rid of Tendulkar for 15. There was an even bigger shock in the next game against Canada, with the best batsman in the world out for two, the victim of an unknown 35-

year-old from Granada by the name of Davis Joseph. The team's final total of 157 for 9 owed much to young Amay Khurasia's 83. Fortunately for the Indians, the Canadian batsmen then proceeded to fold up for 45 against Kumble, who finished with 4 for 11.

The last league match against Australia was a do-or-die game for India. Australia were struggling at 84 for 5 before skipper Steve Waugh scored a century, an innings which he said was his 'most satisfying' in one-day cricket—though it will not be in the record books. This time Tendulkar scored 45 before he fell to Damien Fleming. But India could only muster 109 in reply to 255 for 5, and their campaign fizzled out. There is little doubt that the minds of many of the players were in Toronto. The rumour was then floated that the Indians had, in fact, booked their tickets even before their last league match.

Whatever be the truth, it was obvious that the whole thing had been botched up from the start, thanks to the egos of officials on both sides of the fence. And as has always been the case, it was the sportsmen whose reputations suffered the most. Indian cricket had striven in 1998 to overcome the traumas of the year before. Now much of that good work had been undone by this farce. The Pakistani team management had initially objected to India flying in replacements from Kuala Lumpur. But the sponsor's desperation for more star faces, and Tendulkar in particular, saw the protests subsequently shelved.

Sachin landed in Toronto after 20 overs of the fourth game had been bowled. In effect, he had flown across the world for just one match. Still jet-lagged from his marathon flight, he managed to crack 77 in India's total of 256 for 9 in the fifth and final match; skipper Azhar top-scored with 101. But it wasn't enough and Pakistan romped home by five wickets to take the series 4-1.

Subsequently, WorldTel felt constrained to issue a press statement rebutting the harsh comments made by some of the Indian officials against the cricket team, and specifically Tendulkar, for the poor show at Kuala Lumpur. Tendulkar expressed his sentiments in an interview to Vijay Lokapally in the *Sportstar* (10 October 1998): 'I have always taken great pride in representing the country and nothing gives me greater joy than seeing the tri-colour flutter high in the stands.'

Straight from Toronto, it was off to Zimbabwe for the weary Indians.

The one-off Test at Harare was a disaster. It ended in four days; Zimbabwe were winners by 61 runs. Medium-pacer Neil Johnson on his debut got Tendulkar in both innings, for 34 and 7. There was some consolation, though, in the one-day series which India claimed 2-1 at the start of the short tour. And at Bulawayo in the opening game, Tendulkar scored his eighteenth ODI century to overtake West Indian opener Desmond Haynes' world record. It had taken Haynes 16 years to score his 17 tons. Tendulkar's eighteenth came four years after his first in Colombo in 1994. Of course, the number of games played by the Indians in the late 1990s was also a factor. But it took Sachin 46 innings (in his hundred and ninety-eighth ODI) fewer than the West Indian and that is the true barometer. Ten of Tendulkar's tons had come abroad and the rest at home. It meant that Indian batsmen now held the record for most centuries in Tests (34 by Sunil Gavaskar) and ODIs. Sachin's 127 not out in India's eight-wicket win was his sixth of the year, and there would be more to follow.

The golden run of the Indian team had begun in Dhaka. Now it was back to the Bangladeshi capital for the inaugural ICC mini-World Cup knockout tournament. The tournament was a success, with huge crowds at the Bangabandhu Stadium for every match. South Africa lifted the Wills Trophy, beating the West Indies by four wickets in the final. Tendulkar left his mark on the tournament in the third quarter-final where India faced Australia, this time minus Warne and McGrath.

Ganguly and Azhar went early to make it 8 for 2. Then Tendulkar and Dravid began the rebuilding and Jadeja weighed in with 71 to take India past the 300-run mark. Tendulkar was awesome. Some of the shots he pulled off were extraordinary. He hit five cracking fours off Kasprowicz, but early on decided not to take the aerial route. By the time he was smartly run out for 141 from 127 balls, he had smashed 13 fours and three sixes and the Indian total of 307 for 8 was a formidable one.

Australia too began well. They were 145 for 2 when Tendulkar was tossed the ball and started conjuring up wickets with his assortment of 'offies' and 'leggies'. He accounted for Steve Waugh, caught and bowled, and then added Michael Bevan, Damien Martyn and Brad Young to his bag. The final figures: 9.1-0-38-4. Only Viv Richards has scored a century and taken five wickets in an ODI. Tendulkar came pretty close, and the Australians were all out for 263. He listed the 141 as his greatest innings in an interview with Sebastian Coe (*Daily Telegraph,* 6 May 2001): 'Nobody expected us to win. It was the day that everything came together. I can still remember almost every stroke I played that day.'

The innings also took Sachin past his own record for most ODI runs in a year. In 1996 he had 1611 in 32 matches. Now in 1998, in 34 matches (33 innings, four not out) he would compile 1894 runs at 65.31, with nine 100s and seven 50s, at a strike rate of 102.10! But India's run in the tournament came to an end in the next match, the semi-final against the West Indies, in which they were beaten by six wickets with Tendulkar out at eight.

It was back to Sharjah then, for the Coca-Cola Champions Trophy, with Zimbabwe and Sri Lanka as the competition. And it would be another trophy in the bag for the Indians. Despite both their prolific openers falling cheaply, India won their opening match against the Sri Lankans by three wickets. It was an unhappy week for the world champions as they lost all four of their matches to make it a rare Zimbabwe v India final. Tendulkar notched up his twentieth century against Zimbabwe for a grand total of 36 centuries in international cricket, taking him past Sunil Gavaskar, Viv Richards and Desmond Haynes, all of whom had a combined Test and ODI total of 35 centuries.

There was a surprise in the return encounter. By this time, the Sri Lankans were eliminated and the Indians were not at either full strength or full pace. It was the ideal opportunity for Henry Olonga to prove a point and he did so forcefully and dramatically. Chasing a meagre total of 205 for 7, the Indian batsmen were rocked by a searing spell from the dreadlocked fast bowler, in which he had the prize scalps of Ganguly, Tendulkar, Dravid and Jadeja—the cream of the crop. Tendulkar was surprised by one that took off nastily and had him groping with his bat held high, to be caught by Grant Flower for 11. It was Olonga's first match of the tournament and the fact that he made a master like Tendulkar look uncomfortable at the crease was the talking point when the two teams met in the final 48 hours later.

There was no doubt that Tendulkar's ego had been dented. He has always taken it as a personal challenge to go after the best bowler in the opposition, as in the case of McGrath and Warne. This time it was Olonga. Zimbabwe's total of 196 for 9 was never going to be enough. But their bowlers could scarcely have foreseen the hammering ahead of them. The total was passed with contemptuous ease in just 30 overs. And perhaps for the first time in a tournament, without the loss of a single wicket. It was India's fifth tournament title of the year in their record-breaking fortieth ODI in 1998. They also won the ODI series in Zimbabwe.

Tendulkar's 124 not out was virtually double that of his partner Ganguly's contribution (63), a measure of his total domination at the crease. Olonga came in for special treatment. His figures: 6-0-50-0. A far cry from his performance just two days earlier. Tendulkar's century was his fastest (and the fourth fastest of all), from 71 balls, and had a final boundary tally of six sixes and 12 fours. It was close to the Indian record held by Azhar (62 balls). The first 50 took only 28 balls, inclusive of four sixes and five fours. The stand with Ganguly fetched 112 in the first 15 overs as Tendulkar went hell for leather after a dropped catch when he was on 53, off leg-spinner Paul Strang who was carted for 45 runs from his five overs. Forty-one were smashed from Olonga's first four overs, 28 of which came from Tendulkar's bat. One six was slashed over backward point, the ball picked from well outside off stump. Before that came an extra cover drive. Then he pulled the hapless bowler from outside off stump. In desperation, Olonga tried a slower ball, to no avail. The ball landed in the stands, above widish long off. A chastened Olonga was taken off and forced to lick his wounds.

Tendulkar had another world record to his credit—32 Man of the Match awards in 207 matches, against 31 in 187 by Viv Richards. 'I decided to enjoy my batting. I thought that the final was the right time to play some shots. The pitch was really good today and the ball came on nicely,' he said after the magnificent innings. 'Olonga is an international bowler. He can bowl some good deliveries and he got my wicket. I accept that. But I went to the nets and worked on my batting.' As he said later in the year, he had a point to prove: that he could be taken by suprise once, but it wasn't going to happen everyday.

Looking back on that triumphant year, Azhar described Tendulkar as the team's 'pillar of strength'.

There was just enough time in the calendar to squeeze in one final tour, this one to New Zealand for three Tests and five ODIs, which spilled over into January 1999. India had not won a series in New Zealand since the first in 1967-68 and the trend continued as they were beaten 1-0 while the ODI series was locked at 2-2. After the first Test had been completely washed out, New Zealand won the second at Wellington by four wickets, despite centuries by Azhar and Tendulkar. The third ended in a draw.

Following his golden year, Tendulkar made an inauspicious start to 1999, out for a duck in the first ODI at Taupo. He followed with scores of 23, 45 and 5, but had to miss the fifth and final match at Christchurch (the third was a 'no-result') after suffering a wrist injury in the fourth game at Auckland.

It was an ominous beginning to a year that would be marked by tragedy.

24

Trauma

Never leave something that you can do to someone else.—Sunil Gavaskar

At the start of 1999, all the talk in cricket and political circles was whether or not the Pakistanis would make it to India for a Test series for the first time since 1987. The ruling Bharatiya Janata Party had to overcome a dissenting voice in their coalition, from the Shiv Sena, and not for the first time either. In 1991, the Shiva Sena had dug up the pitch at the Wankhede Stadium in their stronghold of Mumbai, forcing the series against Pakistan to be cancelled. The proposed tours of 1993 and 1994 were cancelled too, in the wake of political protests. In 1996, the World Cup organizers made sure not to allot any of the knockout stage matches to Mumbai in case one of them turned out to be an India-Pakistan clash—which is exactly what occurred in the quarter-finals, allotted to Bangalore. As a result, Mumbai cricket fans had to be content with the India v Australia league match.

The Shiv Sena were up to their old tricks this time, too. In a carefully planned pre-dawn raid—having made sure a bevy of reporters, cameramen and photographers had been informed in advance—they proceeded to dig up the pitch at the Feroze Shah Kotla in New Delhi, the venue of the first Test. As a result, venues had to be switched and Chennai hosted the first Test; the second (and final) Test moved to the capital. The Pakistanis would also stay on to play a Test at Kolkata as part of the inaugural Asian Test championships and then a triangular one-day series with India and Sri Lanka. After that it would be off to Sharjah. So India-Pakistan cricket was very much the flavour of the season—all this in the run-up to the big event, the World Cup in

England.

The huge strain on the Indian cricketers would continue for another year—since 1996, they had played a phenomenal number of matches. But this was the last thing on the minds of the politicians and the game's administrators. What mattered was that the Pakistan tour of India should go off without a hitch. In the end, the series was drawn 1-1 and there was much goodwill all around. There was some fantastic cricket too, to match the victories on the diplomatic front.

In 1987, in the last India v Pakistan Test on Indian soil, Pakistan had prevailed by 16 runs at Bangalore despite an epic 96 by Sunil Gavaskar. The target for India, then, was 221. Now, 12 years later, history would repeat itself in another southern city where Pakistan came out on top by 12 runs. And it was the turn of Gavaskar's successor to the tag of 'Little Master' to script an epic innings in vain. 'Another Greek tragedy' was how one Indian writer described the Test, as India fell just short of the victory target of 271.

It was certainly an amazing four days of cricket at the MA Chidambaram Stadium at Chepauk, Chennai—scene of the second tied Test in 1986. The Indians had got back from New Zealand just a week earlier and were now plunged into a Test that was gripping from start to finish. The first day's honours belonged to the hosts. Pakistan were shot out for 238 with Anil Kumble picking up six wickets in a harbinger of things to come. India were 48 for no loss at stumps, with debutant opener S.Ramesh delighting his home crowd with a flurry of boundaries off Wasim Akram and Waqar Younis. On the second day, Tendulkar perished to the third ball he faced, caught by Salim Malik at gully off Saqlain Mushtaq for a rare duck, as he attempted an ambitious shot. The Pakistanis were beside themselves with joy and Saqlain's 5 for 94 restricted the Indian lead to 16.

This time it was the turn of Venkatesh Prasad to do the damage with the ball; he claimed six wickets. Tendulkar too made a couple of important breakthroughs by accounting for Inzamam-ul-Haq and Yousuf Youhanna, whom he had dismissed in the first innings, too. Despite a maiden Test century by Shahid Afridi, Pakistan collapsed from 275 for 4 to 286 all out and the target for India was 271. On a pitch that had turned from day one, it was not likely to be an easy task.

That India got so close was almost entirely due to Tendulkar and his partnership of 136 for the sixth wicket with Nayan Mongia. Only one other batsman reached double figures (Dravid: 10). With Saqlain again collecting five wickets and Waqar and Wasim striking vital blows, India were tottering at 82 for 5 when Tendulkar was joined by the wicketkeeper. What transpired was intensely competitive cricket as the last recognized pair for India sought to keep out the rampaging Pakistani bowlers. It brought the crowd, silenced by the batting collapse, back to life. Tendulkar revealed a new facet of his supreme batsmanship—the ability to graft for runs and play a long innings. Not that he could resist attacking the bowlers. Saqlain went for four fours in an over and both Wasim and Waqar felt the full power of his strokes. In the same over, he had a big slice of luck when on 90 he charged the off-spinner, got an inside edge and saw keeper Moin Khan drop the catch and miss the stumping, too.

By the time he reached his eighteenth century—his first against Pakistan, in his sixty-fifth Test—panic was beginning to surface in the rival camp. Runs were flowing freely. At the other end, Mongia was providing Tendulkar with admirable support. But by now, Sachin was in obvious pain. He could be seen clutching his back and agony was evident on his face when he played his shots. India were just 53 runs away from a famous victory when Mongia had a rush of blood and paid the price. He made a wild slog to mid-off from the bowling of Akram and was caught by Younis for 54. At the other end, Tendulkar was seething with rage at the sight of the rash shot. It would be a long time before he could bring himself to forgive his teammate.

Thirty-six runs were added in the company of Sunil Joshi before Tendulkar, hampered by back spasms, threw away his wicket after an innings spanning 405 minutes and 273 balls. Desperate to finish the match before being overcome by pain, he took a swipe at Saqlain and was held by Akram at mid-off for 136 at 254 for 7.

This was just the breach the Pakistanis were looking for and the rest of the Indian batting subsided meekly to hand over victory to the ecstatic Pakistanis. In the despondent Indian dressing room, Tendulkar was a shattered man. He had battled the heat, the pain and 11 determined Pakistanis to take his side to the doorstep of victory. That he could not complete the task is something that has haunted him ever since.

'I should have reached the target myself. I was striking the ball well but when the strain aggravated, I could not go through with the follow through. Every time I tried, the pain increased,' he said after his epic. Looking on was Raj Singh Dungarpur. 'I saw Gundappa Visvanath make an undefeated 97 in a score of 191 at Chepauk against the West Indies (in 1975). I would rate Tendulkar's innings in adverse circumstances above that. Because we know Tendulkar as an attacking batsman. It is ingrained in him. Today he showed us all a different facet which should make Capt. Hazare, Visvanath and Sunil Gavaskar proud,' he said (*Sportstar*, 13 February 1999).

That 97 not out against a rampaging Andy Roberts and Gavaskar's 96 against Pakistan have long been rated as the best Indian innings against pace and spin. Now Tendulkar was nudging them off the pedestal. But it's interesting to note that only Visvanath's masterpiece had resulted in an Indian victory.

Four days later, the teams were in New Delhi for the second Test. There was speculation whether Tendulkar would be able to play. It was obvious that he was not fully fit, and the final decision was left to the batsman himself. The feeling in the Indian camp was that even a partially fit Tendulkar would be a psychological boost to the side after his masterly display at Chepauk. Though he did eventually make it to the side, he played only a minor role (6 and 29) in India's decisive win by 212 runs.

The match will go down in cricket history for Anil Kumble's fantastic feat in the Pakistan second innings of taking all ten wickets, only the second man to do so after Jim Laker against Australia in 1956.

The first triangular Test tournament since 1912, the Asian Test championship, the brainchild of Jagmohan Dalmiya, got off to a stormy start at Kolkata less than a fortnight after Kumble's 'Perfect Ten'. It was India v Pakistan again in the pressure-cooker atmosphere of Eden

Gardens. The first four days attracted crowds in excess of 100,000. Yet, the end of the Test was played out in front of empty stands.

That Pakistan eventually won by 46 runs was astonishing, considering they found themselves in the doldrums at 26 for 6 after nine overs from Srinath and Prasad on the first morning. Then came the first of many fight-backs by the Pakistanis as they reached 185 all out. India, in its innings, tumbled from 147 for 2 to 223 all out. Shoaib Akhtar created a sensation by bowling Tendulkar for a first ball duck, knocking out his middle stump through sheer pace. It was the third 'golden' duck of Sachin's Test career stretching over a decade. With his previous ball, the fast bowler had bowled Dravid for 24.

The third day belonged to Saeed Anwar and Srinath, both of whom recorded career-best performances. The left-handed opener carried his bat for 188, the highest score by a Pakistani in India, while Srinath returned figures of 8 for 86 for a match haul of 13 wickets. India were left to chase 279 for victory.

On the fourth day, Tendulkar came to the wicket at 134 for 2, openers Ramesh and V.V.S. Laxman having put on 108 runs. He began confidently with a four off Akram, when disaster struck on the thirteenth delivery he faced, also from Akram, which he punched to midwicket. Substitute Nadeem Khan (on for Anwar) made an astonishing throw from 75 yards as Sachin went for the third run, his eyes on the trajectory of the ball. As a result, he did not notice Akhtar who had positioned himself near the stumps for the throw. The two collided and the bat got tangled between the fielder's legs. It was grounded for a split second before the collision which knocked it into the air, even as the throw crashed into the stumps. West Indies umpire Steve Bucknor consulted his colleague Dave Orchard of South Africa and third umpire K.T.Francis was called in. Francis pressed the dreaded red button and a dejected Tendulkar started the walk back.

Azharuddin came to the crease as the crowd roared in fury, accusing Akhtar of having deliberately obstructed Tendulkar. Instead of retreating to the dressing room, Tendulkar stormed into the TWI TV control room to watch the replays in the company of match referee 'Cammie' Smith. Neither was allowed to express his views but

Tendulkar could be seen shaking his head while Smith draped a consoling arm around him. Play had already resumed and there was no way the decision could have been reversed. But by now missiles were raining down on the fielders and Akram led his team off.

ICC president Jagmohan Dalmiya, in his own backyard, persuaded Tendulkar to accompany him round the ground in a bid to pacify the crowd. After a break of over an hour, play re-started, though the crowd and the Indian camp were still seething. So, was the decision correct or not? The rule book states a batsman can be given not out in such a situation only if he leaves the crease to avoid the possibility of being injured. That was not the case, as Tendulkar had not spotted Akhtar in his path. The only question which remained unanswered was whether Akhtar had deliberately obstructed the batsman's path.

Raju Bharathan, writing in the *Sportstar* (13 March 1999), certainly thought so.

> Shoaib Akhtar was showing himself to be no more than a skilful practitioner of the modern-day stratagem of 'crossing the path' of the batsman (running to the bowler's end) in such an artful way as to make it look as if he was doing nothing more than posturing himself to receive the Nadeem Khan throw. That Akhtar (from the pin pointed corner of his left eye) saw Sachin come dashing down and created that 'gap' between his legs for Tendulkar's bat to 'find', is a fact. But then nothing that Akhtar did here could be legally viewed as the action replay of a man studiedly blocking Sachin's way.

Pakistan captain Wasim Akram could have exercised his prerogative and withdrawn the appeal, though there would have been all hell to pay across the border if he had done so. Reportedly, Pakistan manager Shahryar Khan (a career diplomat) and Pakistan Cricket Board chairman Khalid Mehmood were keen to make the gesture of getting Tendulkar recalled. But coach Javed Miandad put his foot down and the decision stayed.

It is doubtful if the crowd would have reacted the way it did if the batsman had been any other than their favourite. V.Srivatsa captured the mood well when he wrote in the *Times of India*: 'Tendulkar is the body and soul of Indian cricket. Every time he gets out cheaply his teammates and millions of cricket fans miss a heartbeat or two and today their hearts must have ached seeing the way he got out.'

Sadly, there was more trouble on the final morning. India needed 65 to win with four wickets in hand. And the match ended up being played virtually 'in camera' with only the media, officials and club members present after the spectators had been brutally chased away by the Kolkata police. Stones and other objects were once again hurled on to the ground when three quick wickets fell and India were on the brink, at 231 for 9. Dalmiya was adamant that there would not be a repeat of the 1996 World Cup semi-final. A recurrence would have proved a huge embarrassment and could have resulted in the blacklisting of Kolkata as an international venue.

So, three hours of police action later, the game resumed. It lasted only ten minutes and following Akhtar's removal of last man Venkatesh Prasad, the frenzied Pakistani celebrations began.

Subsequently, a high-scoring draw ensued in Colombo between India and Sri Lanka. Tendulkar's nineteenth century on the final day must have also been one of his easiest (and most unsatisfying), as the match was dead and buried by then.

Pakistan were already assured of a place in the final when they took on Sri Lanka in the last league match at Lahore. Determined to ensure that India would not meet them in the final at Dhaka, they cynically gifted away bonus points to Sri Lanka. The final, four days later, was a cakewalk as Pakistan romped home by an innings and 175 runs. But the manner of their victory left a sour taste.

By now, the strain on Tendulkar's back was going from bad to worse. The World Cup was not far away and yet, there lay ahead of the team even more one-day tournaments. The Pepsi tri-series with Pakistan and Sri Lanka at home was to be played in March and the BCCI was frantically trying to dispel all talk of Tendulkar's injury keeping him out of action—perhaps to keep the sponsors quiet. Three weeks before the opening match, the inimitable Board secretary J.Y.

Lele came up with one of his characteristic comments on the issue. The report that Sachin's family wanted him to take a break was, he said, 'absolutely bogus. It is absurd and there is no truth in it at all.' Needless to say, the 'bogus' statement turned out to be true, and a reluctant Indian team went through their paces, to be beaten by Pakistan in the final.

There had been rumblings of dissent within the Indian camp about the event, with many players feeling the strain of so much non-stop cricket. The Board, though, would have none of it. The result was a series of listless performances by a jaded Indian team against the rampaging Pakistanis. From there it was back to Sharjah and another tri-series, this time with Pakistan and England, just a month before the start of the World Cup in England. Once again, India were without the still-resting Tendulkar, and once again they lost in the final to Pakistan.

But there was another honour for Sachin that year. On 23 March 1999, he was back at the Rashtrapati Bhavan for another 'audience' with President K.R. Narayanan. This time, it was to receive the Padma Shri, India's fourth highest civilian honour. 'I am very proud of you and carry on the good work,' were the President's words as he handed over the award.

'Will he, won't he?' was the question for millions of fans. With the World Cup round the corner, the speculation over Tendulkar's fitness reached fever pitch. He had flown to England for treatment from a back specialist. It was thought the intense heat and humidity in Chennai might have triggered off the pain. There was a huge sigh of relief, not only from India but the whole cricket world, when he was declared fit for the World Cup. But after the trauma of the back injury, tragedy was lurking round the corner.

25

Tragedy and Tears

It was my mother who prompted me to go and attend the nation's call.
—Sachin Tendulkar

The World Cup returned to England in 1999 after 16 years. In 1983, the Indian team led by Kapil Dev had stunned the world by lifting the Prudential World Cup. The media and the advertising hype in India in the run-up to cricket's biggest event was simply mind-boggling. It seemed that every company worth its salt, from manufacturers of televisions to soft drinks and everything else in between, had spent their annual ad budgets in one massive splurge on cricket. The sum being tossed around was a staggering Rs 250 crores.

Expectations were sky-high and the atmosphere was one of hysteria. Certainly, the Indian team had done little, either at home or abroad, to justify such enthusiasm. The stars of 1983 also had their day in the sun once again. There were reunions galore, and even a match pitting the team of 1983 against the team of 1999 at Mumbai. Sachin Tendulkar was the star—again—with a century. Which only confirmed what he had said a few years earlier—that he took his batting seriously even in exhibition matches.

Once again, Azharuddin led the team, as he had done in 1992 and 1996. There was no doubt in anybody's mind, though, about where the team's hopes actually rested. In May 1999, Tendulkar made it to the cover of the Asian edition of *Time* magazine (16 May 1999). Inside, the players expected to dominate the tournament were profiled.

The Bombay Bomber's blazing batting performances have earned him comparisons with Diego Maradona—it helps that they are both short, stocky and curly-haired. But unlike the Argentine ace, Tendulkar is a levelheaded, even bland professional who does all his hell-raising at the wicket. He wields the heaviest bat in the game, both literally and figuratively and is a quick reader of bowlers and wicket conditions. Ask Shane Warne: regarded by most batsmen as unplayable, the leg spinner was brutalized by Tendulkar throughout the 1998 Australian tour of India. Later, Warne said he had nightmares about Tendulkar's flashing blade.

It's difficult to single out a standout Tendulkar performance, as there are so many—and so many to come. He already owns the record for most ODI centuries, and he has at least 10 years ahead of him. Gulp!

India were in Group A with hosts England, Kenya, South Africa, holders Sri Lanka and Zimbabwe. Group B consisted of Australia, New Zealand, West Indies, Pakistan, Scotland and Bangladesh. The top three teams from each group would advance to the Super Six stage under a complex system of points and the top four would then go on to the semi-finals.

India's opening match at Hove on 15 May was against South Africa, one of the favourites. India started well after electing to bat first and Tendulkar (28) and Ganguly (97) put on 67 runs. Tendulkar was caught behind off Lance Klusener, just after striking a delightful cover drive to the boundary. The final total of 253 for 5 was a challenging one. Openers Gary Kirsten and Herschelle Gibbs were both claimed by Srinath with the score at 22 before Jacques Kallis took over. When he was run out for 96, South Africa needed 27 from 26 balls. Klusener, the new man in, promptly struck the first three deliveries for four and his team were home by four wickets with 2.4 overs to spare.

It was a disappointing start to the Indian campaign. But then, South Africa were undoubtedly one of the strongest teams in the tournament. The next match, four days later, at Leicester, was against Zimbabwe and the Indian camp was confident it would earn its first points. It was not to be. Not only did the African team stun India in a last-over thriller, but there was an even more disturbing piece of news for Tendulkar the night before the game. His father, Dr Ramesh Tendulkar, had died in Mumbai of a heart attack in his home in Bandra, late on 18 May, at the age of 66. He had been ailing for some time.

My first thought on hearing the news was the same that must have crossed the minds of millions of Indian cricket fans—would Sachin continue at the World Cup or return home? I immediately felt a pang of guilt for thinking so, and I am sure I was not alone in that either. Sachin did indeed return to Mumbai to attend his father's funeral and missed the match against Zimbabwe. He left in the early hours of 19 May with tears in his eyes. Few in the team were aware of what had happened. At 10.30 in the night, coach Anshuman Gaekwad took the call from Mumbai, and was asked to convey the tragic news to Sachin. But he did not have the heart to do so, and turned to Anjali for help. Both Anjali and daughter Sara were in London at the time. The three took the first available flight home from London, early on the morning of the Zimbabwe match.

Ironically, it was at Leicester (which has a large Indian population) that Dr Tendulkar, ten years earlier, had given a lecture on Marathi literature. He had retired six years ago from Kirti College in Mumbai, where he taught Marathi. He had also taught at Sidharth College. Sachin's brothers Ajit and Nitin had been with the team at Hove. They were in Chicago when they received the news.

Even as the demoralized Indians were self-destructing against Zimbabwe, the talk on the streets centred on the tragedy. It was as if the nation was in collective grieving with their favourite son. The players had woken up on the morning of 19 May, stunned to hear the news and learn of their teammate's distress and departure. Understandably, Gaekwad was in no mood to ask Sachin if and when he planned to return. There was no pressure from the Board either. 'I know how close he was to his father. We have to wait for the funeral before we can even think of asking him. I shall keep in touch with him,' the coach told the reporters from India.

A minute's silence was observed before the match at the Grace Road ground. S.Ramesh had the unenviable task of replacing Tendulkar at the top of the order and he did a more than competent job as he top-scored with 55. All through the flight from London to Mumbai, Sachin's mind was on the progress of his team. One of the flight pursers kept coming to him with the latest score. 'Through him I came to know that we lost closely. I was sorry I could not do anything under the circumstances.' Chasing Zimbabwe's 252 for 9, India who had been docked four overs for a slow over-rate by their old nemesis, match referee 'Cammie' Smith, lost by three runs with their last three wickets thrown away in the final over bowled by Henry Olonga.

Back in Mumbai, the funeral of Prof. Tendulkar was a family affair with just a few close friends (Vinod Kambli and Amol Muzumdar) and Mumbai cricket officials in attendance. The time had been brought forward to dawn to avoid the media scramble. A sign was put outside the family residence, requesting people not to pay their condolences. Eldest son Nitin performed the last rites at the Shivaji Park electric crematorium in Central Mumbai. The mourners were personally thanked by Sachin who stood at the exit along with Ajit.

In a touching tribute under the headline, 'God Rewarded Prof. Tendulkar', Sunil Gavaskar wrote in the *Times of India* (28 May 1999):

> The late Ramesh Tendulkar did not watch too many of his son, Sachin's innings at a cricket ground. Even at home he used to watch the highlights rather than the live coverage on TV.
>
> Now he would have seen how not only millions and millions of Indians but even the Gods stop everything to watch his son play. He now has a special place to see his youngest son go on to become the greatest batsman the world has ever seen.

Gavaskar recalled how Prof. Tendulkar (when he was teaching at Sidharth College in the 1960s and 1970s) helped the cricketers of Bombay University. 'He would take extra classes and tuition for these cricketers [who were playing in the inter-varsity Vizzy Trophy] to ensure that they were able to catch up with their studies and get through and not lose a year. So when young Tendulkar started to bat the way he does, plenty of people who knew about the senior Tendulkar's contribution were sure it was God's way of rewarding him with a son as talented as Sachin.'

Prof. Tendulkar had last been seen in public with Sachin and Anjali at a cricket awards function in Mumbai a month before his death. A low-profile man, he stayed out of the spotlight even as he watched his son grow up to become a national icon.

Atmaram 'Bapu' Bhende, the doyen of Marathi theatre, had known Prof. Tendulkar for many decades. Mr Bhende is married to my father's sister, Dr Asha Bhende. (In September 2001, when I met Ajit Tendulkar in Mumbai and told him of the relationship, his reaction was, 'Bapu? He is a great legend.') I asked Mr Bhende to share with me his memories.

Mr Bhende recalled in a letter sent to me in November 2001, how he first met Ramesh Tendulkar when he invited him to attend a *kavi sammelan* (poets' meet) organized by the Indian National Theatre (of which he was secretary of the Marathi section) in the mid-1950s.

> I was charmed by his gentle, soft spoken and cordial manner. A true gentleman, ever ready to extend a helping hand to anyone who needed it. I was particularly impressed by his frank but without malice opinions of the work of other poets. I was particularly interested in bringing together budding poets with the specific intention of bringing them into the limelight. Ramesh Tendulkar was helpful in identifying such poets and contacting them.... Those who knew Ramesh Tendulkar intimately, know that Sachin's modesty is a gift from his father.
>
> I met Ramesh quite accidentally just a few days before his untimely death. We were both invited to a suburban college literary function. The car organized by them first picked up Ramesh and then arrived at my residence. Ramesh rushed into my living room and we met like two long lost friends. Certainly, a moment to cherish. And remember, Ramesh had not changed—the same handsome face, winsome smile, the same

warmth, the same genuine friendliness. The long years in between just melted away.

One seldom comes across such a straightforward and unassuming person, who in reality had so much to boast of! His death was not only a great loss to his family and the Marathi literary world, but also to his large circle of friends, admirers and well wishers.

Since his death, his children have brought out a book of his Marathi poems. The eldest, Nitin, is also a poet, obviously inspired by his father.

Meanwhile, the Indian World Cup campaign appeared to be heading for an early and inglorious end after two defeats in the first two matches. In India, there were strident calls for Azharuddin to be axed before the next game against Kenya on 23 May. Passions were running high and the phone calls from viewers to the morning television show I hosted, were getting increasingly irate and abusive. I realized just how ugly things had become when a furious fan at a petrol station near the studios accosted me. He demanded to know why I was calling for the Indian captain to be retained.

Back in Mumbai, Sachin had made the decision to fly back to England. The news came as a huge relief for the team and its followers. For 24 hours after his father's funeral, it seemed no one could talk of anything else. At the *Times of India* office in the heart of New Delhi, traffic came to a standstill. 'Sachin flying back' was the headline on the giant electronic bulletin board. Buses and cars screeched to a halt, people stood and stared as if they could not believe their eyes. Salvation for the beleaguered Indians was on its way.

'It was my mother who prompted me to go and attend the nation's call. She said even my father would have liked me to go and do my duty,' Tendulkar told reporters at Heathrow airport on his arrival back in England, the morning before the crucial game against Kenya. 'I realize this match is important and we are keen to make a winning impression. We have to win all three matches and keep the hopes of our supporters high. It's not going to be easy to put behind the tragedy and concentrate on the job at hand.'

Tendulkar added, 'The entire country wanted me to play. The World Cup is very important to India. I therefore completed all formalities and took the first available flight to be here with the team.' Gaekwad marvelled at Sachin's composure, and said he had no words to describe his star player's gesture. 'We will do everything to keep Sachin's mind occupied. In any case, he is a restless person.'

'I thought he might make it for the match against Sri Lanka on 26 May. Even in this hour of grief Sachin could not resist coming to the rescue of the team which, as has been proved, cannot do without this man.'

Ten days into the World Cup, the first century of the tournament was recorded. And it was scored by a man who had attended his father's funeral just a few days earlier. What more monumental tribute can there be to his skills, discipline and mental strength?

India won by 94 runs to breathe fresh life into its campaign to reach the next stage. A full house at Bristol (8508) gave Tendulkar three standing ovations—first when he walked to the crease, then when he reached his twenty-second century, and finally when he walked off with fellow centurion Rahul Dravid at the end of India's innings of 329 for 2—Tendulkar on 140 and Dravid on 104. The unbroken stand of 237 in 29 overs was the highest ever in the World Cup (until India's next match against Sri Lanka). Sachin's previous ODI centuries had all come when he was opening. This time he came in after Ramesh, for after the young man's half-century against Zimbabwe, it had been decided to retain him as Ganguly's opening partner. Sachin's first 50 came in 54 balls; the second took 30. A look heavenwards in silent tribute to his father marked the completion of the 100. 'I just looked up. It's very difficult to explain what I felt.' The last ball of the innings was flicked disdainfully over midwicket for six, just as Viv Richards had done in the 1979 World Cup finals.

The century was dedicated to his father. Choking with emotion at the post-match awards ceremony—even Tony Greig appeared overcome when interviewing him—he said he had been motivated by his mother's words when he reached Mumbai for the funeral. 'The first question my mother asked me was why did I come back. She said even your father would have wanted you to stay on. I had gone home because I was committed to my family. Similarly, I also have commitment towards my country and countrymen.' He admitted it had not been his best 100. 'But under the circumstances it was special.'

Prime Minister Atal Behari Vajpayee sent a congratulatory fax to the Man of the Match. 'Not only did you not let the deep personal loss caused by your father's sudden demise deter you but you actually used it as an inspiration to scale another summit in cricketing excellence. The whole of India is proud of you.'

Less than three years later, another tragedy would cast its shadow over Tendulkar's life.

India won their next two matches against Sri Lanka and England to make it to the Super Six. They were joined by Zimbabwe and South Africa from Group A and Australia, Pakistan and New Zealand from Group B. Australia simply blew away India in the first match in the Super Stage game. The big breakthrough came when Glenn McGrath had Tendulkar caught behind for his first duck in 22 innings, with just one run on the board. His three previous innings against Australia had produced centuries. Australia had, in its innings, piled up 282 for 6. No team had scored 283 to win an ODI in England and now, with his first four overs, McGrath had ensured it would not happen at the Oval either. India were staggering at 17 for 4 and were all out for 205. The team's chances of qualifying for the semi-finals were now all but dead. But their next match against Pakistan took on an extra edge.

The conflict in Kargil was still raging back home and the Old Trafford authorities were concerned over a flare-up between rival spectators. The flare-up never happened, and India won a tense match by 47 runs. It was the third time India and Pakistan had met in the World Cup and each time India had come out on top. Tendulkar was back in the opener's slot and blazed briefly for 45. Despite the win, India were playing only for pride in their final match against New Zealand, who had to win to reach the last four—which is exactly what they did. Australia went on to win the World Cup for the second time, beating Pakistan in a lopsided final.

The Indian campaign had started and ended with a whimper. In between, there were some wonderful moments, notably Tendulkar's century against Kenya and the victories over England and Pakistan. But overall, the cricket was disappointing and lacked consistency, as always. All the pre-tournament hysteria had rapidly fizzled out. Tendulkar's form too was patchy. He had 253 runs at 42.17. But under the circumstances, it was a huge credit to him that he made it back at all after the loss of his father.

26

Reluctant Messiah

If Sachin says no, he will be making a big mistake.—Ajit Wadekar

'Always bat first, Azhar, always bat first,' was Bishan Singh Bedi's anguished cry as he watched, on television, the Indian captain put Australia in at the start of India's first Super Six match on 4 June. Just as it had happened three years earlier, at Kolkata in the Wills World Cup semi-final, this time too the move backfired. With the huge defeat that followed, India's hopes of making it to the semi-finals were virtually dashed. And so were Azharuddin's hopes of holding on to the captaincy. The fact that he stayed on in England for surgery on his shoulder made the decision of the selectors somewhat easier when they met in Nagpur on 28 July to announce Azhar's successor.

Nothing is what it seems in Indian cricket. There is always a story behind the story, and more so when it concerns the never-ending soap opera that is the captaincy of the Indian cricket team. And so it transpired this time too, as the committee consisting of chairman Ajit Wadekar, Madan Lal, Shivlav Yadav, Anil Deshpande and Ashok Malhotra, with BCCI Secretary J.Y.Lele in attendance, took all of 'two minutes' (Wadekar's words) to hand the mantle to Sachin Tendulkar once again, as they had done three years earlier. This, after taking more than an hour to trace BCCI president Raj Singh Dungarpur to get his telephonic consent.

'Only one name, that of Sachin, figured during the meeting and no other name came up for discussion,' according to the chairman. 'He is the best player in the team, is a thinker and has good rapport with his colleagues.' Then came the crucial question at the press conference, directed at Wadekar. Had Tendulkar's consent been taken by the Board? 'Not yet. But if Sachin says no (to the captaincy) he will be making a mistake. He has not written to the Board for not being chosen as captain.'

'Let's see if he refuses,' was what another selector was reported to have said. The day before the meeting, a number of papers had carried reports stating Tendulkar had informed the selectors he did not want to lead again. Consequently, Ajay Jadeja was considered a shoo-in for the post. 'Tendulkar Not Inclined to Lead India' was the headline in the *Hindu* (28 July). In a Chennai date-lined report, G. Viswanath wrote: '...the little champion has decided to keep himself clear off the hot seat for reasons best known to him and certain people in the BCCI. In the circumstances the selectors are not likely to look beyond Ajay Jadeja....'

On the day of the announcement, however, the plot thickened further. It seemed every sports journalist and cricket official in the country was trying to track down the new appointee. This was cloak-and-dagger stuff, Indian cricket style. There was one problem—no one had a clue as to where he was. And those who did, were tight-lipped. As Alice said in *Alice in Wonderland,* things were getting 'curiouser and curiouser'. Lele, Indian cricket's very own Mad Hatter, was in the thick of things. 'The telephone answering machine at Sachin's residence in Mumbai recorded the message of his appointment as he was away,' he told a PTI reporter in Nagpur.

He was indeed 'away'. But where? And why had he made himself incommunicado for over 24 hours? The air was full of theories and speculation. Was he in the family holiday home in the hill resort of Lonavala, not far from Mumbai? Was he in Bangalore? Or was he seeking the blessings and advice of his spiritual guru, Satya Sai Baba, at Puttaparti in Andhra Pradesh? Only family and close friends knew for sure. And no one was willing to come out with the facts.

Still, after lying low and keeping the country in suspense—will he, won't he?—the reluctant Messiah finally surfaced in Mumbai on 29 July, and announced he would be holding a press conference the next day to give his version of the dramatic events. Raj Singh conveyed the news to an anxious nation that Tendulkar had indeed accepted the appointment. By now, it was also revealed that the Board had earlier tried to persuade him to take up the captaincy, but he had refused. Finally, it had been presented to him as a virtual *fait accompli*.

Even by the normally chaotic standards of cricket press conferences, the one addressed by the new nominee at the Cricket Club of India in Mumbai on 30 July was pandemonium personified. It was a good ten minutes before Tendulkar could speak, as dozens of photographers and TV cameramen jostled for vantage positions.

Sachin disclosed that he had learnt about his appointment from the messages left on his answering machine, from phone calls and watching the news. 'Two days before the selection committee meeting, I told Mr Raj Singh, Mr Lele and Mr Wadekar, that I was not mentally prepared (to be made captain),' he said. 'I was not mentally prepared to take up the captaincy as it is the practice for the vice-captain to be named the next captain. I was not the vice-captain of the team since losing the captaincy [in January 1998].' He stressed four points: that he was proud to lead the country again and that it was an honour; that he had no problem with Azharuddin being in the team; that he would want more say in selection matters; and that he would open the batting in ODIs.

Not everyone was convinced. G.Rajaraman of the *Hindustan Times* (30 July 1999) asked in the headline: 'Is Azhar's Slot the Contentious Issue?'

> Even if it is the last thing we wanted, we will have to contend with the image of a reluctant and sulking leader, too. Sadly, it will stick for some time....If he cannot face pressure at the appointment, can he stand it when the heat is on?

There seemed little doubt, though, that at the back of Sachin's mind was the bitter memory of how he had been let down by the selectors and some teammates during his first tenure including Azhar, whom he would later name when questioned by the CBI. As the October 2000 *Report on Cricket Match-Fixing and Related Malpractices* says on page 89: 'On being asked whether he suspected any Indian player of being involved in match-fixing, Sachin stated that during his tenure as Captain, he had felt that Mohd. Azharuddin was not putting in 100% effort and he suspected that he was involved with some bookies.'

To get to the bottom of the mystery, I asked Wadekar to write down his views on the incident. He had earlier in a column stated that it was a mistake to appoint Sachin the second time round, against his wishes. This is what Wadekar wrote in a letter to me dated 6 October 2001:

> In 1999 it was clear that Azhar couldn't have been made captain as he was not in form. We tried Anil Kumble but he did not measure up to the requirements of the captain nor did he look very aggressive. We wanted Sourav Ganguly to lead instead but Mr Raj Singh, then president of the Board, interfered with our selection and told us point-blank in the selection committee meeting held at Kolkata (*sic*) that Sourav was a selfish person and wasn't liked by some of the players. Since he wouldn't have ratified our decision as president, it was senseless to appoint him as captain. Yes, Mr Raj Singh has a habit of dabbling in the selections all the time.
>
> Since there was nobody to take the reins of the captaincy, including reluctant Sachin, I thought I would persuade him to be the captain. I went to his home for this purpose. He was playing table tennis. He came up to his flat to meet me. When I opened the topic about the captaincy, he did not oppose it vehemently but he also did not show any joy on the matter and was rather hesitant to accept it or not.
>
> What he did not realize was that I wanted him to lead the Indian team for as long as he wanted to. I wanted him to be another Sir Donald Bradman who was not only a legend in batting all over the world but also a great captain....It was unfortunate that when he was appointed as a captain, he did not come out with the acceptance for nearly three days. In fact, he was not traceable at all....

What this meant was that Tendulkar was certainly not the only name in contention. And the selection meeting certainly took more than two minutes to decide! Tendulkar himself confirmed the meeting with Wadekar (though with a different perspective) in an interview to *Cricket Talk*: 'Yes, I did not want it [the captaincy]. When Ajit Wadekar came to my house at the start of the season last year [i.e., 1999], I told him that I was not interested in the job. He was supposed to inform the other selectors but I don't know what happened and I was asked to lead. . . .' (30 March 2000). Later, Wadekar wrote these words in a specially commissioned article for the 2001 Sachin birthday special for the *Indya.com* website where I was sports editor:

> It was really foolish on my part as chairman of the selection committee to force him to accept the captaincy. This despite the fact that he was very reluctant when I spoke to him at his place prior to the selection. He is not interested in the captaincy—he would prefer to relax by eating his favourite crabs at my place and then go out and smash the bowlers.

Questions remained, doubts lingered, about the captaincy controversy. But by late August, it was time for Tendulkar's first outing as captain in his second stint.

The Aiwa Cup in Sri Lanka pitted India against the hosts and Australia. It turned out to be something of a misadventure for the Indians, who won just one of their four matches and failed to make it to the final. India's first match on 23 August saw them trounced by eight wickets by the Aussies. Things hardly improved when they went down by seven wickets to Sri Lanka in their next match. Four Indian batsmen were run out, including the 'new' captain for 37. There was worse to come, however. On the morning of 28 August, when India were to take on Australia again, the captain awoke with a stiff back and ruled himself out of the match. Ajay Jadeja led the side that was beaten this time by 41 runs.

Tendulkar returned for the final league match, the only one which India would win. It was a make-or-break situation for the side and he chose to ignore his troublesome back. The match was marked by his twenty-third century and though India won by 23 runs, they were edged out of a place in the final on the net run rate. The captain had endured tremendous pain to reach his century, but in vain. The discomfort he was in was obvious when he hoicked spinner Uppal Chandana for six over long on, grimaced and clutched his back. Yet he soldiered on. Team doctor Ravinder Chadha treated him on the field after the fall of opener Ramesh's wicket.

There was much speculation in the media about the reasons for the recurrence of his back problem. Doctors, surgeons, physios, ex-players and journalists all had their say. The theories included excessive cricket, hot and humid conditions, the remarkably heavy bat Tendulkar wielded, even the position of his feet while making certain strokes. The general consensus was that the injury could curtail Tendukar's career.

Next stop for the team was the Singapore Challenge against Zimbabwe and the West Indies. Tendulkar (85) picked up another Man of the Match award against Zimbabwe, and the win was enough to ensure that India would meet the West Indies in the final. Tendulkar rested himself the next day for the inconsequential league match against the twice former world champions, and Ganguly led for the first time. The first final was abandoned due to rain with India struggling on 149 for 6 (Tendulkar: 40). It was worse when the match was replayed. Tendulkar was out without scoring, from the sixth ball of the match bowled by Courtney Walsh, who had taken his wicket in the abandoned final, too. This time the batsman took a chance but paid the price as Hendy Bryan held the juggling catch at third man. India's 254 for 6 was easily overhauled.

The Kargil conflict between India and Pakistan meant the two teams would not meet in the annual Sahara Cup at Toronto. Instead, the organizers arranged for two tournaments involving the West Indies—three matches each against India and Pakistan. The Indians and West Indians virtually flew across the planet and spent more than a day travelling between Sri Lanka and Canada. But India was without the services of their captain, who decided instead to fly to Adelaide to have his back examined by Dr Peter Barnes, a specialist at the Australian

Cricket Academy.

The prognosis was troubling. According to Dr Barnes, 'I think it would be a nuisance to him and probably restrict him. I guess in that sense it would probably limit his career... But he is such a great bat that he can probably bat with one leg and still make runs.' He felt Tendulkar had handled the problem pretty well for the last six months.

Dr Barnes said the Indian captain was suffering from spondylosis. 'There is some bony defect on either side of the spine down in the bottom half of the back.' He told a press conference in Adelaide on 4 September that the problem had been there long before it first surfaced in Chennai in January, during the Test match against Pakistan. Sachin had defects in the lower vertebrae and inflamed scar tissue had formed in the lower back region. It would be an estimated three to four weeks before he could return to cricket.

Once again, it was as if the entire nation had only one thing on its mind. As an irritated Sachin was to say (*Sportstar*, 19 February 2001):

> Whoever I met asked the same question, 'How is your back?' before they actually greeted me with a 'Hello'. It got to a point when it started affecting me. I did not feel like meeting anyone. I understood the feelings of the people but if I have to hear it a thousand times, 'How is your back?' and I have to answer it, it's frustrating. I am glad it's all over. It's part of any sportsperson's life. After playing for 11 years these are things which are bound to happen. There is going to be wear and tear. The fact is that the body has been used for so many years.

The break meant Tendulkar missed not only the DMC Cup in Toronto (India, led by Ganguly, beat the West Indies 2-1), but also the LG Cup in Nairobi, where Ajay Jadeja was captain and India lost in the final to South Africa.

27

Double—Then Trouble

I always wanted this double very badly.—Sachin Tendulkar

By October 1999, Sachin Tendulkar was back in the team after his enforced break. His first Test series was at home against New Zealand, a relatively soft start to his second innings as captain—or should one say, follow-on? Tendulkar was joined by a new coach, Kapil Dev, who had taken over from Anshuman Gaekwad. Kapil Dev had been with Tendulkar in his debut series, in Pakistan in 1989, and the two were known to be close. It was hoped this would open a new chapter in Indian cricket and that the dynamic Kapil could transfer his magic as a player to his new role as coach. Their first day in office was, however, anything but pleasant.

On a slightly damp pitch at Mohali, Stephen Fleming won the toss, put India into bat and shot them out for a shocking 83 in a mere 27 overs. Tendulkar (18) was one of only three batsmen to reach double figures. New Zealand's lead was 132. But that was wiped off by new openers Devang Gandhi and S.Ramesh in the second innings. This time, the top five all crossed 50 and two reached double figures—Rahul Dravid and the captain himself. At times, it appeared Tendulkar was batting from memory. Indeed, he survived a vociferous appeal for lbw from the very first ball from Nathan Astle, which was turned down by Sri Lankan umpire Peter Manuel. Eventually, India declared at 505 for 3—the first time that a side dismissed for under 100 in their first innings had crossed 500 in the second. Tendulkar's twentieth century was a sketchy one, perhaps due to lack of batting practice. He stayed at the crease for more than six and a half hours and got the benefit of numerous lbw appeals.

It took a stubborn 73 by captain Stephen Fleming in the second innings to stave off defeat as the visitors struggled to 251 for 7. But an Indian victory was duly delivered by the spin bowlers in the next Test at Kanpur. India coasted to victory by eight wickets, with the captain himself rattling off 44 not out, from 39 balls, in the second innings of 83 for 2.

The third and final Test at Ahmedabad should have been a triumph for both Tendulkar and the team. Instead, after scoring his first Test double century in a decade, Tendulkar courted controversy by his refusal to enforce a follow-on after leading by 275 runs. The match petered out into a draw and India took the series 1-0. The question of why the follow-on was not enforced was later taken up by the CBI in their investigation into match-fixing and corruption in Indian cricket. The coach and captain would eventually be exonerated of all wrongdoing late in 2001.

Sachin had recorded his first double century in first-class cricket in 1998, for Mumbai against the touring Australians. It had taken him five years to score his maiden ODI century and now, after ten years, came his first double ton in an international Test. The New Zealand attack may not have been the most potent in international cricket. But, after all the pain and trauma resulting from his back injury, it was indeed a sweet way to announce to the world of cricket that he was back at his best.

India were 311 for 3 on the first day at Ahmedabad, with S.Ramesh out for 110 and Tendulkar batting on 104. He had earlier been dropped at short third man by Astle on 93. Fleming had said then that his team might pay a price for the lapse and that is precisely what happened. The runs continued to pile up and Ganguly joined in the fun with 125. The 281 stand with Tendulkar for the fourth wicket was an Indian record and the team declared at 583 for 7.

There had been talk earlier that Tendulkar had neither the stamina nor the application to convert his bagful of Test tons into double centuries. Now he answered his critics with his longest innings yet: 494 minutes in all, during which he scored 217 from 343 balls. It was another psychological breakthrough, overtaking his previous highest of 179 against the West Indies at Nagpur in 1994. The 200 was reached when he placed Vettori to mid-on for a single. Non-striker Ajay Jadeja raced back to congratulate his captain. Sachin looked heavenwards in thanks. The Motera Stadium was once again witness to a milestone. This was the same ground where Sunil Gavaskar became the first to reach 10,000 runs and where Kapil Dev broke Sir Richard Hadlee's world Test wicket record. Sachin dedicated the double ton to his brother Ajit: 'He has been there for me for the past 10 years of international cricket.' He said it was only when he crossed 170 that the thought of the 200 entered his mind. 'I always wanted this double very badly.'

Sunil Gavaskar's Indian record of 236 not out was in sight when Tendulkar was dismissed by a brilliant catch, shortly after tea on the second day. It was a full-blooded pull off left-arm spinner Daniel Vettori which was held inches off the ground at midwicket by Nash. The batsman lingered and waited for the umpire's decision as he was not sure the ball had carried to the fielder.

Sadly, the sheen of achievement soon wore off. New Zealand were dismissed for 308. But India batted again in the second innings, finally declaring on 148 for 5. Set 424 to win in a possible 103 overs, New Zealand had no trouble saving the Test and finished on 252 for 2. So why was the follow-on not enforced? The explanation of the captain and the coach was that the four specialist bowlers wanted a rest after toiling in the blazing heat for nearly ten hours in New Zealand's first innings.

Not everyone was convinced. 'No captain of an international team wanting to win a Test convincingly would have wished away such a fine chance,' wrote G. Viswanath in the *Hindu* (2 November 1999). Ravi Shastri, one of Tendulkar's close friends and business associates, admitted he was 'befuddled' by the tactics. Former New Zealand captain Martin Crowe was more scathing in his column in *Rediff.com* (3 November 1999): 'The last thing Test cricket needs is this approach by the Indian captain Sachin Tendulkar. It was a disgrace that the tactical attitude to dismiss the opposition was not as positive as that of the batting.' The delayed declaration in the second innings was also condemned. 'It really shocked me that Tendulkar appeared to have to be cajoled by Kapil Dev before he did finally declare.' Inexplicably, one of the bowlers who had apparently demanded a break, Javagal Srinath (who bowled 35 overs in the first innings) came out to bat in the second innings and hung around for nearly half an hour to score 19 not out. Both he and the other not-out batsman, Jadeja, were constantly looking in the direction of the pavilion for the captain to call them in.

He did, eventually, after the second innings had consumed 32 overs, leaving the Indians with only 13 overs to have a go at their opponents on the fourth evening. He justified his strategy in an interview with Vijay Lokapally (*Sportstar*, 20 November 1999):

> Just spare a thought for the bowlers. They were tired. In the playing XI, we had a couple of players with health problems. There were a couple of others who also carried on despite some health problems....It was extremely hot that day (42 degrees) and they had bowled about 140 overs. Asking them to bowl another 160 at that stage would have meant someone might have had a breakdown. We didn't want that kind of situation and that is why we gave the bowlers a break. They tried their best I would say.

Tendulkar finished the series with a 100-plus average and got another chance to gorge himself on the mediocre Kiwi attack in the one-day series that followed. It was a high-scoring series and India were run close. They sealed a 3-2 verdict by winning the final game in New Delhi by seven wickets. It was a pretty mixed bag for the skipper. In the second match at Hyderabad, he recorded the highest score by an Indian in ODIs and the fourth highest of all time, 186. But in the other four matches he had scores of 32, 1, 2 and 0.

New Zealand had thrashed the Indian bowlers 349 for 9 in the first match at Rajkot—the highest ODI total on Indian soil. That record lasted just three days. India's 376 for 2 was the second highest ODI total of all time and the stand of 331 for the second wicket in 46 overs between Rahul Dravid and Tendulkar was the biggest ever partnership. Ganguly missed out on the run riot when bowler Shayne O'Connor deflected Tendulkar's firm push on to the non-striker's stumps, with the batsman out of his ground, in the second over. Tendulkar carried his bat, in the process erasing Ganguly's previous Indian highest of 183 against Sri Lanka in the 1999 World Cup. There were 20 fours and three sixes from the 150 balls he faced. He was on 182 when Chris Cairns bowled the last over and there was a huge buzz around the ground. Could he score the 13 needed to surpass Saeed Anwar's world record? It was not to be, though the Indian record was his.

The innings was marked by a number of innovative shots behind square leg. Sachin agreed after the innings that his shot selection had changed. 'Your style of batting should not become too predictable and should not be based on some set pattern,' he explained. 'This change in shot selection has come gradually as far as I am concerned.... The 186 was satisfying not because I set an individual mark. It was satisfying because we won the match. Tomorrow, someone may break the record but people would remember me for the contribution I made in winning the match for India.' (*Sportstar*, 20 November 1999)

The New Zealanders had acquitted themselves admirably. They lost the three-Test series narrowly, 1-0, and the five-match ODI series 3-2.

For Tendulkar and his men, the real test was round the corner in Australia, where the world Test and ODI champions were waiting.

28

Debacle Down Under

That bat is so heavy but he's got so much time, he waves it around like a toothpick.—Brett Lee

The team for Australia generated the usual debate and criticism, most of it centred on the exclusion of Mohammad Azharuddin and Nayan Mongia. 'Mongia was thought to be a self-centred cricketer, which could be debated and Azharuddin was obviously held in poor esteem by the new coach and also skipper Tendulkar. To be sidelined without a proper trial was not the best way to treat a senior cricketer like Azharuddin,' wrote Vijay Lokapally in the *Sportstar* (20 November 1999). By now, both the players were under a cloud of suspicion over their role in corrupt cricket practices. As we have seen in the excerpt from the CBI report, Tendulkar did not feel Azhar was giving 100 per cent during his first stint as captain. And Mongia's crazy shot in the closing stages of the Chennai Test against Pakistan was still, no doubt, fresh in his batting partner's mind. Tendulkar would also tell the CBI how furious he was with Prabhakar and Mongia for their notorious go-slow in the Kanpur ODI against the West Indies in 1994.

Bizarrely, Mongia did finally make it to Australia. But not for long. He was flown out as a backup for M.S.K. Prasad when it was thought he might not be fit for the second Test. He played in one match (against Tasmania), hung around for a while and then returned to India despondent, even as Prasad made a miraculous recovery. When he arrived in Australia, his reception by the captain and the coach was frosty. It was obvious that Tendulkar and Kapil Dev were trying to forge a united front against the selectors. But not all their demands were granted at the selection meeting.

The captain wanted Mumbai left-arm spinner Nilesh Kulkarni in the squad, reinforcing the widely held belief that Tendulkar veered towards players from his own side. The claims of all other left-arm spinners were ignored in the process. The selectors put their collective foot down on this.

There was enormous anticipation and excitement in Australia over the visit of the Indian team, with the focus, naturally enough, on the captain. Tendulkar had made a huge impact on his previous tour Down Under in 1991-92, with his brilliant centuries at Sydney and Perth, while still a teenager. The intervening years had seen him mature into the world's greatest batsman and Australians were delighted as well by the stamp of approval accorded to the Indian master from their very own living legend, Sir Don Bradman.

There was an additional edge to the contest, for Australia under Mark Taylor had been ambushed by the Indians on home turf just the year before. Now, guided by Steve Waugh, they were having a vintage year. After their triumph in the World Cup, they had whitewashed New Zealand and Pakistan at home, at the start of a fantastic run of victories that would last till March 2001.

Sadly, as the tour progressed, it became increasingly apparent that the Indians had developed a siege mentality. This was brought about not just by the dazzling quality of the opposition, but also by the hostile local press and highly contentious umpiring. The Australian cricket fraternity always presents a united front at home and this time was no different. Traditionally, the top player or captain is made a special target. Tendulkar fell into both categories and he was made to pay a heavy price. The trend was set even before the first Test, when umpire Darrell Hair decided to stamp his authority on the tourists in the tour match against New South Wales at Sydney.

'Twice in that match, Darrell Hair played the headmaster to perfection, admonishing the tourists as if they were errant children caught smoking in a school toilet,' wrote Harsha Bhogle in *Wisden Cricketers' Almanack Australia* (2000-01). Hair's bullying tactics had long been resented by teams from Asia. The Indian team management made it clear that they would not be happy if he stood in the Test series. He did, though, in the third and final Test at Sydney.

The high esteem in which Tendulkar is held by Australian cricket followers was best illustrated when Sachin was introduced to Sachin Voigt at the Adelaide Oval, venue of the first Test. The seven-year-old had been named by his father Ian Voigt following Tendulkar's exploits on the previous tour to Australia. 'Dear Sachin, keep smiling, Sachin Tendulkar,' Tendulkar signed on the mini-bat presented by his young namesake who had waited patiently for three hours to meet his hero. That would be about the last pleasant memory of Adelaide for Tendulkar.

After a promising start by the Indian pace bowlers—Australia: 52 for 4—it was downhill all the way for the visitors. A crushing defeat by 285 runs set the pattern for the rest of the series. It did not help matters that Tendulkar was the victim, in both innings, of hotly debated decisions handed out by Australian umpire Daryl Harper, which only added to the growing suspicion that he was being unfairly targeted. Replying to Australia's 441, the Indians were 123 for 4 at close on the second day, with Tendulkar and Ganguly both on 12. The skirmish between McGrath and Tendulkar on the second evening had been brief but captivating. In their only previous meeting in a Test match, the Australian speedster had bowled the Indian captain for a duck in New Delhi in 1996. Now Tendulkar, coming in at a shockingly low number five in the order, was in a rare defensive mood as he batted for 89 minutes and 69 balls for 12 runs. Time and again, McGrath tested him outside off stump, and each time the batsman just waved his bat away and let the ball through to the keeper. Having weathered that storm, it was a different Tendulkar who took charge on the third morning.

He hit the first three deliveries of the second over from fast bowler Michael Kasprowicz to the boundary—an on drive, a flick to square leg and a cover drive. With Ganguly for company, 92 runs were added in 22 overs. Tendulkar's 49 came from 64 balls and he was just getting into his stride when he was adjudged to have been caught bat and pad at short leg off Warne for 61. The replays showed he had clearly missed the ball. The score was 215 for 5, and with the wind taken out of the Indian sails, the innings folded up for 285.

Worse was to follow. After Australia declared their second innings at 239 for 8, it became a matter of survival for the Indians. But they folded up for 110 with the captain out for a duck. He ducked under a McGrath delivery—the fifth one he faced—that did not rise as expected, sank to his haunches and was struck on the left shoulder. After some deliberation, Harper raised his finger. The Australian players and media immediately sprang to the defence of their own. The Indian camp, on the other hand, was incensed. 'I was disappointed that I got out,' was Tendulkar's terse comment.

The question was whether the ball would have hit the stumps or not. Sunil Gavaskar was convinced it would not have, the Australians were convinced it would have. Back home, the dismissal was shown over and over again on television, with various pundits passing judgement in the cozy confines of the studio. Mohinder Amarnath's comment was rather pithy. 'I had always been taught that the umpire's verdict is final, so where is the debate?' The Indian journalists travelling with the team were scathing in their dispatches and it seemed paranoia was gripping the team. That, of course, was exactly what the Aussies wanted.

'The Indians had all along feared this kind of situation and when your best batsman becomes a sort of marked man it becomes tough on the team. If the Tendulkar episode took away the sheen from the Aussie victory the fault lay with the umpire. He was not convincing at all,' wrote Lokapally in the *Sportstar* (25 December 1999).

The series was won and lost in the traditional Boxing Day Test at Melbourne. But before that, Tendulkar enthralled one and all with his third century Down Under and his fifth against Australia in 11 Tests. India this time were beaten by 180 runs in a match curtailed by rain. After Australia once again crossed 400 in their first innings, India were struggling at 235 for 9 at the end of the third day, with Tendulkar holding the batting together with his twenty-second Test century. But it was fast bowler Brett Lee, who grabbed five wickets on Test debut, who captured most of the headlines. Lee bowled lightning quick and only Tendulkar—now batting at number four—managed to defy his hostile pace. Ninth out at 212, he was caught in the deep, hooking Damien Fleming. It was the only mistake he made while facing 191 balls. Even as he got a standing ovation from the crowd of 23,000 he was furious with himself for the poor shot. This time, though, there could be no excuse on the umpiring front.

It appeared as if there was a game within the game going on in the middle: Tendulkar v Australia. Only twice was he beaten, prompting Lee to exclaim in awe: 'That bat is so heavy but he's got so much time, he waves it around like a toothpick.'

There was too, a little gem of an innings when India batted to save the Test the second time round. The battle with Warne was once again engrossing stuff. Finlly, the leg-spinner had him lbw for 52 as he padded up to one that went straight on. The Man of the Match award was little consolation. As the world celebrated the dawn of the new millennium, Tendulkar must have looked back at 1999 with decidedly mixed feelings: His father's death, India's disappointing World Cup performance, his back worries, the captaincy drama and the miseries in Australia....All these factors combined to make it a year to forget. The only silver lining was the birth of his second child, Arjun, in Mumbai on 23 September.

Australia completed a 3-0 whitewash with victory by an innings and 141 runs in just three days in the third and final Test at Sydney, the first Test of the year 2000. There was a brief flash of brilliance in Tendulkar's first-innings 45 as he once again duelled with McGrath. He took 14 runs off one over from the fast bowler before being given out lbw for 45, a shocking decision by Zimbabwean umpire Ian Robinson. McGrath sent the batsman on his way with a crude gesture and a mouthful of abuse, and was lucky to get just a slap on the wrist from match referee Ranjan Madugalle. The Sri Lankan had fined Venkatesh Prasad heavily for a much lesser offence in the second Test and all this added to India's frustration. It was the third time in five innings that Tendulkar had got the short end of the stick from the umpires. And despite a defiant century by V.V S. Laxman in the second innings, India's was a lost cause.

Tendulkar's disappointment at the end of the Test was heightened by anger over the behaviour of the two umpires on the final day. Inevitably, Hair was in the thick of things, refusing the Indian captain's request for sawdust to be sprinkled on damp patches behind the stumps. On the boundary line, Prasad was the target for louts throwing shoes. But the umpires ignored Tendulkar's plea to step in. At the post-match press conference, Man of the Series Tendulkar was livid.

'In all the years that I have known Tendulkar—and I have known him since he was 14—I have never known him to be as worked up at a press conference,' said Harsha Bhogle who pinpointed Hair's attitude towards Asian teams as the crux of the problem. Tendulkar was asked after the series if he felt the umpires had targeted him, but he refused to be drawn, saying it was probably a coincidence.

Despite the rout, crowds for the Tests were huge. And they had come to see one player and one player alone. Not even Sir Donald Bradman in his last international summer at home in 1947-48 caused more excitement at the turnstiles, according to veteran Australian journalist Mike Coward. Coward, a man with a deep affection for Indian cricket and cricketers, wrote an impassioned open letter to Tendulkar in the *Weekend Australian* (8-9 January 2000). It concerned his silence over various controversial issues that had bedevilled the season. Interestingly, Sunil Gavaskar wrote a similar critique in one of his columns in 2001. He too gently chided his protégé for not taking a public stand on important cricket issues.

Following are excerpts from Coward's article under the headline 'Sounds of Silence Magnify Mystique of Cultural Divide':

> Dear Sachin,
> These people [the Australian cricket public] also want to hear from you; to know your thoughts on so many matters affecting cricket in India and around the world.
>
> As the game's pre-eminent batsman and your country's captain you are in a priceless position to make a difference. With respect, you have said little to arouse interest since you've been in the country.

Indeed, your press conferences have been little more than well practiced exercises in political and diplomatic correctness. Perhaps you were following instructions laid down by the faceless powerbrokers of Indian cricket....

Or could it have been that you were so badly wounded in your first incarnation as captain that you now simply do your duty?

...there is a need for a powerful, persuasive and contemporary voice from the region [the Indian subcontinent].

Sachin, you are recognized throughout the cricket world as a thoughtful, self-effacing, intelligent young man of great integrity and quiet dignity.

You can be the voice as well as the face of the game in its most populous and increasingly influential region.

Rest assured, the people (of Australia) who await your every stroke will hang on your every word.

And there are serious matters confronting the game which would benefit greatly from your involvement.

Is this [speculation of an anti-Asian sentiment running through the game and one that is most easily identified in Australia] merely a perception or a reality and has it impacted on your visit?

....after much too long, Australian cricket wants to know more about India and Indian cricket and cricketers.

Sachin, you are in a powerful position. You can make a real difference.

Tendulkar's response to these criticisms was that he was more worried about what he did on the ground than off the field; he hadn't accepted the captaincy to be drawn into controversies.

Writing in 2002 (*Sportstar*, 12 January 2002), Sunil Gavaskar made a similar point:

When he was captain of the team to Australia he had the media there looking for a comment or two about how to give the game a new direction. Owing to his phenomenal batting in the home series, the Australian media was waiting to lap up every word of his but he disappointed them by hardly saying anything of consequence....As one India-loving Australian veteran mediaperson said: 'It was as if "no comment" was two words too many for him.' Perhaps Tendulkar was taking shelter under the ICC Code of Conduct regarding comments, but there comes a time when the good of cricket counts before anything else and one has to stick one's neck out for the betterment of the game. For, when Tendulkar speaks the world will stop and listen.

There was further misery in the one-day tri-series where the Indians lost every match to Australia and Pakistan, except one. That was at Adelaide where they beat Pakistan by 48 runs. India's failure was largely put down to Tendulkar's poor run. At one stage he admitted that the pressures of the one-day game and the non-stop cricket were proving too taxing. He had just one substantial innings, 93 against Pakistan at Hobart, where India lost by 32 runs.

There were two other incidents that further upset his frame of mind and must have been factors in his shock decision to step down from the captaincy. Pakistan's young all-rounder Abdul Razzaq accused Tendulkar of tampering with the ball in the Adelaide game on 26 January. The charge was dismissed as 'frivolous and without foundation' by match referee Cammie Smith and umpires Hair and Steve Davis. The Indian camp was furious at Razzaq's impertinence. And the Pakistan team management reacted by dropping him on disciplinary grounds for the next match at Perth, even though the official reason given was that he was injured.

In that match in Perth, Tendulkar received yet another terrible decision, given out caught behind off Waqar Younis by umpire Simon Taufel for 17. He had struck four boundaries off Akram and Waqar and looked to be getting into his stride when he was handed down the latest shocker. For the first time in two months, something snapped and he showed his displeasure before leaving the crease. It had been a gruelling time for the team and the captain in particular, and he must have been relieved when it was all over.

This was the first time since England in 1974 that India had been whitewashed 3-0. The debacle of the ODI tri-series was really the last straw on the captain's tender back.

29

Stepping Down

I as captain take the moral responsibility for the failure.—Sachin Tendulkar

Was Sachin Tendulkar's opposition to the inclusion of Mohammad Azharuddin based on sound reasoning, or was it another aspect of his often stubborn attitude towards the selectors? Confrontation with the selection panel loomed again when the team for the Australian tour was being picked, as we have already discussed in the previous chapter. The bone of contention was the inclusion of Azhar and Nayan Mongia. The wicketkeeper had, of course, made a brief appearance Down Under, but was soon sent packing. The face-off—the five selectors and J.Y. Lele on one side and coach Kapil Dev and his captain on the other—was back in the headlines when the time came to make changes for the one-day tri-series following the whitewash in the Test series.

Here Tendulkar got his way, with Mumbai teammate Sameer Dighe flying out to replace the disappointing M.S.K. Prasad behind the stumps. Considering the batting failures in the Tests, there were also strong indications that Azhar would be part of the one-day team. Kapil and Sachin, however, would have nothing to do with it. 'The plane bringing Azhar to Australia will be the same one taking Kapil and me back home,' Tendulkar is reported to have told his teammates.

But how long could this attitude persist? Sooner or later the two stalwarts were sure to force their way back into the side on the basis of both form and reputation.

The second day of the tour-opening match of the South African team against the Board President's XI at the Brabourne Stadium in Mumbai was on 20 February 2000. It was also the day the selectors would announce the team for the first Test at Mumbai's Wankhede Stadium, starting in four days' time.

But before the team could be announced, Tendulkar walked into the press box at the Brabourne Stadium to make a dramatic announcement of his own. Accompanied by chairman of the Selection Committee Chandu Borde and Lele, he walked up to the microphone and began: 'I have an announcement to make.' He then read out his statement:

> I just want to make a few things very clear. At the beginning of the season when Mr Wadekar, the then chairman of the selection committee, met with me and offered me the captaincy, I showed my reluctance to accept the job as I felt that I was not mentally prepared at that time.
>
> In spite of that, when my name was announced as captain, I took up the task as I was one of the most experienced players and the selectors felt at that time I was the best man to do the job. I accepted the captaincy knowing that this Australian tour would be a very difficult one, judging from the Australian team's recent performance—they had won the World Cup.
>
> I tried my best but nothing worked out for us. I do not want to offer any excuses for a poor performance in Australia, but I as captain take the moral responsibility for the failure. I feel sorry for not living up to the expectations of my countrymen who always support us and wish well for the team.
>
> I have decided after a lot of thought to step down from the captaincy after the forthcoming two Test matches against South Africa. That will give some time to the next captain to get prepared. I assure you that I will give my best as I have always done in the past, and I am ready to play in the team under anyone and with anyone.

The press were stunned for a moment. Then they began firing

questions. Tendulkar stonewalled the more sensitive ones and left the box. Borde then announced the team, and surrprise, surprise, Azhar and Mongia were back in. Now it was Borde's turn to be in the firing line. Inevitably, most questions were about the return of Azhar and the stepping down of the captain. 'We tried to persuade him to continue, but he had made up his mind. It was his decision. There is nothing we can do about it.'

But what was the story behind the scene? Conspiracy theories abounded. Perhaps a loose understanding was reached between Tendulkar, Ganguly and Jadeja at the World Cup, that whoever was made captain would resign if Mohammad Azharuddin was picked; perhaps Tendulkar arrived with two letters in his pocket for the selection meeting, one with the team he wanted, the other his resignation. Told that Azhar was picked, he had his resignation ready. The third theory was that Tendulkar decided to quit after the Test series so that his confidant Jadeja could take over as captain since India were to play only one-day cricket till November. But of course, there was nothing to prove either of these theories right. As Sanjay Manjrekar commented: '[Sachin] has perfect timing when it comes to batting, but don't expect him to be perfect at everything. I think the player Tendulkar is more effective than the captain-player Tendulkar.'

Writing for *Indya.com* after Ganguly was eventually appointed to succeed Tendulkar, this is how Wadekar assessed the man on whose shoulders he had thrust the captaincy just eight months earlier:

> I'm convinced that Sachin will never lead the Indian side in future. And that is sad. He has perhaps all the ingredients to become a good captain. Every member of the team respects his great talent. He is a thinker, an essential factor for a captain. Sachin also leads from the front. He can crush any attack in the world with his batting on any wicket. He also mixes with everyone in the team. What was it then lacking in him that he could hardly win any series?
>
> I think he gets too much involved in the game. He expects his players to perform at the level where he performs. That is just

> not possible. No player in the world can come close to the standards set by him. He also tries to advise his bowlers almost every ball, with the result that the bowlers stop thinking on their own. I do not think his batting gets affected by captaincy. I feel he doesn't have the ambition to captain the team. I tried my level best to convince him to remain as captain, but he wouldn't budge. He kept on saying that he wouldn't like to be the captain again.

Amazingly, there would be another dramatic twist to the tale. Tendulkar was criticized for delaying his resignation till the day the team was chosen with Azhar in it. The very next day, Azhar withdrew from the first Test with an injury suffered in the Mumbai game, when he was hit on the hand by Nantie Hayward. Inevitably, this too was not clear-cut. Was his thumb fractured or was it a simple injury? Now fingers were being pointed at Azhar. Was it a cop-out to avoid a backlash over Tendulkar's resignation? He insisted the injury was serious enough for him to miss the first Test, though it was also obvious he felt he was the victim of a conspiracy hatched by the incumbent to keep him out of the team.

A survey of former players, including former captains Bishan Singh Bedi, K.Srikkanth and Sunil Gavaskar found them backing Tendulkar's decision. The onus for the resignation was placed firmly on the Board, something Wadekar also agreed with. So what of the man in the middle himself?

This is what he had to say in *Cricket Talk* (30 March 2000):

> Q: Why did you surrender the captaincy so suddenly?
>
> A: It had been building up gradually, the pressure to perform well as well as win. We kept losing without competing hard enough and that hurt. Small, small things contributed till I decided that it simply cannot go on like this. I was not enjoying the game at all, so why carry the burden?
>
> Q: You had not been keen to accept the captaincy either…
>
> A: Yes, I did not want it. When Ajit Wadekar came to my house

at the start of the season last year, I told him that I was not interested in the job. He was supposed to inform the other selectors but I don't know what happened and I was asked to lead…

Q: Does this mean that you were always plagued by doubt? Then why did you agree in the first place?

A: I was in two minds initially, but then I thought to myself, why not give it another try. The dream was to win overseas and I chased it. I tried my level best but it did not work out.

Q: Does the sudden decision to resign have something to do with Mohammad Azharuddin's return to the team?

A: Look, I have no problems with Azhar. I have not quit because he is in the team. I have played for more than 10 years and am not given to whim. I spent a lot of time thinking about this [Azhar's exclusion] when I was made captain last year. At that time it seemed reasonable. But I'm of the firm belief that if anybody is good and he has the form to prove it, he should be in the team. The relationship between Azhar and me is as it was all the time. It was needlessly blown into a controversy and blown out of all proportion.

Interviewed by the same magazine (30 September 2000), this is what he said on his differences with the selectors: 'Yes, my views differed with the members of the earlier selection committee. I suppose this led to a degree of disillusionment and loss of interest in the job. After all, I was leading on the field. But now that is all in the past, so why rake it up?'

The two Tests against South Africa were a disaster for India. They lost the first at Mumbai by four wickets and the second at Bangalore by an innings and 71 runs. That was the end of Tendulkar's second stint as captain.

Tendulkar was the only batsman to look comfortable on a bowler-friendly wicket at Mumbai. His 97 in the first innings was the highest score in the match by far. There was only one other half-century—exactly 50 by opener Gary Kirsten. The Indian captain also picked up his best Test bowling analysis of 3 for 10 from five overs as South Africa collapsed for 176 and conceded a lead of 49. He accounted for Kirsten and fellow opener Herschelle Gibbs as well as Shaun Pollock with a mixture of off and leg spin. The performance made him the Man of the Match. But it was South Africa who held their nerve at the end.

The first Test was over in three days; the second just about dragged into the fifth. Azhar was back and hit the only century of the series, his twenty-second in his ninety-ninth Test. It was also destined to be his last. At the end of the year the BCCI would impose a life ban on him.

The defeat meant Tendulkar had lost five Tests in a row as captain. It was shattering for such a proud man and Indian cricket was at one of its lowest ebbs. His record as captain was poor—four Tests won, 12 drawn and nine lost. In the second stint, it stood at 1-2-5. At virtually the same time, in the West Indies, Brian Lara stepped down from the captaincy with a similar record of six won, two drawn and ten lost.

Ganguly took over for the one-day series which India won 3-2. But a few months later would come the revelations by the Delhi Police. South African captain Hansie Cronje, faced with the irrefutable evidence of taped phone calls, would eventually admit his guilt and the world of cricket was thrown into its gravest crisis.

What emerged was that Cronje and his teammates were busy hobnobbing with bookies throughout the short tour. Certainly, the verdict in the one-day series would be forever tainted. India had not been beaten in a Test series at home since losing 1-0 to Pakistan in 1987. Cronje was the man to emulate the great Imran Khan. What an irony then, that he should find himself exiled from the world of cricket.

After failing in the first three ODIs, Tendulkar came good with his twenty-fifth ton at Baroda as India won by four wickets to take an unbeatable 3-1 lead in the series. He followed it up with 93 in the fifth and final match at Nagpur. The next few months would see a familiar whirl of one-day tournaments around the globe—Sharjah (twice), Nairobi and Dhaka. South Africa and India were joined by Pakistan in Sharjah for the Coca-Cola Cup. India recorded a rare win over Pakistan in the first round but lost the second match, as well as both matches against South Africa, and without a single major contribution from its top batsman, failed to make it to the final.

The Pepsi Asia Cup at Dhaka, a few months later, seemed likely to be a total washout with torrential storms lashing the city. June, after all, is hardly the ideal month to play cricket in Bangladesh.

The run-up on the Indian side could not have been worse. On the night before the team's departure, coach Kapil Dev called a press conference in New Delhi at which he launched an extraordinary attack on Manoj Prabhakar. This followed Prabhakar naming Kapil as the man who, he claimed, had offered him a bribe to throw a match in Sri Lanka in 1994.

Kapil called on the Board to withdraw the team, considering its shattered morale. But the players did arrive in Dhaka, though a more dispirited side I have rarely seen. They just did not seem to have their heart in the game, and it showed in their performance on the field. After an unimpressive win over Bangladesh, India succumbed to both Pakistan and Sri Lanka and failed to make the final. Tendulkar's 93 against Sri Lanka was made out of a total of 205, chasing a target of 277.

Considering their poor one-day form, the Indians turned out to be the surprise package of the second ICC knockout mini-World Cup in Nairobi. Once Kenya were brushed aside, India were up against Australia in the first quarter-final. In a stunning upset, the world champions were tumbled out, beaten by 20 runs. Young guns Yuvraj Singh and Zaheer Khan were the batting and bowling heroes. Ganguly and Tendulkar gave the innings a flying start with a rapid stand of 66 runs. Tendulkar (38) decided to take on McGrath and not only with his bat. He hammered the world's leading fast bowler, prompting a frustrated McGrath to unleash his usual string of abuse. He even offensively demonstrated to Tendulkar how to play a stroke.

McGrath and Brett Lee had over the past two days been talking of having a plan ready for Tendulkar, with the former saying that his goal was to remove the openers in the first over. In Australia they had been able to dictate terms, with Tendulkar on the defensive. It was different this time. In McGrath's first over Tendulkar tried to take one from outside off and hit over midwicket. The ball flared off the bat and soared with immense power over a stunned Gillespie at third man, for an amazing six. The furious bowler could be seen mouthing something to his opponent.

In the next over Sachin danced down the wicket as if he were facing an innocuous off-spinner, picked McGrath on the rise, and smashed him over long off for six. On the next ball, back he came down the track for another smashing drive on the up through mid-off. As McGrath stopped in his tracks, Tendulkar took a few steps forward, and very clearly stared at McGrath and said, 'Just fuck off!' McGrath cupped his hands to his ears, perhaps not able to believe what he had just heard. There was one more six off McGrath before Lee sent Sachin back.

It was for only the second time in his career that Sachin had lost his cool on the field. It was a real shock for the Aussies, and the bowler in particular, who had targeted Tendulkar on their own soil just a few months before, in a strategy Steve Waugh liked to refer to ingenuously as 'mental disintegration'.

It backfired on them this time and India were in the final after another shock defeat of South Africa in the semis. Tendulkar was asked by the *Sportstar* (3 February 2001) about that confrontation.

> Q: What is it that fires you? That charge you gave Glenn McGrath at Nairobi. It was a very different Tendulkar we saw that day…
>
> A: That particular innings, I felt the wicket had a lot of bounce and dampness. If I had not adopted an aggressive approach it would have been a different story. That innings I think I took them by surprise. They didn't expect me to do that at all. This will tell you about how the pitch was. McGrath didn't have a mid-on to start with. He had a square-leg, a fine-leg, mid-off, point, three slips and a gully. It reflects on the state of the pitch for a one-day game. If I had tried to hang around he would have attacked at the same spot and I didn't want them to be at

the top. Counter-attack was the best thing. Scoring runs was important and not killing time on that pitch.

The opening pair again put on 66 in the semi-finals. This time Ganguly carried his bat for 141 while Tendulkar's contribution was 39. The final turned out to be an anticlimax for the rampaging Indians. They were beaten in the last over by dark horses New Zealand, with Chris Cairns not out on 102. This overshadowed another century from the Indian captain and an opening stand worth 141. Tendulkar was run out after a mix-up, for 69. It was a sad end to what had been an outstanding tournament for the young team.

Just five days later, India and Sri Lanka were playing the opening match of the Coca-Cola tri-series (with Zimbabwe) in Sharjah and Tendulkar was back in century mode. It was his sixth century in Sharjah where he had already scored over 1500 runs. But this one against the Sri Lankans was no slam-bang affair. His twenty-sixth ton (101) consisted of just six twos, three fours and a six. 71 runs came from singles this time, as the rest of the batting crumbled around him. He was out only in the forty-seventh over, once again the victim of a run-out.

The track at Sharjah had recently been relaid and was not the batting-friendly wicket it used to be. It was very slow, with the ball not coming on to the bat. So, Sachin was forced to change his style, working the ball around the field, nudging behind square and dropping the ball short of fielders, and scampering for singles. He won the Man of the Match award once again, but it was the Sri Lankans who came out on top by five wickets. Sri Lanka won the return match as well, and then crushed India in the final. Following Jayasuriya's huge 189, the Indian batting crashed to their lowest total of 54 all out. The euphoria of Nairobi was suddenly forgotten.

30

Match-fixing and the CBI

I do not know a thing.—Sachin Tendulkar

Tendulkar's stand on the match-fixing controversy and the subsequent CBI probe and report has been consistent from the start. He has steadfastly maintained that he was unaware of anything unsavoury within the team before, during, or after he was captain. It is a line that one finds increasingly hard to accept.

The question then arises: as the leading player in the side and indeed in the world, could he not have taken a moral stand on the issue as did Pakistan's Rashid Latif? This is a question that Sachin and Sachin alone can answer. So far, he has not been very forthcoming on the matter, except to consistently stress not only his innocence, but also his ignorance. But then, as we have seen before, he has never been one to rock the boat. In an interview to *Cricket Talk (*30 September 2000), he declared, 'I have said it before and I am saying it again. I do not know a thing. No one has approached me about any such thing. I don't think they will dare.' In the same interview, he urged, 'Find the guilty and make examples of them. The game is too great for it to be disgraced in this way.' This was shortly before the release of the CBI report on match-fixing. 'I did not think this would happen to the game. I thought that it was impossible. In fact, such a thought never crossed my mind because it is something no cricketer should even contemplate,' he added.

In interviews, Tendulkar has always claimed he did not have an axe to grind with Azharuddin. In private, it was a different matter. The two enjoyed a good rapport till the game of musical chairs for the captain's seat began to put a strain on their relationship. More than that, Tendulkar always felt that Azhar did not perform as well under his captaincy as he had done under Azhar's. Things came to a head in Sharjah in December 1997 when Azhar's batting methods and running between the wickets came under the microscope. That Tendulkar was sacked from the captaincy and Azhar restored to the position shortly afterwards is just another bitterly ironic chapter in the history of Indian cricket. As we saw in the last chapter, Sachin resigned his second term as captain when Azhar was brought back for the home series against South Africa in March 2000. It was obviously the last straw. However, in one of his last interviews as captain, he reiterated that there was no issue between him and Azharuddin. If someone was performing well and could win games for the country, how could he have a problem? He had not had a serious disagreement with any player for the past 10 years. After losing his captaincy he had played under Azhar and then Azhar had played under him, and there had never been a problem—or so he said.

The closest he came to admitting to a rift was when he was asked by V. Srivatsa of the *Times of India* (7 July 2001): 'How do you find him [Azhar] as a man and what are your feelings after what's happened to him? [the match-fixing ban]. Tendulkar replied, 'It's a very touchy topic and I wouldn't like to go into it.'

The first journalist to openly write about the murky activities of bookies and the speculation of match-fixing was Pradeep Magazine, currently sports editor of the *Hindustan Times*. Magazine was sports editor of the *Pioneer* in 1997, and was covering the tour of the West Indies when he broke the story about being approached by a bookie from Delhi who offered him large sums of money. In return, he was asked to introduce the bookie to key players in the side, including captain Tendulkar.

Magazine recounted the encounter and its aftermath in his book *Not Quite Cricket*. There have been many books on the subject since, but his was the very first. He met Tendulkar for an interview in Georgetown, Guyana, at the end of which he asked the captain for his reaction to the bookie's offer. Magazine quotes Tendulkar:

Look, I am earning crores of rupees from the game, from advertising, only to steel myself against these temptations so that at the end of the day I can look people in the eye with a clear conscience. And playing for the country is so important for me that I can't even dream of doing such a thing. Neither can anyone have the courage to approach me with an offer like this. If he did so the next moment he would find himself in jail.

He added: 'Even I have been hearing a lot of things about this whole affair. I don't know what to do. If I were you I wouldn't do the story but would tell the police about the man. Tell them to tap the man's phone and let us see who he talks to.'

Magazine wrote that he was 'impressed by Sachin's presence of mind, his ability to see things in perspective.... Above all, one thing was becoming increasingly clear to me: the rumours of betting and players taking money was not limited to journalistic circles alone; even the team management in the West Indies had heard about it and were quite concerned.'

The team management included coach Madan Lal who too had advised Magazine against writing the article about his bookie encounter. The headline for Magazine's report splashed across the front page of the newspaper was: 'I Was Offered Rs 40 Lakh by a Bookie to "fix" a Match'.

As often happens in the media world, the heading did not quite reflect the contents. He had been offered the money for introductions to key players, not to 'fix' a match. The 'I' in the headline had an unfortunate fallout. While the BCCI brushed aside the story in public, unknown to Magazine himself, a letter was faxed to Tendulkar midway through the West Indies tour, asking him who the bookie was who had offered him the money! A complete misinterpretation of the report.

Tendulkar confronted Magazine with this revelation at the nets before the Independence Cup match in Chennai against Pakistan in May 1997.

His voice [Tendulkar's] was a mixture of anger and hurt. 'What have you written? You have written that I was offered money?' I looked him straight in the eye and replied: 'Who told you that? I wrote exactly what I had told you. Didn't you read the story?' It took only these few words from me for Tendulkar to calm down. 'The Board had taken the "I" in your story to be me [Tendulkar],' he said. I explained to him that it was quite the reverse, the 'I' referred to me, not him.

'How can they interpret it like that?' I exclaimed. 'I have referred to you only in the end, that too quoting you as saying "it is beneath my dignity to talk about such things."'

After the match was over, it was agreed between Tendulkar, Madan Lal and Magazine that the journalist would write a letter to the Board, clarifying the matter. In his letter Magazine wrote: 'I fail to understand how Tendulkar's name was linked with the bookie when my story was clear and at no stage did it even hint that the bookie had met Tendulkar.' He added something to the effect that Tendulkar was not only a great player but also a great ambassador for the country and should be left alone to concentrate on his game.

'After a week or so,' says Magazine, 'I got a reply from the Board that upset me even more. While thanking me for "clarifying" the situation, it read: "Now that you have denied your story, it would have been in the fitness of things if you had also named the bookie whom you had met."'

Magazine wrote that he was reminded of what Madan Lal had told him in the West Indies. 'The only possibility of the truth coming out is when a player gets up and says that his teammates have taken money. Till that happens there is no point in pursuing this story.'

The establishment's duplicity was becoming clear. Worried perhaps that skeletons from its own closet would come tumbling out under the scrutiny of an investigation, everybody acted as if the crisis did not exist. The shabby cover-up of the Chandrachud Commission followed. This, and the public outcry over the next couple of years, and then the Delhi Police tapes implicating Hansie Cronje, made the government call in the CBI to institute its own independent probe, the report of which was released in October 2000.

Outlook weekly picked up the threads of the story from Magazine in 1997, and then in 2000 came the *tehelka.com* videos clandestinely recorded by Manoj Prabhakar.

These tapes achieved precious little, apart from revealing the backbiting and gossip prevalent among India's cricketing fraternity. But two points concerning Tendulkar stood out: firstly, Prabhakar refused to trap Tendulkar on video despite pressure from those at the web site; he said he had too much respect for him. Secondly, amidst all the tawdry talk—much of it influenced by liberal doses of alcohol—not one person pointed a finger at Tendulkar or was critical of him in any form.

Prabhakar had resigned in a huff after the 1996 World Cup, and was seen to have too many axes to grind. The main target of his campaign was Kapil Dev. Further, Prabhakar allowed himself to become a pawn in the hands of certain sections of the media, who cynically manipulated him for their own benefit. His words thus lacked credibility, and ultimately he would be hoist by his own petard. The CBI probe uncovered his own role in match-fixing and the Board banned him from cricket for five years, acting on the report. The ban was, of course, only symbolic, since he had retired by then.

There remained the question mark over Tendulkar's decision to not enforce a follow-on in the third Test against New Zealand at Ahmedabad. The CBI probed coach Kapil Dev's role in it and both the captain and the coach were questioned. The summer of 2000 saw journalists camping outside the CBI headquarters in central Delhi. One after the other, the who's who of Indian cricket were called to the capital and questioned by India's premier investigating agency. The media scrimmage was getting increasingly chaotic as television cameras and reporters with their mikes jostled with print journalists to get quotes from Azharuddin, Mongia, Wadekar, Kapil Dev, Prabhakar and other past and present players and administrators. Most kept their lips sealed.

Tendulkar was spared the ordeal. He was questioned at home in Mumbai. The stampede outside the CBI office if he had been called to

Delhi would have been unmanageable.

The CBI report did not indict either the captain or the coach over the Ahmedabad match, though there were certain intriguing questions that appeared to have been left unanswered. The matter was finally closed in late 2001 with the CBI issuing a brief press release that it had found no evidence of wrongdoing.

After the report came out in October, BCCI president A.C.Muthiah decided to constitute the Board's own one-man commission in the form of former CBI Joint Director, K.Madhavan. Madhavan also probed the matter, and spoke to Tendulkar and Kapil Dev in July 2001. He too came to the same conclusion. It would be relevant here to quote passages from the CBI report directly concerning Tendulkar, which was released to the media on 1 November 2000. (The italics are mine.)

> Bookie Pawan Puri's testimony (pages 45-47):
>
> Once there was a party at his friend Dimpy's house on 31.10.99 to which both he and (fellow-bookie) Rattan Mehta were also invited. Around 11 p.m. on that day he (Puri) picked up Rattan Mehta from his house in Panchsheel Enclave (in New Delhi) to go to Dimpy's house which is at Sainik Farms. On the way, Rattan Mehta asked him to ring up Shobhan Mehta, a Bombay bookie, and asked him to place a bet to the effect that the ongoing match between India-New Zealand at Ahmedabad would end in a draw. He was surprised as to how Rattan Mehta could anticipate this since New Zealand were in a precarious position on 31.10.99 and very few persons would have anticipated that the match would end in a draw. He dialed Shobhan's number and placed a bet to this effect. Even Shobhan Mehta was skeptical and since he was quite close to him, advised him not to place this bet. However, he told Shobhan that he was placing bets on somebody else's behalf. On being asked as to why Rattan placed bets with Shobhan through him and not directly, he stated that Rattan does not have an account with Shobhan and hence he had to place this bet through him. At Dimpy's place, Rattan Mehta, after getting drunk, boasted that he had exact

information about the outcome of the Ahmedabad Test match and also placed bets with some other bookies, whose names he did not remember.

(*The scores on 31 October, the third day of the Test, was India 583 for 7 wickets declared in the first innings and New Zealand 211 for 6 in reply. The match did, of course, end in a draw.*)

Dr Ali Irani (pages 71-76):

Dr Irani stated that he had never heard anything adverse regarding Tendulkar. In fact, in most of the matches where fixing was taking place, the clue was that the game would be 'on' only when Tendulkar got 'out' because he was one player who could single-handedly win the match and upset any calculation.

(*This was later quoted by English journalist Scyld Berry in his profile of Tendulkar for Wisden.com, calling it the 'finest compliment' accorded to him.*)

Kapil Dev (pages 85-88):

About the India-New Zealand Test at Ahmedabad in 1999 where India did not enforce the follow-on, he stated that this decision was taken in consultation with the captain, vice captain and other senior players.

One day prior to the decision, there was absolutely no doubt in his mind that the follow-on should be enforced. At the end of play on the third day, there was no team meeting on the strategy for the next day. Somewhere during lunchtime on the fourth day the bowlers, especially Srinath, complained that they were very tired and India should bat again and score quick runs and make New Zealand bat thereafter.

On being told that the bookies in Delhi allegedly knew about the decision not to enforce follow-on on 31.10.99 night, Kapil stated that no decision to this effect was taken on the 31st and hence it was very surprising. On being asked whether somebody could have subconsciously influenced this decision on the next day, he stated that it could not be ruled out. He could not remember as to who could have done it.

Analysis of evidence (pages 127- 132):

With regard to the 1999 Ahmedabad Test against New Zealand, Sachin Tendulkar has stated that the decision not to enforce the follow-on was collective, influenced by the fact that bowlers, especially Srinath, had expressed that they were too tired. Kapil Dev has corroborated this version. Moreover, both of them have stated that the decision was arrived at during lunch on the 4th day. There is no evidence that Kapil Dev had passed on any information to the betting syndicate about this match.

Sachin Tendulkar (pages 88—89):

Sachin Tendulkar, former Indian captain, when asked about the India-New Zealand Test at Ahmedabad in 1999, stated that by the end of third day's play when New Zealand had lost around 6 wickets, he had thought to himself that he would enforce the follow-on the next day.

However, the New Zealand innings dragged on till after lunch the next day and by then he himself, coach Kapil Dev, Anil Kumble and Ajay Jadeja decided that the follow-on would not be enforced since the bowlers, especially Srinath had insisted that they were very tired.

It was a collective decision not to enforce the follow-on. (There was speculation in the media that he was here trying to protect the coach.) On being asked whether anybody could have influenced this decision since the bookies in Delhi allegedly knew one day in advance that the follow-on would not be enforced, he accepted that it was possible.

About Shobhan Mehta, the Mumbai bookie, he stated that he had never met this person nor did he invite him to his wedding. During his wedding there was tight security and only select persons were invited and nobody without a proper invitation could have gatecrashed.

All speculations about himself and Shobhan Mehta were absolutely rubbish and he had never met this person any time in his life. On being asked whether he suspected any Indian player of being involved in match-fixing, Sachin stated that during his tenure as captain, he had felt that Mohammad Azharuddin was not putting in 100 per cent effort and he suspected that he was involved with some bookies.

On being asked about the India-West Indies match at Kanpur in 1994 when Manoj Prabhakar and Nayan Mongia batted slowly, he stated that he was the vice captain during that match and he was absolutely sure that there were no instructions from the management for Manoj Prabhakar and Nayan Mongia to bat slowly and that he was so upset with their tactics that he did not talk to them after the match.

At the end of it all, Ajay Sharma and Azharuddin were banned from cricket for life by the BCCI while Manoj Prabhakar, Ali Irani and Ajay Jadeja got five-year suspensions.

Ironically, while Kapil Dev was let off (he later resigned as coach of the national side), it was his accuser Prabhakar who found himself briefly behind bars, for his alleged role in a chit fund scam.

By July 2001, the dust had settled on the controversy, but Tendulkar continued to be guarded in his response.

Asked by V. Srivatsa (*Times of India,* 6 July 2001), 'Did you ever suspect such things were happening right under your nose?' his answer was: 'It's very hard to comment on it. I treated whatever has happened as one of those bad phases and happily it's past. I do get this feeling that people have forgotten all that, they look at this team from a different angle altogether, that's very important to all of us.'

How did the team take it?,' asked Srivatsa.

Tendulkar replied, 'The whole team was shocked because none of us could ever think of it.'

31

'The Greatest Series Ever'

I did not feel any pressure.—Sachin Tendulkar

The second and last quarters of 2000 saw two memorable performances on the domestic circuit by Sachin Tendulkar. In April, he helped Mumbai bounce back from a disastrous 1998-99 season to win the Ranji Trophy once again. He could play just two matches, the semi-final against Tamil Nadu and the final against Hyderabad, but in these his scores were phenomenal: 233 (not out), 13 (not out), 53 and 128.

In December, he made a rare appearance, this time virtually in his backyard! For the first time, a Ranji Trophy match—Mumbai v Baroda—was staged at the MIG ground at Bandra, a stone's throw from his home. He marked the occasion with a century, much to the delight of his neighbours in the stands.

The Ranji semi-final against Tamil Nadu had been postponed by two days to allow Tendulkar to return from Dhaka where he had led an Asian XI against a World XI in a one-day exhibition match. Earlier that season, he had relinquished the Mumbai captaincy to Sameer Dighe since he knew the international calendar would keep him away from domestic cricket.

Tamil Nadu had scored 485 in the first innings, and Mumbai were in danger of conceding the first innings lead when their ninth wicket fell at 472. Tendulkar had come in at the fall of the second wicket at 77, and now had only last man Santosh Saxena for company. He pulled Kumaran to the midwicket boundary for four to gain the lead and the celebrations broke out. The last 20 runs of the innings had come entirely off his bat. He was at the crease for 565 minutes—the longest innings of his career—and was unbeaten on his highest first-class score of 233 (334 balls, 21 fours, five sixes) when Saxena was given out without scoring. Mumbai eventually won by eight wickets.

There is a remarkable sequence of four photographs of Tendulkar, taken by Vivek Bendre (*Sportstar*, 29 April 2000), showing him exulting after guiding Mumbai to the first innings lead. The fist pumping and the whoops of joy were unusual—rarely in international cricket does one see him celebrating with such an outward show of emotion. It showed his commitment to Mumbai cricket.

Mumbai coach and former opening batsman Ashok Mankad said he had never seen a better innings in first-class cricket. Tendulkar himself felt it was one of his best. The final against Hyderabad saw Mumbai win by 297 runs. This time Tendulkar's contribution was 53 and 128.

There would be another double ton in November: 201 not out in the second Test at Nagpur against Zimbabwe. It was the fourth double century of his first-class career and coincidentally, the two hundredth in Test cricket history. This followed a century in the first Test at New Delhi and there was another in the third ODI at Jodhpur. India won the Test series 1-0 and the ODIs 4-1. But the visit of the Zimbabweans was just a warm-up session for the real thing as far as the Indian cricketers and fans were concerned. The real test would come with the arrival of Steve Waugh's all-conquering team.

The Aussies landed in India in February 2001 with an awesome record. They had won 15 Tests in succession, an unprecedented feat. But no Australian team had won a series in India since Bill Lawry's 3-1 verdict in 1969-70.

The pre-tour hype was huge. Waugh called India the 'final frontier' of his career. He had been the ODI captain under Mark Taylor when India won the 1998 Test series 2-1 and was determined to keep alive his side's ruthless streak on Indian soil. He also spoke of 'mental disintegration', the infamous Aussie weapon. They used to call it 'sledging'—abusing an opponent on the field. Now a clever play of words had resulted in a new euphemism for the traditional Aussie tactic.

Things were really hotting up for the Indian team. Sourav Ganguly was still new to the job of captaincy, while Waugh was acknowledged as the best captain in world cricket. The Zimbabwe visit had been Ganguly's first Test series as captain. His style was combative and it was obvious this would be a toe-to-toe, eyeball-to-eyeball confrontation between two strong men in charge of their respective sides. Ultimately, the Australian media campaign of targeting Ganguly backfired. They had seen the Indians roll over tamely, without a fight, on their soil just a year ago. But it would be different this time, with Ganguly paying the aggressive Aussies back in their own coin. Even Tendulkar admitted to 'sledging' Steve Waugh on the field!

Australia were without the injured Brett Lee but were still formidable, with Shane Warne and Glenn McGrath bowling in tandem in India for the first time. India too were without one of their spearheads, the injured Anil Kumble. The series of three Tests produced some of the most memorable games in the recent past. No wonder the world media dubbed it 'the greatest series ever'. And in the end, India were 2-1 winners again.

On the eve of the first Test at Mumbai, the death of Sir Donald Bradman cast a pall of gloom over the proceedings. Tendulkar and Warne were immediately sought out for their memories of the 1998 visit to his home. Both teams wore black armbands in mourning. However, the visitors won the first round by a knockout. In less than three days, they tore the stuffing out of the Indian team for win number 16, and another series whitewash seemed apparent. The only saving grace for India in the ten-wicket trouncing was the batting of Tendulkar. His knocks of 76 and 65 were both classics.

On the opening day, the Indian batting crumbled to 176 all out. They had lost four wickets at lunch for 55 even as Tendulkar reached 19 from 53 balls. After the break, he opened up and suddenly the rampaging bowlers found themselves on the back foot. The first ball after lunch from old adversary Warne was cut for four. The next 59 balls went for 57 wondrous runs. Fleming was flayed for three straight fours and then McGrath was back. Tendulkar succumbed yet again to his nemesis in the series Down Under.

The Indian bowlers struck back on the second morning. Australia found themselves precariously placed at 99 for 5 and the last recognized pair of Matthew Hayden and Adam Gilchrist were at the crease. Off-spinner Harbhajan Singh had picked up three wickets in a sign of things to come. Then, the game was turned on its head as the two left-handers tore the Indian bowling apart. Gilchrist raced to the second fastest century by an Australian, from 84 balls, with 19 fours and a six. Hayden had an identical number of boundaries and their stand of 197 came from just 32 overs.

Trailing by 173 runs, the Indian batting once again crumbled. By close on the second day, they had lost both openers. Tendulkar in the company of Dravid began the rebuilding process. They put on 97 for the third wicket and Tendulkar was at his dazzling best. Boundaries flowed off his bat and the bowlers seemed at their wits' end when an amazing piece of luck saw the Aussies gain the upper hand again.

Mark Waugh bowled one of his gentle 'offies' and Tendulkar lashed out with a ferocious pull. Justin Langer at short leg had taken a pounding and now as he turned instinctively, he was struck on the left shoulder. The ball ballooned towards midwicket. Ponting had failed to score, but now he pulled off a miraculous catch that turned the game. He sprinted 20 metres to his right and flung himself forward to grasp the catch an inch above the ground. Once again, it had taken an extraordinary catch to end an extraordinary innings from the maestro. It was obvious by now that his batting genius made rival bowlers and fielders strive to raise their game too.

The rest of the batting was soon mopped up and Slater and Hayden raced to the small target.

By the third morning of the second Test at Kolkata, it looked like Indian cricket's worst nightmare was unfolding. Powered by captain Waugh's first Test century on Indian soil, Australia had piled up 445. India were then sent packing for 171. The follow-on was duly enforced. Enter V.V.S. Laxman to play the innings of a lifetime. His 281 was begun on the third afternoon and stretched till the fifth morning, and was the highest score by an Indian in Test cricket. This followed

Harbhajan Singh's hat-trick, the first by an Indian in Test cricket. Laxman and Dravid batted throughout the fifth day and suddenly the tables were turned on Australia. Dravid's 180 was magnificent too, and his stand with Laxman was worth a massive 376 runs.

Ganguly declared on the fifth morning at 657 for 7. The target was 384 for Australia. Had the declaration come too late? Only twice before had a team lost after enforcing the follow-on in 124 years of Test cricket and on each occasion Australia had been on the receiving end.

Finally, the match was won for India in the last hour of the match. Harbhajan was the bowling hero with figures of 7 for 123 and 6 for 73. Tendulkar too played his part. Though he scored only ten runs in both innings, he picked up three wickets with his spin bowling. Sachin's victims were Hayden, Gilchrist and Warne. It was the second time in Tests that he had three wickets in an innings.

Australia were all out for 212 to lose by 172 runs. It was one of the greatest moments in Indian cricket history. Now it all came down to the third and final Test at Chennai. The amazing turnaround ensured a full house at the M.A.Chidambaram Stadium. Chennai was as hot and humid as ever, though not as bad as in 1986 when the two teams had been involved in only the second tied Test in history. Matches between India and Australia at Chennai have over the years produced some thrilling contests, both in Tests and ODIs. The third Test would live up to that tradition.

Four years earlier, Tendulkar had played a decisive innings in the first Test against Australia at Chennai: 155 not out. This time, his 126 would be the side's highest score, though it was Matthew Hayden's double ton and Harbhajan's 15-wicket haul that took the individual honours in another fantastic finish. A first-day score of 326 for 3 by Australia had them heading for a 500-plus score. But it was not to be. Waugh's handled-the-ball dismissal triggered a collapse and they were all out for 391. With Das, Ramesh and Laxman all going past 50, Tendulkar did not walk into a crisis as he so often has done in his career. Instead, with Dravid for company, he took India past Australia's score with just four wickets lost. It was his twenty-fifth century, but not one of his best. He had told his teammates before the match that he was determined to stick it out and record a century in the series. It was one of his more patient efforts, the runs coming from 230 balls and nearly six hours of concentration. Colin Miller, bowling seamers to Tendulkar and off-spinners to the rest, had the mortification of seeing him dropped at 82 on 396 for 4. He top-edged a sweep and Michael Slater on the midwicket boundary appeared to drop the ball in a premature act of celebration. Miller was immediately smashed over long on for six as Tendulkar jumped from 94 to 100 and two balls later, there was a pull for four.

Steve Waugh had reached his twenty-fifth Test ton at Kolkata. Now Tendulkar became the sixth to reach this landmark in his eighty-second Test and the third fastest after Don Bradman (45 Tests) and Sunil Gavaskar (79 Tests). After reaching the century, he went after Warne. Twice he swept him fine as the leggie aimed for the rough outside the leg stump. Then he cut him cheekily over slip for four. Tendulkar had come to the crease on the second ball of the third day after McGrath had Das lbw first ball for 84. Exactly 80 overs later, he was caught behind off Jason Gillespie. It was his fourth century in five Tests at Chennai, and the sixth against Australia. There were still ten overs to be bowled in the day. But the crowd began to quietly get up and leave. For them, Tendulkar was out, the entertainment for the day was over, and it was time to slip away.

I asked one of them why he was leaving when there was still some play remaining. He appeared surprised to be asked the question. 'But Sachin is out,' he said.

'Soon, very soon, people will be turning up only to watch Tendulkar play,' R. Mohan had written a decade earlier. The prediction had come true. It was a trend that was first noticeable during the Australia series and would manifest itself more starkly against England at the end of the year. Sachin drew crowds the way Bradman had in the previous century, and W.G. Grace in the century before that. Once the master batsman was out, spectators lost interest in the rest of the day's play. It was as if a game of 11 players on each side was reduced to just one.

The first-innings lead was stretched to 110. Openers Slater and Hayden almost wiped it out with a stand worth 82. Once again, there was a collapse engineered by Harbhajan, who had 8 for 84 to finish with a record 32 wickets, the most by a spinner for a three-Test series. The target for India was only 154. But when Tendulkar (17) fended off a fiery bouncer from the tireless Gillespie to Mark Waugh at slip, the tension around the stadium rose to breaking point. Seven down for 135, the Indians were fighting for every run. Finally, and fittingly, Man of the Series Harbhajan squeezed the winning runs from McGrath with only two wickets in hand. Not since the golden years of 1971 and 1983 had Indian cricket celebrated so long and hard and joyously.

After all the drama of the Test, for once the five-match one-day series was looked upon as an anticlimax. However, it turned out to be one of the best played on Indian soil as the players from both sides carried on the intensity from the Tests. The obvious animosity between the two captains gave the series an edge as Waugh and his men resolved not to leave India empty-handed. In the end, just as they had done in 1998, they bounced back from their defeat in the Test series to take the ODIs 3-2. Hayden and Laxman continued their batting heroics, and for Tendulkar the series would bring two very special landmarks.

India won the first game at Bangalore by 60 runs. Australia levelled with a crushing eight-wicket win at Pune. India then took the lead again as they won the third at Indore by 118 runs and then saw their lead pegged back when they went down by 93 runs at Visakhapatnam. The final match at Margao saw Michael Bevan play another of his typical one-day gems as Australia cantered home by four wickets with two overs to spare.

It was a special moment at Indore for Tendulkar in his two hundred and sixty-sixth match (259 innings) as he drove Warne to extra cover for a single. That took him to 34 and he became the first man to score 10,000 runs in ODIs, on his way to his twenty-eighth century. Sunil Gavaskar in 1987 had achieved a similar feat in Tests.

Normally reticent about records, Sachin was candid this time in his post-match comments. 'I would be lying if I said I wasn't aware of the target but I did not feel any pressure.' He seemed to have been biding his time in the over before Warne's, seemingly determined to reach the magic mark off the spinner's bowling. The figures were revealing. Sixteen of his 28 centuries had come abroad, in 178 matches, while 12 were scored at home in 88 matches. Of the 10,105 runs at the end of the Indore game, 3675 were scored at home at an average of 48.36, while 6430 were scored abroad at fractionally under 40. There were some other significant statistics. Twenty-two of the 28 tons had helped India win. His strike rate was a superb 86.26 and his average for final matches/grand finals was a striking 56.13. All these figures were valid until the end of the Indore match.

At Margao, in the fifth game, would come another milestone that gave him immense satisfaction. He picked up three wickets and the one of Steve Waugh was his hundredth. 10,000 runs and 100 wickets—it was a unique double for a unique cricketer.

32

Foot Fault

There cannot be another Sachin Tendulkar.—Virender Sehwag

After the excitement of the home series against Australia, it was time for the Indians to hit the road again. First stop would be Zimbabwe, where they had not won a Test match in the two previous visits, followed by Sri Lanka and then South Africa. In 1992, Zimbabwe's inaugural Test had been drawn; six years later, they had shocked India by 61 runs. Now it was time to make amends.

The Indians started on the right note. The first Test at Bulawayo was won by the visitors by eight wickets, their first victory outside Asia since beating England 2-0 in 1986. Sachin Tendulkar top-scored with 74 in India's first innings of 318. However, opener Shiv Sundar Das was the Man of the Match with 30 and 82 not out. Tendulkar (36) hit the winning runs. It was a special moment, for only twice before in his career had India won abroad—in Colombo in 1993 and in Dhaka in 2000. He pulled out a stump as a souvenir—something he had never done before. Asked why by a journalist, he replied: 'This is a special feeling.'

Indeed it was. But it would not last for long. Harare had been the scene of India's shocking defeat in 1998. Now the batting crumbled in both innings. Totals of 237 and 234 were just not good enough. Zimbabwe swept home by four wickets and India were once again denied series victory on foreign soil. From an individual point-of-view, the one-day tri-series that followed (with the West Indies) was a triumph for Tendulkar. With scores of 70, 9, 81 not out, 122 not out and 0, he was the Man of the Series, bagging three Man of the Match awards as well. His century came in the last round-robin game against the West Indies at Harare, on 4 July, after India had ensured that they would be in the final. Needing 230 to win, Tendulkar stayed until the end (48.1 overs) on 122, as India won by four wickets. But the duck in the final against the same opponents, at the same venue, rankled. Facing a total of 290, India fell short by 16 runs. It was Tendulkar's dismissal at the hands of Man of the Match Corey Collymore that proved vital once again.

It was obvious Sachin was having fitness problems and while fielding, he had made numerous visits to the dressing room for treatment. At the time, it was said that he had a stomach injury.

Back home, an interview that Tendulkar gave to PTI reporter Ashish Shukla was causing waves. In it, Sachin had discussed the sensitive issue of captaincy. Sensitive, because Sourav Ganguly's bad patch with the bat was just beginning to be noticed and commented upon. In the interview (published in newspapers around the country on 3 July 2001), Tendulkar was quoted as saying that he was not thinking about leading the team 'at the moment. But I haven't ruled it out also.' He then sought to dispel suggestions that the burden of captaincy had hampered his batting in the past and said his first double century came when he was captain. 'Only, I think when I was captain, we played South Africa, West Indies and Australia...probably the toughest tours,' he was quoted as saying. Shukla added: 'But he did admit that captaincy had hampered him "as a person" though he did not elaborate.'

Naturally, all the headlines focussed on his comments on the captaincy, a never-ending debate in Indian cricket circles. Earlier, in December 2000, he had been quoted on the issue for the first time by a Bengali paper from Kolkata. 'When I gave up the captaincy, the situation demanded so. However, I have never said that I will not lead India again. I am pretty open to the idea of leading India if the situation comes to such a stage.'

Word quickly got back to Sachin that the interview was making news. The result was damage control in the form of one of his longest newspaper interviews to V. Srivatsa in Harare, run over three parts in the *Times of India* (6-8 July 2001).

Q: Why this sudden speculation about captaincy and you not being averse to step in when you quit the job on your own even as everyone begged of you to stay on?

A: I have never spoken on this issue. I was just asked whether I would be keen on leading the side and I said I have not really thought about it. I didn't step down from the captaincy so I can immediately start thinking about it. I took some time to make this decision, it's not a rash decision taken at the spur of the moment. I just felt what I was doing was right and I just like to close those chapters and enjoy the game.

Q: There's nothing wrong in aspiring to be a captain, just as a politician wanting to become the prime minister, but what were the compelling reasons for quitting in the first place? Were they cricketing reasons or personal?

A: Even when I stepped down I said I wasn't ruling out completely another stint of captaincy at a later stage. Even now I say the same thing, that doesn't mean I want to become captain today. Things are going well and I don't want to disturb anything. The problem is whatever I say is interpreted. If I had said that I am not interested in captaincy it would have become a headline, and if I say no comments then people would have said something is cooking. I feel things are going in the right direction and that's how it should be.

Apart from the sensitive subject of captaincy, there was news being created by Sunil Gavaskar too. In a rare critique of Tendulkar, he came down on him for throwing away his wicket in the defeat in the second Test at Harare. Tendulkar on 69 had carved a widish delivery to point, to trigger another Indian batting collapse on the fourth day. The team had slipped from 197 for 3 to 234, paving the way for Zimbabwe's victory.

Gavaskar felt that the Australians were correct in rating their captain Steve Waugh as the best Test batsman in the world, for his ability to win or save matches for his team on foreign soil. 'Why blame V.V.S. Laxman when the best batsman in the universe [Tendulkar] gets a half-century and then gets out, when a big score from him is the crying need of the team?' Gavaskar wrote in an Australian paper. The criticism was challenged by veteran journalist Raju Bharatan in *Sporstar* (14 July 2001), who made the point that Waugh had failed to come through for his side when they were beaten 2-1 in that fantastic series in India.

There was a more serious matter, though, for the great man and his millions of followers to wrestle with, shortly after the team returned from Zimbabwe. During the last league match against the West Indies at Harare on 4 July, when he scored his twenty-ninth ODI century, Sachin had felt a sharp pain in his foot while setting off for a single. A month later, he invited the press to his new home in Bandra (West) to explain the injury and its implications.

> During the match [on 4 July], I felt pain while batting. I remember telling Rahul [Dravid] about feeling pain in the right toe. I heard a click while batting. After that click the toe began hurting. The next day's practice session I didn't do much except apply ice to the toe. I informed physio Andrew Leipus. I went to hospital for x-rays. Nothing showed in it. It was normal. We also consulted a specialist who said as there was no fracture, I could play. But he said the injury would need rest afterwards. I started feeling pain and was waiting for it to settle down. When I came back to India I had 4-5 days ice treatment but it didn't go down. I decided to go through a diagnosis. Dr Anant Joshi advised a scan.

After a bone scan and CT scan were done in Mumbai, it was revealed that there was a hairline fracture of the right big toe. The 'click' that Tendulkar had heard was most likely of his tiny toe bone (known as the 'medial sesamoid') snapping. Tendulkar felt there may have been more pressure on the area due to the spike-studded sole of his custom-made shoes. One of the seven spikes is located directly under the sesamoid bone of the big toe. The pressure exerted when taking off for a run, up to three to five times the body weight, on one foot, could have impacted and fractured the tiny bone.

The tour to Sri Lanka, consisting of a one-day tri-series followed by three Test matches, was round the corner. Initially, it was hoped Tendulkar would miss only the ODIs and would be fit in time for the Test series. 'I don't mind missing the one-dayers, but please ensure I can make it for the Test series,' he pleaded with Dr B.A.Krishna, chief of nuclear medicine at Hinduja Hospital, where the scans were carried out. It was not to be. On 10 August, by which time the ODI series was over, he announced he would be pulling out of the Test series as the fracture had not healed completely. Six weeks' rest was recommended, so he would hopefully be fit in time for the tour to South Africa in September.

'Sachin could have played the Test series only at the risk of further injury. And even then he wouldn't have been able to give a hundred per cent,' explained Dr Joshi. For a few days, the whole country watched as Tendulkar's fractured toe and Prime Minister Vajpayee's worn out knee competed for space in the media.

Tendulkar had missed some one-day matches just before and after the 1999 World Cup due to back pain. But it was the first time since his debut in Pakistan in November 1999 that he was missing a Test match. By 14 August 2001, when the first Test against Sri Lanka at Galle started without him, he had played a record 84 consecutive Tests since his debut, stretching from Karachi in November 1989 to Harare in June 2001.

Even as he was resting and undergoing treatment, Sachin received a piece of good news from Australia. Writer Roland Perry revealed that shortly before his death in February, Sir Don had listed for him what he considered his all-time greatest team. There was just one Indian and one contemporary player among the twelve named and that was Tendulkar, one of Sir Don's favourites. The news delighted Sachin even as the Indian media went to town. 'It is a great honour. The greatest thing to happen. It is important when Sir Don speaks anything and especially when he selects me in his team, there cannot be a better thing than that,' he said. 'I am very thrilled about it and very excited. There are some great names missing and to see my name in it, I am more than thrilled. After Sir Don and before Garry Sobers [in the batting line-up]—what else can you ask for?'

The Sri Lankan tour produced mixed results in Sachin's absence. India reached the final of the tri-series (New Zealand was the third team), only to lose once again to the hosts. The Test series started with India losing the first Test at Galle, bouncing back to win the second at Kandy, and then being beaten in the decider at Colombo.

There was a significant innings in the last league match in the ODI series against New Zealand, at Colombo, that India had to win to reach the final. The young Delhi batsman Virender Sehwag was asked to open the innings after Yuvraj Singh and Amay Khurasiya had failed in that position. He grabbed the opportunity with glee, smashing the second fastest century by an Indian in ODIs (from 70 balls).

Remarkably similar in height, build and looks, Sehwag also displayed an array of attacking shots normally the preserve of Tendulkar, whose batting spot he had taken in his hero's enforced absence. Tendulkar thrilled Sehwag by sending a message of congratulations. And the press was quick to latch on to the similarity. The 'New Tendulkar', they were already calling him. Sehwag, though, would have none of it.

'How can I be even compared with the great man! Look at the amount of cricket he has played, and see what I have played in comparison. Just see how many matches he's won for India. I mean, he's God when he's out there in the middle. There cannot be another Sachin Tendulkar,' he told Tapan Joshi of *Cricketnext.com.*

33
Year of Controversies

Life without cricket is unthinkable for me.—Sachin Tendulkar

The latter half of 2001 was to see one controversy after another—not all of his own making—dogging Sachin Tendulkar's footsteps. First in Zimbabwe had come the interview where he claimed he had been misquoted on the captaincy issue. There was even some unpleasantness over his fractured toe, with a section of the media claiming the injury was not as serious as it was made out to be; and was merely an excuse to not tour Sri Lanka. This angered both Tendulkar and Dr Joshi, the BCCI doctor who he had been consulting after his return from Zimbabwe. It was all quite unnecessary and mean-minded, really.

Another storm blew in over which he had little control. *Wisden Cricket Monthly*, which had been founded in 1978 by David Frith, was getting set to launch its Indian edition and also *Wisden*'s Internet site, *Wisden.com*. As part of the pre-launch hype, the publishers released at a press conference in Mumbai on 26 July 2001, their own version of the top 100 Test batting and bowling performances of all time. This was presented as the *Wisden Online* 100. Shockingly, none of Tendulkar's 25 Test tons (until then) got into the list. The reaction in India was swift and sharp. 'Oh Jesus! The Cricketing Bible Excludes the Great Indian God' screamed the banner headline in the New Delhi edition of the *Indian Express* (27 July). The controversial aspect of the list got it tremendous space in the media, both in India and abroad.

The formula for deciding the rankings was explained by the man who had invented the system, Y.Ananth Narayan, a virtual unknown in cricket circles.

One *Wisden* official airily dismissed the outraged response from the journalists gathered at the function. 'Tendulkar needs to play more great innings in future to make the list,' he said. Not many in India or abroad were willing to buy that line. V.V.S. Laxman was the highest ranked Indian on the list, at number six, for his stupendous 281 against Australia at Kolkata earlier that year.

It emerged that the people behind the *Wisden* rankings had laid great store by whether the batsman's contribution had been a match-winning one or not. This automatically shut out some of the great match-saving batting performances. Nirmal Shekhar in the *Sportstar* (11 August 2001) raised the pertinent point: 'Surely, you cannot penalize a genius [Tendulkar] for the mediocrity around him!'

In fact, two of Tendulkar's 100s against Australia, both at Chennai, had been instrumental in earning India a victory. So also his century at Colombo in 1993. His 155 not out in 1998 had been ruled out by *Wisden* as the bowling was not considered to be of top quality—Shane Warne, Gavin Robertson and Paul Reiffel being the front line bowlers! Even more baffling was the exclusion of his 126 at Chennai in March 2001 that had helped India clinch the epic series 2-1. The front line bowlers this time were Glenn McGrath, Jason Gillespie, Colin Miller and Warne. Any attack with McGrath and Warne can safely be considered world-class. But the number-crunchers at *Wisden* were unmoved.

In all the heat and dust raised by the rankings, there was one important factor that was obscured. *Wisden Online* was *not* 'the Bible of cricket'. That tag belongs to *Wisden Cricketers' Almanack*, which is the longest running sports yearbook, having appeared continuously since 1864. The launch of *Wisden Cricket Asia* magazine in December 2001 and the *Wisden.com* web site earlier the same year had sought to cash in on the aura surrounding one of the most revered names in sport. But apart from being part of the same publishing house, they bear little resemblance to the *Almanack* as far as reliability, tradition and longevity are concerned.

Not only did Tendulkar not find a place in the top 100 of all time, but he also did not make it to the Indian Top Ten. This is where the matter took on farcical overtones. For, coming in at number ten was Ajit Wadekar's 143 in the third Test against New Zealand at Wellington in 1968.

Raju Bharatan, who attacked the logic (or the lack of it) behind the rankings both in the *Hindu* and its sister publication, the *Sportstar*, had this to say in the daily (4 August 2001):

> Commendable as was that 143 knock by way of being Ajit Wadekar's only Test hundred, pray how did it 'set up India's first overseas series win'? For Wadekar's 143, being in the third Test v New Zealand at Basin Reserve (Wellington) during March 1968, only saw the Junior Nawab of Pataudi's India go up 2-1 in that four-match series. Short point: 'India's first overseas series win' was thus yet to happen after that third Test in which Wadekar hit 143. Actually, only as a result of our 272-run victory in the fourth and final Test at Eden Park (Auckland) did India register its 'first overseas series win'. And, in that deciding fourth Test, Ajit scored just 5 and 1 (as we clinched the rubber 3-1), so the renewed query—how did Wadekar's 'excellent innings set up India's first overseas series win'? It was mainly thanks to Erapalli Prasanna's match analysis of 55.1-26-84-8 and Bishan Singh Bedi's match figures of 34.4-19-35-5 (on top of Farokh Engineer's 48, Rusi Surti's 99 and Chandu Borde's 65 not out) that we won that fourth determinant Test with Ajit Wadekar nowhere in the picture.

In February 2002, the list of top 100 One-day International batting and bowling performances was announced. This time the media paid less attention than the year before. There were only four centuries out of Sachin's career 31 (at that stage) in the list, with the highest coming in at number 23. (His bowling figures of 5 for 35 against Australia at Kochi in 1998 came in at number 35).

This time the match-winning argument was invalid—a

phenomenal 24 of those centuries had helped India win. Missing from the list was his 143 against Australia at Sharjah in 1998 (the so-called 'sandstorm innings') which got India into the final despite losing the game. The reasons trotted out by Ananth Narayan for its exclusion only exposed the hollowness of the system.

We were told the match did not result in a win for India, thus ignoring the fact that the first target had been to get past New Zealand's net run rate and into the final. And that the sandstorm which interrupted Sachin's innings and altered the target, was of no consideration as factors beyond the scorecard itself were not taken note of. In other words, any schoolboy could have come up with his own ranking. Merely attaching the *Wisden* tag gave it no special sanctity.

Interestingly, one of *Wisden*'s own columnists, Kamran Abbasi, now came out with criticism of the Test listing, saying the absence of any innings from Tendulkar and Javed Miandad had not been adequately explained.

Barely a month after the *Wisden Online* Test 100, came the revelation of Sir Don Bradman's 'Dream Team'. Of course, like any 'World XI' selection, this one too evoked controversy. That it had been chosen by cricket's greatest legend only added to the debate. It was to avoid all this that Bradman had stipulated that author Roland Perry release the twelve names only after his death. There were certainly some surprising names on the list. It was heavily biased towards Australians (seven out of 12, including Bradman) and the structure of the team looked unbalanced. While the team was heavily criticized (Sunil Gavaskar expressed his doubts as to whether Bradman himself had made the selection), there was little dispute over Tendulkar's inclusion in the side.

In the chapter on Tendulkar in Perry's book *Bradman's Best*, Perry emphasized Sir Don's fascination with Tendulkar's batting. 'Bradman never missed a chance to see Tendulkar from then [when he first saw and commented on his batting] until the end of the 1999 three-match Test series in Australia,' wrote Perry. Perry adds that by mid-1998, after watching Tendulkar destroy Australia in Tests and one-day games in

India, Bradman ranked him with Barry Richards, Arthur Morris and Garry Sobers. 'Not long after that series against Australia, Tendulkar received the invitation of a lifetime to join Shane Warne in meeting Bradman at his Kensington Park home in Adelaide on his nineteenth birthday. Tendulkar was honoured to be told by Bradman that he was today's best batsman.'

After the meeting Bradman told Perry how impressed he was with Tendulkar and how he expected him to go on to even greater achievements. 'Both players had mutual friendship and respect for each other. Bradman had great respect for the character of Tendulkar.'

Much to everyone's relief, Tendulkar was fit for the tour to South Africa where India were to play three Tests and a one-day tri-series with Kenya. The short break from cricket had obviously weighed on Sachin's mind. He watched all the matches on TV and was clearly frustrated at not being an active part of it all. But the break did give him precious time with his family.

'How was life without cricket for two months?' he was asked by Vijay Lokapally *(Sportstar*, 29 September 2001).

> A: It's been tough. Life without cricket is unthinkable for me, but then the injury left me with no option. I was forced to stay away from cricket and thankfully the return has been as early as possible.
>
> Q: Wasn't it a frustrating period?
>
> A: No doubt. It was very, very tough and very frustrating too. But then it was not that I wasn't in touch with cricket. I watched the team play and I shared their joy and disappointments in victories and defeats.
>
> Q: How would you describe the feeling on missing your first Test series since your debut in 1989?
>
> A: It was a very unusual situation for me. I am not at all used to sitting at home when cricket is on.
>
> Q: Your reflections after the return from Zimbabwe?
>
> A: I was able to focus on a few things away from cricket even

though it was a painful experience, but the greatest joy came out of the period as I could spend a lot of time with my family. It was a bonus actually for me and my family. I may have missed cricket but the gain on the home front was priceless. Looking after my wife and kids and their company made my recovery every bit easy. Honestly it was great to be in the company of Anjali, Sara and Arjun.

The rest certainly recharged his batteries. He was in peak form in the tri-series where he notched up his thirtieth and thirty-first ODI centuries. Tendulkar and Ganguly had two century opening stands and in the process rewrote two records set by the great West Indian opening pair of Gordon Greenidge and Desmond Haynes. Their stand of 258 in the last league match against Kenya at Paarl rewrote their own previous world record of 252 against Sri Lanka in 1997. The 258-run stand was their sixteenth partnership of over 100, surpassing the mark of 15 held by the West Indians. In the same tournament, Greenidge and Haynes' total of 5150 runs in partnership was also eclipsed.

The opening match against South Africa at Johannesburg on 5 October saw both the Indian openers record centuries in a stand worth 193. It was Tendulkar's first international match in three months and he celebrated his return with 101. Yet, India were beaten by six wickets. There was another century stand against South Africa at East London, though once again it was in a losing effort. Kenya shocked the Indians by 70 runs in Port Elizabeth and so, not for the first time in a tournament, it became a must-win situation for them in their final league match. This time, Ganguly and Tendulkar ensured there would be no escape route for Kenya, with their world-record partnership.

The Indians were looking to their openers for another good start in the final against South Africa at Durban. But their twin failures spelt doom for the side. They were beaten by six wickets. It was the ninth final in a row that the Indians had lost and questions were now being asked about Tendulkar's form in crunch games. These were his scores in the finals (he missed four games between 1999 and 2001 due to injuries): Tri-series v South Africa at Durban: 17; Coca-Cola Cup v West Indies at Harare: 0; Coca-Cola Cup v Sri Lanka at Sharjah: 5; ICC Knock-out v New Zealand at Nairobi: 69; Singapore Challenge v West Indies at Singapore: 0. Ninety-one runs in five innings were rather poor returns. There were other centuries, though, under adverse circumstances, such as the two in the 1996 World Cup; the one in 1999 against Kenya, days after his father's death; and two against Australia at Sharjah in 1998. In addition, he had been there with runs in crunch situations, when India desperately needed to win their final league matches or increase their net run rate in order to reach the finals.

India had not won a Test match on two previous tours to South Africa, in 1992 and 1996-97 and they did not look like they were about to change that scenario in 2001 either. The old weaknesses on pitches outside the Asian subcontinent would once again be cruelly exposed on the very first day of the series at Bloemfontein. 4 Indian wickets were down for 68, with the South African pace attack on the rampage. Sachin Tendulkar was now joined by Virender Sehwag who was playing his first Test; they were the last recognized batting pair at the crease. One more wicket down and the tail would be exposed. There followed a savage counter-attack from Tendulkar and the 'new Tendulkar'. Sehwag, from the small town of Najafgarh outside Delhi, had made a huge impact in the one-day series in Sri Lanka. But dubbed a one-day specialist, he had not been retained for the Test series that followed. For this Test too, he had been a marginal selection.

Now, in the presence of his batting idol, he took the South African bowling attack apart in a stand worth 220 glorious runs. Tendulkar took 17 balls to score his first run; the next 101 came from 97 as he unleashed a range of savage shots, including one he had rarely used, the slash over the slips. India finished the opening day at 372 for 7, Tendulkar out for 155 and Sehwag (105)—now dubbed the 'Najafgarh Sachin'—becoming the eleventh Indian to score a century on Test debut. At the end of the day's play, Tendulkar refused to rate his twenty-sixth Test century, saying 'a hundred is a hundred and each has his own place.' He was determined not to allow his own ton to obscure

Sehwag's feat. 'He has shown everything which a batsman should have—patience, technique and strokes,' he said, hastening to add, 'but I don't want to comment too much about him as there's a lot more to come in the future. We can't judge him on just one innings.' That was seen as Tendulkar's way of lessening the pressure on his 23-year-old teammate.

When Sehwag joined him at the crease, Tendukar's words to the debutant had put him at ease. 'I know you must be tense. Even I was when I made my debut. But don't worry too much, just enjoy yourself.'

'I didn't copy Sachin, I learnt from him when I was young,' said Sehwag on television.

Indian coach John Wright was clear in his assessment of Tendulkar's ton. With his cricketing experience stretching over 25 years, he said it was the best Test innings he had ever seen. Tendulkar and Sehwag in their first big stand together made onlookers rub their eyes in bewilderment. Who was who? Pradeep Magazine was quick to point this out in the *Hindustan Times* (5 November 2001): 'He [Sehwag] has something more as well: strokes which remind everyone of Tendulkar. There were moments yesterday when it became difficult to differentiate between the two. Some of the shots he played bore the maestro's stamp.'

The impressive innings of 155 led *Wisden.com* India editor Sambit Bal to rank it third after Sachin's 1992 century at Perth and the 1999 Chennai ton against Pakistan. Ironically, all three failed to prevent defeat for India. Bal was writing on the third day of the Test, by which time the writing was already on the wall for the Indians despite the heroic effort of the first day. It led him to lament in *Wisden Online* (5 November 2001): 'No prizes for guessing that it won't come within sniffing distance of the Wisden 100 if India lose. Pity.' Sure enough, despite scoring a healthy 379 in the first innings, India capitulated by nine wickets in four days.

'Tendulkar has to perform more consistently on bouncy wickets in South Africa and Australia to lay claim to be the best batsman in the world along with Brian Lara,' South African legend Barry Richards had said a couple of months earlier, labelling him 'a good batsman only at home'. This was Tendulkar's answer to Richards, if one was needed. It was his third century on South African soil (in his eighth Test there) to go along with his three in Australia, also in eight Tests.

Defeat in four days was bad enough. But even worse was lurking round the corner for the tourists. Their bogeyman this time wasn't a South African cricketer, it was match referee Mike Denness, the former England captain. India were battling to save the second Test at Port Elizabeth after conceding a first-innings lead of 161 runs when the world of cricket was hit by a bombshell delivered by Denness on the fourth evening of the match.

Six players—captain Sourav Ganguly, Deep Dasgupta, Shiv Sundar Das, Harbhajan Singh, Virender Sehwag and Sachin Tendulkar—were slapped with sentences of varying degrees. The bulk of these came for what the match referee perceived as excessive and intimidatory appealing and showing dissent at the umpires' decisions. Ganguly was hauled up for not being in control of his team. Suspended sentences and fines were handed out. Sehwag, playing in only his second Test match, was banned for the next and fined 75 per cent of his match fee.

Most shocking was the charge against Tendulkar. Denness claimed Tendulkar, during his bowling spell, had tampered with the ball on the third day. In the dry language of the law, this was the charge:

> For alleged interference with the match ball, thus changing its condition. Match Referee's decision: By acting on the match ball, Tendulkar brought the game into disrepute (ICC Players and Team officials Code No. 2) and has been fined 75% of his match fee, plus a one Test ban suspended until the last day of December 2001.

To understand why Indian cricket fans took to the streets in protest, why the Indian media was full of articles and editorials condemning Denness and why the BCCI under its president Jagmohan Dalmiya virtually brought international cricket to a halt, is to understand the esteem in which Tendulkar is held in his country. This esteem has not been earned easily, nor has it been built merely on a mountain of runs. It had been gained the hard way, by being the ideal role model and avoiding the many unsavoury controversies affecting Indian cricket over the years.

Most shocking was the manner in which South African captain Shaun Pollock, in the same match, had pressurized the umpires into handing out decisions against the Indian batsmen with appeals that were loud, prolonged and provocative. The footage of his lbw appeals against Das and Laxman were shown over and over again on TV.

Suddenly, years of resentment at the widely perceived discrimination against Asian players who received harsh punishments from match referees while 'white' nations were let off scot-free, boiled over. Players like Glenn McGrath, Shaun Pollock, Allan Donald, Andrew Flintoff, Ricky Ponting and Michael Slater had been let off lightly in the past for directing abuse at their opponents. Tendulkar himself had been at the receiving end of such behaviour, particularly from the Australians. What made the charge against Tendulkar particularly ludicrous, even invalid, was that it had not been brought to the notice of the match referee by the two on-field umpires as per the law. Technically, the umpires have to report the matter if they notice the shape of the ball has been deliberately altered.

Instead, it was a South African TV producer who instructed his cameraman to focus on Tendulkar as he cleaned the seam of the ball of mud and grass on a wet day. The tapes were then handed over to Denness. This was contrary to the procedure laid down by the ICC and added a diabolical twist to the controversy. Pakistan captain Waqar Younis expressed his outrage at the anomaly. 'How can a match referee take decisions on the basis of television footage when the on-field umpires have not reported ball-tampering? The International Cricket Council must decide on that. How can a match referee take a decision in such a manner?' (*Wisden.com*)

Technically, Tendulkar was at fault. A new rule stipulated that he had to inform the umpires while cleaning the ball. But the punishment did not fit the 'crime'. Denness, once he had returned home, himself admitted Tendulkar's fault was technical, and not a breach of the law.

However, before that, on the fifth morning of the Test, there was a ridiculous press conference attended by Denness, at which he was prohibited by ICC regulations from saying a word or explaining his stand. Amidst all this tension, the Indian batsmen still had a Test and a series to save. This they did admirably, considering the tremendous pressure while batting out the last day.

Dalmiya now demanded that Denness be removed from his post if the third Test at Centurion was to be played. Or, he threatened to bring the team home. The United Cricket Board of South Africa found itself trapped between the BCCI, the ICC, the series sponsors and the television company. Eventually, a compromise was reached with South Africa's Dennis Lindsay standing in for Denness for the third match that was designated an unofficial Test by the ICC. India went down in the Test by an innings and 73 runs. Either way, South Africa had won the series.

Tendulkar's form after that blazing 155 in the first innings of the first Test was something of a let-down. He followed it up with scores of 15, 1, 22 (not out), 27 and 40. Back home, the storm was now brewing around Sehwag and the first Test at Mohali against the touring English team. The stipulation that he be dropped from one Test had not been adhered to according to the ICC, as the Centurion match where he was not played was not deemed to be an official Test. It was only after some brinkmanship that Sehwag was pulled out of the Mohali Test at the eleventh hour and the series went ahead.

The tour had earlier been thrown into doubt with the English cricket board dithering over whether to go ahead following the post-11 September security scenario in the subcontinent. Their indecision had come in for much criticism in the Indian media. Now, with Tendulkar under a cloud, the English and Australian media got a chance to hit back.

On 17 December in Bangalore, Tendulkar in his first statement following his penalty, clarified that he was indeed trying to clean the ball and never intended to do 'anything wrong'. 'Consciously I never wanted to do anything wrong. I only took the ball to remove the dust in it but the laws (about cleaning the ball) are different,' Tendulkar said while receiving the Castrol Indian Cricketer of the Year Award.

One Australian journalist, among others, brushed aside the fury of Indian fans as 'knee-jerk hubris'. It was as if they were gloating at the thought that the Indian icon had finally been found guilty after a spotless record all these years. The English media's favourite whipping boy, Dalmiya, was once again a convenient target.

One of the few English writers who tried to understand what Sachin meant to the Indian psyche was Simon Barnes. Writing in the *Cricketer International* (January 2002), Barnes drew parallels between what Sir Don Bradman meant to Australia in the 1930s and 1940s and Tendulkar's place in modern India. He also revealed that he had been told by that doyen of cricket writers, John Woodcock, that he felt Tendulkar was as good a batsman as Bradman. 'Not the view of a nutcase, not even an Indian,' wrote Barnes. 'I heard it from John Woodcock, former cricket correspondent of the *Times* and former editor of *Wisden*. So I take it seriously.' He continued, 'In India's turbulent present he [Sachin] means as much as Bradman did to Australia in the years of the Depression and incipient nationhood. In India's nationalistic climate, Tendulkar stands for Indian aspiration and India's desire to fling off subservience and take a new station in the world.'

Harsha Bhogle in *Wisden Cricket Monthly* (January 2002), lucidly explained India's case in an article headlined 'Why India Has Been Wronged.'

'Somebody [in the Western media] should have had the sagacity to stand up and say that if liberal, intelligent, moderate Indians were feeling outraged by what had happened, then maybe they should try to see why….By Denness' own admission he was not tampering with the ball, nor even picking the seam. He was merely taking the grass off the seam—an offence but a minor one….The punishment was extraordinary, not so much because of the fine and suspended sentence, but because of the opportunity it gave the world to call an honest man a cheat. Worse still, Denness had no complaint from the on-field umpires and refused to trust Tendulkar.'

While the storm was still brewing, the England team under Chennai-born Nasser Hussain arrived in India—one of the most inexperienced teams to tour the country. Nobody in the team had previously played a Test match in India. Alec Stewart, Robert Croft, Darren Gough and Andrew Caddick all withdrew from the Test series for one reason or the other, though the last two would be back for the one-day series that followed. In the first Test at Mohali, India swept to victory by ten wickets on the strength of their batting and spin bowling, inside of four days. All the predictions of another whitewash (England had been routed 3-0 when they toured last in 1993) appeared to be coming true.

Once again, it was obvious the spectators had eyes for only one man. When India batted in reply to England's 238, Deep Dasgupta scored his maiden Test century and, with Rahul Dravid, put on 136 runs. The going was slow as the batsmen sought to build up a big lead. Not that those in the stands on the second day of the match had much patience for these tactics. Both Dravid and the wicketkeeper-opener were regularly booed. It was not very pleasant and the most embarrassed person there was probably the next man to come in. Dravid, at the vital number three slot, had a new burden to bear: he was coming in just before Tendulkar. There was polite applause for Dasgupta when he reached his century in close to six hours. But when he was out for exactly 100, the man everyone in the ground had been waiting for made his grand appearance to a tumultuous applause.

Most of the English mediamen were watching Tendulkar play at home for the first time. The build up to the series in the English press had almost solely focussed on Tendulkar and his place in Indian cricket and Indian society. For them, it was a novel experience to watch the stands erupt in joy at the mere sight of their hero.

The huge hype surrounding Tendulkar obviously had an effect on the English players too, for they appeared to be initially overawed in his presence. Tendulkar came in with the score at 212 for 3. It had been quite a crawl till then. But in the short time he was at the crease before stumps on the second day, he thumped five sizzling boundaries to get 31 of the 50 runs that were scored after his arrival at the wicket. There was a great deal of overnight anticipation of his twenty-seventh

Test century, and the biggest crowd for the match turned up for it. Hussain, in a desperate bid to plug the flow of runs from Sachin's bat had his seamers, particularly Matthew Hoggard, bowl a consistent outside off-stump line with an 8-1 field in place. Tendulkar's free-flowing stroke play was stifled and he faced 144 balls before being caught behind off the persistent Hoggard for 88.

England's tactics and Tendulkar's reaction to them were an ominous sign of things to come. After the debacle at Mohali, England showed great heart in getting the better of draws, both at Ahmedabad and Bangalore. England's batsmen bounced back from their first Test trauma to pile up 407 when they batted first at Ahmedabad. India lost 4 wickets for 93 before Tendulkar and Laxman's century stand hauled them back. Once again, Hussain switched to containing tactics. Hoggard, Craig White and Andrew Flintoff bowled well outside off stump to a 7-2 and 8-1 field—two slips, two gullies, backward point, point, cover and mid-off.

It was obvious by now that England's intention was not so much for their bowlers to get Sachin out, but rather to frustrate him so much that he would throw away his wicket. Tendulkar was not flustered, though, and got his runs steadily though not particularly quickly. His first 50 came from 128 balls. Then he decided to break free of the shackles in the post-lunch session of the third day.

Hoggard's negative line was brilliantly negated in one magical over. The ball was twice worked outside off, through the vacant leg side field, for boundaries. For the last ball of the over, Hussain was forced to move a fielder across. It made no difference. Once again, the ball was whipped across his stumps and Sachin made three runs. England's fielders appeared awestruck as Hoggard went for 11 in that over.

Another 11 followed from off-spinner Richard Dawson's over and Tendulkar got to his almost inevitable century with a savage pull off Hoggard. The second 50 had taken just 55 balls. His dismissal for 103, caught by Hussain at mid-on off Hoggard, was disappointing, just when he had got on top of the bowling and the tactics. 'I was very disappointed,' the centurion said at the press conference at the end of the day. 'I made a hundred but I was hoping to keep going so that we could get as close to England's total as possible.'

The century brought him level with Steve Waugh and Allan Border in his eighty-eighth Test. Now only Bradman (29) and Gavaskar (34) were ahead of him. Significantly, it was also the fiftieth century of his first-class career since his first on debut in 1988 against Gujarat. This was his two hundred and seventy-third innings in his one hundred and seventy-sixth match, and he joined four other Indians with 50-plus centuries.

England delayed their declaration to set India an improbable target of 374 from 97 overs. Behind the delay—no team had scored 300-plus to win a Test in India—was the fear in the England captain's mind of another flurry of runs from Tendulkar. In the event, he scored 26 from 81 balls as India were determined not to go for the runs.

It was obvious by now that just one player out of 22 was dictating the trend of the entire series. Hussain's obsession with Tendulkar had become all-consuming.

Former England captain Mike Brearley summed up quite beautifully in the *Guardian* (16 December 2001), the special place Tendulkar enjoys in India: 'Perhaps it is in his Hindu roots that Tendulkar finds the peace of mind to carry without either arrogance or panic the load of national fervour that lands on his stocky shoulders. If it is in one's karma to be the Indian Bradman, then all that is to be done is to try one's best and thank God.'

The Bangalore Test was severely curtailed by rain and a draw was always on the cards. Once again, though, England gained a healthy first innings lead. India had won the series 1-0, but there was talk of a 'moral' victory for the raw Englishmen. Hussain was being described as the best England captain since Brearley. There were comparisons with Douglas Jardine, the proponent of the hated 'Bodyline' bowling in the 1932-33 series in Australia. There were indeed some uncanny similarities: the peaked cap, the angular nose and the place of birth (Jardine too was born in India, though of Scottish parents). But most striking of all was what the press, both in India and England, were referring to as 'Bodyline II'.

Jardine's attempt to stem the massive flow of runs from the blade of the incomparable Sir Donald Bradman had worked to the extent that his average was cut from 100-plus to just over 50, and England won the 'Ashes' back. The sour taste left by the negating of fair play, however, threatened to cause a split in the Empire. Now, 70 years later, there was no Empire left and no unfair intimidation either. But there was one common motive—a batsman with the ability to dominate had to be stopped at any cost. The bowler entrusted with keeping Tendulkar on a leash was the tall left-arm spinner Ashley Giles. Giles operated to a leg-side line with a packed on-side field, bowling over the wicket in the rough behind Tendulkar's legs in order to frustrate him. Even wicketkeeper James Foster stationed himself well outside the leg stump.

'A Moral Win, but at What Price?' was the headline to Brearley's report of the Test in *Wisden Cricket Monthly* (February 2002). 'Nasser Hussain is an inventive thinker, a superb motivator, a steely leader. But his Bodyline II tactics against Tendulkar took the fun out of cricket,' he wrote. Tendulkar made a mockery once again of the off-stump line of England's pace attack, forcing Hussain to change tactics and switch the field. Flintoff began to pepper the batsmen round the wicket down the leg side as the fast bowlers had done in 1932-33, though not to such devastating physical effect. The rules had been altered shortly after the 'Bodyline I' series to restrict the number of fielders allowed to crouch around the bat, waiting for the ball to be fended off. Hussain's tactics were perhaps the supreme compliment to the supreme batsman of the modern era. Not that Tendulkar was in any mood to appreciate it at the time.

By the close of the truncated second day, Tendulkar was on 50. He had failed to score off 75 of the first 92 balls he had faced. Things got out of hand and the umpires had to intervene to cool things down at the final drinks interval of the day when Tendulkar and Das indulged in a finger-wagging session with Hussain. The subject of the heated discussion was obvious. It was one of the very rare occasions when Tendulkar was seen to lose his temper on the field of play.

On the third morning, he managed just 27 runs in 90 minutes.

Time and again, he used his backside or his pads instead of his bat to knock Giles' deliveries away. It was obvious he was trying to make a point. You bowl this line all day and I will keep using my 'backside' play. As Brearley explained in the *Wisden Cricket Monthly* (February 2002): 'Legside attack precludes almost all the classical strokes of batting. It becomes impossible to swing the arms freely at the ball if it is constantly leaping at your ribs or scuttling around behind your calves. The sweep is hard to control because the bounce of the ball is unpredictable.' Both Brearley and Sunil Gavaskar called for legislation to outlaw such bowling. They felt the umpires should have been empowered to call 'wide'.

Tendulkar was joined at the crease by Sehwag. Remarkably, the man with just two Tests behind him proceeded to show just how Giles could be mastered. Admittedly, the 'new Tendulkar' was living dangerously. He was dropped at slip on one, and time and again he was beaten outside the off stump. But he brought the first signs of forceful batting into the Indian innings. Six of his 13 boundaries in an innings of 66 from 88 balls were off the spinner. He went over midwicket, he played a cross-bat slog and there was a reverse sweep that went with the speed of a tracer bullet to the boundary.

His ego piqued by this audacious display—perhaps all the talk of the 'new Tendulkar' was getting on his nerves—the role model decided to finally chance his arm. He succeeded briefly, smashing 12 in an over from Giles. But in the next, trying another heave, he was stranded outside the crease and Foster had him stumped for 90.

It was the first time in 89 Tests that he had been dismissed thus. Judging by the celebrations, one would have thought England had got him for a first ball duck. .

Gavaskar has long attacked the attitude of English cricket and cricketers and this display of theirs gave him ample fodder. 'They once again confirmed (with their tactics) that they are a boring side that drives spectators to despair,' he declared in the *Hindustan Times* (21 December 2001).

None, though, was more scathing than former Somerset captain Peter Roebuck, one of the most perceptive cricket writers. As he observed in the *Age*, Melbourne (22 December 2001):

> England pretends to be the guardian of the game, yet does more harm than all the rest put together. That the batsman in these instances was Sachin Tendulkar hardly needs saying. After all, the Poms did not hesitate to attack The Don's skull when they couldn't get him out, an approach so effective that it was promptly used against less gifted willow-wielders, and then the Poms sacked their captain and fastest bowler. Tendulkar is the modern master of batting. It is a privilege to watch him and bowl to him. To see him reduced to kicking the ball away like a dopey tail-ender in the closing minutes of a tight contest was to see the game betrayed. England has lots of young players and it hasn't been much of an education for them. If Tendulkar has any sense he'll bat till Christmas. If the game has any sense it will outlaw these puritanical practices. Tendulkar gives the bowlers a chance and he is human. Let them try to get him out with skill and not cleverness.

Wrote former Hampshire captain Mark Nicholas in the *Daily Telegraph* (21 December 2001):

> What we were watching was a legal, non-violent bodyline-type tactic, an attempt to minimise the impact of an awesome opponent. It was well thought out and applied with accuracy.... With a terrific performance at Ahmedabad they proved to themselves that they could match 10 of the Indian team but admitted the 11th, Tendulkar, had the wood on them. So they resolved to keep him in check. The line Giles bowled in Ahmedabad was very good, consistently on or around leg stump, and with the seamers sticking to a line outside off stump the master batsman was tested fair and square. He made an unforgettable hundred.
>
> The differences from Ahmedabad and here in Bangalore are that England have increased the distance between him and the

ball and have at times bowled the same line from both ends. This compromises the entertainment which, we must continue to assume, is the point of it all. The line in this case between what is fair and what compromises the spirit of the game is as fine as it gets.

Not surprisingly, Tendulkar was the Man of the Series with 307 runs at 76.75. He would also be Man of the Series in the one-day games that followed, after Christmas, in which the visitors came back from 1-3 down to finish on 3-3. Sachin had scores of 36, 45, 68, 87 (not out), 18 and 12. An ODI century against England was still elusive, however, after ten years.

There were two memorable century opening stands between Sachin and Sehwag in the ODIs, during which, but for the names on their shirts, it would have been virtually impossible to tell the two apart. In the third match at Chennai, they hammered 107 in the first 19 overs; at Kanpur in the next it was 134 in 18, Tendulkar scoring 87 not out from 67 balls and Sehwag 82 from 62.

The talk of 'moral victory' for the English camp was more valid this time.

34

Global Brand

Tendulkar works.—Hemant Kenkre

When Sachin Tendulkar was signed up by WorldTel chief Mark Mascarenhas in October 1995 for a five-year deal (starting in 1996) worth $7.5 million (Rs 31.5 crores), it made the front pages of all the national papers in India. The sum was considered astronomical, more than any other Indian sportsperson could have ever dreamed of, and was of as much news value as another century from Indian cricket's latest superstar. In May 2001, the contract was renewed, this time reportedly for $17.5 million. Eight months later, on 26 January 2002, Mascarenhas was killed in a road accident near Nagpur. He was 44.

It was a shattering blow for Tendulkar. Mascarenhas had used his marketing genius to transform his client's iconic status on the cricket field into the number one brand name in the Indian marketplace. His death came in the middle of the one-day series against England. 'I met him as an agent, but he became a very close friend of mine,' said Tendulkar. 'I had a very emotional relationship with him. I will never forget him because he always stood by me and wished well for me. Often, he went out of the way to make things comfortable for me. Overall he was more a family member than an agent.'

Tendulkar flew between one-day matches to Bangalore, where he delivered a moving eulogy at St. Patrick's Chruch. 'He was like my elder brother,' Tendulkar said at the 40-minute service, attended by a large gathering. 'He always treated me as a family member.…He always told me to concentrate on my cricket and never bother about the commercial aspect and never forced me to do any commercials.'

By the time he died, Mascarenhas's empire was beginning to show numerous cracks. There had been income tax raids on his business premises in Bangalore and accusations of rigged telecast deals. The last straw was when, at the height of the match-fixing scandal, he was publicly referred to as a 'bookie' by a Union minister. As usual, he threatened to sue. His weekly magazine, *Cricket Talk,* and the website *total-cricket.com,* both launched in characteristically flamboyant fashion, had shut down in six months in the wake of financial scandals. He had also lost numerous TV deals including telecast rights in the lucrative Sharjah market and had been left with the crumbs of only Bangladesh. A far cry from his glory days which began with the acquisition of telecast rights to the 1996 Wills World Cup. He had paid $10 million for the rights, and made twice that in profits.

The renewal of the contract with Tendulkar was seen as the last chance to salvage his business. He got the signature he wanted in the face of stiff competition from sports marketing giant IMG, who also manage Tiger Woods, Michael Jordan and the Williams sisters. It was a measure of the faith Tendulkar had in him. 'I don't believe in what has been said about Mark,' Tendulkar said in an interview, shortly after renewing the deal. 'I am very comfortable working with him. He is a nice guy.'

'Larger than life' was the phrase that popped up in almost every obituary. Binoo John, who had worked with Mascarenhas at *Cricket Talk*, used the most apt comparison in an article on the web site *HTcricket.com* (27 January 2002); he described Masceranhas as the 'Don King of Indian cricket'.

'He was tough as nails as a negotiator. But once he got you to sign on the dotted line, he was the perfect host. He made his clients feel like royalty with lavish gifts and extravagant parties,' I was told by the marketing man of a multinational company, who had extensive dealings with Mascarenhas.

He was also a man in a hurry, with flamboyant traits and idiosyncrasies, which would drive his colleagues to dismay. Many of the obits were written by ex-employees who highlighted these traits. Dues had been left unpaid to employees and contributors after the magazine and website had folded up, including to some high-profile international cricketers. One person who worked with him told me that Mascarenhas had a habit of booking four or five airline tickets in a day. 'As the day wore on he would cancel one after the other. That gave him a sense of power. Then when it was time for his last flight he would curse and howl at the poor driver to speed things up. That was Mark for you.'

WorldTel, with its base in Connecticut—where Sachin and his family enjoyed occasional holidays—was a one-man show. Mascarenhas's ego and love for power and prestige meant he controlled the day-to-day running of the company.

In an interview shortly after Tendulkar's contract was renewed in 2001, Mascarenhas said he was initially attracted by the 'angelic quality' of his star client, evident in the few commercials he shot before 1995. Mascarenhas, of course, used the 'national icon' cliché in abundance, and outlined his plans to merchandize the Tendulkar brand name in a chain of restaurants. The idea has probably been put in cold storage now.

The entry of multinational companies into the Indian market after the opening up of the economy in 1991, the massive appeal cricket enjoys all over India, and the explosion in the number of one-day matches combined with the birth of cable TV—were all factors in the marketing success of Tendulkar. His clean image and status as a role model for the young generation, in particular, was the clincher. But back in 1995, Mascarenhas's offer to him was perceived as a huge gamble. Many felt the WorldTel chief had priced his client out of the market.

It was Ravi Shastri who first introduced Tendulkar to Mascarenhas in a Bangalore pub. The first deal was struck soon after that. 'I'm betting on the power of Sachin and the power of the Indian economy,' Mascarenhas said in an interview (*Outlook,* 15 November 1995). 'TV spending is growing at the rate of 50 per cent per annum. Even if you account for 15 per cent inflation, that's a high figure.' In 1995, Tendulkar was considered to be in the second rung of cricket's superstars, a shade behind Brian Lara and Shane Warne. But the

Tendulkar mania went from strength to strength in the intervening years and the Bangalore-born maverick businessman got handsome returns on his canny investment.

The brands Tendulkar currently endorses represent a wide variety of products. Only liquor and cigarettes have always been taboo. 'If people look up to me, I've got to set the right example,' he said in an interview to the *Telegraph* (1998). The public today identifies him by his TV commercials for Pepsi, Adidas, Fiat and a host of others, as much as for his cricketing achievements. That is, of course, what the marketing men aim for.

The car industry has been going through a recession in India with a glut of new models flooding the market and most flopping miserably. It took an Italian manufacturer to cash in on the Tendulkar magic. As a result, the Fiat Palio is the only car for which there is a waiting list. A high-priced limited signature edition (the S10) was unveiled in early 2002 and was snapped up in a jiffy. Never mind that Tendulkar's favourite cars are his two Mercedes Benz luxury models (a silver SL600 and a maroon C36 AMG600—he has a passion for driving them himself). As far as the buying public is concerned, Pialo is at the top of his list.

Reportedly, Tendulkar's contract is worth Rs 3 crores per year. (Amitabh Bachchan is said to earn Rs 5 crores annually from the Maruti Versa ad campaign.) After the first contract was finalized in 1995, Mascarenhas claimed in an interview that only Tendulkar and Bachchan had the power to endorse everything from bicycles to luxury cars, 'but Bachchan has faded away and Sachin has just risen'.

It's doubtful whether Tendulkar has ever ridden a two-wheeler, except perhaps bicycles in his schooldays. That did not stop him from endorsing the TVS Ltd. range of motorbikes. The deal was struck in the wake of the Sourav Ganguly/Hero Honda endorsement. Then, just before the 1996 Wills World Cup, the Chennai-based MRF tyre company proposed a bat logo deal. It was clinched in a matter of seconds. This has been one of the most lucrative and high-profile deals for Sachin. The back of his broad bat is prime advertising space. He had some problems initially in regard to ICC regulations. But now, the world cricket body has ratified such logos and MRF have since signed up Steve Waugh as well. Every other deal is peanuts compared to the original one, though.

If Tendulkar is known as the 'god of Indian cricket' (one ad even depicted him in a Lord Krishna-like avatar), then Alyque Padamsee is considered the 'god' of the world of Indian advertising. This is what Padamsee told me about the Tendulkar marketing phenomenon: 'When a cricketer achieves the status of Don Bradman, he becomes a global brand. In other words, he is instantly recognizable as the Coke bottle or the Marlboro Cowboy. He becomes more than a personality. He becomes a saleable persona. Sachin and Gavaskar have both imprinted themselves on the global emotional retina.'

'What does money mean to you?' Tendulkar was asked by Sanjay Karhade in the *Times of India Sunday Review* (10 June 2001).

> I guess it is important. But it doesn't mean you can do *anything* to earn it. I play cricket from the bottom of my heart because I enjoy it a great deal and I am compensated in the process. One thing most people do not understand is that I started playing at the age of 11. Do you think at that age, any kid can think of the money aspect of the game? You will see thousands of kids playing cricket, do you think they have money on their mind?

There is no doubt that companies that sign on Tendulkar for astronomical sums get more than their money's worth. Fiat is just one example. Adidas, the German sports clothing and equipment firm, is another. 'Adidas has grown by over 200% after signing on Tendulkar in 1998,' according to Managing Director Tarun Kunzru (*Mid Day*, 27 June 2000). 'Growth has been significant and one reason could be the association between Adidas and Sachin.' More than just 'one reason', one suspects!

Interviewed for the same article, marketing man Hemant Kenkre (Tendulkar's captain at the CCI in the late 1980s) had this to say: 'Sachin's a real person, someone who delivers imagery with attitude—not some "make believe" screen persona who acts a part. That's what a brand is all about—being real with imagery, attitude and delivery. Tendulkar works.'

He certainly does—even with that squeaky, boyish voice he has had since childhood. The current list of endorsements includes Visa, Britannia, Pepsi, Fiat, Adidas, MRF, TVS and Boost. His first, for Action Shoes ten years ago, earned him Rs 2 lakhs a year. Now the money is in the region of Rs 2 crores.

Sachin's wife Anjali, her father Anand Mehta, and his elder brother Ajit are known to handle deals on Sachin's behalf. WorldTel steps in to finalize the arrangement. Tendulkar is thus free to concentrate on cricket. Sachin, of course, has the final say. 'His strength is that he listens carefully and he knows very clearly what he wants to do and what he doesn't,' Mascarenhas said in 2001. 'Is there a parallel to Tendulkar on the cricket field? So judge it from there,' was his comment in *Mid Day* (17 May 2001) when asked, 'Would you say this deal will be unparalleled in the history of world cricket?'

The renewed contract also saw a new-look Sachin appearing in commercials for the likes of *Home Trade,* with the Sydney Cricket Ground as a backdrop. Gone were the boyish curls, in was the goatee, complete with designer stubble and a new hairstyle—the close-cropped look known as the 'Caesar cut'. The boy-to-man image makeover was handled by 'Team Tendulkar': hair stylist Monisha Naegamvala, photographer Atul Kasbekar, fashion consultant Rocky S. (credited with styling the new look) and ad film-maker Prahlad Kakkar.

'Sachin had a great recall value among men and kids. But after the *Home Trade* commercials, even women go "wow Sachin",' said Kasbekar in an article on the Sachin makeover in the *Times of India Sunday Review* (21 October 2001). Though he looked stiff in the early commercials, Sachin is now comfortable in front of the camera. He comes across as a natural. It was not always like that, as he himself admits. He used to get nervous in the beginning and it took him a while to relax before the camera and be himself. It was, after all, a whole new ball game.

Sachin's priorites in life have always been clear: Family, cricket and commercials—in that order. His life is cricket, but not without his family. They go with him everywhere. What he does off the ground is private....And only when he has enough time to switch off from cricket or when he's not playing the game does he do commercials, never in the middle of a cricket series.

Mascarenhas's American widow Karen has inherited his empire. Whether she will be able to keep the big bucks flowing in their star client's direction is the big question now.

35

Man and Myth

My family is altogether a different issue.—Sachin Tendulkar

It's not easy being Sachin Tendulkar. In a vast country like India, cricket and movies are about the only outlets for a population of a billion-plus, of whom most lead a mundane, often perilous existence. Life can get pretty claustrophobic for us ordinary folk. Imagine what is must be like for cricketers and movie stars.

I have seen Tendulkar mobbed wherever he goes. Yet, he rarely loses his cool. And the adulation is not confined to India either. In Dhaka, Sachin, Sourav Ganguly and Wasim Akram are the reigning deities. During the October 2000 inaugural Test match, I witnessed this adulation first-hand. In a country where cricket fanaticism rivals even the kind witnessed in India, it can sometimes get scary. Certainly, Ganguly looked terrified as he raced the short distance from the dressing rooms at the Bangabandhu Stadium to the team bus. Thousands of hands sought him out from the crowd of fans milling inside and outside the stadium. It was equally hysterical when it came to Sachin's turn to run the gamut of the hordes. 'Sochin, Sochin,' they screamed. I could not help but notice his beatific smile. He was actually lapping up the adulation. It reminded me of old film clips depicting the Beatles mania of the 1960s.

'It would be terrible if only 10 people came to watch. As a cricketer I try to give pleasure, and the more people that watch and applaud, the more pleasure I get myself. I wouldn't swap it,' Tendulkar told Mark Nicholas in an interview in the *Daily Telegraph* (11 December 2001). Nicholas, the former Hampshire captain, spent the whole interview seemingly probing for a chink in the Tendulkar armour. He exulted after the answer above: 'So there's an ego, at last, saved for the stage and the curtain calls.'

How could it be any different? Every entertainer, whether on stage, screen or field of play, has an ego. Tendulkar has accomplished what all superstars strive for, to harness that ego in a positive manner. Ego has driven some international sports persons, when they visit India, to bring the media in tow as they do their good deed for the day. It is the done thing to be seen and heard attempting to alleviate the misery of India's teeming downtrodden. When was the last time you saw even a photograph of Tendulkar at a charity function? Yet, he gives of his spare time unstintingly.

Journalist Joe Hoover knows this hidden side of Tendulkar well. Sports editor of *Deccan Herald*, Hoover has organized numerous charity auctions and functions where Tendulkar is the star attraction. 'He is so approachable and he never says no,' Hoover told me. 'He doesn't need the publicity because unlike some other sportspersons, he sees no need to use these acts to improve his image.' Hoover recalled an incident in Pakistan in 1997 when he telephoned Tendulkar in his hotel room and asked him if he could give some signed bats for a charity auction. 'Within minutes he was on the phone, informing his bat manufacturers in Meerut to send over a dozen to New Delhi for this purpose.'

Throughout this book there have been excerpts from numerous interviews with Tendulkar by Vijay Lokapally. As the cricket correspondent for the *Hindu* and the *Sportstar*, Lokapally has undoubtedly interviewed him more often than any other journalist. He spoke to me about his interaction with Sachin over the years:

> Sachin once said to me, *"Kiti lihishil?"* (How much will you write)?...I first met him at a Wills Trophy match at Kanpur. This was before his 1989 Test debut. The next occasion was in New Delhi just before the Pakistan tour, his first. He and Vivek Razdan, the other debutant were very excited. And do you know, he has that same excitement about playing cricket after all these

years?

I have always been impressed by the dignified way he carries himself both on and off the field. Despite all his fame and wealth, he is very down to earth. That has not changed a bit in all the years I have known him.

Friends, family, food (particularly seafood—he enjoys a spot of cooking too), cricket and music. These are Tendulkar's passions in life. Lokapally says you can guess which hotel room is his by the music blaring from it. '*Dire Straits* used to be his favourite group. But these days he is into old Hindi songs. He seeks these out and gets them specially recorded.'

(This incidentally is another trait he shares with Sir Don Bradman, who would lock himself up in his hotel room and play his gramophone records after the day's play.)

'Sachin Tendulkar is an important person of our country. He is our country's wealth and we will protect him,' said Mumbai's Commissioner of Police, M.N.Singh. This followed reports that Tendulkar and Ganguly were kidnap targets for militant groups.

Another heavy price of fame is the loss of privacy. 'Ask me anything you want about cricket, but keep my family out of this,' he has told journalists repeatedly.

Wife Anjali, daughter Sara and son Arjun are the centre of Sachin's existence, just as his parents and siblings were when he was growing up. 'My family life is altogether a different issue. I have always kept it a very private affair and I don't want that to be public. Everybody is watching whatever I do on the field,' he told the *Week* (29 November 1998). 'Even today they [his family] look after me and ensure that my feet are on the ground,' he said when asked how he copes with all the hopes and adulation of the fans. 'Not Tiger Woods, not even Michael Jordan lives with such a following,' wrote Nicholas in the *Daily Telegraph* interview.

'It has been harder for my family than for me to be honest. I've known no other way. A couple of times I tried going out for the evening in Bombay in disguise but that didn't work too well, so now I just stay in. Now when I go to pray I go late at night to the temples which are empty and quiet,' he told Nicholas. His favourite temple is the Uddan Ganesh temple in Bandra which he visits with Anjali, often after midnight.

Sachin has spent all his life in Bandra, first with his parents, brothers and sisters at *Sahitya Sahawas* in Bandra (East) and since the middle of 2001, at the swank *Le Mer* apartments in Bandra (West). They may share virtually the same address, but Bandra (East) and Bandra (West) are worlds apart. 'West looks down its nose at East,' says one long-time resident of the more upmarket side of town. For the first few years of their marriage, Sachin and Anjali stayed in a separate flat in the same building where he grew up. *Le Mer* was recommended to him by Prahlad Kakkar who has been directing Sachin's commercials for a decade now. The Tendulkars bought a duplex apartment there in mid 2001. 'The apartment block has more glittering stars than the milky way,' one Mumbai sports journalist told me. In that sense, Sachin has made the transformation from his solid middle-class youth to the world of Mumbai's glitterati.

The influence of Anjali and her parents, Anand (an international bridge player) and Annabelle Mehta (who is English and a leading philanthropist) has played a large part in this transition. According to a family friend, when Anjali and he first met and started dating, Mrs Mehta would disguise Sachin in a wig and beard and smuggle the couple out to the family's holiday homes in Lonavalla and Goa. The Mehtas are among Mumbai's wealthiest families, a fixture on the city's social circuit. Which is very distant from Sachin's roots. But he still keeps in touch with his old school friends and often drops by to enjoy his mother's seafood dishes, which he relishes. ('Favourite Food: Anything cooked by mother.') Anjali was a practising paediatrician till the birth of Arjun in 2000. Now she looks after the two kids. It is the daughter who has inherited her father's curly hair. As for Arjun, his father has already gifted him a plastic bat and ball. 'It may be a batsman's game. But I would want him to become a good all-rounder,' says the proud father with characteristic determination.

Wife and kids (accompanied by a maid) fly out to be with Sachin on long tours abroad. He obviously cannot be parted from them for long.

So how good a father is he?

'It's not just bull about spending "quality time" with his children,' neighbour and friend Kakkar says. 'While other kids are rocked to sleep with a pat on the back, Sachin drives Arjun round and round the building in his Merc at night and puts him to sleep.' (*Times of India Sunday Review*, 9 December 2001)

Epilogue

Qua Vadis, Sachin?

'The moment that I start thinking I am the best batsman in the world, that will be the end of my career'—Sachin Tendulkar

Sachin Tendulkar made his twenty-eighth century against Zimbabwe at Nagpur in March 2002 in his ninetieth Test match. India won the Test by an innings and 101 runs, and the second Test in New Delhi by four wickets, Sachin's contribution being 36 and 42. The century put him ahead of Allan Border and Steve Waugh and one behind Sir Donald Bradman.

He was rested for the five-match one-day series that followed the two Tests. BCCI secretary Niranjan Shah explained that he was suffering from 'Patellofemoral Syndrome', an injury to his knees. 'Tendulkar has been experiencing discomfort in both his knees since the Test series against England. While this is not a serious problem, it is necessary to give him rest. However, with prescriptive exercises and physiotherapy, he will be available for the tour of the West Indies,' we were told. Having played first-class cricket non-stop (there were three short breaks earlier for health reasons) for half his life, it was hardly surprising that the body was beginning to show signs of wear-and-tear. Still, there were whispers that it was more than just 'discomfort in both knees' that Tendulkar was suffering from. There was also the issue of discomfort against left-arm spinners.

We have seen in Chapter 33 how England captain Nasser Hussain sought to bottle up Tendulkar by using his left-arm spinner Ashley Giles in a negative leg-stump attack (it was revealed in March 2002 that this tactic was shortly to be outlawed). Now it was the turn of unheralded Zimbabwe left-arm spinner Ray Price to get the better of Tendulkar. Right through his career, Sunil Gavaskar had encountered difficulties in tackling left-arm spinners. England's Derek Underwood claimed his wicket on more occasions (12) than any other Test bowler. In the 1981-82 Ranji Trophy semifinal at Bangalore, Gavaskar attracted a barrage of criticism by switching to batting left-handed for Mumbai for one hour to stave off an innings defeat. He explained it was the only way to thwart the negative line bowled by Karnataka left-arm spinners Raghuram Bhat and B.Vijaykrishna. Tendulkar too has been seen batting (and bowling) left-handed in the nets—and pretty effectively at that—and indeed, he writes with his left hand.

Bradman's wicket was similarly claimed eight times by England left-arm spinner Headley Verity, more than by any other bowler. Bishan Singh Bedi—arguably the greatest left-arm spinner of them all—has claimed that short batsmen have traditionally had problems against this type of bowling, citing the case of Dilip Doshi and Javed Miandad. At Nagpur, Tendulkar batted the whole of the second day for 137 runs. It was a side of him that surprised many. He said the slow nature of the Nagpur pitch, with its low bounce, made batting difficult, especially when driving in front of the wicket. As a result, he did not loft the ball even once.

Tendulkar's 176 was the highest of three Indian tons in the match. At the same venue and against the same team, two years earlier, he had scored a double century and this time he let out a yell of frustration when he was caught off Price. Test double-century number three was obviously his target.

After picking up five of the seven Indian wickets to fall at Nagpur, Price posed problems for all the batsmen on a spinning track at Delhi's Ferozeshah Kotla. 'I have never seen Sachin batting so tentatively,' was Andy Flower's comment after Tendulkar had scratched around for 119 balls for 36 in the first innings. Twice, he was lucky to survive lbw appeals off Price who finally got him trapped in front with one that kept low. At the start of the tour, Zimbabwe captain Stuart Carlisle had sent out a warning that he would attempt to emulate Hussain's tactics. But Price did not bowl negatively. There was no bowling outside the batsmen's legs, no packed on-side field.

Once again, it was Virender Sehwag who proved a point or two when it was his turn to bat in the second Test (he had not played at Nagpur). Playing in his usual streaky style, he blasted 74 from 118 balls, including 16 boundaries in the first innings. India were set a small target of 122 to win the Test. But with Sehwag injured, they struggled to get home by four wickets. For 45 minutes on the final day, Tendulkar did not face Price. He had batted attractively for his 42. But the first over the left-arm spinner bowled to him, he had him lbw. There were murmurs in the press box at the Kotla as Sanjay Bangar and Harbhajan Singh took India home with some shaky batting amidst rising tension. 'Why was Tendulkar not around at the end? He never finishes a game for India,' said one journalist in disgust.

Tendulkar had been there at the end when India beat Zimbabwe at Bulawayo the year before. But when India squeaked home by two wickets at Chennai in the third Test against Australia earlier that year, it was the tailenders who had had to finish the job. And there were some who were yet to forgive Sachin for not being able to guide India to victory against Pakistan in Chennai in 1999—despite his heroic century played in intense pain. A spate of articles had appeared in the Indian media towards the end of 2001, partly as a fallout of the *Wisden* 100 rankings, questioning Tendulkar's greatness, specifically his match-winning capabilities. The misgivings had some validity, going by figures alone.

India had won 26 of the 91 Test matches (till the end of the 2002 Zimbabwe series at home) in which Tendulkar had played (just three of these abroad—he did not play in the 2001 Kandy Test). Only seven of his 28 centuries had resulted in a victory (nine were scored in Tests which India lost) and his batting average in Tests won was only marginally higher than his career average (He would go on to score his twenty-ninth century in India's win in the Port-of-Spain Test in April 2002). This is in stark contrast to the records of Sir Garry Sobers, Steve Waugh and Greg Chappell whose averages were close to or over 20 more than their career average in matches won by their teams.

All this sounds rather arcane, but the whole point of the exercise was perhaps to de-mystify Tendulkar, not a bad thing in India where, of course, he has long enjoyed god-like status. It was also pointed out that just seven of his 28 centuries had been scored in the second innings. The statistics for his first and second innings in his 91 Tests make interesting reading:

First: Innings: 89; not out: 3; runs: 5, 578; highest score: 217; average: 64.86; 100s: 20; 50s: 23; 0s: 4.

Second: Innings: 57; not out: 12; runs: 2, 095; highest score: 155 not out; Average: 46.55; 100s: 8; 50s: 7; 0s: 3.

(These figures are taken from an article headlined 'Is Sachin an all-time great?' by C. Rammanohar Reddy in the *Hindu*, Sunday Magazine, 20 January 2002).

Another analysis of Sachin's career appeared in the *Indian Express* Sunday Magazine of 2 December 2001. Headlined 'God, no please', the piece written by Vikrant Gupta and Sandeep Dwivedi set out to find fault. Every achievement was downplayed, every drawback magnified. This was evident in its dismissal of Bradman's famous quote in 1996, 'Sachin reminds me of myself,' which was brushed aside with the comment: 'But that might have come at the end of a long day watching TV.'

The article reminded me of a comment by cricket historian Ramachandra Guha in an article about the giants of the game, from W.G.Grace to Bradman, Sobers and Tendulkar. 'Grace was loved by 15 million Englishmen. Bradman was idolised by 10 million Australians. Sobers worshipped by a like number of West Indians. But Sachin is answerable to a billion hyper-expectant and too-easily dissatisfied Indians,' observed Guha in the *Hindu*, Sunday Magazine, 25 November 2001.

At the other end of the scale from the *Indian Express* attack were the fanciful views of H.Natarajan in *Cricketnext.com* and Chris Ryan in *Wisden Cricket Monthly*. Natarajan's tongue-in-cheek article in May 2001 under the headline 'Crystal ball gazing into Tendulkar's future' used statistics initially to look towards the end of his career and what he could achieve if he played till 2010. According to the writer's calculations he would end up with 48 Test centuries and over 17,000 runs. His ODI record would read 22,595 runs with 39 centuries. Natarajan then listed 'a few things in the realms of fantasy but which could well become a reality in the years to come.' The list ran to a total of 39. Among them:

- Tendulkar will be the first Indian sportsperson to be granted Bharat Ratna (the nation's highest civilian honour).
- The Reserve Bank of India will mint a special 100 rupee coin with Tendulkar's face on one side.
- A stamp and a first day cover featuring Tendulkar.
- Bandra, the place where the hero spent all his life, will be renamed Sachin Tendulkar Nagar.
- April 24, Tendulkar's birthday, will be declared as Ekta Din. A day when all differences—political, linguistic, religious, etc.—are set aside to foster national pride. 'That is what Tendulkar was able to achieve when he was at the crease and that is what the day aims to achieve in his honour.'

Mark Waugh predicted in a column in 1998 that Tendulkar would play another 10 years and score more than 40 Test centuries. Like many of his rivals, Waugh too admitted he got pleasure watching Tendulkar bat. 'While I keep hoping he gets out, I must admit that his strokeplay is a treat to watch from that (slips) position.'

Ryan in the June 2001 issue of *Wisden Cricket Monthly* looked back on Tendulkar's 28 'most prolific' years 'and 27 of the most prodigious months in the history of batting.' At 28, Tendulkar had 25 Test centuries in his kitty. His nearest rivals at the same age, Bradman and Neil Harvey, both had 15. Average-wise, of course, no one could touch Bradman who had 3,849 runs at 98.69 by his twentieth birthday. (Tendulkar: 6,720 at 56.94).

'But even that gap is closing. In the past 27 months, since February 1999, Tendulkar has piled up 1,720 runs in 15 Tests at a Bradmanesque 71.67. Should he continue at this rate for the next decade, at age 38 he will have amassed 20,480 runs and 81 centuries in 202 Tests. His average will be a cool 66.06, placing him on a unique second tier of champion batsmen—still behind Bradman (99.94) but distinctly ahead of Pollock, Headley and Sutcliffe (60-odd).'

What this projection did not take into account was that many batsmen see their career graphs dipping dramatically after they cross 30. The reasons are obvious—reflexes, footwork, eyesight, all tend to decline at this stage. A perfect example is the career graph of Sunil Gavaskar. His first 50 Tests saw him score 20 centuries; his last 75, just 14. Tendulkar himself is uncertain about the future. When asked in an interview in 2001 if he had another 10 years to go, he replied: 'I will try. But you know the idea is to enjoy the game and the years will fly by I am sure.'

What of the captaincy? As we have seen in Chapter 32, the question had cropped up again, as recently as mid-2001. Tendulkar, while denying he was eyeing it, did not rule out the possibility of taking up the reins again, sometime in the future. When Sourav Ganguly was retained as captain for the series against Zimbabwe at home in early 2002, chairman of the selection committee, Chandu Borde, made it clear that Tendulkar's name had not come up for discussion. Borde said Tendulkar had told him that he was not interested in the post. Still, it is conceivable that if Ganguly's form continues to be shaky in Test matches, Tendulkar—who will be 30 in 2003—could once again take up the job. Perhaps this time he will be allowed to make a better job of it.

The major landmark of 100 Tests should be reached very soon, on the tour to England, in the fourth Test at the Oval starting on 5 September 2002—fitness (and match referees) permitting. That will make him the youngest ever to reach the landmark, and the fourth Indian after Sunil Gavaskar, Kapil Dev and Dilip Vengsarkar. Gavaskar made an impassioned plea to BCCI president Jagmohan Dalmiya to ensure that the historic Test was staged at the Wankhede Stadium at home in Mumbai. But that appears unlikely unless Sachin misses a Test in the West Indies where India play five from April 2002, and then in England where there will be four later in the year.

And what of life after cricket? The only time Tendulkar made a comment on his future career, he said he was interested in 'some business connected to cricket.'

Journalist Vijay Lokapally feels he has a future as an expert TV commentator: 'I have watched matches sitting by his side and seen how astutely he reads the game. Often he will uncannily predict a move by the fielding captain.'

In September 2001, Ajit Tendulkar launched a coaching scheme in Mumbai and promised Sachin would drop by occasionally to share his insights. The name alone would surely bring in hordes of youngsters desperate for some of that Sachin magic to rub off on them.

Whichever path Sachin Tendulkar chooses once his playing days are over, he is sure to make a success of it. Such is the spirit and determination of the Little Champion.

Sachin Tendulkar in Figures

(All statistics are up to 31 March 2002)

by S. Pervez Qaiser

INNINGS BY INNINGS PERFORMANCE IN TESTS

Runs	*Min*	*Balls*	*4s*	*6s*	*Opponent*	*Venue*	*Season*	*Result*	*Match*	*Innings*
15	29	24	2	-	Pakistan	Karachi	1989-90	Drawn	1	1
59	248	165	4	-	Pakistan	Faisalabad	1989-90	Drawn	2	2
8	24	16	1	-						3
41	124	90	5	-	Pakistan	Lahore	1989-90	Drawn	3	4
35					Pakistan	Sialkot	1989-90	Drawn	4	5
57	195	136	5	-						6
0	1	1	-	-	New Zealand	Christchurch	1989-90	Lost	5	7
24										8
88	324	266	4	-	New Zealand	Napier	1989-90	Drawn	6	9
5					New Zealand	Auckland	1989-90	Drawn	7	10
10					England	Lord's	1990	Lost	8	11
27										12
68	216	136	8	-	England	Manchester	1990	Drawn	9	13
119*	225	189	17	-						14
21					England	The Oval	1990	Drawn	10	15
11					Sri Lanka	Chandigarh	1990	Won	11	16
16	47	42	3	-	Australia	Brisbane	1991-92	Lost	12	17
7	30	28	1	-						18
15	33	23	-	-	Australia	Melbourne	1991-92	Lost	13	19
40	122	107	5	-						20
148*	298	215	14	-	Australia	Sydney	1991-92	Drawn	14	21

Runs	Min	Balls	4s	6s	Opponent	Venue	Season	Result	Match	Innings
6	20	8	1	-	Australia	Adelaide	1991-92	Lost	15	22
17	36	29	2	-						23
114	228	161	16	-	Australia	Perth	1991-92	Lost	16	24
5	12	9	1	-						25
0					Zimbabwe	Harare	1992-93	Drawn	17	26
11					South Africa	Durban	1992-93	Drawn	18	27
111	375	270	19	-	South Africa	Johannesburg	1992-93	Drawn	19	28
1										29
6					South Africa	Port Elizabeth	1992-93	Lost	20	30
0	1	1	-	-						31
73	272	208	8	1	South Africa	Cape Town	1992-93	Drawn	21	32
50	158	118	6	-	England	Kolkata	1992-93	Won	22	33
9*	17	19	2	-						34
165	316	296	24	1	England	Chennai	1992-93	Won	23	35
78	285	213	10	-	England	Mumbai	1992-93	Won	24	36
62	128	114	7	-	Zimbabwe	Delhi	1992-93	Won	25	37
-	-	-	-	-	Sri Lanka	Kandy	1993-94	Drawn	26	
28					Sri Lanka	Colombo (SSC)	1993-94	Won	27	38
104*	217	163	11	1						39
71	204	152	10	-	Sri Lanka	Colombo (RPS)	1993-94	Drawn	28	40
142	260	224	22	-	Sri Lanka	Lucknow	1993-94	Won	29	41
96	189	138	15	-	Sri Lanka	Bangalore	1993-94	Won	30	42
6					Sri Lanka	Ahmedabad	1993-94	Won	31	43
43	55	47	7	-	New Zealand	Hamilton	1993-94	Drawn	32	44
11*										45
34	68	43	7	-	West Indies	Mumbai	1994-95	Won	33	46
85	176	139	10	1						47

Runs	Min	Balls	4s	6s	Opponent	Venue	Season	Result	Match	Innings
179	212	158	12	-	West Indies	Nagpur	1994-95	Drawn	34	48
54	180	138	3	-						49
40	67	55	9	-	West Indies	Mohali	1994-95	Lost	35	50
10	37	24	2	-						51
4	6	4	1	-	New Zealand	Bangalore	1995-96	Won	36	52
0*	1	0	-	-						53
52*	95	72	5	-	New Zealand	Madras	1995-96	Drawn	37	54
2	7	8	-	-	New Zealand	Cuttack	1995-96	Drawn	38	55
24	71	41	4	-	England	Birmingham	1996	Lost	39	56
122	263	176	19	1						57
31	81	59	5	-	England	Lord's	1996	Drawn	40	58
177	462	360	26	-	England	Nottingham	1996	Drawn	41	59
74	111	97	11	1						60
10	12	11	2	-	Australia	Delhi	1996-97	Won	42	61
0	6	7	-	-						62
42	79	74	7	-	South Africa	Ahmedabad	1996-97	Won	43	63
7	44	33	1	-						64
18	91	62	3	-	South Africa	Kolkata	1996-97	Lost	44	65
2	29	25	-	-						66
61	211	173	4	1	South Africa	Kanpur	1996-97	Won	45	67
36	128	98	4	-						68
15	57	45	2	-	South Africa	Durban	1996-97	Lost	46	69
4	31	25	1	-						70
169	333	254	26	-	South Africa	Cape Town	1996-97	Lost	47	71
9	39	28	1	-						72
35	72	55	7	-	South Africa	Johannesburg	1996-97	Drawn	48	73
9	13	11	2	-						74

Runs	*Min*	*Balls*	*4s*	*6s*	*Opponent*	*Venue*	*Season*	*Result*	*Match*	*Innings*
7	40	30	1	-	West Indies	Kingston	1996-97	Drawn	49	75
15*	43	36	1	-						76
88	306	233	9	-	West Indies	Port of Spain	1996-97	Drawn	50	77
92	223	147	14	1	West Indies	Bridgetown	1996-97	Lost	51	78
4	25	14	-	-						79
-	-	-	-	-	West Indies	St John's	1996-97	Drawn	52	
83	287	221	9	-	West Indies	Georgetown	1996-97	Drawn	53	80
143	292	247	20	-	Sri Lanka	Colombo (RPS)	1997-98	Drawn	54	81
139	397	267	16	-	Sri Lanka	Colombo (SSC)	1997-98	Drawn	55	82
8	43	44	1	-						83
23	129	93	2	-	Sri Lanka	Mohali	1997-98	Drawn	56	84
15	38	20	1	1	Sri Lanka	Nagpur	1997-98	Drawn	57	85
148	320	244	20	3	Sri Lanka	Mumbai	1997-98	Drawn	58	86
13	28	16	1	-						87
4	7	5	1	-	Australia	Chennai	1997-98	Won	59	88
155*	286	191	14	4						89
79	110	86	12	2	Australia	Kolkata	1997-98	Won	60	90
177	306	207	29	3	Australia	Bangalore	1997-98	Lost	61	91
31	75	64	4	-						92
34	103	68	3	-	Zimbabwe	Harare	1998-99	Lost	62	93
7	27	14	-	-						94
47	87	72	7	-	New Zealand	Wellington	1998-99	Lost	63	95
113	200	151	13	2						96
67	118	93	9	1	New Zealand	Hamilton	1998-99	Drawn	64	97
0	5	3	-	-	Pakistan	Chennai	1998-99	Lost	65	98
136	405	273	18	-						99
6	13	11	1	-	Pakistan	Delhi	1998-99	Won	66	100

Runs	Min	Balls	4s	6s	Opponent	Venue	Season	Result	Match	Innings
29	99	65	4	-						101
0	2	1	-	-	Pakistan	Kolkata	1998-99	Lost	67	102
9	18	13	1	-						103
53	94	54	10	-	Sri Lanka	Colombo (SSC)	1998-99	Drawn	68	104
124*	308	235	10	1						105
18	46	34	3	-	New Zealand	Mohali	1999-00	Drawn	69	106
126*	397	248	14	-						107
15	76	54	3	-	New Zealand	Kanpur	1999-00	Won	70	108
44*	58	39	8	-						109
217	494	343	29	-	New Zealand	Ahmedabad	1999-00	Drawn	71	110
15	16	10	3	-						111
61	181	133	8	-	Australia	Adelaide	1999-00	Lost	72	112
0	6	5	-	-						113
116	283	191	9	1	Australia	Melbourne	1999-00	Lost	73	114
52	162	122	4	-						115
45	82	53	8	-	Australia	Sydney	1999-00	Lost	74	116
4	6	4	1	-						117
97	208	163	12	2	South Africa	Mumbai	1999-00	Lost	75	118
8	20	11	2	-						119
21	119	76	3	-	South Africa	Bangalore	1999-00	Lost	76	120
20	76	53	2	-						121
18	63	41	1	-	Bangladesh	Dhaka	2000-01	Won	77	122
122	283	233	19	-	Zimbabwe	Delhi	2000-01	Won	78	123
39	45	39	8	-						124
201*	392	284	27	-	Zimbabwe	Nagpur	2000-01	Drawn	79	125
76	139	114	13	-	Australia	Mumbai	2000-01	Lost	80	126
65	154	107	11	-						127

Runs	*Min*	*Balls*	*4s*	*6s*	*Opponent*	*Venue*	*Season*	*Result*	*Match*	*Innings*
10	25	17	2	-	Australia	Kolkata	2000-01	Won	81	128
10	26	23	2	-						129
126	346	230	15	2	Australia	Chennai	2000-01	Won	82	130
17	27	17	3	-						131
74	177	128	12	-	Zimbabwe	Bulawayo	2000-01	Won	83	132
36*	42	49	4	-						133
20	77	46	2	1	Zimbabwe	Harare	2000-01	Lost	84	134
69	184	35	9	-						135
155	233	184	23	1	South Africa	Bloemfontein	2001-02	Lost	85	136
15	60	35	2	-						137
1	10	4	-	-	South Africa	Port Elizabeth	2001-02	Drawn	86	138
22*	54	45	4	-						139
88	229	144	13	-	England	Mohali	2001-02	Won	87	140
103	254	197	12	1	England	Ahmedabad	2001-02	Drawn	88	141
26	87	81	4	-						142
90	263	198	13	-	England	Bangalore	2001-02	Drawn	89	143
176	441	316	23	-	Zimbabwe	Nagpur	2001-02	Won	90	144
36	124	119	5	-	Zimbabwe	Delhi	2001-02	Won	91	145
42	79	52	7	1						146

BATTING AND FIELDING PERFORMANCE AGAINST EACH TEAM IN TESTS

Opponent	*Matches*	*Innings*	*N.O.*	*Runs*	*Avg.*	*H.S.*	*100s*	*50s*	*0s*	*Ct*
Australia	15	28	2	1406	54.07	177	6	5	2	8
Bangladesh	1	1	-	18	18.00	18	-	-	-	-
England	12	18	2	1282	80.12	177	5	6	-	13
New Zealand	12	19	5	891	63.64	217	3	3	1	7
Pakistan	7	12	-	395	32.91	136	1	2	2	1
South Africa	14	26	1	948	37.92	169	3	3	1	10
Sri Lanka	13	16	2	1124	80.28	148	6	3	-	8
West Indies	8	12	1	691	62.81	179	1	5	-	10
Zimbabwe	9	14	2	918	76.50	201*	3	3	1	5
Total	**91**	**146**	**15**	**7673**	**58.57**	**217**	**28**	**30**	**7**	**62**
As captain	25	43	3	2054	51.35	217	7	7	2	16
As a player	66	103	12	5619	61.74	201*	21	23	5	46

N.O.: Not out, H.S.: Highest Score, Ct: Catches

BATTING AND FIELDING PERFORMANCE IN EACH COUNTRY IN TESTS

Country	*Matches*	*Innings*	*N.O.*	*Runs*	*Avg.*	*H.S.*	*100s*	*50s*	*0s*	*Ct*
In Australia	8	15	1	646	46.14	148*	3	2	1	5
In Bangladesh	1	1	-	18	18.00	18	-	-	-	-
In England	6	10	1	673	74.77	177	3	2	-	5
In India	42	68	7	3888	63.73	217	14	14	3	33
In New Zealand	6	9	1	398	49.75	113	1	2	1	2
In Pakistan	4	6	-	215	35.83	59	-	2	-	1
In South Africa	9	16	1	636	42.40	169	3	1	1	7
In Sri Lanka	6	8	2	670	111.66	143	4	2	-	4
In West Indies	5	6	1	289	57.80	92	-	3	-	5
In Zimbabwe	4	7	1	240	40.00	74	-	2	1	-
Total	**91**	**146**	**15**	**7673**	**58.57**	**217**	**28**	**30**	**7**	**62**
Home	42	68	7	3888	63.73	217	14	14	3	33
Away	49	78	8	3785	54.07	177	14	16	4	29

N.O.: Not out, H.S.: Highest score, Ct: Catches

POSITION-WISE BATTING PERFORMANCE IN TESTS

Position	*Matches*	*Innings*	*N.O.*	*Runs*	*Avg.*	*H.S.*	*100s*	*50s*	*0s*
Opening	1	1	-	15	15.00	15	-	-	-
Fourth	69	107	13	5850	62.23	217	23	21	4
Fifth	13	16	-	988	61.75	169	3	5	2
Sixth	12	18	2	703	43.93	148*	2	4	1
Seventh	3	4	-	117	29.25	41	-	-	-
Total	**91**	**146**	**15**	**7673**	**58.57**	**217**	**28**	**30**	**7**
First innings	42	42	2	2967	74.17	217	10	11	-
Second innings	48	47	1	2611	56.76	176	10	12	4
Third innings	29	29	4	1424	56.96	155*	6	6	1
Fourth innings	34	28	8	671	33.55	136	2	1	2

N.O.: Not out, H.S.: Highest score

SEASON-WISE BATTING AND FIELDING PERFORMANCE IN TESTS

Season	*Matches*	*Innings*	*N.O.*	*Runs*	*Avg.*	*H.S.*	*100s*	*50s*	*0s*	*Ct*
1989-90	7	10	-	332	33.20	88	-	3	1	2
1990-91	4	6	1	256	51.20	119*	1	1	-	3
1991-92	5	9	1	368	46.00	148*	2	-	-	5
1992-93	9	12	1	566	51.45	165	2	4	2	8
1993-94	7	8	2	501	83.50	142	2	2	-	5
1994-95	3	6	-	402	67.00	179	1	2	-	5
1995-96	3	4	2	58	29.00	52*	-	1	-	3
1996-97	15	25	1	1134	47.25	177	3	5	1	11
1997-98	8	12	1	935	85.00	177	5	1	-	5
1998-99	7	13	1	625	52.08	136	3	2	2	1
1999-00	8	16	2	859	61.35	217	3	3	1	4
2000-01	6	10	1	684	76.00	201*	3	2	-	4
2001-02	9	15	2	953	73.30	176	3	4	-	6
Total	**91**	**146**	**15**	**7673**	**58.57**	**217**	**28**	**30**	**7**	**62**
Matches won	26	41	6	2156	61.60	176	7	9	1	19
Matches drawn	39	53	9	3343	75.97	217	13	14	1	27
Matches lost	26	52	-	2174	41.80	177	8	7	5	16

N.O.: Not out, H.S.: Highest score, Ct: Catches

BATTING PERFORMANCE AT EACH GROUND IN TESTS

Ground	*Matches*	*Innings*	*N.O.*	*Runs*	*Avg.*	*H.S.*	*100s*	*50s*	*0s*
Adelaide Oval	2	4	-	84	21.00	61	-	1	1
Brisbane Cricket Ground	1	2	-	23	11.50	16	-	-	-
Melbourne Cricket Ground	2	4	-	223	55.75	116	1	1	-
Sydney Cricket Ground	2	3	1	197	98.50	148*	1	-	-
W.A.C.A. Ground,Perth	1	2	-	119	59.50	114	1	-	-
In Australia	**8**	**15**	**1**	**646**	**46.14**	**148***	**3**	**2**	**1**
National Stadium, Dhaka	1	1	-	18	18.00	18	-	-	-
In Bangladesh	**1**	**1**	**-**	**18**	**18.00**	**18**	**-**	**-**	**-**
Edgbaston, Birmingham	1	2	-	146	73.00	122	1	-	-
Kennington Oval, London	1	1	-	21	21.00	21	-	-	-
Lord's London	2	3	-	68	22.66	31	-	-	-
Old Trafford, Manchester	1	2	1	187	187.00	119*	1	1	-
Trent Bridge, Nottingham	1	2	-	251	125.50	177	1	1	-
In England	**6**	**10**	**1**	**673**	**74.77**	**177**	**3**	**2**	**-**
Barabati Stadium, Cuttack	1	1	-	2	2.00	2	-	-	-
Eden Gardens, Kolkata	5	9	1	187	23.37	79	-	2	1
Feroz Shah Kotla, Delhi	5	9	-	346	38.44	122	1	1	1
Green Park, Kanpur	2	4	1	156	52.00	61	-	1	-
K.D. Singh Babu Stadium, Lucknow	1	1	-	142	142.00	142	1	-	-
M. Chinnaswamy Stadium, Bangalore	5	8	1	439	62.71	177	1	2	-
M.A. Chidambaram Stadium, Chennai	5	8	2	655	109.16	165	4	1	1
Punjab C.A. Stadium, Mohali	4	6	1	305	61.00	126*	1	1	-
Sardar Patel Stadium, Ahmedabad	4	7	-	416	59.42	217	2	-	-
Sector 16 Stadium, Chandigarh	1	1	-	11	11.00	11	-	-	-
Vidarbha C.A. Ground, Nagpur	4	5	1	625	156.25	201*	3	1	-
Wankhede Stadium, Mumbai	5	9	-	604	67.11	148	1	5	-

Ground	*Matches*	*Innings*	*N.O.*	*Runs*	*Avg.*	*H.S.*	*100s*	*50s*	*0s*
In India	**42**	**68**	**7**	**3888**	**63.73**	**217**	**14**	**14**	**3**
Basin Reserve, Wellington	1	2	-	160	80.00	113	1	-	-
Eden Park, Auckland	1	1	-	5	5.00	5	-	-	-
Jade Stadium, Christchurch	1	2	-	24	24.00	24	-	-	1
McLean Park, Napier	1	1	-	88	88.00	88	-	1	-
Westpac Trust Park, Hamilton	2	3	1	121	60.50	67	-	1	-
In New Zealand	**6**	**9**	**1**	**398**	**49.75**	**113**	**1**	**2**	**1**
Gaddafi Stadium, Lahore	1	1	-	41	41.00	41	-	-	-
Iqbal Stadium, Faisalabad	1	2	-	67	33.50	59	-	1	-
Jinnah Stadium, Sialkot	1	2	-	92	46.00	57	-	1	-
National Stadium, Karachi	1	1	-	15	15.00	15	-	-	-
In Pakistan	**4**	**6**	**-**	**215**	**35.83**	**59**	**-**	**2**	**-**
Goodyear Park, Bloemfontein	1	2	-	170	85.00	155	1	-	-
Kingsmead, Durban	2	3	-	30	10.00	15	-	-	-
New Wanderers, Johannesburg	2	4	-	156	39.00	111	1	-	-
Newlands, Cape Town	2	3	-	251	83.66	169	1	1	-
St George's Park, Port Elizabeth	2	4	1	29	9.66	22*	-	-	1
In South Africa	**9**	**16**	**1**	**636**	**42.40**	**169**	**3**	**1**	**1**
Asgiriya Stadium, Kandy	1	-	-	-	-	-	-	-	-
P. Saravanamuttu Stadium, Colombo	1	1	-	71	71.00	71	-	1	-
R. Premadasa Stadium, Colombo	1	1	-	143	143.00	143	1	-	-
Sinhalese Sports Club, Colombo	3	6	2	456	114.00	139	3	1	-
In Sri Lanka	**6**	**8**	**2**	**670**	**111.66**	**143**	**4**	**2**	**-**
Recreation Ground, St John's, Antigua	1	-	-	-	-	-	-	-	-
Bourda, Georgetown, Guyana	1	1	-	83	83.00	83	-	1	-
Kensington Oval, Bridgetown, Barbados	1	2	-	96	48.00	92	-	1	-
Queen's Park Oval, Port of Spain, Trinidad	1	1	-	88	88.00	88	-	1	-

Ground	*Matches*	*Innings*	*N.O.*	*Runs*	*Avg.*	*H.S.*	*100s*	*50s*	*0s*
Sabina Park, Kingston, Jamaica	1	2	1	22	22.00	15*	-	-	-
In West Indies	**5**	**6**	**1**	**289**	**57.80**	**92**	**-**	**3**	**-**
Harare Sports Club, Harare	3	5	-	130	26.00	69	-	1	1
Queens Sports Club, Bulawayo	1	2	1	110	110.00	74	-	1	-
In Zimbabwe	**4**	**7**	**1**	**240**	**40.00**	**74**	**-**	**2**	**1**
Total	**91**	**146**	**15**	**7673**	**58.57**	**217**	**28**	**30**	**7**

N.O.: Not out, H.S.: Highest score

BATTING MILESTONES IN TESTS

Runs	*Tests*	*Innings*	*Score*	*Opponent*	*Venue*	*Season*	*Age*
1000	19	28	111	South Africa	Johannesburg	1992-93	19 years 217 days
2000	32	44	43	New Zealand	Hamilton	1993-94	20 years 331 days
3000	45	67	61	South Africa	Kanpur	1996-97	23 years 228 days
4000	58	86	148	Sri Lanka	Mumbai	1997-98	24 years 223 days
5000	67	103	9	Pakistan	Kolkata	1998-99	25 years 302 days
6000	76	120	21	South Africa	Bangalore	1999-00	26 years 313 days
7000	85	136	155	South Africa	Bloemfontein	2001-02	28 years 193 days

PERFORMANCE AS CAPTAIN IN TESTS

Opponent	*Matches*	*Won*	*Lost*	*Drawn*	*Success %*	*Toss*
Australia	4	1	3	-	25.00	2
South Africa	8	2	5	1	31.25	6
West Indies	5	-	1	4	40.00	2
New Zealand	3	1	-	2	66.66	1
Sri Lanka	5	-	-	5	50.00	4
Total	**25**	**4**	**9**	**12**	**40.00**	**15**
Home	12	4	3	5	54.16	7
Away	13	-	6	7	26.92	8
First time	17	3	4	10	47.05	10
Second time	8	1	5	2	25.00	5

TOP FIFTEEN BATSMEN BY RUNS IN TESTS

Batsman	*Matches*	*Innings*	*N.O.*	*Runs*	*Avg.*	*H.S.*	*100s*	*50s*	*0s*
Allan Border (Australia)	156	265	44	11174	50.56	205	27	63	11
Sunil Gavaskar (India)	125	214	16	10122	51.12	236*	34	15	12
Steve Waugh (Australia)	148	233	41	9600	50.00	200	27	44	20
Graham Gooch (England)	118	215	6	8900	42.58	333	20	46	13
Javed Miandad (Pakistan)	124	189	21	8832	52.57	280*	23	43	6
Vivian Richards (West Indies)	121	182	12	8540	50.23	291	24	45	10
David Gower (England)	117	204	18	8231	44.25	215	18	39	7
Geoff Boycott (England)	108	193	23	8114	47.72	246*	22	42	10
Gary Sobers (West Indies)	93	160	21	8032	57.78	365*	26	30	12
Mark Waugh (Australia)	125	205	17	7949	42.28	153*	20	46	18
Mike Atherton (England)	115	212	7	7728	37.69	185*	16	46	20
Sachin Tendulkar (India)	91	146	15	7673	58.57	217	28	30	7
Colin Cowdrey (England)	114	188	15	7624	44.06	182	22	38	9
Gordon Greenidge (West Indies)	108	185	16	7558	44.72	226	19	34	11
Mike Taylor (Australia)	104	186	13	7525	43.49	334*	19	40	5

N.O.: Not out, H.S.: Highest score

TOP TEN BATSMEN BY AVERAGES IN TESTS

(Minimum 1500 runs)

Batsman	*Matches*	*Innings*	*N.O.*	*Runs*	*Avg.*	*H.S.*	*100s*	*50s*	*0s*
Don Bradman (Australia)	52	80	10	6996	99.94	334	29	13	7
Graeme Pollock (South Africa)	23	41	4	2256	60.97	274	7	11	1
George Headley (West Indies)	22	40	4	2190	60.83	270*	10	5	2
Herbert Sutcliffe (England)	54	84	9	4555	60.73	194	16	23	2
Adam Gilchrist (Australia)	31	44	8	2160	60.00	204*	6	11	4
Edward Paynter (England)	20	31	5	1540	59.23	243	4	7	3
Ken Barrington (England)	82	131	15	6806	58.67	256	20	35	5
Everton Weekes (West Indies)	48	81	5	4455	58.61	207	15	19	6
Sachin Tendulkar (India)	91	146	15	7673	58.57	217	28	30	7
Wally Hammond (England)	85	140	16	7249	58.45	336*	22	24	4

N.O.: Not out, H.S.: Highest score

BOWLING PERFORMANCE AGAINST EACH COUNTRY IN TESTS

Opponent	*Matches*	*Overs*	*Mds*	*Runs*	*Wkts*	*Avg.*	*5WI*	*10WM*	*Best*
Australia	15	106.2	16	338	8	42.25	-	-	3-31
Bangladesh	1	10	2	34	1	34.00	-	-	1-34
England	12	30	8	88	1	88.00	-	-	1-27
New Zealand	12	30	6	98	4	24.50	-	-	2-7
Pakistan	7	20	2	88	4	22.00	-	-	2-35
South Africa	14	42.4	7	138	5	27.60	-	-	3-10
Sri Lanka	13	16	2	29	0	-	-	-	-
West Indies	8	6	-	28	0	-	-	-	-
Zimbabwe	9	62	15	172	2	86.00	-	-	1-19
Total	**91**	**323**	**58**	**1013**	**25**	**40.52**	**-**	**-**	**3-10**
Home	42	181.2	35	538	13	41.38	-	-	3-10
Away	49	141.4	23	475	12	39.58	-	-	2-7

5WI: 5 wickets in an innings, 10WM: 10 wickets in a match

MAN OF THE MATCH AWARDS IN TESTS

No.	*Performance*		*Opponent*	*Venue*	*Season*	*Match No.*
	Runs	*Wkts*				
1	187	-	England	Manchester	1990	9
2	165	-	England	Chennai	1992-93	23
3	52*	-	New Zealand	Chennai	1995-96	37
4	159	-	Australia	Chennai	1997-98	59
5	136	3	Pakistan	Chennai	1998-99	65
6	232	-	New Zealand	Ahmedabad	1999-00	71
7	168	-	Australia	Melbourne	1999-00	73
8	105	3	South Africa	Mumbai	1999-00	75

INNINGS BY INNINGS PERFORMANCE IN ODIs

Runs	*Balls*	*4s*	*6s*	*Opponent*	*Venue*	*Date*	*Result*	*Match*
0	2	-	-	Pakistan	Gujranwala	18-12-1989	Lost	1
0	2	-	-	New Zealand	Dunedin	01-03-1990	Lost	2
36	39	5	-	New Zealand	Wellington	06-03-1990	Won	3
10	12	-	-	Sri Lanka	Sharjah	25-04-1990	Lost	4
20	25	1	-	Pakistan	Sharjah	27-04-1990	Lost	5
19	35	1	1	England	Leeds	18-07-1990	Won	6
31	26	3	-	England	Nottingham	20-07-1990	Won	7
36	22	3	2	Sri Lanka	Nagpur	01-12-1990	Won	8
53	41	7	1	Sri Lanka	Pune	05-12-1990	Won	9
30	29	1	2	Sri Lanka	Margao	08-12-1990	Lost	10
-	-	-	-	Bangladesh	Chandigarh	25-12-1990	Won	11
4	11	-	-	Sri Lanka	Cuttack	28-12-1990	Lost	12
53	70	-	-	Sri Lanka	Kolkata	04-01-1991	Won	13
52*	40	5	-	Pakistan	Sharjah	18-10-1991	Won	14
22	27	3	-	West Indies	Sharjah	19-10-1991	Won	15
11*	27	1	-	West Indies	Sharjah	22-10-1991	Won	16
49	38	3	2	Pakistan	Sharjah	23-10-1991	Lost	17
0	1	-	-	Pakistan	Sharjah	25-10-1991	Lost	18
62	73	8	1	South Africa	Kolkata	10-11-1991	Won	19
4	8	-	-	South Africa	Gwalior	12-11-1991	Won	20
1	3	-	-	South Africa	New Delhi	14-11-1991	Lost	21
1	9	-	-	West Indies	Perth	06-12-1991	Tied	22
36	65	3	-	Australia	Perth	08-12-1991	Won	23
57*	99	1	-	Australia	Hobart	10-12-1991	Lost	24
48	57	2	-	West Indies	Adelaide	14-12-1991	Won	25
21	35	3	-	Australia	Adelaide	15-12-1991	Lost	26

Runs	*Balls*	*4s*	*6s*	*Opponent*	*Venue*	*Date*	*Result*	*Match*
77	127	5	-	West Indies	Brisbane	11-01-1992	Lost	27
31	44	1	-	Australia	Sydney	14-01-1992	Lost	28
57	88	2	-	West Indies	Melbourne	16-01-1992	Won	29
4	10	-	-	Australia	Melbourne	18-01-1992	Lost	30
69	100	3	-	Australia	Sydney	20-01-1992	Lost	31
35	44	5	-	England	Perth	22-02-1992	Lost	32
-	-	-	-	Sri Lanka	Mackay	28-02-1992	Ab'd	33
11	19	1	-	Australia	Brisbane	01-03-1992	Lost	34
54*	62	3	-	Pakistan	Sydney	04-03-1992	Won	35
81	77	8	1	Zimbabwe	Hamilton	07-03-1992	Won	36
4	11	-	-	West Indies	Wellington	10-03-1992	Lost	37
84	107	6	-	New Zealand	Dunedin	12-03-1992	Lost	38
14	14	1	-	South Africa	Adelaide	15-03-1992	Lost	39
39	56	7	-	Zimbabwe	Harare	25-10-1992	Won	40
15	27	1	-	South Africa	Cape Town	07-12-1992	Lost	41
10	33	-	-	South Africa	Port Elizabeth	09-12-1992	Lost	42
22	24	2	-	South Africa	Centurion	11-12-1992	Won	43
21	44	1	-	South Africa	Johannesburg	13-12-1992	Lost	44
32	52	1	-	South Africa	Bloemfontein	15-12-1992	Lost	45
23	39	-	-	South Africa	Durban	17-12-1992	Lost	46
21	38	3	-	South Africa	East London	19-12-1992	Won	47
82*	81	6	1	England	Jaipur	18-01-1993	Lost	48
1	5	-	-	England	Chandigarh	21-01-1993	Won	49
3	6	-	-	England	Bangalore	26-02-1993	Lost	50
24	32	1	-	England	Jamshedpur	01-03-1993	Lost	51
5	6	1	-	England	Gwalior	04-03-1993	Won	52
34	30	2	1	England	Gwalior	05-03-1993	Won	53

Runs	Balls	4s	6s	Opponent	Venue	Date	Result	Match
3	9	-	-	Zimbabwe	Faridabad	19-03-1993	Won	54
8*	6	-	-	Zimbabwe	Guwahati	22-03-1993	Won	55
-	-	-	-	Zimbabwe	Pune	25-03-1993	Won	56
21	39	1	-	Sri Lanka	Colombo (RPS)	25-07-1993	Won	57
15	30	-	-	Sri Lanka	Colombo (RPS)	11-08-1993	Lost	58
25	39	1	-	Sri Lanka	Moratuwa	14-08-1993	Lost	59
26*	30	4	-	Sri Lanka	Kanpur	07-11-1993	Won	60
2	8	-	-	West Indies	Ahmedabad	16-11-1993	Lost	61
24	16	1	1	Zimbabwe	Indore	18-11-1993	Tied	62
3	25	-	-	South Africa	Chandigarh	22-11-1993	Won	63
15	31	3	-	South Africa	Kolkata	24-11-1993	Won	64
28*	43	2	-	West Indies	Kolkata	27-11-1993	Won	65
1	5	-	-	Sri Lanka	Rajkot	15-02-1994	Won	66
11*	18	-	-	Sri Lanka	Hyderabad	18-02-1994	Won	67
52	63	3	-	Sri Lanka	Jalandhar	20-02-1994	Lost	68
15	19	1	-	New Zealand	Napier	25-03-1994	Lost	69
82	49	15	2	New Zealand	Auckland	27-03-1994	Won	70
63	75	9	-	New Zealand	Wellington	30-03-1994	Won	71
40	26	8	-	New Zealand	Christchurch	02-04-1994	Lost	72
63	77	7	1	Emirates	Sharjah	13-04-1994	Won	73
73	64	10	3	Pakistan	Sharjah	15-04-1994	Lost	74
6	7	1	-	Australia	Sharjah	19-04-1994	Won	75
24	26	4	-	Pakistan	Sharjah	22-04-1994	Lost	76
11*	-	-	-	Sri Lanka	Colombo (RPS)	04-09-1994	Ab'd	77
6	5	-	-	Sri Lanka	Colombo (RPS)	05-09-1994	Lost	78
110	130	8	2	Australia	Colombo (RPS)	09-09-1994	Won	79
0	2	-	-	Sri Lanka	Colombo (SSC)	17-09-1994	Won	80

Runs	*Balls*	*4s*	*6s*	*Opponent*	*Venue*	*Date*	*Result*	*Match*
0	4	-	-	West Indies	Faridabad	17-10-1994	Lost	81
0	4	-	-	West Indies	Mumbai	20-10-1994	Won	82
8	24	-	-	West Indies	Chennai	23-10-1994	Won	83
115	136	9	-	New Zealand	Baroda	28-10-1994	Won	84
34	47	7	-	West Indies	Kanpur	30-10-1994	Lost	85
62	54	13	-	New Zealand	Delhi	03-11-1994	Won	86
66	68	8	-	West Indies	Kolkata	05-11-1994	Won	87
54	64	5	-	West Indies	Visakhapatnam	07-11-1994	Won	88
88	112	10	-	West Indies	Cuttack	09-11-1994	Won	89
105	134	10	-	West Indies	Jaipur	11-11-1994	Won	90
13	15	3	-	New Zealand	Napier	16-02-1995	Lost	91
37	51	3	1	South Africa	Hamilton	18-02-1995	Lost	92
47	40	7	-	Australia	Dunedin	22-02-1995	Won	93
48	30	9	1	Bangladesh	Sharjah	05-04-1995	Won	94
4	9	1	-	Pakistan	Sharjah	07-04-1995	Lost	95
112*	107	15	1	Sri Lanka	Sharjah	09-04-1995	Won	96
41	41	5	-	Sri Lanka	Sharjah	14-04-1995	Won	97
30	19	5	-	New Zealand	Jamshedpur	15-11-1995	Lost	98
39	51	4	-	New Zealand	Amritsar	18-11-1995	Won	99
7	11	1	-	New Zealand	Pune	24-11-1995	Won	100
65	60	9	1	New Zealand	Nagpur	26-11-1995	Lost	101
1	4	-	-	New Zealand	Mumbai (BS)	29-11-1995	Won	102
127*	136	15	1	Kenya	Cuttack	18-02-1996	Won	103
70	91	8	-	West Indies	Gwalior	21-02-1996	Won	104
90	88	14	1	Australia	Mumbai	27-02-1996	Lost	105
137	137	8	5	Sri Lanka	Delhi	02-03-1996	Lost	106
3	12	-	-	Zimbabwe	Kanpur	06-03-1996	Won	107

Runs	*Balls*	*4s*	*6s*	*Opponent*	*Venue*	*Date*	*Result*	*Match*
31	59	3	-	Pakistan	Bangalore	09-03-1996	Won	108
65	88	9	-	Sri Lanka	Kolkata	13-03-1996	Lost	109
28	31	3	1	Sri Lanka	Singapore	03-04-1996	Won	110
100	111	9	1	Pakistan	Singapore	05-04-1996	Lost	111
1	5	-	-	Pakistan	Sharjah	12-04-1996	Lost	112
2	15	-	-	South Africa	Sharjah	14-04-1996	Lost	113
118	140	8	2	Pakistan	Sharjah	15-04-1996	Won	114
17	26	2	-	South Africa	Sharjah	17-04-1996	Lost	115
57	71	6	-	South Africa	Sharjah	19-04-1996	Lost	116
30	19	5	1	England	The Oval	23-05-1996	Ab'd	117
6	19	1	-	England	Leeds	25-05-1996	Lost	118
1	11	-	-	England	Manchester	26-05-1996	Lost	119
110	138	5	1	Sri Lanka	Colombo (RPS)	28-08-1996	Lost	120
40	46	8	-	Zimbabwe	Colombo (SSC)	01-09-1996	Won	121
7	11	1	-	Australia	Colombo (SSC)	06-09-1996	Lost	122
89*	89	9	3	Pakistan	Toronto	16-09-1996	Won	123
20	23	3	-	Pakistan	Toronto	17-09-1996	Lost	124
2	13	-	-	Pakistan	Toronto	18-09-1996	Won	125
3	9	-	-	Pakistan	Toronto	21-09-1996	Lost	126
23	44	-	1	Pakistan	Toronto	23-09-1996	Lost	127
11	8	2	-	South Africa	Hyderabad (I)	17-10-1996	Lost	128
88	111	9	-	Australia	Bangalore	21-10-1996	Won	129
64	93	3	-	South Africa	Jaipur	23-10-1996	Lost	130
28	38	5	-	South Africa	Rajkot	29-10-1996	Lost	131
62	61	8	-	Australia	Mohali	03-11-1996	Won	132
67	89	6	-	South Africa	Mumbai	06-11-1996	Won	133
114	126	14	-	South Africa	Mumbai	14-12-1996	Won	134

Runs	*Balls*	*4s*	*6s*	*Opponent*	*Venue*	*Date*	*Result*	*Match*
0	4	-	-	South Africa	Bloemfontein	23-01-1997	Lost	135
6	8	1	-	Zimbabwe	Paarl	27-01-1997	Tied	136
1	14	-	-	South Africa	Port Elizabeth	02-02-1997	Lost	137
14	24	2	-	South Africa	East London	04-02-1997	Lost	138
41	56	1	1	Zimbabwe	Centurion	07-02-1997	Lost	139
104	97	8	1	Zimbabwe	Benoni	09-02-1997	Won	140
32	27	6	-	South Africa	Durban	12-02-1997	Ab'd	141
45	33	7	1	South Africa	Durban	13-02-1997	Lost	142
13	15	-	1	Zimbabwe	Bulawayo	15-02-1997	Lost	143
44	43	10	-	West Indies	Port of Spain	26-04-1997	Lost	144
65*	70	6	-	West Indies	Port of Spain	27-04-1997	Won	145
9	15	1	-	West Indies	Kingstown	30-04-1997	Lost	146
1	11	-	-	West Indies	Bridgetown	03-05-1997	Lost	147
117	137	13	2	New Zealand	Bangalore	14-05-1997	Won	148
2	4	-	-	Sri Lanka	Mumbai	17-05-1997	Lost	149
4	7	1	-	Pakistan	Chennai	21-05-1997	Lost	150
21	28	3	-	Sri Lanka	Colombo (RPS)	18-07-1997	Lost	151
-	-	-	-	Pakistan	Colombo (SSC)	20-07-1997	Ab'd	152
28	21	5	-	Bangladesh	Colombo (SSC)	24-07-1997	Won	153
53	67	2	-	Sri Lanka	Colombo (RPS)	26-07-1997	Lost	154
27	28	3	-	Sri Lanka	Colombo (RPS)	17-08-1997	Lost	155
6	6	1	-	Sri Lanka	Colombo (RPS)	20-08-1997	Lost	156
27	31	4	-	Sri Lanka	Colombo (SSC)	23-08-1997	Ab'd	157
39	32	3	2	Sri Lanka	Colombo (SSC)	24-08-1997	Lost	158
17	54	2	-	Pakistan	Toronto	13-09-1997	Won	159
25*	45	3	-	Pakistan	Toronto	14-09-1997	Won	160
-	-	-	-	Pakistan	Toronto	17-09-1997	Ab'd	161

Runs	*Balls*	*4s*	*6s*	*Opponent*	*Venue*	*Date*	*Result*	*Match*
0	10	-	-	Pakistan	Toronto	18-09-1997	Won	162
6	7	1	-	Pakistan	Toronto	20-09-1997	Won	163
51	64	4	1	Pakistan	Toronto	21-09-1997	Lost	164
2	11	-	-	Pakistan	Hyderabad (P)	28-09-1997	Lost	165
21	18	2	1	Pakistan	Karachi	30-09-1997	Won	166
7	11	1	-	Pakistan	Lahore	02-10-1997	Lost	167
91	87	4	2	England	Sharjah	11-12-1997	Lost	168
3	4	-	-	Pakistan	Sharjah	14-12-1997	Lost	169
1	2	-	-	West Indies	Sharjah	16-12-1997	Lost	170
82*	86	6	-	Sri Lanka	Guwahati	22-12-1997	Won	171
-	-	-	-	Sri Lanka	Indore	15-12-1997	Ab'd	172
6	13	-	-	Sri Lanka	Margao	28-12-1997	Lost	173
54	76	4	-	Bangladesh	Dhaka	10-01-1998	Won	174
67	44	11	-	Pakistan	Dhaka	11-01-1998	Won	175
95	78	6	5	Pakistan	Dhaka	14-01-1998	Won	176
1	6	-	-	Pakistan	Dhaka	16-01-1998	Lost	177
41	26	7	1	Pakistan	Dhaka	18-01-1998	Won	178
8	11	1	-	Australia	Kochi	01-04-1998	Won	179
5	17	-	-	Zimbabwe	Baroda	05-04-1998	Won	180
100	89	5	7	Australia	Kanpur	07-04-1998	Won	181
1	2	-	-	Zimbabwe	Cuttack	09-04-1998	Won	182
15	24	2	-	Australia	Delhi	14-04-1998	Lost	183
40	41	5	1	New Zealand	Sharjah	17-04-1998	Won	184
80	72	9	-	Australia	Sharjah	19-04-1998	Lost	185
38	58	2	-	New Zealand	Sharjah	20-04-1998	Lost	186
143	131	9	5	Australia	Sharjah	22-04-1998	Lost	187
134	131	12	3	Australia	Sharjah	24-04-1998	Won	188

Runs	*Balls*	*4s*	*6s*	*Opponent*	*Venue*	*Date*	*Result*	*Match*
33	29	6	-	Bangladesh	Mumbai	25-05-1998	Won	189
18	25	2	-	Kenya	Gwalior	28-05-1998	Lost	190
100*	103	13	-	Kenya	Kolkata	31-05-1998	Won	191
65	50	9	-	Sri Lanka	Colombo (RPS)	19-06-1998	Won	192
53	36	3	3	New Zealand	Colombo (RPS)	23-06-1998	Ab'd	193
17	16	4	-	Sri Lanka	Colombo (SSC)	01-07-1998	Lost	194
-	-	-	-	New Zealand	Colombo (SSC)	03-07-1998	Ab'd	195
128	131	8	2	Sri Lanka	Colombo (RPS)	07-07-1998	Won	196
77	109	9	-	Pakistan	Toronto	20-09-1998	Lost	197
127*	130	13	1	Zimbabwe	Bulawayo	26-09-1998	Won	198
29	21	4	1	Zimbabwe	Bulawayo	27-09-1998	Won	199
2	6	-	-	Zimbabwe	Harare	30-09-1998	Lost	200
141	128	13	3	Australia	Dhaka	28-10-1998	Won	201
8	14	1	-	West Indies	Dhaka	31-10-1998	Lost	202
3	6	-	-	Sri Lanka	Sharjah	06-11-1998	Won	203
118*	112	14	2	Zimbabwe	Sharjah	08-11-1998	Won	204
18	28	2	-	Sri Lanka	Sharjah	09-11-1998	Won	205
11	12	2	-	Zimbabwe	Sharjah	11-11-1998	Lost	206
124*	92	12	6	Zimbabwe	Sharjah	13-11-1998	Won	207
0	5	-	-	New Zealand	Taupo	09-01-1999	Lost	208
23	60	3	-	New Zealand	Napier	12-01-1999	Won	209
45	42	2	2	New Zealand	Wellington	14-01-1999	Ab'd	210
5	12	1	-	New Zealand	Auckland	16-01-1999	Won	211
28	46	5	-	South Africa	Hove	15-05-1999	Lost	212
140*	101	16	3	Kenya	Bristol	23-05-1999	Won	213
2	3	-	-	Sri Lanka	Taunton	26-05-1999	Won	214
22	40	2	-	England	Birmingham	29-05-1999	Won	215

Runs	*Balls*	*4s*	*6s*	*Opponent*	*Venue*	*Date*	*Result*	*Match*
0	4	-	-	Australia	The Oval	04-06-1999	Lost	216
45	65	5	-	Pakistan	Manchester	08-06-1999	Won	217
16	22	2	-	New Zealand	Nottingham	12-06-1999	Lost	218
14	33	-	-	Australia	Galle	23-08-1999	Lost	219
37	58	1	-	Sri Lanka	Colombo (RPS)	25-08-1999	Lost	220
120	141	11	2	Sri Lanka	Colombo (SSC)	29-08-1999	Won	221
85	72	7	3	Zimbabwe	Singapore	04-09-1999	Won	222
40	65	6	-	West Indies	Singapore	07-09-1999	Ab'd	223
0	6	-	-	West Indies	Singapore	08-09-1999	Lost	224
32	31	2	1	New Zealand	Rajkot	05-11-1999	Lost	225
186*	150	20	3	New Zealand	Hyderabad (I)	08-11-1999	Won	226
1	23	-	-	New Zealand	Gwalior	11-11-1999	Won	227
2	10	-	-	New Zealand	Guwahati	14-11-1999	Lost	228
0	3	-	-	New Zealand	Delhi	17-11-1999	Won	229
13	26	2	-	Pakistan	Brisbane	10-01-2000	Lost	230
12	11	2	-	Australia	Melbourne	12-01-2000	Lost	231
1	11	-	-	Australia	Sydney	14-01-2000	Lost	232
93	103	10	-	Pakistan	Hobart	21-01-2000	Lost	233
41	46	5	-	Pakistan	Adelaide	25-01-2000	Won	234
18	28	2	-	Australia	Adealdie	26-01-2000	Lost	235
17	14	4	-	Pakistan	Perth	28-01-2000	Lost	236
3	21	-	-	Australia	Perth	30-01-2000	Lost	237
26	25	4	-	South Africa	Kochi	09-03-2000	Won	238
21	31	3	-	South Africa	Jamshedpur	12-03-2000	Won	239
12	28	1	-	South Africa	Faridabad	14-03-2000	Lost	240
122	138	12	-	South Africa	Baroda	17-03-2000	Won	241
93	89	7	4	South Africa	Nagpur	19-03-2000	Lost	242

Runs	*Balls*	*4s*	*6s*	*Opponent*	*Venue*	*Date*	*Result*	*Match*
5	8	-	-	South Africa	Sharjah	22-03-2000	Lost	243
11	28	1	-	Pakistan	Sharjah	23-03-2000	Won	244
10	18	1	-	Pakistan	Sharjah	26-03-2000	Lost	245
39	68	3	-	South Africa	Sharjah	27-03-2000	Lost	246
36	25	4	2	Bangladesh	Dhaka	31-05-2000	Won	247
93	95	10	-	Sri Lanka	Dhaka	01-06-2000	Lost	248
25	30	4	-	Pakistan	Dhaka	03-06-2000	Lost	249
25	35	4	-	Kenya	Nairobi	03-10-2000	Won	250
38	37	3	3	Australia	Nairobi	07-10-2000	Won	251
39	50	4	-	South Africa	Nairobi	13-10-2000	Won	252
69	83	10	1	New Zealand	Nairobi	15-10-2000	Lost	253
101	140	3	1	Sri Lanka	Sharjah	20-10-2000	Lost	254
8	15	1	-	Zimbabwe	Sharjah	22-10-2000	Won	255
4	10	-	-	Zimbabwe	Sharjah	26-10-2000	Won	256
61	54	7	-	Sri Lanka	Sharjah	27-10-2000	Lost	257
5	11	-	-	Sri Lanka	Sharjah	29-10-2000	Lost	258
44	49	7	-	Zimbabwe	Cuttack	02-12-2000	Won	259
8	20	-	-	Zimbabwe	Ahmedabad	05-12-2000	Won	260
146	153	15	2	Zimbabwe	Jodhpur	08-12-2000	Lost	261
62	86	9	-	Zimbabwe	Kanpur	11-12-2000	Won	262
27	38	5	-	Zimbabwe	Rajkot	14-12-2000	Won	263
35	26	6	1	Australia	Bangalore	25-03-2001	Won	264
32	29	6	1	Australia	Pune	28-03-2001	Lost	265
139	125	19	-	Australia	Indore	31-03-2001	Won	266
62	38	11	-	Australia	Visakhapatnam	03-04-2001	Lost	267
12	15	2	-	Australia	Margao	06-09-2001	Lost	268
70*	70	13	-	Zimbabwe	Harare	24-06-2001	Won	269

Runs	*Balls*	*4s*	*6s*	*Opponent*	*Venue*	*Date*	*Result*	*Match*
9	27	-	-	Zimbabwe	Bulawayo	27-06-2001	Won	270
81*	110	8	-	West Indies	Bulawayo	30-06-2001	Won	271
122*	131	12	-	West Indies	Harare	04-07-2001	Won	272
0	4	-	-	West Indies	Harare	07-07-2001	Lost	273
101	129	9	-	South Africa	Johannesburg	05-10-2001	Lost	274
38	57	5	-	South Africa	Centurion	10-10-2001	Won	275
-	-	-	-	Kenya	Bloemfontein	12-10-2001	Won	276
3	20	-	-	Kenya	Port Elizabeth	17-10-2001	Lost	277
37	35	5	-	South Africa	East London	19-10-2001	Lost	278
146	132	17	-	Kenya	Paarl	24-10-2001	Won	279
17	42	3	-	South Africa	Durban	26-10-2001	Lost	280
36	43	6	-	England	Kolkata	19-01-2002	Won	281
45	60	6	-	England	Cuttack	22-01-2002	Lost	282
68	79	10	-	England	Chennai	25-01-2002	Won	283
87*	67	13	1	England	Kanpur	28-01-2002	Won	284
18	16	3	-	England	Delhi	31-01-2002	Lost	285
12	18	1	1	England	Mumbai	03-02-2002	Lost	286

BATTING AND FIELDING PERFORMANCE AGAINST EACH TEAM IN ODIs

Opponent	*Matches*	*Innings*	*N.O.*	*Runs*	*Avg.*	*H.S.*	*100s*	*50s*	*0s*	*Ct*
Australia	33	33	-	1626	49.27	143	6	7	1	17
Bangladesh	6	5	-	199	39.80	54	-	1	-	2
England	20	20	2	650	36.11	91	-	4	-	9
Kenya	8	7	3	559	139.75	146	4	-	-	1
New Zealand	31	30	1	1279	44.10	186*	3	7	3	5
Pakistan	43	41	4	1335	36.08	118	2	9	3	24
South Africa	40	40	-	1310	32.75	122	3	5	1	7
Sri Lanka	45	43	5	1760	46.31	137	6	9	1	15
U.A.E.	1	1	-	63	63.00	63	-	1	-	1
West Indies	29	29	6	1046	45.47	122*	2	8	4	6
Zimbabwe	30	29	5	1242	51.75	146	5	4	-	5
Total	**286**	**278**	**26**	**11069**	**43.92**	**186***	**31**	**55**	**13**	**92**
As captain	73	70	5	2454	37.75	186*	6	12	4	31
As a player	213	208	21	8615	46.06	146	25	43	9	61

N.O.: Not out, H.S.: Highest score, Ct: Catches

BATTING AND FIELDING PERFORMANCE IN EACH COUNTRY IN ODIs

Opponent	*Matches*	*Innings*	*N.O.*	*Runs*	*Avg.*	*H.S.*	*100s*	*50s*	*0s*	*Ct*
In Australia	23	22	2	713	35.65	93	-	6	-	12
In Bangladesh	10	10	-	561	56.10	141	1	4	-	9
In Canada	12	11	2	313	34.77	89*	-	3	1	8
In England	12	12	1	340	30.90	140*	1	-	1	4
In India	96	93	10	4015	48.37	186*	12	23	3	30
In Kenya	4	4	-	171	42.75	69	-	1	-	1
In New Zealand	16	16	-	575	35.93	84	-	4	2	2
In Pakistan	4	4	-	30	7.50	21	-	-	1	3
In South Africa	22	21	-	729	34.71	146	3	-	1	4
In Sri Lanka	26	24	1	980	42.60	128	4	3	1	8
In Singapore	5	5	-	253	50.60	100	1	1	1	-
In Emirates	42	42	5	1778	48.05	143	7	7	1	10
In West Indies	4	4	1	119	39.66	65*	-	1	-	-
In Zimbabwe	10	10	4	492	82.00	127*	2	2	1	1
Total	**286**	**278**	**26**	**11069**	**43.92**	**186***	**31**	**55**	**13**	**92**
Home	96	93	10	4015	48.37	186*	12	23	3	30
Away	82	82	4	2551	32.70	128	5	11	5	24
Neutral	108	103	12	4503	49.48	146	14	21	5	38

N.O.: Not out, H.S.: Highest score, Ct: Catches

YEAR-WISE BATTING AND FIELDING PERFORMANCE IN ODIs

Year	*Matches*	*Innings*	*N.O.*	*Runs*	*Avg.*	*H.S.*	*100s*	*50s*	*0s*	*Ct*
1989	1	1	-	0	0.00	0	-	-	1	-
1990	11	10	-	239	23.90	53	-	1	1	3
1991	14	14	2	417	34.75	62	-	4	1	4
1992	21	20	2	704	39.11	84	-	6	-	5
1993	18	17	4	319	24.53	82*	-	1	-	4
1994	25	25	2	1089	47.34	115	3	9	3	8
1995	12	12	1	444	40.36	112*	1	1	-	6
1996	32	32	2	1611	53.70	137	6	9	-	13
1997	39	36	3	1011	30.63	117	2	5	2	14
1998	34	33	4	1894	65.31	143	9	7	-	14
1999	22	22	2	843	42.15	186*	3	1	4	4
2000	34	34	-	1328	39.05	146	3	6	-	11
2001	17	16	3	904	69.53	146	4	3	1	3
2002	6	6	1	266	53.20	87*	-	2	-	3
Total	**286**	**278**	**26**	**11069**	**43.92**	**186***	**31**	**55**	**13**	**92**
Matches won	136	133	24	6717	61.62	186*	24	31	4	47
Matches tied	3	3	-	31	10.33	24	-	-	-	-
Matches ab'd	12	7	1	238	39.66	53	-	1	-	2
Matches lost	135	135	1	4083	30.47	146	7	23	9	43

N.O.: Not out, H.S.: Highest score, Ct: Catches

POSITION-WISE BATTING PERFORMANCE IN ODIs

Position	*Matches*	*Innings*	*N.O.*	*Runs*	*Avg.*	*H.S.*	*100s*	*50s*	*0s*
Opening	193	193	14	8743	48.84	186*	30	38	8
Third	4	4	-	49	12.25	21	-	-	-
Fourth	41	41	4	1369	37.00	140*	1	12	2
Fifth	36	36	8	797	28.46	82*	-	5	3
Sixth	3	3	-	91	30.33	36	-	-	-
Seventh	1	1	-	20	20.00	20	-	-	-
Did not bat	8	-	-	-	-	-	-	-	-
Total	**286**	**278**	**26**	**11069**	**43.92**	**186***	**31**	**55**	**13**
Day matches	189	182	19	7010	43.00	186*	17	38	11
Day/night matches	97	96	7	4059	45.60	146	14	17	2
First innings	139	138	7	5416	41.34	186*	17	22	3
Second innings	143	140	19	5653	46.71	143	14	33	10

BATTING PERFORMANCE AT EACH GROUND IN ODIs

Ground	*Matches*	*Innings*	*N.O.*	*Runs*	*Avg.*	*H.S.*	*100s*	*50s*	*0s*
Adelaide Oval	5	5	-	142	28.40	48	-	-	-
Bellerive Oval, Hobart	2	2	-	150	75.00	93	-	2	-
Brisbane Cricket Ground	3	3	-	101	33.66	77	-	1	-
Harrup Park, Mackay	1	-	-	-	-	-	-	-	-
Melbourne Cricket Ground	3	3	1	73	36.50	57*	-	1	-
Sydney Cricket Ground	4	4	1	155	51.66	69	-	2	-
W.A.C.A. Ground, Perth	5	5	-	92	18.40	36	-	-	-
In Australia	**23**	**22**	**2**	**713**	**35.65**	**93**	**-**	**6**	**-**
National Stadium, Dhaka	10	10	-	561	56.10	141	1	4	-
In Bangladesh	**10**	**10**	**-**	**561**	**56.10**	**141**	**1**	**4**	**-**
Toronto Cricket, Skating & Curling	12	11	2	313	34.77	89*	-	3	1
In Canada	**12**	**11**	**2**	**313**	**34.77**	**89***	**-**	**3**	1
County Ground, Hove	1	1	-	28	28.00	28	-	-	-
County Ground, Taunton	1	1	-	2	2.00	2	-	-	-
Edgbaston, Birmingham	1	1	-	22	22.00	22	-	-	-
Headingley, Leeds	2	2	-	25	12.50	19	-	-	-
Kennington Oval, London	2	2	-	30	15.00	30	-	-	1
Old Trafford, Manchester	2	2	-	46	23.00	45	-	-	-
County Ground, Bristol	1	1	1	140	-	140*	1	-	-
Trent Bridge, Nottingham	2	2	-	47	23.50	31	-	-	-
In England	**12**	**12**	**1**	**340**	**30.90**	**140***	**1**	**-**	**1**
Barabati Stadium, Cuttack	6	6	1	309	61.80	127*	1	1	-
Barkatullah Khan Stadium, Jodhpur	1	1	-	146	146.00	146	1	-	-
Brabourne Stadium, Mumbai	1	1	-	1	1.00	1	-	-	-
Roop Singh Stadium, Gwalior	6	6	-	132	22.00	70	-	1	-
Eden Gardens, Kolkata	8	8	2	425	70.83	100*	1	4	-

Ground	*Matches*	*Innings*	*N.O.*	*Runs*	*Avg.*	*H.S.*	*100s*	*50s*	*0s*
Feroz Shah Kotla, Delhi	5	5	-	232	46.40	137	1	1	1
Gandhi Sports Complex, Amritsar	1	1	-	39	39.00	39	-	-	-
Gandhi Ground, Jalandhar	1	1	-	52	52.00	52	-	-	-
Green Park, Kanpur	6	6	2	312	78.00	100	1	2	-
I.P.C.L. Sports Complex, Baroda	3	3	-	242	80.66	122	2	-	-
Indira Priyadarshini, Visakhapatnam	2	2	-	116	58.00	62	-	2	-
Jawaharlal Nehru Stadium, New Delhi	1	1	-	1	1.00	1	-	-	-
Keenan Stadium, Jamshedpur	3	3	-	75	25.00	30	-	-	-
Lal Bahadur Shastri Stadium, Hyderabad	3	3	2	208	208.00	186*	1	-	-
M.Chinnaswamy Stadium, Bangalore	5	5	-	274	54.80	117	1	1	-
M.A.Chidambaram Stadium, Chennai	3	3	-	80	26.66	68	-	1	-
Municipal Stadium, Rajkot	4	4	-	88	22.00	32	-	-	-
Nahar Singh Stadium, Faridabad	3	3	-	15	5.00	12	-	-	1
Nehru Stadium, Fatorda, Margao	3	3	-	48	16.00	30	-	-	-
Nehru Stadium, Guwahati	3	3	2	92	92.00	82*	-	1	-
Nehru Stadium, Indore	3	2	-	163	81.50	139	1	-	-
Nehru Stadium, Kochi	2	2	-	34	17.00	26	-	-	-
Nehru Stadium, Pune	4	3	-	92	30.66	53	-	1	-
Punjab C.A. Stadium, Mohali	2	2	-	65	32.50	62	-	1	-
Sardar Patel Stadium, Ahmedabad	2	2	-	10	5.00	8	-	-	-
Sawai Mansingh Stadium, Jaipur	3	3	1	251	125.50	105	1	2	-
Sector 16 Stadium, Chandigarh	2	1	-	1	11.00	1	-	-	-
Vidarbha C.A. Ground, Nagpur	3	3	-	194	64.66	93	-	2	-
Wankhede Stadium, Mumbai	7	7	-	318	45,42	114	1	2	1
In India	**96**	**93**	**10**	**4015**	**48.37**	**186***	**12**	**23**	**3**
Gymkhana Club Ground, Nairobi	4	4	-	171	42.75	69	-	1	
In Kenya	**4**	**4**	**-**	**171**	**42.75**	**69**	**-**	**1**	-

Ground	*Matches*	*Innings*	*N.O.*	*Runs*	*Avg.*	*H.S.*	*100s*	*50s*	*0s*
Basin Reserve, Wellington	4	4	-	148	37.00	63	-	1	-
Carisbrook, Dunedin	3	3	-	131	43.66	84	-	1	1
Eden Park, Auckland	2	2	-	87	43.50	82	-	1	-
Jade Stadium, Christchurch	1	1	-	40	40.00	40	-	-	-
McLean Park, Napier	3	3	-	51	17.00	23	-	-	-
Owen Delany Park, Taupo	1	1	-	0	0.00	-	-	-	1
Westpac Trust Park, Hamilton	2	2	-	118	59.00	81	-	1	-
In New Zealand	**16**	**16**	**-**	**575**	**35.93**	**84**	**-**	**4**	**2**
Gaddafi Stadium, Lahore	1	1	-	7	7.00	7	-	-	-
Jinnah Stadium, Gujranwala	1	1	-	0	0.00	0	-	-	1
National Stadium, Karachi	1	1	-	21	21.00	21	-	-	-
Niaz Stadium, Hyderabad (Sind)	1	1	-	2	2.00	2	-	-	-
In Pakistan	**4**	**4**	**-**	**30**	**7.50**	**21**	**-**	**-**	**1**
Boland Bank Park, Paarl	2	2	-	152	76.00	146	1	-	-
Buffalo Park, East London	3	3	-	72	24.00	37	-	-	-
Goodyear Park, Bloemfontein	3	2	-	32	16.00	32	-	-	1
Kingsmead, Durban	4	4	-	117	29.25	45	-	-	-
New Wanderers, Johannesburg	2	2	-	122	61.00	101	1	-	-
Newlands, Cape Town	1	1	-	15	15.00	15	-	-	-
St George's Park, Port Elizabeth	3	3	-	14	4.66	10	-	-	-
Super Sport Park, Centurion	3	3	-	101	33.66	41	-	-	-
Willowmoore Park, Benoni	1	1	-	104	104.00	104	1	-	-
In South Africa	**22**	**21**	**-**	**729**	**34.71**	**146**	**3**	**-**	**1**
Galle International Stadium, Galle	1	1	-	14	14.00	14	-	-	-
R.Premadasa Stadium, Colombo	14	14	1	663	51.00	128	3	3	-
Sinhalese Sports Club, Colombo	10	8	-	278	34.75	120	1	-	1
Tyronne Fernando Stadium, Moratuwa	1	1	-	25	25.00	25	-	-	-

Ground	*Matches*	*Innings*	*N.O.*	*Runs*	*Avg.*	*H.S.*	*100s*	*50s*	*0s*
In Sri Lanka	**26**	**24**	**1**	**980**	**42.60**	**128**	**4**	**3**	**1**
Kallang Ground, Singapore	3	3	-	125	41.66	85	-	1	1
The Padang, Singapore	2	2	-	128	64.00	100	1	-	-
In Singapore	**5**	**5**	**-**	**253**	**50.60**	**100**	**1**	**1**	**1**
Sharjah Cricket Stadium, Sharjah	42	42	5	1778	48.05	143	7	7	1
In United Arab Emirates	**42**	**42**	**5**	**1778**	**48.05**	**143**	**7**	**7**	**1**
Arnos Vale Ground, Kingstown, St Vincent	1	1	-	9	9.00	9	-	-	-
Kensington Oval, Bridgetown, Barbados	1	1	-	1	1.00	1	-	-	-
Queen's Park Oval, Port of Spain, Trinidad	2	2	1	109	109.00	65*	-	1	-
In West Indies	**4**	**4**	**1**	**119**	**39.66**	**65***	**-**	**1**	**-**
Harare Sports Club, Harare	5	5	2	233	77.66	122*	1	1	1
Queens Sports Club, Bulawayo	5	5	2	259	86.33	127*	1	1	-
In Zimbabwe	**10**	**10**	**4**	**492**	**82.00**	**127***	**2**	**2**	**1**
Total	**286**	**278**	**26**	**11069**	**43.92**	**186***	**31**	**55**	13

N.O.: Not out, H.S.: Highest score

BATTING MILESTONES IN ODIs

Runs	*Match*	*Innings*	*Score*	*Opponent*	*Venue*	*Date*	*Age*
1000	36	34	81	Zimbabwe	Hamilton	07-03-1992	18 years 318 days
2000	73	70	63	Emirates	Sharjah	13-04-1994	20 years 354 days
3000	96	93	112*	Sri Lanka	Sharjah	09-04-1995	21 years 350 days
4000	115	112	17	South Africa	Sharjah	17-04-1996	22 years 359 days
5000	141	138	32	South Africa	Durban	12-02-1997	23 years 294 days
6000	176	170	95	Pakistan	Dhaka	14-01-1998	24 years 265 days
7000	196	189	128	Sri Lanka	Colombo	07-07-1998	25 years 74 days
8000	217	209	45	Pakistan	Manchester	08-06-1999	26 years 45 days
9000	242	235	93	South Africa	Nagpur	19-03-2000	26 years 330 days
10000	266	259	139	Australia	Indore	31-03-2001	27 years 341 days
11000	284	276	87*	England	Kanpur	28-01-2002	28 years 279 days

TOP TEN BATSMEN BY RUNS IN ODIs

Batsman	*Matches*	*Innings*	*N.O.*	*Runs*	*Avg.*	*H.S.*	*100s*	*50s*	*0s*
Sachin Tendulkar (India)	286	278	26	11069	43.92	186*	31	55	13
Mohammed Azharuddin (India)	334	308	54	9378	36.92	153*	7	58	9
Desmond Haynes (West Indies)	238	237	28	8648	41.37	152*	17	57	13
Mark Waugh (Australia)	244	236	20	8500	39.35	173	18	50	16
Aravinda de Silva (Sri Lanka)	275	266	26	8430	35.12	145	11	57	13
Saeed Anwar (Pakistan)	230	227	17	8348	39.75	194	19	41	13
Inzamam ul Haq (Pakistan)	257	242	35	8243	39.82	137*	8	60	12
Steve Waugh (Australia)	325	288	58	7569	32.90	120*	3	45	15
Sourav Ganguly (India)	191	185	14	7522	43.98	183	18	45	7
Arjuna Ranatunga (Sri Lanka)	269	255	47	7454	35.83	131*	4	49	18

TOP TEN BATSMEN BY AVERAGES IN ODIs

(Minimum 1500 runs)

Batsman	*Matches*	*Innings*	*N.O.*	*Runs*	*Avg.*	*H.S.*	*100s*	*50s*	*0s*
Michael Bevan (Australia)	172	152	52	5653	56.53	108*	6	37	3
Zaheer Abbas (Pakistan)	62	60	6	2572	47.62	123	7	13	2
Vivian Richards (West Indies)	187	167	24	6721	47.00	189*	11	45	7
Glenn Turner (New Zealand)	41	40	6	1598	47.00	171*	3	9	1
Gordon Greenidge (West Indies)	128	127	13	5134	45.03	133*	11	31	3
Dean Jones (Australia)	164	161	25	6068	44.61	145	7	46	6
Sourav Ganguly (India)	191	185	14	7522	43.98	183	18	45	7
Sachin Tendulkar (India)	286	278	26	11069	43.92	186*	31	55	13
Jacques Kallis (South Africa)	147	142	25	5156	44.06	113*	8	35	6
Brian Lara (West Indies)	193	189	18	7257	42.43	169	14	47	11

N.O.: Not out, H.S.: Highest score

TOP TEN BATSMEN BY STRIKE RATES IN ODIs

(Minimum 1000 runs)

Batsman	*Matches*	*Innings*	*N.O.*	*Runs*	*Avg.*	*H.S.*	*100s*	*50s*	*S/R*
Shahid Afridi (Pakistan)	142	138	5	3266	24.55	109	2	19	99.45
Ian Smith (New Zealand)	98	77	16	1055	17.29	62*	-	3	99.43
Kapil Dev (India)	225	198	39	3783	23.79	175*	1	14	95.07
Ricardo Powell (West Indies)	51	47	3	1006	22.86	124	1	4	93.06
Lance Klusener (South Africa)	132	108	37	3006	42.33	103*	2	17	90.59
Vivian Richards (West Indies)	187	167	24	6721	47.00	189*	11	45	90.09
Adam Gilchrist (Australia)	130	125	5	4039	33.65	1546	6	22	88.94
Sanath Jayasuriya (Sri Lanka)	252	244	9	7235	30.78	189	11	47	88.95
Wasim Akram (Pakistan)	324	255	47	3372	16.21	86	-	6	87.72
Sachin Tendulkar (India)	286	278	26	11069	43.92	186*	31	55	86.66

N.O.: Not out, H.S.: Highest score, S/R: Strike rate

BOWLING PERFORMANCE AGAINST EACH COUNTRY IN ODIs

Opponent	*Matches*	*Overs*	*Mds*	*Runs*	*Wkts*	*Avg.*	*4WI*	*R/O*	*Best*
Australia	33	135.1	1	645	18	35.83	2	4.76	5-32
Bangladesh	6	16.3	-	78	5	15.60	-	4.72	2-8
England	20	59.5	-	326	2	163.00	-	5.44	1-30
Kenya	8	18	-	112	0	-	-	6.22	-
New Zealand	31	108.3	3	540	13	41.53	-	4.97	3-34
Pakistan	43	140.4	1	725	13	55.76	-	5.15	3-45
South Africa	40	171	4	843	13	64.84	1	4.92	4-56
Sri Lanka	45	134.5	4	615	15	41.00	-	4.56	3-43
Emirates	1	5	-	22	0	-	-	4.40	-
West Indies	29	118	6	514	16	32.12	1	4.35	4-34
Zimbabwe	30	92.2	-	530	10	53.00	-	5.74	1-6
Total	**286**	**999.5**	**19**	**4950**	**105**	**47.14**	**4**	**4.95**	**5-32**
Home	96	394.5	10	1977	51	38.76	2	5.00	5-32
Away	82	209	5	1058	16	66.12	-	5.06	3-34
Neutral	108	396	4	1915	38	50.39	2	4.83	4-34

4WI: Four wickets in an innings, R/O: Runs per over

PERFORMANCE AS CAPTAIN IN ODIs

Opponent	*Matches*	*Won*	*Lost*	*Tied*	*No Result*	*Success %*	*Toss*
Sri Lanka	13	2	9	-	2	23.07	7
Australia	8	2	6	-	-	25.00	3
Zimbabwe	6	3	2	1	-	58.33	3
Pakistan	21	8	11	-	2	42.85	11
New Zealand	6	4	2	-	-	66.66	4
West Indies	7	1	5	-	1	21.42	5
South Africa	10	2	7	-	1	25.00	7
England	1	-	1	-	-	00.00	1
Bangladesh	1	1	-	-	-	100.00	1
Total	**73**	**23**	**43**	**1**	**6**	**36.30**	**42**
In India	18	9	8	-	1	52.77	10
Outside India	55	14	35	-	5	30.00	32
First time	54	17	31	1	5	37.03	30
Second time	19	6	12	-	1	34.21	12

MAN OF THE MATCH AWARDS IN ODIs

No.	Performance		Opponent	Venue	Date	Match No.
	Runs	Wkts				
1	53	2	Sri Lanka	Pune	05-12-1990	9
2	11*	4	West Indies	Sharjah	22-10-1991	16
3#	62	1	South Africa	Kolkata	10-11-1991	19
4	57*	-	West Indies	Melbourne	16-01-1992	29
5	54	1	Pakistan	Sydney	04-03-1992	35
6	81	1	Zimbabwe	Hamilton	07-03-1992	36
7	82	-	New Zealand	Auckland	27-03-1994	70
8	110	-	Australia	Colombo	09-09-1994	79
9	115*	-	New Zealand	Baroda	28-10-1994	84
10	62	2	New Zealand	Delhi	03-11-1994	86
11	66	2	West Indies	Kolkata	05-11-1994	87
12	112*	-	Sri lanka	Sharjah	09-04-1995	96
13	127*	-	Kenya	Cuttack	18-02-1996	103
14	70	-	West Indies	Gwalior	21-02-1996	104
15	118	2	Pakistan	Sharjah	15-04-1996	114
16	89*	-	Pakistan	Toronto	16-09-1996	123
17	88	1	Australia	Bangalore	21-10-1996	129
18	114	-	South Africa	Mumbai	14-12-1996	134
19	104	-	Zimbabwe	Benoni	09-12-1997	140
20	117	-	New Zealand	Bangalore	14-05-1997	148
21	95	3	Pakistan	Dhaka	14-01-1998	176
22	8	5	Australia	Kochi	01-04-1998	179
23	100*	-	Australia	Kanpur	07-04-1998	181
24	80	-	Australia	Sharjah	19-04-1998	185
25	142	1	Australia	Sharjah	22-04-1998	187

No.	*Performance* *Runs*	*Wkts*	*Opponent*	*Venue*	*Date*	*Match No.*
26	134	-	Australia	Sharjah	24-04-1998	188
27	100*	-	Kenya	Kolkata	31-05-1998	191
28	128	-	Sri Lanka	Colombo	07-07-1998	196
29	127*		Zimbabwe	Bulawayo	26-09-1998	198
30	141	4	Australia	Dhaka	28-10-1998	201
31	118*	-	Zimbabwe	Sharjah	08-11-1998	204
32	124*	1	Zimbabwe	Sharjah	13-11-1998	207
33	140*	-	Kenya	Bristol	23-05-1999	213
34	85	-	Zimbabwe	Singapore	04-09-1999	222
35	186*	-	New Zealand	Hyderabad	08-11-1999	226
36	122	-	South Africa	Baroda	17-03-2000	241
37	101	-	Sri Lanka	Sharjah	20-10-2000	254
38	139	-	Australia	Indore	31-05-2000	266
39	70*	-	Zimbabwe	Harare	24-06-2001	269
40	81*	-	West Indies	Bulawayo	30-06-2001	271
41	122*	-	West Indies	Harare	04-07-2001	272
42	146	-	Kenya	Paarl	24-10-2001	279
43	68	-	England	Chennai	25-01-2002	283

Shared the award with South African Allan Donald

CENTURIES IN FIRST-CLASS CRICKET

Score	Mins	Balls	4s	6s	For	Against	Venue	Season
100*	186	129	12	-	Mumbai	Gujarat	Mumbai	1988-89
103*	174	145	14	1	Rest of India	Delhi	Mumbai	1989-90
119*	225	189	17	-	India	England	Manchester	1990
108	156	140	18	-	India	Rest of World	Scarborough	1990
159	267	174	23	2	West Zone	East Zone	Guwahati	1990-91
131	226	174	17	1	West Zone	South Zone	Rourkela	1990-91
125	203	155	13	5	Mumbai	Delhi	Delhi	1990-91
148*	298	215	14	-	India	Australia	Sydney	1991-92
114	228	161	16	-	India	Australia	Perth	1991-92
100	-	97	16	-	Yorkshire	Durham	Durham	1992
111	375	270	19	-	India	South Africa	Johannesburg	1992-93
131	210	183	3	1	India	Student's XI	East London	1992-93
165	316	296	24	1	India	England	Chennai	1992-93
104*	217	163	11	1	India	Sri Lanka	Colombo (SSC)	1993-94
138	257	211	20	2	Mumbai	Maharashtra	Thane	1993-94
142	260	224	22	-	India	Sri Lanka	Lucknow	1993-94
179	212	158	12	-	India	West Indies	Nagpur	1994-95
175	185	141	22	8	Mumbai	Baroda	Mumbai	1994-95
166	220	153	27	1	Mumbai	Tamil Nadu	Mumbai	1994-95
109	180	157	4	1	Mumbai	Uttar Pradesh	Mumbai	1994-95
140	203	130	14	5	Mumbai	Punjab	Mumbai	1994-95
139	124	91	15	7	Mumbai	Punjab	Mumbai	1994-95
151	163	105	12	9	Mumbai	Maharashtra	Thane	1995-96
122	263	176	19	1	India	England	Birmingham	1996
177	462	300	26	-	India	England	Nottingham	1996
169	333	254	26	-	India	South Africa	Cape Town	1996-97

Score	*Mins*	*Balls*	*4s*	*6s*	*For*	*Against*	*Venue*	*Season*
143	292	247	20	-	India	Sri Lanka	Colombo (RPS)	1997-98
139	397	267	16	-	India	Sri Lanka	Colombo (SSC)	1997-98
177	223	174	30	3	Mumbai	Gujarat	Bulsar	1997-98
148	320	244	20	3	India	Sri Lanka	Mumbai	1997-98
135	199	159	19	1	Mumbai	Orissa	Mumbai	1997-98
204*	269	192	25	2	Mumbai	Australians	Mumbai	1997-98
155*	286	191	14	4	India	Australia	Chennai	1997-98
177	306	207	29	3	India	Australia	Bangalore	1997-98
154	175	120	20	3	India	C.Districts	Napier	1998-99
113	200	151	13	2	India	New Zealand	Wellington	1998-99
136	405	273	18	-	India	Pakistan	Chennai	1998-99
124*	308	235	10	1	India	Sri Lanka	Colombo	1998-99
126*	397	248	14	-	India	New Zealand	Mohali	1999-00
217	494	344	29	-	India	New Zealand	Ahmedabad	1999-00
116	283	191	9	1	India	Australia	Melbourne	1999-00
233*	565	334	21	5	Mumbai	Tamil Nadu	Mumbai	1999-00
128	173	124	13	3	Mumbai	Hyderabad	Mumbai	1999-00
122	283	233	19	-	India	Zimbabwe	Delhi	2000-01
201*	392	284	27	-	India	Zimbabwe	Nagpur	2000-01
108	195	95	11	3	Mumbai	Baroda	Mumbai	2000-01
199	299	214	30	4	West Zone	East Zone	Pune	2000-01
126	346	230	15	2	India	Australia	Chennai	2000-01
155	233	184	23	1	India	South Africa	Bloemfontein	2001-02
103	254	197	12	1	India	England	Ahmedabad	2001-02
176	441	316	23	-	India	Zimbabwe	Nagpur	2001-02

BATTING AND FIELDING PERFORMANCE IN FIRST-CLASS CRICKET

Type	*Matches*	*Innings*	*N.O.*	*Runs*	*Avg.*	*H.S.*	*100s*	*50s*	*0s*	*Ct*
Tests	91	146	15	7673	58.57	217	28	30	7	62
Ranji Trophy	30	45	6	3591	92.07	233*	14	17	-	33
Duleep Trophy	7	10	-	600	60.00	199	3	1	-	5
Irani Cup	2	3	1	155	77.50	103*	1	-	-	1
County Cricket	16	25	2	1070	46.52	100	1	7	1	10
Other Matches	33	49	5	2437	56.42	204*	4	17	1	14
Total	**179**	**278**	**29**	**15526**	**62.35**	**233***	**51**	**72**	**9**	**125**

BOWLING PERFORMANCE IN FIRST-CLASS CRICKET

Type	*Overs*	*Mds*	*Runs*	*Wkts*	*Avg.*	*5WI*	*10WM*	*Best*
Tests	323	58	1013	25	40.52	-	-	3-10
Ranji Trophy	132.3	19	444	2	222.00	-	-	1-8
Duleep Trophy	118	19	364	7	52.00	-	-	3-60
Irani Cup	22	6	53	1	53.00	-	-	1-6
County Cricket	62.3	10	195	4	48.75	-	-	2-35
Other Matches	195.1	24	731	10	73.10	-	-	3-79
Total	**853.1**	**136**	**2800**	**49**	**57.14**	**-**	**-**	**3-10**

N.O.: Not out, H.S.: Highest score, Ct: Catches, 5WI: 5 wickets in an innings, 10WM: 10 wickets in a match

* Indicates not out

Select Bibliography

Bamzai, Sandeep, *Gavaskar and Tendulkar: Shaping India's Cricket Destiny* (Jaico Publishing House, New Delhi, 1996).

Benaud, Richie, *Anything but...an Autobiography* (Hodder and Stoughton, UK, 1998).

Bhogle, Harsha, *Azhar: The Authorized Biography of Mohammad Azharuddin* (Penguin Books India, New Delhi, 1995).

Bhogle, Harsha, *The Joy of a Lifetime—India's Tour of England, 1990* (Marine Sports Publications, Mumbai, 1991).

Boycott, Geoffrey, *Geoffrey Boycott on Cricket: Yorkshire's Greatest Son Hits Out* (Ebury Press, Random House, UK, 1999).

Donald, Allan, *White Lightning : The Autobiography* (Collins Willow, HarperCollins Publishers, UK, 1999).

Guha, Ramachandra, *An Anthropologist Among Marxists and Other Essays* (Permanent Black, New Delhi, 2000).

Guha, Ramachandra and Vaidyanathan T.G. (ed.) *An Indian Cricket Omnibus* (OUP, New Delhi, 1994).

Haigh, Gideon (ed.), *Wisden Cricketers' Almanack Australia 2000-2001* (3rd edition, Hardie Grant Books, Australia).

Indian Cricket Annual (various editions), Chennai.

Magazine, Pradeep, *Not Quite Cricket* (Penguin Books India, New Delhi, 1999).

Perry, Roland, *Bradman's Best* (Bantam Press, UK, 2001).

Rajan, Sunder (ed.), *Lord Harris Shield Cricket Tournament Commemoration Volume 1897-1997* (Marine Sports Publications, Mumbai, 1997).

Ramchand, Partab, *Indian Cricket: The Captains—From Nayudu to*

Tendulkar (Marine Sports Publications, Mumbai, 1997).

Tendulkar, Ajit, *The Making of a Cricketer: Formative Years of Sachin Tendulkar in Cricket* (Published by Ajit Tendulkar for ten' Promotions, 1996).

Warne, Shane, *Shane Warne—My Autobiography* (Hodder and Stoughton, UK, 2001).

Wisden Cricketers' Almanack (various editions), Wright, Graeme (ed.) (John Wisden & Co. Ltd., UK).

Index

Aaj Kal, 170,176
Abbasi, Kamran, 295
Achrekar, Ramakant, 13-18, 24, 31, 109-110
Adams, Jimmy, 134
Adelaide, 81, 83, 90, 92, 141, 243-44, 252, 257
Afridi, Shahid, 170, 222
Agarkar, Ajit, 206
Age, the, 309
Ahmed, Ijaz, 178, 193
Ahmed, Mushtaq, 50
Ahmedabad, 153, 155, 172, 246, 305
Aiwa Cup, in Sri Lanka, 242
Akai Singer Champions Trophy, 179
Akhtar, Shoaib, 225-26
Akram, Wasim, 45, 47-48, 51-52, 124, 142, 151, 178, 222-23, 225-26, 257, 318
Aldridge, Brian, 122
Ali, Basit, 124
Alleyne, 60
Alter, Tom, 39
Amarnath, Mohinder, 41, 253
Ambrose, Curtly, 81-82, 91, 128, 162-63, 215
Amre, Pravin, 8, 13, 75, 104, 106
Anjuman-E-Islam, 13, 26, 28
Ankola, Salil, 35-36, 43-44, 46, 105, 160
Antigua, 164, 215
Anwar, Saeed, 142, 169-70, 193, 213, 225, 249
Apte, Madhav, 10
Arbab Niaz Stadium, Peshawar, 52
Asia Cup, 69, 136, 170, 184, 186
Asian Test Championship, 221, 224-28
Association of Cricket Statisticians and Scorers of India, 25
Astle, Nathan, 245-46
Ata-ur-Rehman, 124, 143, 145
Atherton, Mike, 57-58, 148, 171, 213-14
Auckland, 55, 87, 92, 120, 220, 294
Austral-Asia Cup, 55, 123-25
Ayub, Arshad, 37, 46, 70
Azad Maidan, Mumbai, 11, 17-18, 24, 109
Azharuddin, Mohammad, 36, 43-44, 46-47, 53-54, 57-60, 62, 65-68, 80-81, 83-84, 88-91, 102-03, 105, 107-08, 112, 116-18, 120, 122, 124, 131-33, 135, 138, 141, 143, 145, 147-50, 152, 156-58, 163, 166, 168-72, 176, 179-80, 182-94, 196-97, 200-01, 204, 206, 213, 216, 219-20, 225, 229, 234, 238, 240, 250, 259-62, 272, 276

BCA Colts, 21
Bacher, Aaron 'Ali', 75
Bacher, Adam, 157
Bahutule, Sairaj, 24-25
Baig, Abbas Ali, 83, 86, 92
Bal, Sambit, 299
Baloch, Aftab, 44
Bamzai, Sandeep, 11, 36
Banerjee, Ajay, 73
Banerjee, Sambaran, 175, 186
Banerjee, Subroto, 81, 88
Bangabandhu Stadium, Dhaka, 217, 318
Bangalore, 142-43, 169, 197, 221-22, 263, 284, 302, 305, 313
Bangar, Sanjay, 325
Baptiste, Eldine, 215
Barbados, 129, 162, 164
Barker, Lloyd, 162
Barnes, Peter, 243-44
Barnes, Simon, 303
Barnett, Kim, 56
Baroda, 122, 135-36, 264

Basin Reserve, Wellington, 55, 294
Bedi, Bishan Singh, 1-2, 53, 58, 64 238, 262, 294, 324
Benaud, Richie, 64
Benjamin, Kenneth, 132, 134-35, 215
Benoni, 158
Benson and Hedges World Cup, 87-93
Berbice, 81
Berry, Scyld, 27, 63, 137, 274
Bevan, Michael, 197-98, 201, 218, 284
Bhandari, Yogendra, 73
Bharat CC, 19
Bharathan, Raju, 226, 289, 294
Bhat, Raghuram, 324
Bhave, Surendra, 35, 40
Bhende, Asha, 233
Bhende, Atmaram 'Bapu', 233
Bhogle, Harsha, 60, 84, 181-82, 203, 251, 255, 303
Bishop, Ian, 42, 56, 162-63
Bloemfontein, 298
BCCI, 42-43, 175, 184-91, 214-15, 300
Bodyline, 306-7
Bombay Cricket Association, 17
Bombay Junior Cricket Tournament, 21
Boon, David, 77-78, 83, 85-86, 90
Borde, Chandu, 260-61, 294, 328
Border, Allan, 77-78, 80, 83, 86, 89, 92, 104, 174, 306, 323
Border-Gavaskar Trophy, 151, 197
Botham, Ian, 88
Boycott, Geoffrey, 57, 146, 174, 185
Brabourne Stadium, Mumbai, 5, 26-27, 194, 260
Bradman, Donald, 2, 11, 64, 106, 113, 126, 131, 138, 141, 201, 203-04, 207-10, 212, 241, 251, 255, 280, 283, 290, 295-96, 303, 306-07, 320, 323-24, 326, 327
    death, 280
    invitation to Sachin, 208-09
    World XI, 295-96
Bradman, John, 212
Bradman's Best, 130-31, 295-96
Brearly, Mike, 129, 306-07
Bridgetown, 162
Brisbane, 77-78, 82, 89, 140
Bristol, 60, 235
Browne, 139
Bryan, Hendy, 243
Buckner, Steve, 225
Bulawayo, 217, 286, 325
Burge, Peter, 107

Caddick, Andrew, 304
Cairns, Chris, 249, 267
Calcutta Cricket Club, 8
Campbell, Sherwin, 162
Canada, 151
Cape Town, South Africa, 156-57
Carisbrook, 55, 92
Carlisle, Stuart, 324
Carrick, Phil, 137
Central Bureau of Investigation, 268-277
Centurion, 302
Chadha, Ravinder, 243
Chandana, Uppal, 177
Chandrachud, Y.V., 177
Chandrachud Commission, 271
Chanderpaul, Shivnarine, 161-62, 213
Chandigarh, 67, 103
Chappell, Greg, 28, 174, 325
Chappell, Ian, 83
Chauhan, Rajesh, 178, 184
Chennai, 140, 147, 169, 195, 208, 221, 250, 270, 282, 293, 299, 309, 325
Chepauk, 103, 170, 195, 222
Christchurch, 123, 220
Coca-Cola Champions Trophy, Sharjah, 218
Coca-Cola Cup, Harare, 298
Coca-Cola Cup tri-series at home, 204
Coca-Cola Cup tri-series at Sharjah, 200, 267, 269, 298
Coe, Sebastian, 44, 218
Collymore, Corey, 287
Colombo, 107, 112, 124-26, 147, 176, 205-06, 217, 286, 293
Commonwealth Games, Kuala Lumpur, 214-16
Compton, Dennis, 62
Contractor, Nari, 8, 149
Cooch-Behar Trophy, 35
Cork, Dominic, 147
Cosmopolitan Shield, 21

Coward, Mike, 255
Cricket Board Patron's XI, 43
Cricket Club of India (CCI), 27, 240
Cricket Talk, 86, 242, 262-63, 268, 312
Cricketer International, 28, 34, 62, 108, 153, 201, 303
Cricketnext.com, 291, 326-27
Croft, Robert, 304
Cronje, Hansie, 117, 156, 172, 264, 271
Cross Maidan, Mumbai, 11, 17
Crowe, Martin, 88, 247
Cullinan, Daryll, 158
Cummins, Anderson, 81-82
Cuttack, 105, 114

DMC Cup, Toronto, 244
D'Monte, Gregory, 35
Dadar Union CC, 7, 11, 19
Daily Telegraph, the, 44, 218, 309-10, 318-19
Dalmiya, Jagmohan, 75, 224, 226-27, 300, 302, 329
Dandekar, 17
Das, Shiv Sundar, 282-83, 286, 300, 307
Dasgupta, Deep, 300, 304
Dattu Phadkar XI, 23
David, Noel, 160-61, 172, 184
Davis, Heath, 169
Davis, Steve, 257
Dawson, Richard, 305
Defreitas, Phil, 57, 105
DeSilva, Aravinda, 107, 144, 175, 206, 213
DeSilva, Sanjeeva, 169
De Villiers, Fanie, 117
Deccan Herald, 319
Denness, Mike, 193, 300-03,
Deodhar Trophy, 69
Derbyshire, 56, 66
Desai, Ramakant, 175-76, 182, 185-91
Deshpande, Anil, 238
Dev, Kapil, 3, 31, 44-46, 52-54, 58-59, 63-65, 69-71, 72-73, 77, 83-85, 89-91, 104, 117, 131, 172, 175, 198, 229, 245-46, 250, 259, 265, 272-73, 274-75, 329
Dhaka, 108, 217, 227, 264-65, 278, 286
Dhanraj, 133
Dharmasena, Kumara, 169
Diana Princess of Wales Memorial Match, 212-13
Dighe, Sameer, 29, 259, 276
Dillon, Merv, 163
Donald, Allan, 75-76, 117, 152, 155-57, 213-14, 301
Doshi, Dilip, 324
Dravid, Rahul, 147-48, 158-59, 161-67, 169, 171-72, 187, 191, 196, 217-18, 223, 225, 235, 245, 281-82, 289, 303-04
Dujon, Jeff, 74
Duleep Trophy, 69
Dungarpur, Raj Singh, 26, 29-31, 33, 42, 55, 188, 211, 228, 242, 244-45
Durban, 173, 297
Durham, 128
Dwivedi, Sandeep, 326
Dyson, John, 174

East London, 297
Eden Gardens, Kolkata, 75, 103, 143, 183, 196, 204
Eden Park, Auckland, 294
Edgbaston, 128, 146
Emburey, John, 105
Engel, Matthew, 157-58
Engineer, Farokh, 94, 294
England tour to India, 9, 102-05, 302, 303-10

Faridabad, 133
Fazal, Zahid, 91
Feroze Shah Kotla, Delhi, 71, 142, 152, 221, 324
Fleming, Damien, 140, 216, 254, 280
Fleming, Stephen, 246
Flintoff, Andrew, 301, 305, 307
Flower, Andy, 324
Flower, Grant, 218
Foster, James, 307, 308
Francis, K.T., 225
Fraser, Angus, 59, 61-62, 64
Frith, David, 60, 62, 80, 292

G.R. Visvanath Trophy, 19
Gaekwad, Anshuman, 34, 192, 231, 235, 245

Galle, Sri Lanka, 126, 205, 290-91
Gandhi, Devang, 245
Ganesh, D., 160, 162, 172-73
Ganguly, Dona, 188
Ganguly, Sourav, 69, 114, 147-48, 151, 158, 162, 165-66, 169, 171-72, 177-78, 187, 189, 192-93, 198, 200-01, 204-05, 210-11, 213, 217-19, 230, 235, 241, 243-44, 246, 249, 252, 261, 264, 280, 297, 300, 314, 318, 320, 328
Gardiner, H., 144
Gattani, Kailash, 29
Gavaskar, Sunil, 2, 3, 7-8, 11, 21-22, 24, 31, 34, 39, 41, 44, 62-63, 105-06, 150, 113, 153, 170, 174, 177, 185, 190, 207-08, 217-18, 221-22, 224, 232, 247, 253, 255, 257, 262, 283-84, 288, 295, 306, 308, 315, 323-24, 328-29
Gavaskar and Tendulkar:Shaping Indian Cricket's Destiny, 11, 36
Geoffrey Boycott on Cricket, 130
Georgetown, 164, 269
Ghije, Laxmibai, 4-5
Gibbs, Herschelle, 230, 264
Gilchrist, Adam, 281-82
Giles, Ashley, 307-09, 323
Giles Shield, 11, 13, 19, 20, 23, 25
Gillespie, Jason, 194, 202, 266, 283-84, 293
Gloucestershire, 60
Gohil, Virbhadran, 33
Gondhalekar, 17
Gooch, Graham, 56-61, 63-65, 88, 102, 104, 127
Gordhandas Shield, 18, 21
Gough, Darren, 304
Gowariker, Avinash, 6
Gower, David, 57-58, 65
Grace, W.G., 213-14, 283, 326
Greatbatch, Mark, 65
Green Park, Kanpur, 198
Greenidge, Gordon, 65, 297
Greig, Tony, 82, 235
Guardian, the, 306
Guha, Ramachandra, 1, 10, 326
Guinness Book of World Records, 25
Gujranwala, 49, 52
Gupta, Vikrant, 326
Gurusinghe, 174
Guwahati, 179
Guyana, 164, 269
Gwalior, 139, 204

Htcricket.com, 312
Hadlee, Richard, 53, 85, 131, 247
Hair, Darrell, 251, 255, 257
Hall, Wes, 128
Hamilton, 58, 91
Hammond, Wally, 106
Hampshire, John, 43, 56
Harare, 217, 286-90, 298
Harper, Daryl, 252-53
Harper, Roger, 65
Harris, Lord, 9
Harris Shield inter-school tournament, 9, 11, 19-20, 23-24, 26-27, 33, 109
Harshe, Sunil, 6
Hart, Matthew, 122
Harvey, Neil, 79, 327
Hattangadi, Shishir, 32-34, 37-38
Hayden, Matthew, 1, 281-82, 284
Haynes, Desmond, 81, 110, 204, 217-18, 297
Hayward, Nantie, 262
Haywards Heath CC, 29
Hazare, 224
Headingley, 57
Headly, George, 13, 328
Healy, Ian, 90, 141
Hemmings, Eddie, 57, 59, 61-63
Hero Cup 1993, 112, 116-25
Hind Sevak CC, 18
Hindu, the, 49, 115, 177, 239, 247, 294, 319, 326
Hindustan Times, 240, 269, 299, 308
Hirwani, Narendra, 39, 58-60, 65, 78
Hobart, 81, 257
Hodgson, 60
Hoggard, Matthew, 305
Holder, John, 43
Holding, Michael, 174
Home series against
  Australia, 194-199, 279-85
  England, 9, 102-06, 302-10
  New Zealand, 138, 245-49

Pakistan, 221-24
South Africa, 74-78, 153-54, 263-66
Sri Lanka, 67-68, 131-32
West Indies, 132-35
Zimbabwe, 106, 279, 323-25
Hooper, Carl, 133
Hoover, Joe, 319
Horsham CC, 30
Hove, 230-31
Hudson, Andrew, 116, 155-57
Hughes, Kim, 174
Hughes, Merv, 77, 80, 83, 89
Hussain, Nasser, 146, 148, 171, 304-07, 323, 324
Hyderabad, 36, 248
Hyderabad (Sind), 178

ICC Mini-World Cup knock out tournament, Nairobi, 217-18, 265-66, 298
Independence Cup, 168-69, 176, 184, 270
India Today, 2
Indian Cricket: the Captains, 150
Indian Cricket Annual, 57, 74
Indian Cricket Omnibus, An, 10
Indian Education Society, 17
Indian Express, the, 25, 36, 292, 326
Indian Olympic Association (IOA), 214-15
Indian tour to
Australia, 77-86, 250-58
England, 56-66, 145-48
New Zealand, 53-55, 118-123, 219-220
Pakistan, 7, 43-52
South Africa, 155-60, 295-303
Sri Lanka, 106-08, 290-91
West Indies, 42, 159-167, 172-74
Zimbabwe, 217, 286-87, 291
Indore, 284-85
indya.com, 242, 261
International Cricket Council (ICC), 214, 301-02, 314-15
Inzamam-ul-Haq, 91-92, 192, 222
Iqbal Stadium, Faisalabad, 46
Irani, Ali, 274, 276
Irani, Mehli Dinshaw, 10
Irani Trophy, 21, 39, 69
Jadeja, Ajay, 72-73, 87, 90, 105, 116, 120-24, 139-40, 142, 158, 187, 189, 197, 200-01, 211, 215, 220, 222-23, 239, 242, 244, 247, 261, 276
Jadeja, Bimal, 33
Jadeja, Rajesh, 33
Jaffar, Saleem, 46
Jaipur, 102, 111, 135-36
Jamaica, 159-60
Jamshedpur, 70
Jardine, Douglas, 306-07
Jarvis, Paul, 104
Javed, Aaqib, 45, 74
Jayasuriya, Sanath, 141-44, 150, 169, 175, 177, 183, 205, 213, 267
Jinnah Cup, 184
Jodhpur, 279
Johannesburg, 147, 297
John, Binoo, 312
John Bright CC, 19
Johnson, David, 172
Johnson, Neil, 217
Jolly Cricketers, 10
Jones, Dean, 78, 85, 89
Jordan, Michael, 312, 320
Joseph, Davis, 216
Joshi, Anant, 289-90, 292
Joshi, Sunil, 172-73, 223
Joshi, Tapan, 291

Kakkar, Prahlad, 316, 321
Kallis, Jacques, 230
Kaluwitharana, Romesh, 141-43, 150
Kamat Club, 14
Kamat Memorial CC, 13, 16
Kamath, P.K. Joe, 37
Kambli, Vinod, 8, 13, 17, 19, 24-27, 29, 39, 72, 73-74, 75, 87-88, 102-16, 118, 122, 124-25, 132-33, 139, 140-41, 143, 153, 169, 175-76, 232
friendship with Sachin, 109-115
Kandy, Sri Lanka, 106, 108, 161, 291, 325
Kanga League, 9-13, 16, 18, 22, 27, 30
Kanpur, 152, 198, 250, 276, 310
Karachi, 49, 51-52, 178, 290
Karhade, Sanjay, 315
Karim, Syed Saba, 40, 170

Kasbekar, Atul, 316
Kasliwal, 31-32
Kasprowicz, Michael, 217, 252
Kenkre, Hemant, 311
Kensington Oval, 163
Kent, 56-57, 128
Khan, Imran, 43-49, 87, 92, 264
Khan, Iqbal, 32
Khan, Moin, 223
Khan, Nadeem, 225-26
Khan, Shahryar, 226
Khan, Zaheer, 265
Kher, 31
Khettarama, 124
Khurasia, Amay, 216
King, Chris, 122
Kingsmead, Durban, 155
Kingston, 159-61
Kirsten, Gary, 155-56, 230, 263-64
Klusener, Lance, 156-57, 230
Kochi, 197, 294
Kolkata, 143, 153, 221, 227, 238, 281, 283, 293
Krishna, B.A., 290
Kulkarni, Nilesh, 251
Kulkarni, Raju, 30
Kumaran, 278
Kumble, Anil, 57, 70, 104, 107, 117-18, 133, 141-42, 144, 146, 172-73, 177, 195, 198, 213-16, 222, 224, 241, 275, 280
Kunzru, Tarun, 315
Kuruvilla, Abey, 73, 160, 162, 165, 172-73

L.G. Cup, Nairobi, 244
Lahore, 48, 50, 178, 227
Laine, Tim, 77, 86
Laker, Jim, 224
Lal, Akash, 38
Lamb, Allan, 57-60
Lamba, Raman, 38, 44, 70-71
Lambert, Clayton, 74
Lancaster Park, Christchurch, 53
Langer, Justin, 281
Lara, Brian, 81, 105, 118-19, 127-28, 134, 161-64, 209, 264, 299, 313
  highest score in test and first-class cricket, 127-28
Larson, Gavin, 122
Latif, Rashid, 176
Lawry, Bill, 279
Laxman, V.V.S. 161, 163, 172, 196, 201, 225, 254, 281-82, 284, 289, 293, 301, 305
Lee, Brett, 250, 253-54, 265, 280
Lehmann, Darren, 198
Leicester, 231
Leipus, Andrew, 289
Lele, J.Y., 175-76, 191, 227-28, 238-40, 259-60
Lele, Jaywant, 185-86
Lewis, Chris, 59, 61- 62-65, 105, 146-47
Lewis, Tony, 5
Lillee, Dennis, 22, 72
Lindsay, Dennis, 302
Lloyd, Clive, 143-44, 183
Lloyd, David, 64
Logie, Gus, 74
Lokapally, Vijay, 115, 122-23, 136, 164, 216, 248, 250, 253, 296-97, 319-20
Lord Harris Shield Cricket Tournament Commemoration Volume 1897-1997, 26-27
Lord's, 23, 58-60, 62-63, 81, 147, 213-14
Lucknow, 131, 147

M.A. Chidambaram Stadium, Chennai, 103, 222, 282
MCG, 92
MIG Cricket Club, 17
MRF Pace Academy, 22
Mackay, 88, 111
Madan Lal, 38, 40, 152, 163, 166, 175-77, 238, 270-71
Madhavan, K., 273
Madugalle, Ranjan, 145, 254
Magazine, Pradeep, 268-72, 299
Mahanama, Roshan, 68, 175, 177
Mahim-Dadar Shield, 21
Mahmood, Azhar, 193
Malcolm, Devon, 103
Malhotra, Ashok, 238
Malik, Aamir, 44-45, 47
Malik, Salim, 46, 50, 52, 123, 222
Manchester, 63
Manjrekar, Sanjay, 8, 11, 34-35, 37-38, 40,

45-48, 53-54, 57-58, 61, 70, 72, 74, 79, 81-82,89, 105, 132-34, 140, 143, 146, 148, 171-72, 261
Manjrekar, Vijay, 8, 11, 48
Mankad, Ashok, 279
Mankad, Vinoo, 3
Mantri, Madhav, 57
Manuel, Peter, 205, 245
Maradona, Diego, 230
Margao, 68, 131, 179, 181, 284-85
Marks, Vic, 104
Marsh, Geoff, 152
Marsh, Rodney, 174
Marshall, Malcolm, 81
Martin-Jenkins, Christopher, 62
Martyn, Damien, 198, 218
Mascarenhas, Mark, 138, 311-14, 317
Match-fixing controversy and CBI, 185, 187, 268-77
Matunga Shield, 22
McDermott, Craig, 77, 83-85, 89-90, 125
McEnroe, John, 6
McGrath, Glenn, 124-25, 140, 194, 213, 217, 219, 236, 352-54, 265-66 280, 283-84, 293, 301
McMillan, Brian, 117, 156-57
Mehmood, Khalid, 226
Mehta, Anand, 316
Mehta, Anjali, 137
Mehta, Annabelle, 321
Mehta, Rattan, 273-74
Mehta, Shobhan, 273
Melbourne, 78-79, 81-82, 152, 174
Merchant, Vijay, 3, 8, 10
Miandad, Javed, 45, 47, 91, 92-93, 204, 226, 295, 324
Mid Day, 21, 45, 60, 80, 315
Miller, Colin, 283, 293
Minor Counties, 56
Mistry, Bharat, 32
Modi, Rusi, 8
Mohali, 116, 131, 133-34, 169, 245, 302-05
Mohammad, Hanif, 48
Mohammad, Mushtaq, 44, 54, 63
Mohammad, Shoaib, 44-46, 48
Mohan, R., 49, 75-76, 149, 153, 159, 168-69, 177, 283
Mohinder Amarnath benefit game at Mumbai, 154
Mokashi, Kiran, 37
Mongia, Nayan, 132, 148, 170-72, 175-76, 195, 198, 201-02, 223, 250, 259, 261, 272, 276
Moody, Tom, 82, 85, 90, 196
More, Kiran, 34, 46, 54, 57, 65, 69, 90-91, 172
Morris, Arthur, 296
Morrison, Danny, 54, 122
Moseley, Ezra, 65
Motera Stadium, 247
Motz, Dick, 294
Mulye, R., 24
Mumbai, 7-10, 132, 140, 147, 207, 210, 221, 229, 263-64
Muralitharan, Muthiah, 126, 143
Murray, Junior, 133
Murzello, Clayton, 10
Mushtaq, Saqlain, 145, 178, 192, 222-23
Muthiah, A.C., 276
Muzumdar, Amol, 16, 24, 226

Nadkarni, Bapu, 23
Nadkarni, Shirish, 28, 34
Naegamvala, Monisha, 316
Nagpur, 67, 133, 238-39, 247, 264, 279, 324
Naik, Sudhir, 10, 23, 30
Nairobi, 114, 264-66
Napier, 54, 120, 122
Narayan, Y. Ananth, 293, 295
Narayanan, K.R., 210-11, 228
Nash, 247
Natarajan, H., 326-27
National stadium, Karachi, 44
National stadium, New Delhi, 193
Navroze Cricket Club, 17
Nayak, Suru, 33, 37-38
Nayudu, C.K., 3
Nayyar, Manu, 38
Nazar, Mudassar, 65
Neely, Don, 54, 120
New South Wales, 77
New Zealand Cricket Annual, 54
Nicholas, Mark, 185, 309-10, 318-20
Nicholls, Eddie, 165

Not Quite Cricket, 269-71

O'Connor, Shayne, 249
O'Neill, Norman, 86
O'Reilly, Bill, 208
Old Trafford, Manchester, 60, 65, 79, 145, 147, 236
Olonga, Henry, 218-20, 232
Orchard, Dave, 225
Oriental Cricket Club, 9
Outlook, 6, 16, 31, 39, 45, 209, 272, 313
Oval, the, 61, 65, 236

P.J. Hindu Gymkhana, 19
Paarl, 297
Padamsee, Alyque, 315
Palkar, Abhay, 34
Palton, T., 25
Pandit, Chandrakant, 13, 34-35, 37
Pandove, M.P., 175
Panicker, Prem, 160, 182-91
Parkinson, Michael, 65
Parsi Cyclists, 11
Pataudi, 'Tiger', 3, 130, 149
Patel, Dhansukh, 31
Patel, Dipak, 88
Patel, Min, 146
Patel, Nisarg, 32
Patel, Rashid, 34, 70-71
Pathak, S.D., 32
Patherya, Mudar, 42
Patil, Madhu, 11
Patil, Sandeep, 8, 11, 23, 152
Patil, Sanjay, 71-72
Patterson, Patrick, 81
Pedang, Singapore, 144
Pepsi Aŝia Cup, Dhaka, 265
Pepsi cup matches, 136, 197, 200, 202, 206, 227
Perry, Roland, 130, 290, 295-96
Perth, 81, 86, 146, 196, 257, 299
Peshawar, 50-52
Pioneer, the, 269
Pollard, Vic, 294
Pollock, Shaun, 156, 264, 301, 328
Ponting, Ricky, 281, 301
Port Elizabeth, 297, 300
Port-of-Spain, 128, 161, 165
Prabhakar, Manoj, 38, 45, 47, 50, 54, 58, 61-62, 78, 80, 84, 89-90, 102, 107, 117, 125, 132-33, 172, 185, 250, 265, 272, 276
Prasad, M.S.K., 250, 259
Prasad, Venkatesh, 142, 159-60, 152, 165, 172-73, 177, 190, 222, 225, 227, 254-55
Prasanna, Erapalli, 294
Press Trust of India, 176
Price, Ray, 324
Pringle, Chris, 122
Pringle, Meyrick, 30, 65
Prudential World Cup, 5, 229
Pukekura Park, New Plymouth, 53
Pune, 68, 284
Puri, Pawan, 273

Qadir, Abdul, 42, 47, 50-52
Qasim, Iqbal, 44

R.Premadasa Stadium, Colombo, 124, 150, 177
Raja, Rameez, 178
Rajan, Sanjay, 208
Rajan, Sunder, 25
Rajaraman, G., 240
Rajkot, 33, 135, 248
Rajput, Lalchand, 12, 31, 35-35, 37, 40, 70
Raju, Venkatapathy, 37, 41, 60, 67, 70, 78, 83, 90, 130, 176
Raman, W.V., 54, 57, 105, 172
Ramchand, Partab, 150
Ramesh, S., 222, 225, 232, 235, 243, 245-46, 282
Ranade, Atul, 6, 24
Ranatunga, Arjuna, 52, 67, 141, 144, 174
Ranatunga, Dhammika, 68
Randall, Steve, 162
Ranji Trophy, 7-8, 9-10, 21, 31, 69-73, 135-36, 194, 278-79, 324
Rao, M.V. Narasimha, 37
Rathore, 148, 172
Rawalpindi, 43
Raza, Akram, 124
Razdan, Vivek, 41, 43, 46, 48, 319
Razzaq, Abdul, 257
Reddy, C. Rammanohar, 326

Rediff.com, 111, 182, 189, 247
Rege, Milind, 19, 30
Reid, Bruce, 78
Reiffel, Paul, 194, 293
Reliance World Cup, 138
Report on Cricket Match Fixing and Related Malpractices, 240-41
Reporter, Piloo, 10-11
Rice, Clive, 75
Richards, Barry, 207, 296, 299-300
Richards, Vivian, 21, 39, 49, 80-81, 104, 202-04, 207, 211, 215, 218, 235
Richardson, Dave, 116, 155, 157
Richardson, Richie, 74, 80, 117-18
Rippon, N., 25
Roberts, Andy, 224
Robertson, Gavin, 293
Robinson, Ian, 254
Roebuck, Peter, 308-09
Romaines, 60
Rose, 163
Rourkela, 70
Row, Raman Subba, 131
Rungta, Kishen, 175, 187-90
Russell, Jack, 57
Rutherford, Ken, 122
Rutnagar, D.J., 196
Ryan, Chris, 326

Sabnis, 31
Sahara Cup, Toronto, 114, 149, 177, 185, 208, 214-17, 243
Sanghani, 24-25
Sardesai, Dilip, 9
Sardesai, Rajdeep, 9-10
Sassanian Cricket Club, 13, 18, 24
Satya Sai Baba, 239
Saxena, Ramesh, 40
Scotland, 56
Secunderabad, 36
Sehwag, Virender, 286, 291, 298-99, 302, 308, 310, 325
Shah, Niranjan, 323
Sharadashram Vidyamandir (English), 13-14, 16-17, 19-20, 24, 26-27, 76, 111
Sharjah, 2, 52, 55, 74, 110, 114, 123-24, 135-36, 144-45, 179, 181, 185-86, 188, 192, 198-204, 208, 221, 265, 267, 295, 298, 312
Sharma, Chetan, 65, 72-73
Sharma, Deepak, 72
Sharma, Gopal, 37
Sharma, Sanjay, 38
Sharma, Sanjeev, 40
Shastri, Ravi, 35, 37-38, 45-48, 52, 59, 65-66, 69, 78-81, 83-84, 86-88, 90, 172, 247, 313
Shekhar, Nirmal, 293
Shivaji Park, Mumbai, 7, 11, 14, 18, 19
Shukla, Ashish, 287
Sialkot, 48
Sidhu, Navjot Singh, 45-46, 48-49, 57, 59, 61, 78, 102, 104, 106-07, 120, 124, 131-34, 142-43, 145-46, 161-63, 166, 170, 172, 174, 176, 183, 189, 192, 195-96
Silver Jubilee Independence Cup, 192
Simpson, Bobby, 152
Singapore, 114, 136, 144
Singapore Challenge Cup, 243, 298
Singer Cup, 112, 124-25, 149, 204-05
Singh, Bantoo, 71
Singh, Gursharan, 40-41
Singh, Harbhajan, 281-82, 284, 300, 325
Singh, M.N., 320
Singh, Maninder, 38, 40-41, 46
Singh, Robin, 70, 160, 193, 215
Singh, Yuvraj, 265, 291
Sippy, Alan, 32-33
Sivaramakrishnan, Laxman, 44, 195
Slater, Michael, 281, 288, 301
Sleep, Peter, 65
Smith, 'Cammie', 225-26, 232, 257
Smith, Robin, 57-58, 60, 88
Snell, Richard, 116
Sobers, Garry, 58, 105, 127, 204, 207, 291, 296, 326
Sohail, Aamir, 91, 124, 142, 214
Sportstar, 35, 49, 75, 86, 108, 112, 114, 118, 120-23, 149-50, 159, 163-64, 168-69, 177, 181, 203, 28, 216, 224, 226, 244, 248-50, 253, 256-57, 289, 293-94, 296-97, 319-320
Sportstar Trophy, 22
Sportsweek, 30

Sportsworld, 3, 42, 49, 105, 118-19, 130, 152
Srikkanth, Krishnamachari, 42, 44-46, 48, 50-51, 82, 84, 88-90, 91, 149, 172, 262
Srinath, Javagal, 70, 78, 88, 90-91, 116-17, 132-34, 146, 159-60, 172-73, 177, 184, 213, 225, 230, 248, 275
Srivatsa, V., 226, 269, 278, 287-88
St. John's, Antigua, 127, 164
St. Vincent, 166, 168, 184
Star CC, 29, 56
Stewart, Alec, 88, 147, 307
Strang, Paul, 219
Streak, Heath, 141
Sunday Mid Day, 10-11
Surendran, C.P., 1
Surti, Rusi, 294
Sutcliffe, Herbert, 113, 328
Sydney, 78, 82, 86, 90, 128, 147, 196, 251-52

Talim Shield, 31
Talpade, Sameer, 32-33
Tamhane, Naren, 29-30, 40
Taufel, Simon, 257
Taupo, 220
Taylor, Bruce, 294
Taylor, Mark, 83, 140, 152, 195, 251, 279
Taylor, Peter, 78, 85
tehelka.com, 272
Telegraph, the, 182, 314
Tendulkar, Ajit, 4-8, 10, 13-19, 23, 109, 114, 231-33, 247, 316, 329
Tendulkar, Anjali, 187, 211, 231, 233, 297, 316, 320-21
Tendulkar, Arjun, 320, 322
Tendulkar, Mangala, 7
Tendulkar, Nitin, 4-5, 231-32, 234
Tendulkar, Rajini, 4
Tendulkar, Ramesh, 4, 16, 231-34
Tendulkar, Sachin Ramesh,
  Abdul Qadir on, 51-52
  about his technique, 324
  Achrekar on, 14-15
  acting captain, 108
  Allan Donald on, 130, 214
  as global brand, 311-17
  back injury, 227, 242-449
  birth of, 4-5
  Bishan Singh Bedi on, 1-2, 15
  Brian Lara and, 126-27
  CBI report concerning, 273-77
  captain of Indian team, 149-54, 238-42
  captain of Mumbai in Ranji Trophy, 135-36
  captain of Rest of India Team, 105
  Castrol Indian Cricketer of the Year award, 302-03
  century on debut in Ranji, Irani and Duleep trophy, 69
  child cricketer, 7
  childhood friends, 5-6
  choice of bat, 16
  confrontation with McGrath, 265-66
  Dave Richardson on, 157
  deal with WorldTel, 137, 311-13, 316
  death of father, 231-34
  debut, 17
  Donald Bradman and, 131, 20-10, 290-91
  family life, 318-22
  first century on foreign soil, 29
  first interview, 21
  first Man of the Match award, 68
  first match in Kanga league, 18
  first organized match, 15
  first sporting hero, 6
  first test wicket, 80
  first to score 10,000 runs in ODIs, 122-23, 284
  first tour abroad, 29
  friendship with Vinod Kambli, 109-15
  Imran Khan on, 92-93
  in Bradman's all time World XI, 210
  interview by Tom Alter, 39
  in West Zone under-15 team, 106
  knee injury, 323
  maiden international century, 62-63
  maiden test appearance at home, 67
  Man of the Match awards record, 219
  Maninder Singh on, 38-39
  marriage, 137
  Mike Coward open letter to, 255-56

Norman O'Neill on, 86
on captaincy issue, 147-48, 151, 287-88, 292
on criticism of his captaincy, 147 48
on selection of Indian team, 170 75, 259-63
opening batsman in ODIs, 119-21
Padma Shri award, 228
Partab Ramchand on, 150-51
Prem Panicker on his removal from captaincy, 182-91
Raj Singh Dungarpur on, 27-28
Rajiv Gandhi *Khel Ratna* award, 210-12
resignation from captaincy, 259-63
schooling, 13, 16
selection in Indian team, 40
selection in Mumbai Ranji team, 30-31
Shane Warne on, 197, 203
signed by WorldTel, 137, 311-13, 316
Steve Waugh on, 202-03
test debut, 3, 109
toe injury, 289-90, 292
tribute to Harris Shield, 26-27
vice captain of Indian team, 106
Wadekar on, 261-62
with Star CC team in England, 29 30
World Cup debut, 87-93
World record with Kambli, 25, 109
youngest Indian test player, 44
to score century on debut in first-class matches, 33
to score century in Irani trophy, 41
youngest player in West Zone Ranji Trophy league, 23
Tendulkar, Sara, 231, 297, 320
Tendulkar, Suresh, 7
Texaco series, 56
Thorpe, Graham, 146
Tillekeratne, Hashan, 141, 175
Time, 229-30
Times of India, 11, 21, 25, 147-48, 171, 227, 232, 234, 269, 287-88
Times of India Sunday Review, 315, 316
Times Shield, 11
Titan Cup, 151-52, 183
Toronto, 149-54, 165, 177, 184, 208, 214-17, 243-44
total-cricket.com, 312
Traicos, John, 91, 99
Trent Bridge, 57, 147
Trinidad, 128, 161
Tufnell, Phil, 105
Turner, Glenn, 15

Umrigar, Polly, 8
Underwood, Derek, 324
United Cricket Board of South Africa, 302

Vaas, 169
Vaidyanathan, T.G., 10
Vajpayee, Atal Behari, 236, 290
Vengsarkar, Dilip, 11, 31, 34, 37-38, 42, 44, 54, 58-59, 69-70, 72-73, 79, 84, 172, 329
Verity, Headley, 324
Vernon, G.F., 9
Vettori, Daniel, 247
Vijay Hazare Tournament, 30
Vijay Merchant inter-zonal tournament, 19, 22
Vijayakar, Pradeep, 8, 10
Vijaykrishna, B., 324
Visakhapatnam, 105, 284
Visvanath, G.R., 40, 105, 224
Viswanath, G., 114, 239, 247
Vizzy Trophy, 232
Voigt, Ian, 252
Voigt, Sachin, 252

WACA, 88
WSC one-day tournament, 77, 80-83
Wadekar, Ajit, 9, 11, 13, 23, 30, 115, 117, 120, 125, 238-43, 260-62, 272, 294
Walsh, Courtney, 113, 129, 131-35, 161-62, 243
Walters, Doug, 174
Wankhede Stadium, Mumbai, 26, 30, 38,

72-74, 105, 140, 204, 221, 260, 329
Warnaweera, 107
Warne, Shane, 79, 103, 125, 140-41, 152, 194-99, 208-10, 212, 217, 219, 230, 252, 254, 280, 282-84, 293, 296, 313
Warrier, Sunil, 21
Warwickshire, 128
Wassan, Atul, 40-41, 71
Waugh, Mark, 141-42, 201, 281, 284-85
Waugh, Steve, 2, 82, 90, 197-98, 202-03, 216, 218, 251, 266, 279-83, 288-89, 306, 315, 323, 325
Week, the, 2, 4, 186, 320
Weekend Australian, the, 255
Weekes, Everton, 113
Wellington, 91, 123, 220, 294
Wessels, Kepler, 75, 116
White, Craig, 305
Whitney, Mike, 65, 77-78, 82, 85
Wickramesinghe, 107
Wijesinghe, Mahinda, 108
Williams, Neil, 65
Wills Challenge Cup, 178, 238
Wills Trophy, 69, 74, 135-36, 217, 319
Wills World Cup, 238, 312, 314
Wills World Series, 131, 135-36
Wisden Cricket Asia, 293
Wisden Cricket Monthly, 27, 37, 60, 62, 80, 137, 146, 157-58, 164, 196, 292, 303, 307, 326
Wisden Cricketers' Almanack, 21, 63, 150, 161, 256, 298
Wood, Graeme, 174
Woodcock, John, 157, 303
Woods, Tiger, 312, 320
World Cup 1979, 235
World Cup 1983, 198
World Cup 1992, 110-11
World Cup 1996, 114, 129, 138-44, 174, 221, 227, 298
World Cup 1999, 130, 228-37, 249
WorldTel, 311, 313, 316
Wright, John, 54-55, 299

Yadav, Shivlal, 175, 186, 191, 238
Yadav, Vijay, 117
Youhanna, Yousuf, 222
Young, Brad, 218
Young Parsee Cricket Club, 18
Younis, Waqar, 46-48, 50-51, 53-54, 144, 181, 226-27, 262

Zinto, Joy, 32